Assuring the Safety of Sys

Related Titles

Chris Dale • Tom Anderson

Editors

Assuring the Safety of Systems

Proceedings of the Twenty-first
Safety-critical Systems Symposium,
Bristol, UK, 5-7th February 2013

Safety-Critical
Systems Club

The publication of these proceedings is
sponsored by BAE Systems plc

BAE SYSTEMS

Editors
Chris Dale
Dale Research Ltd
2 Reppersfield Row
Breage
Helston TR13 9PG
United Kingdom

Tom Anderson
Centre for Software Reliability
Newcastle University
Newcastle upon Tyne NE1 7RU
United Kingdom

ISBN 978-1481018647

Preface

This volume contains the papers presented at the twenty-first Safety-critical Systems Symposium (SSS 2013). This year's authors have, as usual, delivered informative material touching on many topics that are of current concern to the safety-critical systems community; we are grateful to them for their contributions.

The first day of the event focused on safety certification and related issues. Four of the papers consider these issues in a particular industry sector: defence, civil aviation, automotive and rail. The other is more generic, being concerned with safety assurance measures within international standard IEC 61508.

The keynote paper written by John Thomas and Nancy Leveson defines a formal mathematical structure can be used to identify potentially hazardous control actions in a system. This is followed by a paper describing the development of a safety case for the Airborne Collision Avoidance System, and by three papers that discuss potential advances in safety cases, safety arguments and safety assurance.

Jonathan Storey's keynote address describes the approach to developing the safety case for the London Underground Victoria Line resignalling project. Two papers then deal with safety management: first, BAE Systems' product safety principles, then the UK Military Aviation Authority's risk management approach.

The keynote paper from Yoshiki Kinoshita and Makoto Takeyama proposes a novel framework for formal assurance cases. The next paper puts forward a new approach to hazard analysis, while the third paper in this group looks at how proof and testing can be combined in the context of safety assurance.

The final group of papers looks at some 'softer' issues that are – of course – no less important: the balance between designed-in and procedural approaches to safety; human factors; and safety culture.

We are grateful to our sponsors for their valuable support and to the exhibitors at the Symposium's tools and services fair for their participation. And we thank Joan Atkinson and her team for laying the event's foundation through their exemplary planning and organisation.

CD & TA
November 2012

A message from the sponsors

BAE Systems is pleased to support the publication of these proceedings. We recognise the benefit of the Safety-Critical Systems Club in promoting safety engineering in the UK and value the opportunities provided for continued professional development and the recognition and sharing of good practice. The safety of our employees, those using our products and the general public is critical to our business and is recognised as an important social responsibility.

The Safety-Critical Systems Club

organiser of the

Safety-critical Systems Symposium

What is the Safety-Critical Systems Club?

This 'Community' Club exists to support developers and operators of systems that may have an impact on safety, across all industry sectors. It is an independent, non-profit organisation that co-operates with all bodies involved with safety-critical systems.

Objectives

The Club's two principal objectives are to raise awareness of safety issues in the field of safety-critical systems and to facilitate the transfer of safety technology from wherever it exists.

History

The Club was inaugurated in 1991 under the sponsorship of the UK's Department of Trade and Industry (DTI) and the Engineering and Physical Sciences Research Council (EPSRC). Its secretariat is in the Centre for Software Reliability (CSR) at Newcastle University, and its Meetings Coordinator is Chris Dale of Dale Research Ltd. Felix Redmill of Redmill Consultancy is the Newsletter Editor.

Since 1994 the Club has been self-sufficient, but it retains the active support of the Health and Safety Executive, the Institution of Engineering and Technology, and BCS, the Chartered Institute for IT. All of these bodies are represented on the Club's Steering Group.

The Club's activities

The Club achieves its goals of awareness-raising and technology transfer by focusing on current and emerging practices in safety engineering, software engineering, and standards that relate to safety in processes and products. Its activities include:

- running the annual Safety-critical Systems Symposium each February (the first was in 1993), with Proceedings published in book form.
- organising a number of full day seminars each year
- providing tutorials on relevant subjects
- publishing a newsletter, *Safety Systems*, three times annually (since 1991), in January, May and September
- a web-site www.scsc.org.uk providing member services, including a safety tools, products and services directory.

Education and communication

The Club brings together technical and managerial personnel within all sectors of the safety-critical systems community. Its events provide education and training in principles and techniques, and it facilitates the dissemination of lessons within and between industry sectors. It promotes an inter-disciplinary approach to the engineering and management of safety, and provides a forum for experienced practitioners to meet each other and for the exposure of newcomers to the values, roles and actions of the safety-critical systems industry.

Influence on research

The Club facilitates communication among researchers, the transfer of technology from researchers to users, feedback from users, and the communication of experience between users. It provides a meeting point for industry and academia, a forum for the presentation of the results of relevant projects, and a means of learning and keeping up-to-date in the field.

The Club thus helps to achieve more relevant research, a more rapid and effective transfer and use of technology, the identification of best practice, the definition of requirements for education and training, and the dissemination of information. Importantly, it does this within a 'club' atmosphere of cooperation and support rather than a commercial environment.

Membership

Members pay a reduced fee (well below the commercial level) for events and receive the newsletter and other mailed information. Not being sponsored, the Club depends on members' subscriptions: these can be paid at the first meeting attended, and are almost always paid by the individual's employer.

To join, please contact Mrs Joan Atkinson at: The Centre for Software Reliability, Newcastle University, Newcastle upon Tyne, NE1 7RU, UK; telephone: +44 191 221 2222; fax: +44 191 222 7995; email: csr@newcastle.ac.uk.

Contents

Safety Certification in the Defence Sector

Allan Bain

Defence Safety and Environment Authority, Ministry of Defence

Bristol, UK

Abstract This is a review of safety certification and approval process within UK defence systems and forms part of a set of papers describing certification regimes across a number of industries for the Safety-critical Systems Symposium 2013. Since the range of transportation and infrastructure used within the defence sector draws from all other environmental domains combined, the safety regimes of each UK defence system reflects the civil domains they are drawn from. For this reason, the paper describes the system safety regime within UK warships, including their software-intensive systems.

1 Introduction

The UK Ministry of Defence (MOD) requires safety and environmental management to occur during the acquisition[1] phases so that harm can be minimised (so systems are shown to be 'safe to operate') and during operations phases (so systems can be 'operated safely'). This paper gives a high level summary of each defence safety regulatory regime, with particular reference to defence maritime activities and how the legislation that frames it has influenced departmental policy.

MOD departmental policy is to comply with legislation, and has been shaped by a series of 'watershed accidents' that have led to specific principles and techniques being required to discharge departmental responsibilities. Crown servants play key roles as 'duty holders', who hold responsibilities for managing safety; as standards setters providing guidance to those managing risk (the *why* and *how*); and as internal MOD regulators specifying *what* should be done to manage safety.

Software intensive systems are not usually certified or regulated independently of the system they reside in. However they are often procured separately and extensive effort can be expended assessing and assuring compliance with standards. This becomes important in mission-critical functions or where they have been

---

[1] The concept, design, manufacture, trials, support and disposal of equipment/major systems/ platforms.

associated with safety-critical features, often resulting in program delays or even cancellations.

2 Legislation

2.1 National legislation

The Health and Safety at Work etc, Act 1974 (HSWA) and its associated regulations apply to the MOD, its agencies and to the armed forces operating within the territory of Great Britain. This Act extends out to the 12 mile territorial limit but is disapplied from maritime activities, subject to merchant shipping law. Certain regulations also 'disapply' training for war, transition to war and war-fighting. The MOD has the same duty of care as any other employer, and Section 2 of the HSWA requires:

> 'all employers to ensure, so far as is reasonably practicable, the health, safety and welfare at work of all its employees'.

Section 3 of the HSWA requires that innocent parties are not exposed to the 'conduct of any activity' which risks their health or safety. In particular, Section 2(2) has an explicit duty to:

> 'provide and maintain facilities and safe systems of work, without risks to health, the working environment and to make adequate arrangements for employee welfare'.

It is an offence to fail to discharge the duties established by the HSWA. The Secretary of State for Defence has powers, in the interests of national security, to exempt the armed forces from some of its requirements. As a government department, the MOD also enjoys crown privilege (Section 48). Instead of prosecution, administrative arrangements (crown censures) are applied to government departments who fail to discharge their duties. Whilst the MOD has legal duties as an organisation, it cannot itself be criminally prosecuted. Individual crown servants may still be prosecuted for failures to discharge their duties (under Section 40), where they are shown to be un-cooperative, take unreasonable care of their own health and safety or of others likely to be affected by their acts or omissions. The Health and Safety Executive (HSE) will not generally prosecute individual employees when an employer clearly holds the principal duties under the Act.

A health and safety measure must be demonstrated as not reasonably practicable if it is to be a legal defence[2]. Such a 'safety argument' needs defendants to present evidence that a health and safety measure was not practical[3] by demonstrating that reducing that quantum of risk was grossly disproportionate to the cost

---

[2] R v D Janway Davies [2002] EWCA 2949

[3] Practicality must mean in the interests of national security and the need to maintain operational capability. MOD can only dispense of legislative provisions if legislation explicitly permits it.

of mitigating it[4]: the ALARP justification. This concept is useful for military activities where equivalent measures can be as common as direct compliance.

The HSE publishes 'Approved Codes of Practice' (ACOP) to aid compliance. Failure to comply with an ACOP is not an offence in itself, but it has special legal status (Section 16 of the HSWA). HSE Inspectors (or a court) can regard failure to follow advice within an ACOP as evidence of guilt unless compliance with the law can be shown in some other way. The MOD uses the safety case both to prove direct compliance with the law and with defence standards, demonstrated to be 'at least as good' as the statutory goals, in a similar manner to ACOP.

The Corporate Manslaughter and Corporate Homicide Act (CMCHA-2007) creates certain offences, which may duplicate offences in the HSWA or other primary legislation (MSA95, CAA, etc). Corporate manslaughter requires proof of a *gross* breach of duty of care and *senior management failings* to be a substantial element in that breach. Such prosecutions will generally be shown to be systemic failures.

Any offence from CMCHA-2007 is rooted in the breach of the duty of care owed from 'common law negligence' and from which there is no crown immunity. Section 12 of that Act states that the armed forces are to be treated as MOD employees, but that any offence committed during the 'preparation, training, and conduct of operations or any activity of the special forces' is not covered. The Act does not cover public policy decisions (Section 3(1)) including strategic funding decisions and other matters involving competing public interests, but does apply to how decisions about resources were managed. MOD's internal governance and regulation does however seek to consider all these aspects.

2.2 International legislation

There are international regulations for transport by air and sea and for the carriage of dangerous goods. UN conventions for maritime safety are formed by the International Maritime Organization (IMO) and International Labour Organization (ILO). These maritime conventions concern transportation safety, pollution prevention and specific regional issues (e.g. the Arctic or EU) which apply to ships visiting that region. Whilst warships are generally disapplied, some clauses are partially applied e.g. the polluter pays.

2.2.1 Treaties dealing with the ship

SOLAS (International Convention for the Safety of Life at Sea, 1974) sets a comprehensive range of minimum standards for:

---

[4] Edwards v National Coal Board [1949] 1 All ER 743

- safe construction of ships
- the basic types and levels of safety equipment (e.g. fire protection, navigation, lifesaving and radio) to be carried on board
- regular ship surveys
- the issue of certificates of compliance by flag states.

MARPOL (International Convention for the Prevention of Pollution from Ships, 1973/1978) sets minimum standards to prevent pollution caused accidentally or in the course of routine operations. MARPOL concerns:

- preventing pollution from oil, bulk chemicals, dangerous goods, sewage, garbage and atmospheric pollution,
- architectural provisions e.g. for oil tankers to have double hulls.

LOAD-LINE (International Convention on Load-lines, 1966) sets minimum permissible freeboards, according to the season and the ship's trading pattern.

ISPS (International Ship and Port Facility Security Code, 2002) sets requirements to ensure ships and port facilities are secure at all stages during a voyage.

The naval ship code is a militarised version of the major conventions (NATO, 2010), which establishes a 'militarised' baseline for many NATO navies.

2.2.2 Treaties dealing with the shipping company

ISM (The International Safety Management Code, 1993) requires shipping companies to have a 'licence to operate'. Companies and their individual ships must undergo regular audits to ensure that the safety management systems they have in place include adequate procedures and lines of communication between ships and their managers ashore.

This code forms part of MOD Maritime Regulations (MOD, 2012a).

2.2.3 Treaties dealing with the seafarer

COLREG (Convention on the International Regulations for Preventing Collisions at Sea, 1972) specified basic 'rules of the road', rights of way and actions to avoid collisions.

STCW (International Convention on Standards of Training, Certification and Watch keeping for Seafarers, 1978/1995) establishes uniform standards of competence for seafarers.

ILO 147 (The ILO Merchant Shipping (Minimum Standards) Convention, 1976) requires national administrations to legislate on labour issues such as hours of work, medical fitness and seafarers' working conditions. This will be superseded when the ILO Maritime Labour Convention, 2006, comes into force.

Simplistically no legislation applies to military activities outside 12 nautical miles of GB (HSE 1999). However successive Secretaries of State for Defence have made policy statements that 'where derogations and exemptions exist, standards shall be applied which are at least as good as statute'. This requires the intelligent application of safety goals and principles, to achieve levels of risk at least as good as statute to be justified within the safety case. Safety principles and goals may be shared with civil practice but the defence imperative may require similar activities to be managed differently because they have a different application. In addition to benchmarking national legislation, hazardous activities need to be risk assessed and shown that they are 'at least as good as' that legislation (MOD 2012b).

3 Complying with policy and legal obligations

3.1 Regulatory principles

The MOD's overarching policy statement by the Secretary of State is published within Joint Service Publication (JSP) 815, Defence Environment and Safety Management. The policy statement requires:

> 'within the UK it is policy for MOD to comply with all legislation which applies in the
> UK (including legislation giving effect to the UK's international obligations)'.

The MOD seeks to apply UK standards overseas, where reasonably practicable, unless relevant host nations' standards[5] set a more onerous safety level (MOD 2012a). Where there are exemptions or derogations from either domestic or international law, its policy is that defence standards and management arrangements will be at least as good as those required by legislation. The MOD will only exempt itself from legal requirements when such action is essential to maintain operational capability[6]. Where no relevant legislation exists, standards are to be selected, so that the balance between risk and military benefit is optimized (MOD 2006), recognising MOD does not seek zero risk, but that the risk is responsibly managed to:

- work-related fatalities and to minimise work-related injuries and ill-health
- maintaining effective emergency arrangements
- protecting the environment

---

[5] For equipment, stringent application of host nation standards is not always required as long as partner nations are aware and content with the degree of compliance with our own legislation.

[6] Where the statute refers to the Secretary of State (SofS) as having authority to apply for an exemption, this power can only be exercised by the SofS or in some cases a crown servant on his behalf.

• delivering the government's commitments for sustainable development.

Corporate policy (JSP815) assumes standards (DefStan 00-56, 2007) will be followed as a means to achieve this.

3.2 Domain specifics

A series of safety regulations sit below corporate policy for individual operating environments (or domains). These defence regulations are published in Joint Service Publications (JSP 430 for maritime, JSP 454 for land, JSP 800 for movements and transport, JSP 309 for bulk fuels and gases storage, JSP 482 for explosives storage, JSP 520 for intrinsic WOME (Weapons, Ordnance, Munitions and Explosives), and JSPs 518 and 538 for nuclear). The air domain sets its own series of Military Aviation Authority (MAA) Regulatory Publications (MRP).

Generic requirements have been articulated (DefStan 00-56, 2007) since the mid-1980s. Each domain has its own specific safety regulations (e.g. NATO 2011) but follows a set of common concepts (Inge 2007) which are:

• the safety case concept
• generic requirements for risk management, governance and management of change, supplemented with additional domain-specific elements that can range from the content and format of documents to reporting requirements
• specific 'regulatory' and/or certification requirements.

Following the Haddon-Cave inquiry (2009), the MOD has established independent regulatory organisations within the MAA and the Defence Safety and Environment Authority (DSEA). Both write regulations for defence activities that emulate their statutory counterparts (and seek outcomes at least as good as the goals of statute) for each domain. Whilst it has always been a requirement to periodically review the safety case, the new role of the independent regulator in this process is evolving to improve the rigour of such reviews.

3.3 Warship and submarine safety

Safety policy within the maritime domain is set by the DSEA's Defence Maritime Regulator (DMR) (MOD 2012a). The most significant hazards (termed key hazards[7]) are certified on behalf of the DMR by the Naval Authority Group, (MOD 2012b) which is an authorised certification body embedded within the Defence Equipment and Support organisation (DE&S). Key hazard certification (see Fig-

---

[7] Those which could potentially lead to significant loss of life, entire loss of a vessel or significant environmental damage.

ure 1) is the outcome of independent reviews of part of the safety case, submitted by the DE&S project teams designated platform duty holders (responsible for the materiel of a ship) to the regulator's agent (the naval authority). A suite of certification should prove a ship is materially seaworthy (safe to operate) and mandates certain accident sequences to have been assessed. These currently are loss of structural strength; stability; weapons magazine integrity; propulsion and manoeuvring; that there is sufficient escape, evacuation and lifesaving provision; and fire-fighting. Submarines additionally have certified the loss of watertight integrity, atmospheric control and dynamic control. Warships should not normally be operated without valid naval authority certificates for all those key hazard areas.

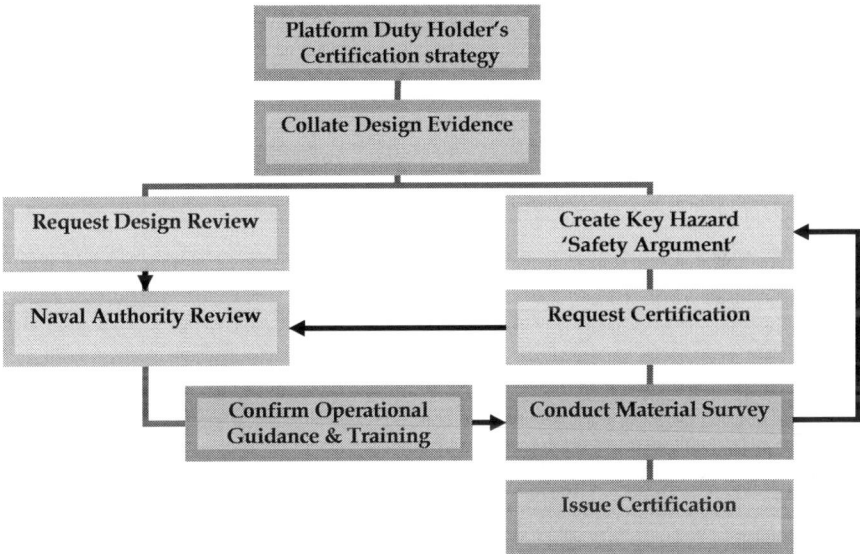

Fig-1. Key hazard certification (JSP430 (MOD 2012b))

The DMR with its naval authority is equivalent to the regulatory activities of the Maritime and Coastguard Agency for UK civil shipping. The requirement for certificates to be re-submitted, on a 5 to 10 year cycle, roughly aligned with ship refits allows the maritime domain to address ageing systems (HSE 1999) in an efficient manner. The assessment that warships are 'operated safely' will be assessed by ship inspectors within DMR. The MOD organisations in control of these maritime activities have been mapping established practices against the regulatory risk control systems, as required by regulation (MOD 2012a).

3.4 Nuclear safety

Nuclear propulsion systems and nuclear weapons have their own regulatory policy set by the Defence Nuclear Safety Regulator (DNSR) (within the DSEA). Defence nuclear safety (JSPs 518 and 538) emulates the civil licensing model of the Office of Nuclear Regulation (ONR)[8]. Certain personnel are recognised to be 'in control' of nuclear activities (e.g. transport and heads of establishments for different sites). The DNSR conducts four regulatory activities:

1. authorisation (equivalent to ONR's licensing) of Operating Duty Holders (ODHs)
2. inspections to verify those authorised are adhering to the 36 authorisation conditions required by DNSR regulations
3. assessment of specified safety documentation, including emergency response exercises to assess how effective arrangements are in a dynamic environment
4. permissioning high consequence activities affecting present or future safety.

The DNSR also regulates project teams from DE&S who control the 'safe to operate' part of the safety regime including design, systems approval, business processes (for naval reactor plants, propulsion and nuclear weapons). The DNSR specifies 'authorisation conditions' that mirror civil licensing conditions, requiring adequate safety management arrangements to be in place.

DNSR controls and influences each authorisee by a form of certification or more correctly 'permission' for certain activities to progress, given the evidence within nuclear safety cases showing that risks are ALARP. The authorisation of nuclear reactor operation at sea mirrors the US Department of Defence protocols, recognising control and responsibilities sit where the expertise lies. DNSR's successful safety regime has helped keep nuclear submarines safe for as long as they have existed.

3.5 Land systems safety

The Land Systems Safety Regulator (also part of the DSEA federation) regulates all land-based activities within JSP 454 for systems. Specific regulations address the carriage of dangerous goods (JSP 800) and bulk storage (JSP 309), broadly mirroring statute, with some licensing and authorisation processes. There is no specific certification process for land systems but JSP 454 requires a three part safety case for requirements capture and design; manufacture and test; and usage. The operational safety case is scrutinised by the ODH and can be audited by the regulator. The regulator also facilitates a comprehensive legislation exemption committee process.

---

[8] Contractor-managed defence nuclear activities are jointly regulated by ONR and the DNSR.

3.6 Weapon systems safety

The Defence Ordnance Safety Regulator is responsible for the intrinsic safety of weapons and explosives, their safe storage and transportation (DOSR is another federated part of the DSEA). It does this by a tiered certification of the riskiest elements (explosives chain). The classification of the explosive components is achieved through the Explosive Storage and Transportation Committee (ESTC) which certifies to United Nations tests, defence standards, performance, safety, insensitive munitions, etc. The weapons safety case demonstrates the weapon is inherently safe by controlling the initiation of the explosives train. The safety case is peer-reviewed by the Ordnance Safety Review Panel and certification then considers that weapon's integration within military platform as part of that regulatory domain. Their resupply (factory to foxhole) is shown in Figure 2 (MOD 2009).

3.7 Duty holders

The Permanent Under-Secretary of Defence has personally delegated each Chief Executive to ensure their arm of defence discharges its safety responsibilities in accordance with departmental policy. In their capacity as senior duty holders they use 'letters of delegation' to cascade responsibilities down to individual DE&S project team leaders and front-line ODHs. Below this level, responsibilities are specified in individual job descriptions and terms of reference. The MAA requires a similar process using letters of authorisation.

Competent contractors may identify potential issues and recommend how they can be managed, but only the owner and operator (crown servants) can own the risks, in accordance with their legal duties. A relatively small number of crown servants occupy positions where they can be defined as the 'controlling mind', responsible and accountable for:

1. the acquisition of a product or service, with a risk of harm to life, loss of capability or to the environment
2. oversight of a safety case formally identifying the measures required to make risks broadly acceptable *or* tolerable and ALARP (through a safety argument[9])
3. the control and acceptance of such risks
4. control over activities.

MOD terms such individuals 'duty holders'. Each of regulators places similar requirements upon duty holders to operate a safety management system and define individual responsibilities. Although roles may change (during acquisition phases,

---

[9] The nuclear industry states a safety case should contain 'an analysis of possible faults using the complementary approaches of design basis and probabilistic analyses, so that severe accidents are analyzed as appropriate, demonstrating that control of hazards and residual risks are ALARP'(HSE 2006, S92(f)).

defined activities or defined operations), duty holders must demonstrate that risks within their control are either broadly acceptable *or* tolerable and ALARP. In discharging such duties, duty holders must control:

- the commissioning of the act, start or stop an activity, manage the programme
- the design intent/material state, the programming of a risky activity and the finance or other resource

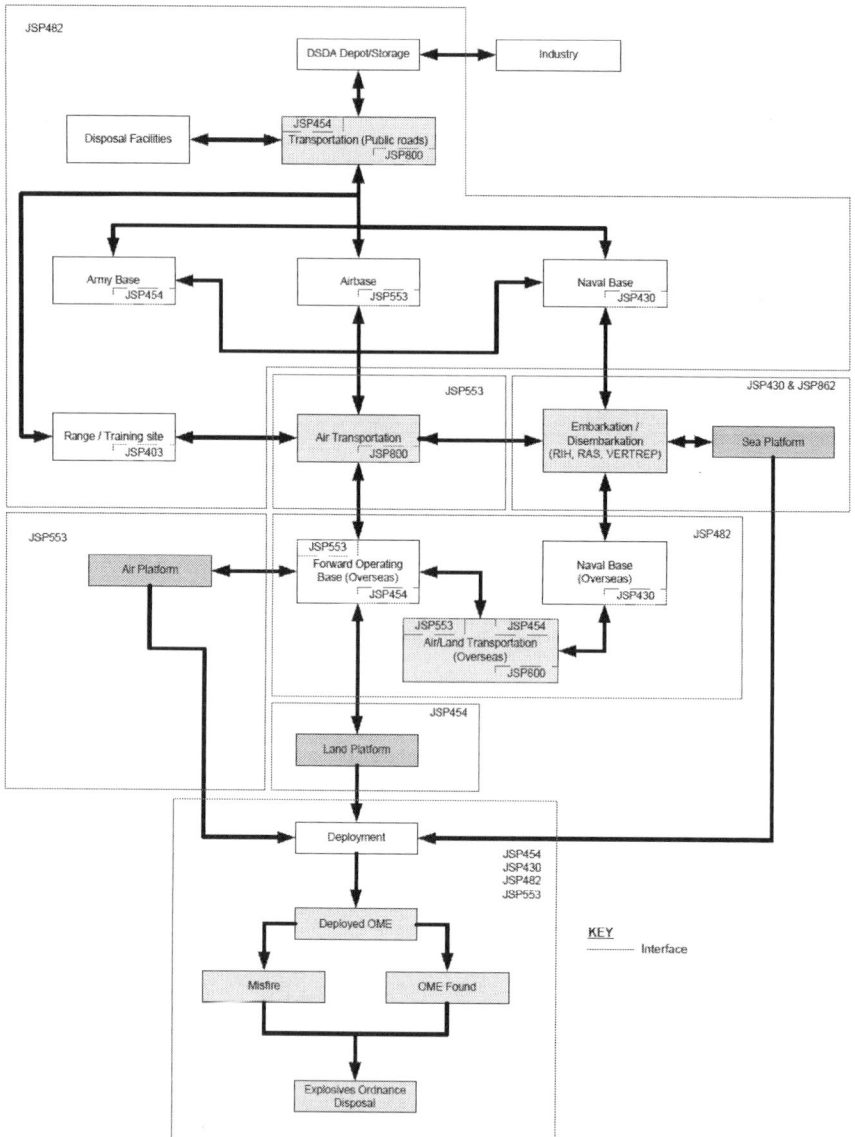

Fig-2. Weapons safety certification

- their safety management system
- the process for accepting, tolerating risk or requiring further work
- how mitigation actions are implemented and appropriately managed
- the accountability, authority and resources necessary to discharge their duties.

In order to comply with safety policies and instructions, duty holders (e.g. heads of establishment and project team leaders at certain acquisition stages) need to demonstrate their control of activities which pose significant risk of harm.

4 A systems view?

The people, software, hardware and management that form effective military systems are predicated on clear performance requirements and sound organisation, provided by competent people, working co-operatively, from the earliest stage of the system lifecycle to produce and maintain physical systems that are fit for purpose. Safety or environmental management cannot be considered in isolation and is founded on good programme management and planning, good requirements specification and engineering design, and effective quality management (including configuration management, conformance management, quality control and assurance). Most safety cases rely upon this multidisciplinary systems approach.

4.1 Reliability?

Defence safety and environmental management shares much in common with system survivability, dependability and ensuring mission success. Respected safety thinkers fear that systems safety engineering can be confused with component reliability (Leveson 2011). Whilst this is undoubtedly true in the minds of some practitioners, it is not UK policy. Safety-critical systems may need to be available on demand or depend on a level of system availability (Dalzell 2012).

Risk mitigation needs effective design, robust human factors, reliability or maintainability and procedural improvement, maintained with a competent, multidisciplinary workforce within a good safety culture. Each organisational component can be certified to improve its robustness.

4.2 Goals or precise targets?

The different sides of the Atlantic appear superficially to have opposed philosophies in defining what a compliant standard should be. There are ethical and moral questions (Leveson 2011) about risk acceptance by cost benefit analysis (underlying an ALARP argument). Yet any effective risk control should not assume risk is tolerable just because it is compliant with a standard nor that it is safe merely by passing a test or being accepted by the regulator. A better risk control measure is for risk owners to prove what else is 'reasonably practicable' after a standard 'method, test and scrutiny' are met and that the regulator endorses this strategy.

Such certification can support parts of a 'safety case' approach, as evidence that elements have met objective standards, or have followed a risk mitigation hierarchy and can then be regulated for compliance using a performance-based regulation. Perhaps this viewpoint might help temper such fears of 'irrational safety calculation', which no safety regime should tolerate?

4.3 Risk mitigation hierarchy

The risk mitigation hierarchy (HSE 1999, Schedule 1, Regulation 4) used across defence is the same as that used by most UK statutory safety regimes (Dalzell 2012) and specifies the general principles of prevention.

4.4 Why goals?

Simple compliance is only the first step in reaching a safe system. Dalzell (2012) eloquently expresses this evolution in thinking as: 'I do, therefore I comply; I understand, therefore we are safe; I think, therefore we are all safer. Adherence to four key principles of safety management (Leadership, Independence, People-focussed, Simplicity – LIPS) make safety cases better (Haddon-Cave 2009) and focus the safety argument on proving that clear thinking has occurred.

For UK defence, the historic problem has been that the overhead in maintaining defence standards has not kept pace with the technology and many, if not all, European industries have moved from prescriptive to goal-based standards since the 1980s. Mere compliance against increasingly obsolescent standards had stifled innovation and had become (or was accused of becoming) a barrier to adopting new technologies and solutions. Certification has become more to do with the safety argument and less to do with compliance. Certainly most defence standards have shifted from 'do it this way to be safe' to 'meet these principles'. Regrettably there has been less consensus on what effective software safety might be.

Attempts to reverse-engineer prescriptive standards for hardware have helped clarify 'why' things were safe and the original design intent (Hoppe 2005). Although the safety case can be critiqued (Haddon-Cave 2009) the idea of focussing on risks and prioritising effort remains the focus of UK defence regulations (Inge 2007).

Good safety cases are built by staged product certification and procedural compliance. Dalzell (2012) summarises this as: 'I know why it is dangerous so now we make it safe'. This shift in defence thinking reflects civil practice. Successive International Marine Organisation (IMO) committees 'MSC79' and 'MSC80' agreed some basic principles for future IMO goal-based standards, which were:

1. a broad overarching safety, environmental and/or security management standard that ships are required to meet during their lifecycle
2. the required standard to be achieved in rules applied by 'recognised organisations' such as class societies, or with other administrations via the IMO
3. clear, demonstrably verifiable, long-standing and achievable regulations, irrespective of ship design or technology
4. specific enough that requirements are not to be open to differing interpretations.

Such basic principles are applicable to both goal-based standards for new construction standards and in-service by recognising these concepts' application in machinery, equipment, and fire protection, so that future standards for organisations follow the same principles.

4.5 Using standards

Leveson (2011) classifies safety standards as 'product, process or performance standards'. Defence standards have encoded the *specific designs and features* to pass on knowledge about past experience and lessons learned from past lessons. She correctly observes that different industries face different safety problems and therefore have different *general approaches to determining what is safe*. Yet as defence has standardised its practices across each defence sector, and has adopted civil practice, it has been expected that individual safety cases would capture the understanding of the standards selected.

Prior to Haddon-Cave, increased use of *process standards* was the preferred strategy. However standards that only specify the method to produce a product rather than how the system will operate has had mixed success. Assurance solely based on process compliance cannot substitute for the design standard or performance standard and should be used in combination with these. *Performance-based or goal-setting approaches* focus on desired, measurable outcomes, rather than required product features and remain common in the maritime sector (Roberts et al. 2007). The IMO safety committees agreed a hierarchy of five tiers:

- **Tier I** goals
- **Tier II** functional requirements
- **Tier III** verification of compliance criteria
- **Tier IV** technical procedures and guidelines, classification rules and industry norms or standards
- **Tier V** codes of practice, quality systems for shipbuilding, safe ship operation, maintenance, training, manning, etc.

4.6 Selecting standards and codes of practice

Proper selection of standards in the defence maritime sector comes with an expectation (MOD 2006) that relevant standards and codes of practice should be used wherever practicable, because they provide relevant and clear examples of good practice (Dalzell 2012). To paraphrase this guidance, the safety case is built upon evidence, which shows that a selected standard is relevant; any risks not covered by that standard is managed according to the risk mitigation hierarchy. Duty holders are required to demonstrate that the standards and codes of practice used adequately control the risks claimed to be mitigated.

The evidence underpinning selection of a particular standard or code of practice should show that the resulting level of safety risk is 'at least as good as' a relevant statutory regulation (a shore-based regulation, a merchant shipping statutory regulation or similar best practice standard). This can use appropriate quantitative analysis or direct comparison to a deterministic standard (see Figure 3), such that the safety requirement is addressed. A duty holder's safety managers can seek external expertise to successfully complete such a detailed analysis.

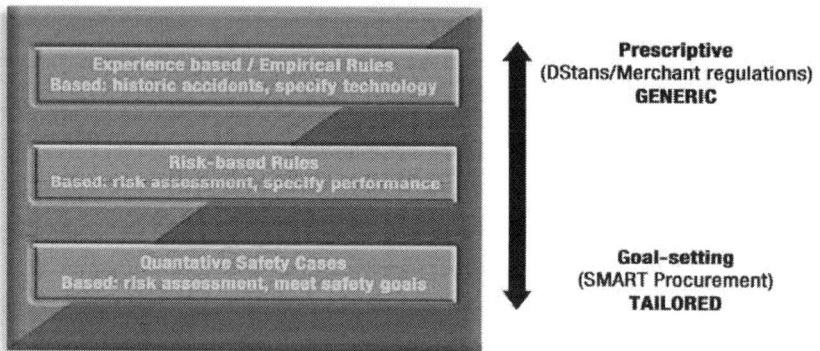

Fig. 3. Empirical versus quantitative assessment (MOD, 2006)

Performance-based standards align well with the goal setting principles. However, the application of prescriptive/deterministic rules remains a core element of the safety regime for specific risks, as they:

1. are often widely used and understood, representing good practice to control a set of specified risks
2. may not require advanced knowledge or deep competence to apply and they can be easy to contract against
3. enable 'traditional' designs to be quickly and repeatedly generated and surveyed in a reliable/predictable format
4. capture expertise/historic lessons learnt into a readily useable format or formulae, permitting benchmarking

5. support established feedback and review systems from in-service experience, permitting easier survey, verification and acceptance into service
6. provide a clear-cut route to achieving a safety requirement, less susceptible to corruption by programme or resource considerations.

4.7 Managing software

Software is regulated via a recently published policy leaflet (MOD 2012b) requiring for

'any activity that relies on the integrated use of equipment or sub-systems that includes software, the risks associated with software and its integration into the equipment or subsystem are properly managed and assurance is provided that the software is safe to use for the activity for which it was developed'.

It states:

'Where equipment or sub-systems use software in the delivery of some or all functionality, an assessment shall be made to determine whether by failure or unspecified behaviour, the software could credibly trigger:

a. an event that escalates to a key hazard,
b. impairment of the mitigation of a key hazard, or
c. impairment of recovery from a key hazard.

'The way software could be a stimulus event to a key hazard, impair the mitigation of a key hazard, or impair recovery following such a key hazard event shall be communicated to the appropriate parties so that the contribution to the overall system risk can be properly assessed and alternative designs or mitigation considered, where necessary. The appropriate parties include those responsible for the overall system development, the safety of the system, and the Defence Security and Assurance Services. Provision shall be made to protect systems against:

d. intentional or unintentional viruses or unauthorised code,
e. unauthorised installation, change, or deletion of software,
f. the installation or use of unauthorised software, and
g. modification of the software function.'

This adapts system safety justification to manage risks posed by the use of software and links to configuration management, development and testing of changes to the software, including specific arrangements for on-board testing, release and installation of software and the importance of communicating, cooperating, and sharing information and documentation, prior to operational use.

Clearly prescriptive or deterministic standards may not address all issues or be entirely relevant to every application (MOD 2006), since:

1. Deterministic standards are based on past practice, often making them inappropriate for new technology or unusual circumstances, and stifling innovative approaches or solutions.

2. The original purpose of the standard can be hidden or may no longer apply, and the reasons for specific criteria may not be expressed.
3. Compliance with the standard may discourage work to seek safety improvements.
4. They often do not account for human error or violation of procedures.

A successful safety case requires consideration of how hardware or software safety requirements are affected by military operations, particularly during selecting appropriate design or material-state standards. When it is necessary to maintain a selected capability to specified requirements, the way the system is used may require levels of redundancy or ruggedisation, enhanced fire protection, graceful degradation, reparability, recoverability, shock protection, consideration of system interaction, ballistic protection, etc.

Adequate consideration of the safety features will affect military capability and the ultimate survivability of the warship as a fighting unit. Conversely ships designed without any military features and subsequently used for military operations can easily find themselves to be working outside the scope of their design envelope and 'known, safe material state'.

In either case, the original basis for the safety case may need to be revisited. The selection of key naval defence standards has been codified. Duty holders are required to consider the use of appropriate Category 1 to 3 Naval Defence Standards. When a Category 1 standard is not selected the duty holder must satisfy the naval authority. The categorisation of these standards depends on the effect the standard may have on safety, operational performance, through life support or fleet commonality. The safety case must also demonstrate how equivalent compliance has been achieved with MOD and civil statutory regulations, as applicable.

5 Conclusions

Despite significant differences in environmental domains, there is consistency in the principles and legislative base of much defence safety certification. The certification and approval of safety cases within UK defence maritime systems follows common principles, whilst continuing to evolve best practice.

Since defence activities occur across many environmental domains, the safety regimes of each UK defence system must also reflect multiple civil counterparts. The certification of UK warships, including their software-intensive systems, follows a set of general principles based on civil law. The defence sector considers certification during 'safe to operate' and has begun to consider the operational function to prove that it can be 'operated safely'. Legislation influences departmental policy, which must respond to significant accidents to include principles and techniques that duty holders are required to discharge. Certification helps crown servants playing key roles as duty holders, by adapting and complying with standards under regulations set by internal MOD regulators.

Acknowledgments   The support of colleagues in DSEA and specialist across MOD, who have supported me in developing the thinking behind this paper, is acknowledged.

References

Dalzell GA (2012) Safety leadership – what it should mean to engineers. http://webcommunities. hse.gov.uk/connect.ti/riskeducation/viewdocument?docid=451173. Accessed 6 November 2012

Haddon-Cave C (2009) The Nimrod review. HC1025. Stationery Office Ltd, London

Hoppe H (2005) Goal-based standards – A new approach to the international regulation of ship construction. www.imo.org/ourwork/safety/shipdesign/documents/goal.pdf. Accessed 12 November 2012

HSE (1999) Approved code of practice and guidance for the 'management of health and safety at work regulations'

HSE (2006) Safety assessment principles for nuclear facilities, 2006 Edition, Revision 1

Inge JR (2007) The safety case: its development and use in the United Kingdom. Equipment Safety Assurance Symposium, Bristol

Leveson N (2011) White paper on the use of safety cases in certification and regulation. Aeronautics and Astronautics/Engineering Systems, MIT

MOD (2006) JSP 430 Ship safety management policy guidance, Issue 3, Part 2, Amdt 1

MOD (2009) Guidance for UK MOD's Ordnance, Munitions & Explosives Safety Management system, JSP520, Part2, Issue3

MOD (2012a) MOD ship safety and environmental protection regulations, JSP430 Part-1, Issue 4, Amendment 1

MOD (2012b) Naval authority certification, JSP430 Part-3, Issue 5, Amendment B

NATO (2011) Naval ship code, allied naval engineering publication 77, Issue 3, International Naval Safety Association. www.nakmo.co.uk. Accessed 7 November 2012

Roberts G, Smaller A, Simpson R, Plaskitt M (2007) The assurance afforded to a risk-based naval authority certification regime by commercial and naval class. http://media.bmt.org/ bmt_media/resources/89/RINAPaperClassificationandSafetyCase17OctFinalDraft.pdf. Accessed 6 November 2012

Steinzor R (2010) Lessons from the North Sea: should 'safety cases' come to America? Boston College Symposium on Environmental Affairs Law Review

IEC61508: Assessment, Certification and Other Assurance Measures

Ron Bell

Engineering Safety Consultants Ltd

London, UK

Abstract   This paper focuses on the safety assurance measures within international standard IEC 61508, 'Functional safety of electrical, electronic and programmable electronic safety-related systems'. IEC 61508, and other sector and product standards developed from it, have had a major impact on the application of electrical, electronic and programmable electronic safety-related systems. In particular, the paper examines the safety assurance measures that are part of the compliance requirements within IEC 61508. The paper provides an overview of the key features of IEC 61508 which are relevant to effective assurance as well as covering the explicit assurance measures such as functional safety assessment, functional safety audit, verification and validation. The paper also covers various models for certification that have developed in relation to IEC 61508.

1 Background

IEC 61508 applies to safety-related systems when one or more of such systems incorporate electrical, electronic or programmable electronic (E/E/PE) devices. E/E/PE safety-related systems are intended, with the other risk reduction measures and risk parameters, to prevent the specified hazardous event or to mitigate the consequences of the specified hazardous event.

Parts 1 to 7 of IEC 61508 were published during the period 1998-2000. A review process to update and improve the standard was initiated in 2002 and was completed with the publication of IEC 61508 Edition 2 (IEC 2010a) in April 2010.

The application of IEC 61508 and sector and product implementations are increasingly being recognised as 'accepted good practice' and have also influenced sectors which have developed their own standards and have incorporated some of the core concepts that exist within IEC 61508 into their own standards.

2 Structure of IEC 61508

The overall title of IEC 61508 is 'Functional safety of electrical, electronic and programmable electronic (E/E/PE) safety-related systems'. The Parts are as listed in Table 1.

Table 1. The Parts of IEC 61508

Part	Title
0	Functional safety and IEC 61508
1	General requirements
2	Requirements for electrical/electronic/programmable electronic safety-related systems
3	Software requirements
4	Definitions and abbreviations
5	Examples of methods for the determination of safety integrity levels
6	Guidelines on the application of parts 2 and 3
7	Overview of techniques and measures

In IEC standards, a requirement that has to be satisfied if compliance is to be claimed is referred to as a normative requirement. Such requirements are prefaced by 'shall'. A requirement prefaced by 'should' is informative and can be considered as a recommendation. However, a recommendation may, over time, become normative when that edition of the standard is revised and this should be taken into account.

Parts 1, 2 and 3 contain all the normative requirements and some informative requirements. Parts 0, 5, 6 and 7 do not contain any normative requirements.

IEC 61508 can be used as a standalone standard. Also, as Parts 1, 2, 3 and 4 have been designated as IEC basic safety publications, IEC Technical Committees have, wherever practicable, to make use of IEC 61508 in the preparation of their own sector or product standards that have E/E/PE safety-related systems within their scope. In its role as a basic publication, IEC 61508 has, for example, been used to develop standards for the process (IEC 61511) and nuclear (IEC 61513) sectors and for machinery (IEC 62061) and power drive systems (IEC 61800-5-2).

The application of IEC 61508 as a standalone standard includes the use of the standard:

- as a set of general requirements for E/E/PE safety-related systems where no application sector or product standards exist or where they are not appropriate
- by suppliers of E/E/PE elements for use in all sectors (e.g. hardware and software of sensors, smart actuators, programmable controllers)
- by providing a technical framework for conformity assessment and certification services as a basis for carrying out assessments of safety lifecycle activities.

3 Scope of IEC 61508

IEC 61508 is mainly concerned with E/E/PE safety-related systems whose failure could have an impact on the safety of persons and/or the environment. However, it was recognized that the consequences of failure could have serious economic implications and in such cases the standard could be used to specify any E/E/PE system used for the protection of equipment or product (asset protection). Some of the key features of IEC 61508 are set out below.

- It enables the development of product and sector international standards, dealing with E/E/PE safety-related systems. This should lead to a high level of consistency (for example, of underlying principles, terminology etc.) both within and across application sectors; this will have both safety and economic benefits.
- It provides a method for the development of the safety requirements specification necessary to achieve the required functional safety for E/E/PE safety-related systems.
- It uses safety integrity levels (SILs) for specifying the target level of safety integrity for the safety functions to be implemented by the E/E/PE safety-related systems.
- It adopts a risk-based approach for the determination of the safety integrity level requirements.
- It sets numerical target failure measures for E/E/PE safety-related systems that are linked to the safety integrity levels.

4 Concept of functional safety

Safety is defined as the freedom from unacceptable risk of physical injury or of damage to the health of people, either directly or indirectly, as a result of damage to property or to the environment.

Functional safety is part of the overall safety that depends on a system or equipment operating correctly in response to its inputs. In essence, this means the achievement of safety through application of control systems. This requires identifying *what has to be done* and *how well it should be done*.

5 Strategy to achieve functional safety

The strategy for achieving functional safety is made up of the following key elements:

- management of functional safety including competence

- technical requirements for relevant phases of the applicable safety lifecycles
- assurance measures such as verification, validation, functional safety audit and functional safety assessment.

IEC 61508 uses three safety lifecycles in order that all relevant phases are addressed. They are:

- the overall safety lifecycle (see Figure 1)
- the E/E/PE system safety lifecycle (see Figure 2)
- the software safety lifecycle (see Figure 3).

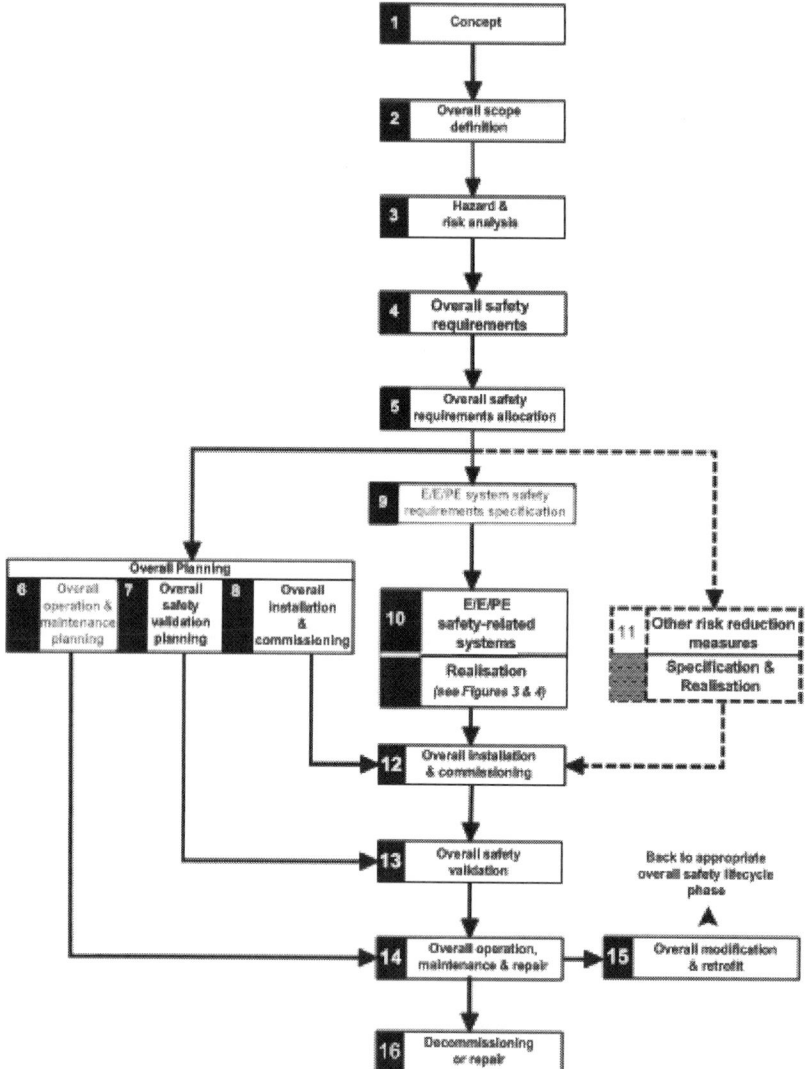

Fig. 1. Overall safety lifecycle from IEC 61508 Edition 2

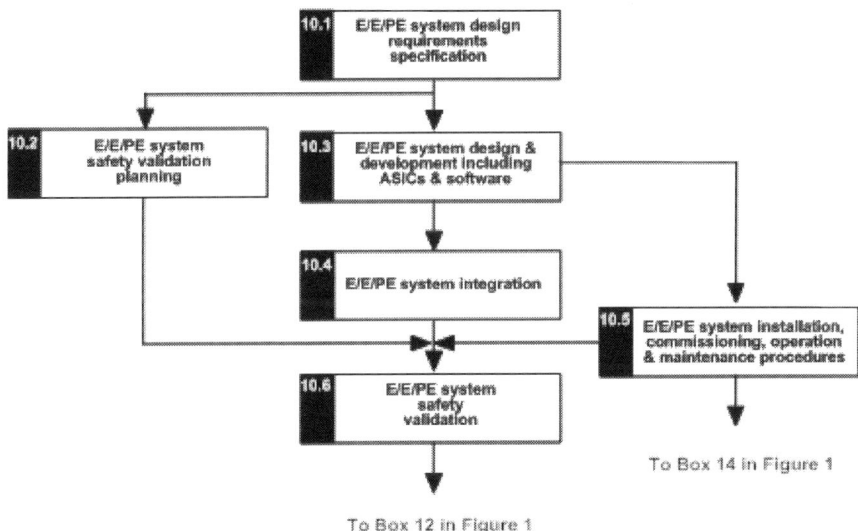

Fig. 2. E/E/PE system safety lifecycle (in realisation phase) from IEC 61508 Edition 2

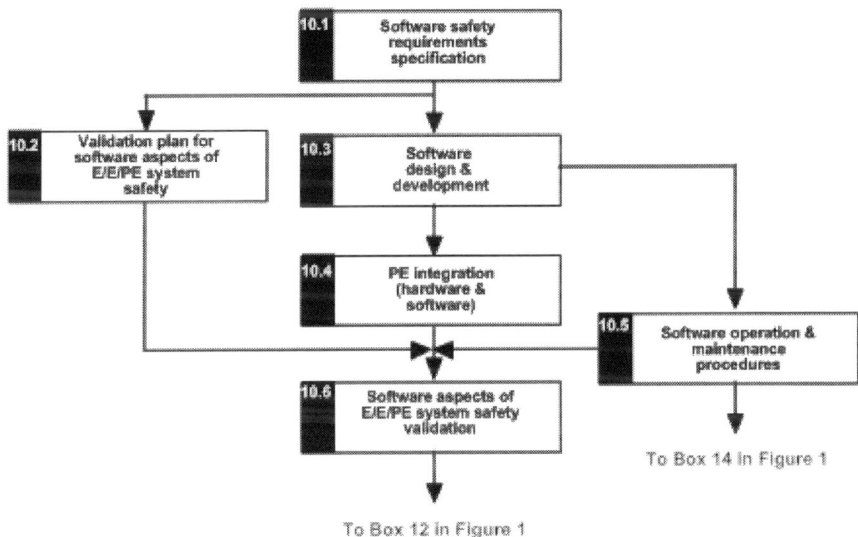

Fig. 3. Software safety lifecycle (in realisation phase) from IEC 61508 Edition 2

In order to deal in a systematic manner with all the activities necessary to achieve the required safety integrity for the E/E/PE safety-related systems, IEC 61508 adopts the overall safety lifecycle indicated in Figure 3 as the technical framework. The overall safety lifecycle specified in IEC 61508 should be used as a basis for claiming conformance to the standard, but a different overall safety lifecycle can be used to that given in Figure 3, providing the objectives and requirements of each clause of the standard are met.

The overall safety lifecycle encompasses the following risk reduction model:

- E/E/PE safety-related systems
- other risk reduction measures.

Whilst IEC 61508 provides design requirements for the achievement of functional safety for E/E/PE safety-related systems, it does not provide design requirements for 'other risk reduction measures' but does take into account the risk reduction achieved by such measures.

The portion of the overall safety lifecycle dealing with E/E/PE safety-related systems is expanded and shown in Figure 2. This is termed the E/E/PE system safety lifecycle and forms the technical framework for IEC 61508-2. The software safety lifecycle is shown in Figure 3 and forms the technical framework for IEC 61508-3.

It is very important to recognize that the overall, E/E/PE system safety and software safety lifecycle figures are simplified views of reality and as such do not show all the iterations relating to specific phases or between phases. Iteration, however, is an essential and vital part of development through the overall E/E/PE system safety and software safety lifecycles.

Activities relating to the management of functional safety, verification and functional safety assessment are not shown on the overall E/E/PE system safety and software safety lifecycles. This has been done in order to reduce the complexity of the safety lifecycle activities. These activities will need to be applied at the relevant phases of the safety lifecycles.

Evidence of the need to adopt an approach that covers all phases of the overall safety lifecycle is illustrated in a study undertaken by the UK Health and Safety Executive (HSE 2003). The study analyzed a number of accidents and incidents involving safety-related control systems. Figure 4 shows the primary cause of failure for each lifecycle phase.

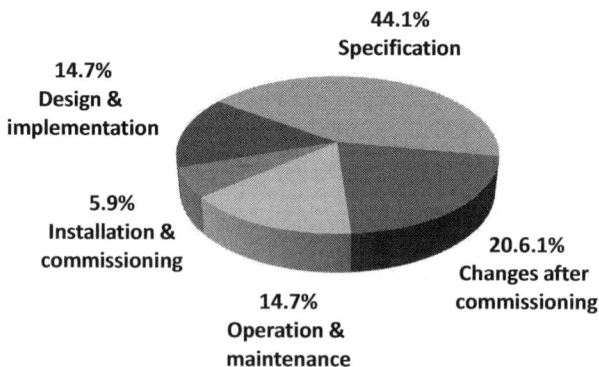

44.1%
Specification

14.7%
Design &
implementation

5.9%
Installation &
commissioning

20.6.1%
Changes after
commissioning

14.7%
Operation &
maintenance

Fig. 4. Primary cause, by phase, of control system failures

The analysis suggests that most control system failures may have their root cause in an inadequate specification. In some cases this was because insufficient hazard analysis of the equipment under control had been carried out; in others it was because the impact on the specification of a critical failure mode of the control system had not been assessed.

Based on the HSE study, more than 60% of failures were 'built in' to the safety-related system before being taken into service. Whilst the primary causes by phase will vary depending upon the sector and complexity of the application, what is self-evident is that it is important that all phases of the lifecycle be addressed if functional safety is to be achieved.

6 Essence of functional safety

A cornerstone of functional safety is the safety function. The safety function is defined as follows:

> 'Function to be implemented by an E/E/PE safety-related system, or other risk reduction measures, that is intended to achieve or maintain a safe state for the equipment under control in respect of a specific hazardous event.'

There is a need to specify the functional safety performance requirements for each safety function and this is the objective of the E/E/PE system safety requirements specification which contains the requirements for all the safety functions being carried out by the E/E/PE safety-related system.

If the safety function is performed the hazardous event will not take place. The safety function is determined from the hazard analysis. It is the safety function that determines *what has to be done* to achieve or maintain a safe state for the equipment under control.

IEC 61508 adopts a risk-based approach to the development of the specification of the required safety performance of each safety function. The safety performance is referred to as the safety integrity and is determined from the risk assessment. This is illustrated in Figure 5.

7 Safety-related systems

A safety-related system is a system that is capable of carrying out the various specified safety functions and also capable of carrying them out with the required safety integrity. It is the safety integrity requirement of the safety function that sets the safety integrity requirements for the safety-related system. A safety-related system will carry out many safety functions and must be of sufficient safety integrity to carry out the safety function with the highest safety integrity requirement (unless special measures are taken).

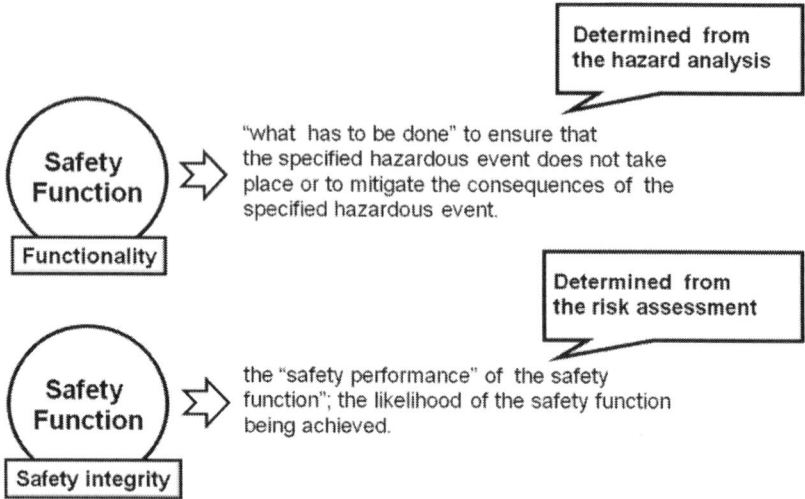

Fig. 5. The functionality and safety integrity of a safety function

Safety integrity is made up of hardware safety integrity (in relation to random failures) and systematic safety integrity (in relation to systematic failures).

8 Safety Integrity Levels (SILs)

Each safety function to be carried out by an E/E/PE safety-rated system is specified in terms of the Safety Integrity Level (SIL). Tables 2 and 3 relate the target failure measures to the SIL.

Table 2. Safety integrity levels: target failure measures for a safety function operating in a low demand mode of operation

SIL	Average probability of a dangerous failure on demand of the safety function (PFD_{avg})
4	10^{-5} to $< 10^{-4}$
3	10^{-4} to $< 10^{-3}$
2	10^{-3} to $< 10^{-2}$
1	10^{-2} to $< 10^{-1}$

The target failure measure is specified as either:

- the average probability of dangerous failure on demand of the safety function, (PFD_{avg}), for a low demand mode of operation (see Table 2)
- the average frequency of a dangerous failure of the safety function [h_{-1}], (PFH), for a high demand mode of operation (see Table 3)

- the average frequency of a dangerous failure of the safety function [h_{-1}], (PFH), for a continuous mode of operation (see Table 3).

Table 3. Safety integrity levels: target failure measures for a safety function operating in a high demand or continuous mode of operation

SIL	Probability of dangerous failure per hour (PFH)
4	10^{-9} to $< 10^{-8}$
3	10^{-8} to $< 10^{-7}$
2	10^{-7} to $< 10^{-6}$
1	10^{-6} to $< 10^{-5}$

It can be seen from Tables 2 and 3 that the SILs are related to the target failure measures depending upon the 'mode of operation'. The mode of operation has important implications when determining the SIL of a safety function to meet a target risk frequency.

9 Compliance to IEC 61508

The compliance model for IEC61508 is indicated in Figure 6.

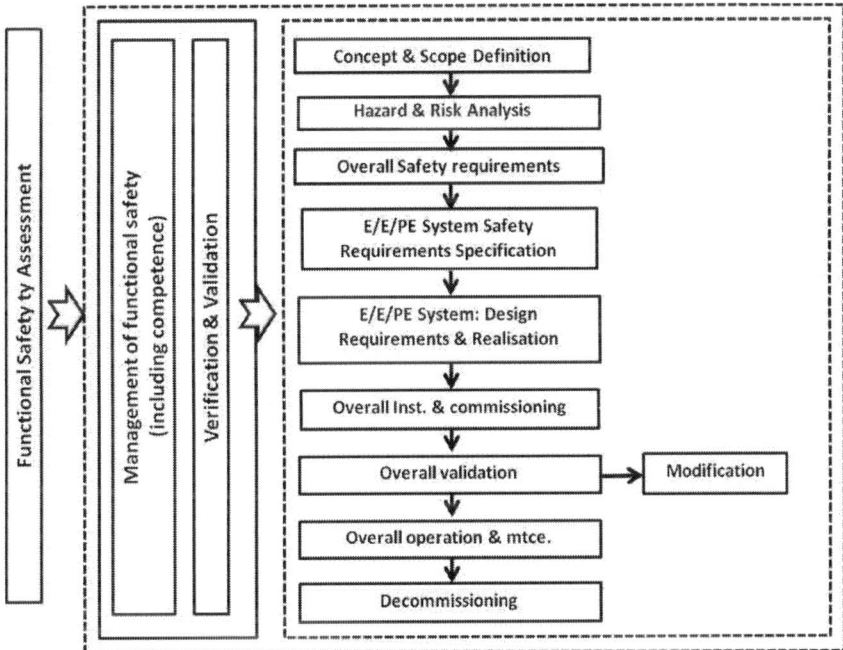

Fig.6. Compliance to IEC 61508, showing a simplified overall safety lifecycle (compare with Figure 1)

It can be seen that compliance to IEC 61508 in respect of any safety life-cycle clauses for which compliance is to be claimed requires the following.

Technical requirements. All relevant clauses in relation to any safety lifecycle phase (i.e. overall safety lifecycle, E/E/PE system safety lifecycle and software safety lifecycle) have to be met.

Functional safety management. The requirements relating to management have to be met in the context of the relevant safety life cycle phases.

Verification is required to be undertaken for each relevant safety lifecycle phase.

Validation is required to be undertaken with respect to the E/E/PE safety-rated system in respect of the specified safety functions.

Functional safety assessment is required to be carried out for all relevant safety life cycle phases.

Competence. All persons with responsibilities (i.e. including all persons involved in any overall, E/E/PE system or software lifecycle activity, including activities for verification, validation, management of functional safety, functional safety audit and functional safety assessment), have to have the appropriate competence. This would include training, technical knowledge, experience and qualifications relevant to the specific duties that they have to perform.

10 Key safety assurance measures

The key assurance measures in the achievement of functional safety, in compliance with IEC 61508, are:

- functional safety assessment;
- functional safety audit;
- verification;
- validation;

These are considered in Sections 10.1 to 10.4.

10.1 Functional safety assessment

The objective is to arrive at a judgement on the adequacy of the functional safety achieved by the E/E/PE safety-related system(s) or compliant items (e.g. elements, subsystems) based on compliance with the relevant clauses of this standard.

All relevant safety life cycle phases are within scope of the functional safety assessment including functional safety management, verification, validation and documentation.

Those undertaking a functional safety assessment have to meet specific independence requirements. There are three levels of independence which are:

- independent person
- independent department
- independent organization.

The criteria for the above three levels of independence are specified in IEC 61508-1.

The degree of independence depends upon:

- the consequence in the event of a hazardous event arising, with the consequence parameter being used as a factor in the degree of independence (see Table 4)
- the SIL or the systematic capability of the safety function (see Table 5).

With respect to Tables 4 and 5:

- 'X' is the level of independence specified is the minimum for the specified consequence (Table 4) or safety integrity level or systematic capability (Table 5). If a lower level of independence is adopted, then the rationale has to be specified.
- 'Y' is the level of independence specified that is considered insufficient for the specified consequence (Table 4) or safety integrity level or systematic capability (Table 5).

Table 4. Minimum levels of independence of those carrying out functional safety assessment (overall safety lifecycle phases 1 to 8 and 12 to 16 inclusive (see Figure 1))

Minimum level of independence	Consequence			
	A	B	C	D
Independent person	X	X1	Y	Y
Independent department		X2	X1	Y
Independent organization			X2	X

Table 5. Minimum levels of independence of those carrying out functional safety assessment (overall safety lifecycle phases 9 and 10, including all phases of E/E/PE system and software safety lifecycles (see Figures 1, 2 and 3))

Minimum level of independence	SIL/systematic capability			
	1	2	3	4
Independent person	X	X1	Y	Y
Independent department		X2	X1	Y
Independent organization			X2	X

The functional safety assessment may be carried out after each safety lifecycle phase or after a number of safety lifecycle phases subject to the overriding requirement that a functional safety assessment be undertaken prior to the determined hazards being present.

10.2 Functional safety audit

In IEC 61508, a functional safety audit is defined as:

'Systematic and independent examination to determine whether the procedures specific to the functional safety requirements to comply with the planned arrangements are implemented effectively and are suitable to achieve the specified objectives'

The evidence obtained from the functional safety audit will form part of the evidence assessed as part of the functional safety assessment.

It will be necessary that periodic functional safety audits be specified for:

- the frequency of the audits
- the level of independence of those carrying out the audits
- the necessary documentation and follow-up activities after an audit has been completed.

10.3 Verification

In IEC 61508, verification is the activity of demonstrating for each phase of the relevant safety lifecycle (overall, E/E/PE system and software), by analysis, mathematical reasoning and/or tests, that, for the specific inputs, the outputs meet in all respects the objectives and requirements set for the specific phase.

An example of verification activities will include:

- reviews on outputs (documents from all phases of the safety lifecycle) to ensure compliance with the objectives and requirements of the phase, taking into account the specific inputs to that phase
- design reviews
- tests performed on the designed products to ensure that they perform according to their specification
- integration tests performed where different parts of a system are put together in a step-by-step manner and by the performance of environmental tests to ensure that all the parts work together in the specified manner.

The documentation related to verification would be assessed as part of the functional safety audit and the functional safety assessment.

10.4 Validation

In IEC 61508, validation is the activity of demonstrating that the safety-related system under consideration, before or after installation, meets in all respects the safety requirements specification for that safety-related system.

Therefore, for example, validation of the E/E/PE safety-rated system means confirming by examination and provision of objective evidence that the E/E/PE safety-rated system satisfies the E/E/PE system design requirements specification.

In IEC61508 there are three validation phases:

- overall safety validation (see Figure 1)
- E/E/PE system validation (see Figure 2)
- software validation (see Figure 3).

The documentation related to validation would be assessed as part of the functional safety audit and the functional safety assessment.

10.5 Conformity assessment and certification

10.5.1 The fundamentals

The terms 'conformity assessment' and 'certification' are often misunderstood. In this paper the term conformity assessment is defined as[1]:

'... activity that provides demonstration that specified requirements relating to a product, process, system, person or body are fulfilled'

Conformity assessment may be undertaken by:

- a first party: this could be manufacturer of a specified product
- a second party: this could be user of a specified product
- a third party: this is a body that is independent of the first and second parties.

A body that carries out third-party conformity assessment within the framework of ISO/IEC 17065:2012 is referred to as a certification body. The scope of ISO/IEC 17065:2012 is specified as follows:

'This International Standard contains requirements for the competence, consistent operation and impartiality of product, process and service certification bodies. Certification bodies operating to this International Standard need not offer all types of products, processes and services certification. Certification of products, processes and services is a third-party conformity assessment activity (see ISO/IEC 17000:2004, definition 5.5).

---

[1] ISO/IEC 17000:2004 Conformity assessment – vocabulary and general principles

'In this International Standard, the term "product" can be read as "process" or "service", except in those instances where separate provisions are stated for "processes" or "services" (see ...).'

Therefore, certification bodies carrying out conformance assessment in compliance with ISO/IEC 17065: 2012 are undertaking third-party conformity assessment[2].

There is no requirement in IEC 61508 for compliance to be attested by a certification body as defined previously. It is a compliance requirement in IEC 61508 that an independent functional safety assessment be undertaken with respect to all relevant clauses applicable to the entity in question. The degree of independence, as part of that assessment process, will depend upon the criteria set out in IEC 61508 (see Section 10.1).

However, although there is no requirement within IEC 61508 that conformity assessment be undertaken by a certification body, companies often seek conformity assessment to IEC 61508 from a certification body operating within the framework of ISO/IEC 17065:2012.

When a third-party undertaking conformity assessment has been accredited as being in compliance with ISO/IEC 17065:2012 they are referred to as accredited certification bodies. Accreditation is carried out by a nationally appointed body such as the United Kingdom Accreditation Service (UKAS).

In the context of a specified product (e.g. sensor containing hardware and software) that is deemed to be in compliance with IEC 61508, the product manufacturer may request that an accredited certification body undertake the functional safety assessment. This approach is often adopted on the basis that conformity assessment by an accredited certification body provides a high level of confidence of compliance, which is valuable in terms of their own legal position and also valuable commercially by providing strong and supportable evidence of compliance to IEC 61508.

Companies procuring elements to IEC 61508 will, as a first priority, usually seek to procure elements that have been certified as complying with IEC 61508 by an accredited certification body.

10.5.2 What can be certified?

Certification can be undertaken on:

1. A specified product (e.g. sensor comprising complex electronics (hardware and software)). This will be referred to as a 'certified sensor'.

---

[2] ISO/IEC 17065: 2012 'Conformity assessment – Requirements for bodies certifying products, processes and services' is the international standard for certification bodies operating third-party conformity assessment schemes. This standard will be used by accreditation bodies as the basis of their accreditation of certification bodies and supersedes ISO/IEC Guide 65:1996 'General requirements for bodies operating product certification systems'. Within Europe, EN ISO/IEC 17065:2012 will replace EN 45011:1998.

2. The functional safety management system in respect of the specified scope of the activities of:

- a systems integrator
- an end user with respect to the operation and maintenance phase requirements.

The certification model in item 2 above is essentially a capability assessment of the organisation involved and provides confidence that, in the context of a systems integrator, they have the capability within the defined scope on the certificate of being able to comply with relevant clauses in IEC 61508.

11 Documentation and traceability

The documentation clause in IEC 61508 states:

'**5.1.1** The first objective of the requirements of this clause is to specify the necessary information to be documented in order that all phases of the overall, E/E/PE system and software safety lifecycles can be effectively performed.

'**5.1.2** The second objective of the requirements of this clause is to specify the necessary information to be documented in order that the management of functional safety (see Clause 6), verification (see 7.18) and the functional safety assessment (see Clause 8) activities can be effectively performed.'

The focus of the documentation clause is on information rather than physical documents. The clause, as written, provides explicit forward traceability but by indicating the necessary information is documented 'in order that all phases of the overall, E/E/PE system and software safety lifecycles can be effectively performed' it is clear that both forward and backward traceability is a necessary requirement of IEC 61508.

The information, and the traceability of the information relating to the relevant phases of the various safety lifecycles, is a prerequisite to effective safety assurance. This cannot be underestimated since it will be necessary to manage the equipment for possibly 25 years and probably within that time a number of modifications will necessitate impact analyses to be undertaken. Without robust traceability it would not be possible to assure that the target risk is being maintained.

Although documentation and traceability are not usually seen as an explicit safety assurance measure it is a cornerstone on which an effective safety assurance policy has to be based.

12 Concluding comments

IEC 61508 has a number of key compliance requirements which can be regarded as explicit safety assurance measures (i.e. functional safety assessment, functional safety audit, verification and validation) and these are all necessary as part of robust safety assurance strategy. However, a vital part of the safety assurance is the ability to understand the processes that have been undertaken in the relevant phases of the safety lifecycles. That is, robust information and traceability of the information is a cornerstone of an effective safety assurance strategy.

The holistic approach adopted in IEC 61508 to the achievement of functional safety provides a sound basis for ensuring that the initial design, the ongoing maintenance of the design and subsequent modifications to the design are managed in a systematic manner. The documentation clause which focuses on information rather than physical documents provides requirements that facilitate forwards and backward traceability.

Acknowledgments The author thanks the International Electrotechnical Commission (IEC) for permission to reproduce information from its international publication IEC 61508 ed.2.0 parts 1 to 7 (2010). All such extracts are copyright of IEC, Geneva, Switzerland. All rights reserved. Further information on the IEC is available from www.iec.ch. IEC has no responsibility for the placement and context in which the extracts and contents are reproduced by the author, nor is IEC in any way responsible for the other content or accuracy therein.

References

HSE (2003) Out of control: why control systems go wrong and how to prevent failure, 2nd edn. HSE Books. http://www.hse.gov.uk/pubns/books/hsg238.htm. Accessed 10 October 2012

IEC (2010a) IEC 61508 Functional safety of electrical/electronic/programmable electronic safety-related systems, Parts 1 to 7, Edition 2.0. International Electrotechnical Commission

Certification in Civil Aviation

Dewi Daniels

Verocel Limited

Trowbridge, UK

Abstract   This paper describes how system safety is addressed in the design of civil airliners, particularly of software-intensive avionics systems. This paper is intended to be one of a set of papers that describe how certification is carried out in a number of industries.

1 Introduction

There are over 20,000 certified jet airliners in service worldwide (Boeing 2012). Modern airliners are very complex machines. The majority of airliners in service today rely on software to carry out many flight critical functions, including:

- flight control systems
- full authority digital engine control systems
- primary flight displays
- landing gear systems
- fuel management systems
- flight management systems.

This paper describes how civil airliners are certified, with a particular emphasis on how the safety of complex, software-intensive systems is assured.

2 Regulation

2.1 International Civil Aviation Organization (ICAO)

The top-level regulator for civil aviation is ICAO, which is a specialized agency of the United Nations, established by the Chicago Convention in 1944.

ICAO sets international standards that national authorities have to follow. These regulations range from the specific (aircraft give way to the right) to the general (all pilots shall be licensed and all aircraft shall have a certificate of airworthiness).

2.2 Federal Aviation Administration (FAA)

Regulation is the responsibility of the individual authorities in each country, such as the FAA in the USA. This was created by the Federal Aviation Act of 1958, following a mid-air collision between a United Airlines DC-7 and a TWA Super Constellation over the Grand Canyon in 1956. The FAA, like all national aviation authorities, has separate sets of rules and regulations covering topics such as:

- pilot licensing
- airworthiness
- aircraft maintenance
- air traffic rules
- licensing of air carriers and commercial operators.

The focus of this paper will be on the certification of large airliners, which is covered by airworthiness regulation.

In the US, large airliners are certified according to Part 25 of the Federal Aviation Regulations (FARs) (FAA 2007). Other Parts define airworthiness standards for other types of aircraft and equipment:

- Part 23 normal, utility, acrobatic and commuter category airplanes
- Part 25 transport category airplanes
- Part 27 normal category rotorcraft
- Part 29 transport category rotorcraft
- Part 31 manned free balloons
- Part 33 aircraft engines
- Part 35 propellers.

It is a common misconception that FAR 25 requires that avionic software has to demonstrate a failure rate of 1×10^{-9} failures per hour or less.

Part 25 states that the aeroplane systems must be designed so that 'the occurrence of any failure condition which would prevent the continued safe flight and landing of the airplane is extremely improbable'. Part 25 does not mention software, nor does it define 'extremely improbable'. Advisory Circular AC 25.1309-1A (FAA 1988) describes various acceptable means for showing compliance with FAR 25.1309. These means are not mandatory. AC 25.1309-1A suggests that, when using quantitative analyses, extremely improbable failure conditions should be considered to be those having a probability on the order of 1×10^{-9} or less.

CS-25 (EASA 2012) describes the rationale for this target of 1×10^{-9}:

'Historical evidence indicated that the probability of a serious accident due to operational and airframe-related causes was approximately one per million hours of flight.

Furthermore, about 10 percent of the total were attributed to Failure Conditions caused by the aeroplane's systems. It seems reasonable that serious accidents caused by systems should not be allowed a higher probability than this in new aeroplane designs. It is reasonable to expect that the probability of a serious accident from all such Failure Conditions be not greater than one per ten million flight hours or 1×10^{-7} per flight hour for a newly designed aeroplane. The difficulty with this is that it is not possible to say whether the target has been met until all the systems on the aeroplane are collectively analysed numerically. For this reason it was assumed, arbitrarily, that there are about one hundred potential Failure Conditions in an aeroplane, which could be Catastrophic. The target allowable Average Probability per Flight Hour of 1×10^{-7} was thus apportioned equally among these Failure Conditions, resulting in an allocation of not greater than 1×10^{-9} to each. The upper limit for the Average Probability per Flight Hour for Catastrophic Failure Conditions would be 1×10^{-9}, which establishes an approximate probability value for the term "Extremely Improbable".'

To summarise, AC 25.1309-1A suggests that the probability of a *specific failure condition* (one of 100 potential failure conditions on the aeroplane) *actually resulting in a serious accident* should be 1×10^{-9} per flight hour or less. It does not state that the *overall failure rate* of any system needs to be anywhere near 1×10^{-9} per flight hour. Indeed, since each subsystem has a number of potential failure conditions and only a small proportion of defects will result in serious accidents, the overall failure rate will usually be much higher.

The ten-year average accident rate is 0.88 hull loss accidents per million departures, while less than 4% of fatal aircraft accidents have been caused by system/component failure or malfunction (Boeing 2012). This is better than the target assumed in CS-25 of the probability of a serious accident of approximately one per million hours of flight, and about 10% of that total being attributed to failure conditions caused by the aeroplane's systems.

The FAA certifies aircraft and engines. The FAA does not approve the software as a unique, stand-alone product. Once the FAA has determined that the aircraft or engine satisfies its airworthiness regulations, the FAA issues a type certificate for that aircraft or engine.

2.3 European Aviation Safety Agency (EASA)

In Europe, regulation was formerly the responsibility of national aviation authorities such as the Civil Aviation Authority (CAA) in the United Kingdom (UK) and the Direction Générale de l'Aviation Civile (DGAC) in France. European regulation is increasingly coming under the remit of EASA, which was created in 2002. Certification of large transport aircraft is already the responsibility of EASA. EASA Certification Specifications (CSs) are structured similarly to the FARs:

- CS-22 sailplanes and powered sailplanes
- CS-23 normal, utility, aerobatic and commuter aeroplanes
- CS-25 large aeroplanes
- CS-27 small rotorcraft

- CS-29 large rotorcraft
- CS-31GB gas balloons
- CS-31HB hot air balloons
- CS-APU auxiliary power units
- CS-E engines
- CS-LSA light sport aeroplanes
- CS-P propellers
- CS-VLA very light aeroplanes
- CS-VLR very light rotorcraft

2.4 Other national aviation authorities

There are, of course, many other national aviation authorities, including the Agência Nacional de Aviação Civil (ANAC) in Brazil and Transport Canada.

3 Applicable standards

Both the FAA and EASA recognise a set of related standards that cover systems, software and hardware aspects of complex systems:

- ARP4761 Guidelines and methods for conducting the safety assessment on civil airborne systems and equipment (SAE 1996)
- ARP4754A/ED-79A Guidelines for development of civil aircraft and systems (SAE 2010, EUROCAE 2010)
- DO-178C/ED-12C Software considerations in airborne systems and equipment certification (RTCA 2011, EUROCAE 2012)
- DO-254/ED-80 Design assurance guidance for airborne electronic hardware (RTCA 2000, EUROCAE 2000).

For example, AC 20-115B (FAA 1993) recognises RTCA DO-178B as a means, but not the only means, to secure FAA approval of digital computer software. Likewise, AMC 20-115B (EASA 2003) recognises EUROCAE ED-12B as a means, but not the only means to secure EASA approval of software. It is expected that the FAA and EASA will recognise DO-178C/ED-12C shortly.

3.1 SAE

ARP4761 and ARP4754A are published by SAE International. This is a global association of more than 128,000 engineers and related technical experts in the aerospace, automotive and commercial vehicle industries. Its core competencies include voluntary consensus standards development.

3.2 RTCA

DO-178C and DO-254 are published by RTCA, Inc. This is a not-for-profit corporation formed to advance the art and science of aviation and aviation electronic systems for the benefit of the public. The organization functions as a Federal Advisory Committee and develops consensus-based recommendations on contemporary aviation issues.

3.3 EUROCAE

ARP4754A, DO-178C and DO-254 are also published by the European Organisation for Civil Aviation Equipment (EUROCAE) as ED-79A, ED-12C and ED-80 respectively. This non-profit making organisation was formed at Lucerne (Switzerland) in 1963 to provide a European forum for resolving technical problems with electronic equipment for air transport. EUROCAE deals exclusively with aviation standardisation (airborne and ground systems and equipment) and related documents required for use in the regulation of aviation equipment and systems.

ARP4761 is in the process of being updated. The updated document will be published by SAE as ARP4761A and by EUROCAE as ED-135 respectively.

3.4 Standards, guidance, recommended practices and guidelines

To be pedantic, neither DO-178C nor DO-254 is a standard; they are stated to contain guidance. RTCA, Inc. defines guidance to be 'material that could be recognized by the authorities as a means of compliance to the regulations' (RTCA 2009). The legal status of ARP4761 and ARP4754A is similar, although SAE International seems to be happy to classify its documents as standards.

3.5 Consensus-based

These standards are all consensus-based. A large number of experts representing government and industry were involved in their production. For example, 100–150 members attended each meeting of SC-205/WG-71, the committee that wrote DO-178C/ED-12C.

3.6 Objective-based

ARP4754A/ED-79A, DO-178C/ED-12C and DO-254/ED-80 are all objective-based. They do not prescribe any particular system, software or hardware processes or lifecycles. Rather, they describe the objectives that the chosen system, software or hardware lifecycle has to satisfy.

For example, DO-178C/ED-12C:

- emphasises requirements-based testing as a means of verification
- requires that traceability be provided between system requirements, software requirements and source code, to ensure that all of the requirements have been implemented, and that there are no unintended functions
- requires that traceability be provided between software requirements, test cases, test procedures and test results, to ensure that the tests demonstrate correct implementation of all the software requirements
- requires structural coverage analysis, up to and including Modified Condition/ Decision Coverage (MC/DC) at Level A, to establish the thoroughness of the requirements-based testing, to support demonstration of absence of unintended functions and to ensure that the code structure was verified.

3.7 Quantitative Risk Assessment (QRA)

The use of QRA in aircraft certification tends to be restricted to the use of techniques such as Fault Tree Analysis (FTA) and Failure Mode Effect Analysis (FMEA) to calculate the effect of random hardware failures such as component wear-out. For example, the author was involved in developing fault trees for the Lockheed C-130J. He found FTA, particularly cut set analysis, to be a useful technique for identifying and fixing common mode failures that compromised ostensibly independent subsystems.

DO-178C purposely does not assign probabilities to software failure. DO-178C section 2.3 states:

> 'Development of software to a software level does not imply the assignment of a failure rate for that software. Thus, software levels or software reliability rates based on software levels cannot be used by the system safety assessment process as can hardware failure rates.'

Rather, it was the consensus of SC-167/WG-12, the committee that wrote DO-178B (the revision that introduced those words) that if the software could cause or contribute to a catastrophic failure condition for the aircraft, then it had better satisfy all of the objectives defined for Level A software. No claim was made as to the resulting failure rate. This consensus belief has been confirmed by the fact that the hull loss accident rate remains very low and that no hull loss accidents have been ascribed to software failure.

The Communication, Navigation, Surveillance and Air Traffic Management (CNS/ATM) community seems to make more use of QRA (for example, to set risk budgets) than we tend to do in the airborne community.

3.8 Safety cases

Aircraft certification also makes little use of safety cases. None of the SAE or RTCA standards require the use of safety cases. ARP4761 does not mention safety cases at all. ARP4754A mentions that the aircraft safety assessment forms part of what is sometimes called a safety case. DO-178C mentions that one technique for presenting the rationale for using an alternative method is an assurance case. The author was involved in writing a safety case for the Lockheed C-130J.

4 In-service experience

Modern airliners are very safe. The accident rate remains extremely low at 0.88 hull loss accidents per million departures (0.39 fatal accidents per million departures). Not a single hull loss accident in passenger service has been ascribed to software failure, although software has been a contributing factor in a small number of accidents and implicated in a small number of in-flight upsets. This is a remarkable achievement given the number of aircraft in service:

- 21,538 certified jet aeroplanes greater than 60,000 pounds maximum gross weight in service in 2011
- 23.6 million departures in 2011
- 50.9 million flight hours flown in 2011
- 36 accidents in 2011 (of which 13 were hull loss accidents) resulting in 175 onboard fatalities and no external fatalities.

These statistics (Boeing 2012) show that the present regulatory regime has served the civil aviation community well for several decades.

5 Challenges for the future

5.1 New technologies

There are a number of emerging technologies that pose a challenge to the existing regulatory regime. These technologies include:

- Unmanned Aircraft Systems (UASs)

- Next-generation CNS/ATM systems, notably the FAA's NextGen and the EUROCONTROL's Single European Sky ATM Research (SESAR).

5.1.1 Unmanned Air Systems

Take UASs as an example. Most of the discussion that follows is based on medium and large UASs that are operated beyond line of sight, rather than small and micro UASs that are operated within visual line of sight of the launch point. A UAS consists of

2. an airborne component (the airframe)
3. a ground-based component (the control segment)
4. a control link
5. the pilot/UAS operator.

A UAS differs from a manned aircraft in a number of respects:

- The *airframe*, or Unmanned Air Vehicle (UAV) and its associated avionic systems are relatively similar to those on a manned aircraft. Avoiding the need to carry a pilot results in significant size and weight savings. Some argue that a UAV does not need to be built to the same level of integrity as a manned aircraft. However, the third party risk (of mid-air collision with a manned aircraft, or the UAV crashing in a built-up area) is the same as for a manned aircraft of the same weight and size. It therefore follows that while some of the aircraft systems can be built to a lower level of integrity, most of the aircraft systems need to be developed to the same level of integrity as for an equivalent manned aircraft and should therefore be developed to equivalent standards. Airworthiness regulation for manned aircraft has tended to focus on the first party risk (to the pilot and passengers), while the only risk with a UAS is third party risk (to pilots and passengers of other aircraft, and to people on the ground). The airworthiness regulations for UASs will therefore need to reflect this change in risk.
- The *ground control segment* is unique to UASs. This component is unregulated at present, since the ground control segment is neither an airborne system (which would be subject to DO-178C) nor is it a CNS/ATM system (which would be subject to DO-278A). Many of the systems, such as primary flight displays, which are fitted to manned aircraft, have been moved to the ground control segment in a UAS. The effect on safety is the same, regardless of where the system is fitted. It seems to the author that each system should be built to the same level of integrity, regardless of whether it is installed in the airframe or in the ground control segment. The author concedes that some flight-specific requirements, such as the ability to read primary flight displays in bright sunlight, might not apply to a ground control segment. New regulations will therefore need to be introduced for UAS ground control segments.

- The *control link* is also unique to UASs. UASs will need a voice link (and in the future, data link) to the Air Traffic Controller (ATC), just as for a manned aircraft, for flight in controlled airspace. However, UASs also need a control link so that the pilot/UAS operator can issue instructions to the UAS and receive feedback on the UAS's status. In the case of a Remotely Piloted Vehicle (RPV), the control link needs to pass instructions to the control surfaces throughout the flight. In the case of autonomous and semi-autonomous UASs, the control link needs only to communicate changes to the flight plan to the UAS. While manned aircraft can cope with loss of voice communications (with some degradation in safety if flying in controlled airspace), the loss of the control link to a UAS is much more serious. Present UASs, which were mostly designed for military applications in combat zones, are designed to variously climb in a spiral, return to the launch point or continue on their pre-programmed flight plan on loss of data link. None of these actions may be acceptable when flying in civilian airspace, especially controlled airspace. The author suspects that large civilian UASs will need to have redundant control links so that loss of the control link on a UAS is even less likely than loss of voice communications on a manned aircraft.
- Finally, the relationship between the *pilot/UAS operator* and a UAS can be very different to that between a pilot and a manned aircraft. Remotely Piloted Air Systems (RPASs) are much like manned aircraft, except that the pilot is sitting on the ground. Semi-autonomous and autonomous UASs may not be able to be hand-flown at all. In many designs, the UAS operator is only able to direct the UAS by selecting a waypoint on a map. For example, the British Army is deploying the Watchkeeper, which is an autonomous UAS. It follows a flight plan entered by the UAS operator on the ground. Watchkeeper does not provide a facility for the UAS operator to hand-fly the UAV. The Watchkeeper will be operated by Bombardiers and Non-Commissioned Officers (NCOs) who do not hold a Private Pilot Licence (PPL), but who have received specialised training in how to operate Watchkeeper. In contrast, the Royal Air Force (RAF) operates the Predator, which is an RPAS. The Predator is flown by fully qualified RAF pilots with fast jet experience. RPASs and UASs both offer challenges when operated in unsegregated civilian airspace. In the case of an RPAS, two critical challenges are loss of the ground control segment and loss of the data link. For example, a Predator B operated by the US Department of Homeland Security (DHS) crashed in Arizona in 2006 after the ground control segment locked up (NTSB 2007). For an autonomous UAS, loss of the control link is less of an issue. However, the UAS operator may have limited ability to intervene in an emergency. For example, if the engine were to fail on a Watchkeeper, the operator can only select a nearby airfield and command the UAS to land there. Both types of UAS depend heavily on the on-board automated aircraft systems in an emergency. This suggests that those systems need to be built to a higher level of integrity, not less, than the equivalent systems on a manned aircraft. For example, were a light aircraft to suffer an engine failure, the pilot would select a suitable field in which to land. If an autonomous UAS

were to suffer an engine failure, how do we ensure that it does not crash in a built-up area? Another area where the division of responsibility between the pilot and automated systems differs as compared to manned aircraft is in the area of sense and avoid. Within uncontrolled (Class G) airspace, pilots are responsible for collision avoidance. The field of vision of a RPAS pilot is limited, while an autonomous UAS might be expected to sense and avoid other aircraft without any operator intervention. It is difficult to imagine how a UAS could comply with the rules of the air in Class G airspace without an effective sense and avoid system. A UAS operator may require less training (or at least different training) than the pilot of a manned aircraft, but at the cost of moving some tasks that were previously performed by the pilot to new aircraft systems such as sense and avoid. This has implications for both pilot licensing and aircraft certification. The author believes that the availability of practicable sense and avoid systems will also improve the safety of manned aviation.

The military has gained a lot of experience of flying UASs of various sizes in combat theatres such as Iraq and Afghanistan. Many military and civilian operators now wish to fly UASs in unsegregated civilian airspace. The FAA Modernization and Reform Act of 2012 set a deadline for the FAA to develop a comprehensive plan to safely accelerate the integration of civilian unmanned aircraft systems into the national airspace system by 30 September 2015. EUROCONTROL's roadmap is partial integration of UAS in 2016–2020, and full integration in 2021–2050. The author believes the following will be necessary to achieve these goals:

Rules for the airworthiness certification of UAVs. This could be done by introducing a new FAR Part and a new EASA CS for UASs. It is likely that UASs will be split into several categories, for example:

1. UAV under 150 kg and Visual Line of Sight (VLOS) operations
2. UAV over 150 kg or Beyond Line of Sight (BLOS) operations.

Rules for certification of the ground control segment. This could be done by incorporating the requirements in the relevant FAR Parts and EASA CSs, or by developing separate documents.

Rules for certification of the control link. Again, this could be done by incorporating the requirements in the FAR Part and EASA CS, or by developing separate documents.

Deployment of effective sense and avoid systems. The author believes that the development of affordable, low-power sense and avoid systems will be beneficial to General Aviation (GA) and Commercial Air Transport (CAT), as well as to UAS.

Pilot licensing for UAS operators/pilots. Appropriate training and licensing could be introduced for UAS operators/pilots, perhaps including a National Private Pilot Licence (Unmanned Air System) (NPPL (UAS)).

5.2 Safety and security

Another challenge is the growing concern over cyber security, especially with the increased reliance on air-ground data links by next-generation CNS/ATM systems and by UAVs. The aviation industry needs to ensure that safety is not compromised through breaches of security. With the increasing sophistication of cyber-attacks, and the introduction of data links between the aircraft and the ground, we can expect terrorists and others to launch cyber-attacks in addition to physical attacks on airliners.

RTCA SC-216/EUROCAE WG-72 was established in 2007 to address aeronautical systems security. The committee has published:

- DO-326/ED-202, Airworthiness security process specification.

SC-216/WG-73 is now working on:

- DO-XXX/ED-XXX, Security assurance and assessment methods for safety-related aircraft systems
- DO-XXX/ED-XXX, Security guidance for continuing airworthiness
- DO-326A/ED-202A, Update to security assurance and assessment processes for safety-related aircraft systems.

One would think that the safety and security communities would have much in common (and they do). However, historically, the emphasis of the aviation safety community has been on proactively demonstrating that aircraft systems are safe for their intended purpose before they enter service. The emphasis of much of the Information Technology (IT) security community has been more reactive – issuing security patches to address vulnerabilities as they are discovered.

For example, suppose a zero-day exploit were discovered in a safety-critical avionic system that could be exploited over a communications link. Should the airframe manufacturer:

1. Rush out a security update and risk introducing a defect that causes an accident?
2. Ground the aircraft fleet until an update can be tested thoroughly?
3. Continue flying with the existing software until the update is thoroughly tested, accepting there is a zero-day exploit?

Given that the members of SC-216/WG-73 come from an avionics background rather than a mainstream IT security background, the author expects that the avionics industry will continue to ensure that avionic systems are safe (and secure) before they are deployed, minimising the need to publish security updates.

6 Conclusion

The aviation industry has achieved exceptionally high levels of safety over the last several decades. The hull loss rate is less than one hull loss accident per million departures. This has been achieved through regulation that is a mix of goal-based, objective-based and prescriptive. The aviation industry uses consensus-based standards that are developed in partnership between certification authorities and industry. Aircraft certification does not make much use of safety cases and quantitative risk assessment, and avoids making quantitative claims for software reliability. There are new technologies emerging that pose challenges to the existing certification regime, though these should be surmountable.

References

Boeing (2012) Statistical Summary of Commercial Jet Airplane Accidents, Worldwide Operations 1959 - 2011. Boeing Commercial Airplanes. http://www.boeing.com/news/techissues/pdf/statsum.pdf. Accessed 15 August 2012
EASA (2003) AMC 20-115B Recognition of Eurocae ED-12B / RTCA DO-178B. European Aviation Safety Agency
EASA (2012) CS-25 Certification Specifications and Acceptable Means of Compliance for Large Aeroplanes. European Aviation Safety Agency
EUROCAE (2000) ED-80: Design Assurance Guidelines for Airborne Electronic Hardware. EUROCAE
EUROCAE (2010) ED-79A: Guidelines for Development of Civil Aircraft and Systems. EUROCAE
EUROCAE (2012) ED-12C: Software Considerations in Airborne Systems and Equipment Certification. EUROCAE
FAA (1988) Advisory Circular 25.1309-1A System Design and Analysis. Federal Aviation Administration
FAA (1993) Advisory Circular 20-115B RTCA, Inc. Document RTCA/DO-178B. Federal Aviation Administration
FAA (2007) Code of Federal Regulations, Part 25 Airworthiness Standards: Transport Category Airplane, Sec. 25.1309 Equipment, systems, and installations. Federal Aviation Administration
NTSB (2007) CHI06MA121. 2007, National Transportation Safety Board
RTCA (2000) DO-254: Design Assurance Guidance for Airborne Electronic Hardware. RTCA, Inc.
RTCA (2009) RTCA Paper No. 234-09/PMC-758. Terms of Reference for Software Joint Special Committee/Working Group Software Considerations in Aeronautical Systems (Revised SC-205 TOR V4). RTCA, Inc.
RTCA (2011) DO-178C: Software Considerations in Airborne Systems and Equipment Certification. RTCA, Inc.
SAE (1996) ARP4761: Guidelines and Methods for Conducting the Safety Assessment Process on Civil Airborne Systems and Equipment. SAE International
SAE (2010) ARP4754A: Guidelines for Development of Civil Aircraft and Systems. SAE International

Automotive Regulations

Roger Rivett

Jaguar Land Rover

Gaydon, UK

Abstract   This paper describes the different approaches that countries use to regulate the sale of passenger cars in their domestic markets. It also describes some of the other pressures on manufacturers and suppliers to produce products that do not cause injury. This paper is intended to be one of a set of papers that describe how certification is carried out in a number of industries.

1 Introduction

Current passenger car production stands at approximately 80 million vehicles per annum, and of these virtually all will use software for some of their systems, ranging from relatively small amounts in a low-cost utility vehicle, to more lines of code in a premium vehicle than occurs in a modern airliner (Rivett 2012). These are sold into all the countries of the world, each of which has the right to control the sale of vehicles in their own country; they are not subject to any wider constraints. Consequently there is a wide variation in the detail of how regulations are written and what different countries require, although there is commonality in the major established markets.

The regulations that have to be met in order to sell a vehicle represent a minimum standard although in practice the performance of vehicles exceeds that required by the regulations due to other pressures. These pressures are for both primary and secondary safety measures and arise from consumer protection laws, product liability legislation, reports published by independent non-governmental agencies and the feature content of competitor vehicles. There is also much media attention from newspapers, magazines and television programmes; this means that if a customer has a bad experience it can be a very public event.

In 1997 I presented a paper at the Safety-critical Systems Symposium held in Brighton (Rivett 1997) which included a summary of the automotive regulations, and although there have been some changes in the intervening years, the basic approach remains the same. This is in contrast to the extent that the vehicle has changed, particularly with regard to the exponentially increasing use of software.

2 Regulations

Most governments control the sale of vehicles in their countries by mandating a set of regulations that the vehicle must meet, although some countries do not mandate any regulations. Where they exist, these regulations relate to either safety or environmental issues. Safety regulations are intended to help avoid accidents or lessen the injuries resulting from an accident. Environmental regulations are mainly concerned with exhaust gas emissions but they also include the prohibition of some materials and recycling requirements.

The regulations specify performance criteria that must be met, and depend on the type of vehicle (there is no globally agreed scheme for defining vehicle types). The regulations relate to one of the following:

- a particular component where legislative requirements can be assessed without vehicle fitment, for example horns, headlights, tyres
- a system, for example braking, which may contain components which are themselves subject to individual legislation and for which there may also be an installation criteria
- the whole vehicle, for example emissions and EMC.

For some countries there may be hundreds of regulations that have to be met before the vehicle can be sold. The safety regulations are normally introduced as a result of issues experienced in service. The prompt for these may come from government bodies, international groups or lobby organisations. Some regulations, particularly crash protection, are driven by accident statistics. Most bodies that produce regulations invite public comment prior to publication. The regulations are worded as black box performance requirements, in that they do not address how an item is designed, verified or manufactured. In general, regulations do not make requirements concerning the technology used, and specifically electronics and software as technologies are never mentioned.

A country may write its own regulations or mandate that a regulation authored elsewhere be met. Most of the regulations that are used in Europe are published by the United Nations Economic Commission for Europe (UNECE 2012) and these are also used in many countries throughout the world. The European Union also writes regulations and also issues directives which require member nations to adopt specific regulations in their own legislation. Countries that have written their own particular regulation may accept that a regulation not authored by them is equivalent and accept vehicles that meet the equivalent regulation. Of the developing countries, Russia are mandating existing UNECE regulations, China, India and Brazil are all creating their own with the Chinese and Indian regulations being heavily based on European regulations.

Vehicle manufacturers have to decide four years in advance of when work begins on the design of a new vehicle which markets they will sell in, and then compile a list of all the relevant regulations that must be met, taking into account where different markets accept common regulations. They have to try and anticipate how the regulations in all these countries may change before production begins.

3 Enforcement of regulations

There are two different approaches that countries use to enforce compliance with the regulations they have placed on vehicles. One is to mandate that compliance with each regulation is checked by a third party; this is referred to as homologation or type approval. The other approach is to allow the manufacturer to make an explicit claim that the vehicle is compliant with all the relevant regulations; this is referred as self-certification.

3.1 Type approval

This is the most common way that regulations are enforced and is used throughout Europe. Agencies are registered to perform a third party check and they witness tests, using production representative parts, that demonstrate that the performance criteria contained in the regulation have been met. Some countries appoint additional 'technical services'. In the UK the Vehicle Certification Agency (VCA 2012) is the agency appointed by the UK government; however a vehicle manufacturer in the UK is not obliged to use the VCA.

The manufacturer also has a conformity of production requirement to ensure that all the parts sold perform the same as those used for the witnessed test. Conformity of production means the ability to produce series products in conformity with the specification, performance and marking requirements in the type approval. The manufacturer's quality systems and procedures are assessed in order to verify that there are robust controls in place to ensure that all products made conform to the approved type during the life of the approval.

When the agency has witnessed a successful test, a certificate is awarded. For the manufacturer to get permission to sell the vehicle in a country, all the relevant certificates corresponding to the mandated regulations have to be given to the relevant government body.

Reported incidents are investigated and may lead to recalls for service fixes. In the UK, the Vehicle and Operations Services Agency (VOSA 2012) support the police by examining vehicles involved in accidents to identify contributory defects, but this does not include detailed scrutiny of the electrical/electronic systems. There is no data that relates road deaths to failures of particular systems of their components. VOSA also undertake technical investigations into potential manufacturing or design defects, highlighting safety concerns and monitoring safety recalls.

3.2 Whole vehicle type approval

Whole vehicle type approval was introduced by the European Union in 1996 to cut down on paperwork. Rather than issuing individual certificates for each regulation applicable to the vehicle, a single certificate is given if all the individual regulations have been met; it is only necessary to send this one certificate to the relevant government body. Whole vehicle type approval only applies in EU territories, Israel and some former Soviet countries excluding Russia.

3.3 Self-certification

The USA is the largest market that uses this approach. The government agency, the National Highways Traffic Safety Agency (NHTSA 2012) buys vehicles and checks that the regulations are met. If they find that a regulation is not being met they can order recalls, fine the company or halt sales until the issue is resolved. This approach involves less bureaucracy than type approval.

NHTSA evaluates effectiveness of the life-saving technologies mandated by the Federal Motor Vehicle Safety Standards (FMVSS) and a report it published in 2004 concluded that an estimated 328,551 lives had been saved from 1960 to 2002 (NHTSA 2004).

Accidents are also investigated by National Transportation Safety Board (NTSB 2012) and again may lead to recalls for service fixes

3.4 TREAD Act

In 2000 the US passed the Transportation Recall Enhancement, Accountability and Documentation (TREAD) Act in response to a well publicised issue related to SUVs and tyres. This is intended to provide an early warning system by enabling NHTSA to collect and analyse data in order to identify trends and warn consumers of potential defects in vehicles.

This act requires vehicle manufacturers to report to NHTSA all safety recalls or safety campaigns in foreign countries. Vehicle manufacturers also have to report all information related to defects, reports of injury or death related to its products.

4 UNECE regulations

In order to facilitate free trade in Europe, UNECE, based at Geneva, set up Working Party 29 in 1952 as the World Forum for Harmonization of Vehicle Regulations. It produced an agreement in 1958 which relates to parts and equipment for motor vehicles. The agreement is based on reciprocal recognition by signatory countries of approvals of motor vehicle parts included in the agreement. Since 1958 more and more countries have become signatories and the scope is European in its widest geographical sense, e.g. it now includes Russia and former communist countries. Currently there are about 50 signatories (an increase from 28 in 1997). The UK signed in 1963, the United States has not signed. The agreement now includes approximately 126 different regulations. The parts and systems covered are wide-ranging and include lights, noise, radio interference, locks, exhaust emissions, seats, brakes and even motor-cycle rider's helmets and advance warning triangles. Some of them concern motorbikes, trucks or buses. Different regulations apply to different classes of vehicle, example regulations for cars are:

- Regulation 10   – EMC
- Regulation 13-H   – braking
- Regulation 79   – steering
- Regulation 100   – battery electric vehicles

Working Party 29 continues to work on the harmonization of vehicle regulations with a wide national representation including countries which have not signed the 1958 Agreement.

5 US regulations

NHTSA was officially established by the Highway Safety Act of 1970. NHTSA issues Federal Motor Vehicle Safety Standards (FMVSS). Vehicles not certified by the maker or importer as compliant with US safety standards cannot legally be sold or imported into the United States. Rather than an UNECE-style system of type approvals, the US automotive safety regulations operate on the principle of self-certification; no prior verification is required by a third party before the vehicle or equipment can be imported, sold, or used. NHTSA tests vehicles on a random basis to ensure the regulations are being met. If a non-compliance is discovered NHTSA have the power to halt sales, order a recall and fine the company. The fine can be punitive, e.g. more than $10,000 per vehicle per day until they are recalled.

The FMVSS are structured as follows:

- crash avoidance 1xx
- crashworthiness 2xx
- post crash standards 3xx
- other regulations.

6 Complex electronic vehicle controls

There is only one piece of UNECE regulation that acknowledges the use of electronic control. This goes by the title of 'Special requirements to be applied to the safety aspects of complex electronic vehicle control systems'. This defines a complex electronic vehicle control system as '... electronic control system ... subject to a hierarchy of control in which a controlled function may be over-ridden by a higher level electronic control system/function'.

This regulation was first added as an annex to the braking regulation ECE-13 'Uniform provisions concerning the approval of: vehicle of categories M, N and O with regard to braking'. It was later added as an annex to steering regulation ECE-79 'Uniform provisions concerning the approval of: vehicles with regard to steering equipment'. It is considered applicable to these systems because both of them perform a base function (braking and steering) but in addition they may also provide yaw control functions which are seen as being higher level functions.

This regulation requires the manufacturer to provide documentation describing the design of the system and its safety concept and '... provide evidence that the design and development has had the benefit of expertise from all the system fields which are involved'. The safety concept is defined as '... a description of the measures designed into the system, for example within the electronic units, so as to address system integrity and thereby ensure safe operation even in the event of an electrical failure. The possibility of a fall-back to partial operation or even to a back-up system for vital vehicle functions may be a part of the safety concept.'

During the witness testing, the type approval authority may '... apply output signals to electrical units or mechanical elements in order to simulate the effects of internal faults within the unit'. and check that the response is as documented in the safety concept.

In the US, FMVSS 126 requires the fitment of Electronic Stability Control (ECS) systems; this is an example of what the UNECE terms complex electronic vehicle control systems. The FMVSS definition is 'ESC augments vehicle directional stability by applying and adjusting the vehicle brakes individually to induce correcting yaw torques to the vehicle.' FMVSS mandates that a driver warning be given after the occurrence of one or more ESC malfunctions.

7 Standards and guidelines

In addition to the regulations there are many other documents that are used in the development of automotive products. Where these are used, it is done so voluntarily on the basis that they are considered to represent best practice. If any of these documents were to be referenced by a regulation they would then become a *de facto* part of the regulation with the legal force associated with the regulation in each market.

7.1 The code of practice for Advanced Driver Assistance Systems

Advanced Driver Assistance Systems (ADAS) systems are intended to provide the driver with additional information. In some cases they perform aspects of the driving task while still allowing the driver to be in control of the vehicle. The driver being in control is a key principle established by the Vienna Convention (Vienna 1968). Examples of these systems are adaptive cruise control, blind spot monitoring, lane departure warning, parking assist, electronic stability control, and autonomous emergency braking. Whereas the emphasis previously has been on increasing the survival rates for those involved in road traffic accidents, these systems are seen as helping to prevent accidents from happening in the first place.

Original Equipment Manufacturers (OEMs) started developing this technology over 10 years ago and these developments were supported by governments, including the UK DfT, which believed it would help prevent road accidents on the basis that the vast majority of accidents are caused by human error, for example lack of attention, driving too fast, being under the influence of alcohol or drugs.

The new issues that arose in developing these technologies concerned the interaction of the driver with the vehicle and the increasing complexity in the Human Machine Interface (HMI) that arises as ADAS systems are fitted. However, the regulations at the time only covered vehicle behaviour rather than the HMI of ADAS systems. The standards that existed were very high level and generic, e.g. font size for readability, loudness, and colour contrasts. This lack of regulation was seen as hampering the deployment of these technologies to production vehicles as manufacturers were concerned about the lack of documented best practice to follow. This led, via a number of EU Response projects, to the publication of a code of practice for the design and evaluation of ADAS (ADAS 2009). A draft was published in 2006, trials were held between 2007 and 2008 and the final version was published in 2009.

Although the ADAS Code of Practice (CoP) does not change any legal requirements it helps the OEMs address the legal concepts of being 'reasonably safe' and exercising 'duty of care'. It does this by providing many checklists of questions to be answered, thus providing a common consistent approach. Note, the ADAS CoP only considers one system at a time, it does not consider the effect of multiple systems operating at the same time.

7.2 ISO 26262 road vehicles – functional safety

This ISO standard was published in November 2011 (ISO 2011). It is an automotive sector-specific version of the generic safety standard IEC 61508 (IEC 2010). It has nine normative parts and one informative guideline part. It has adapted the IEC 61508 safety lifecycle to fit in with typical automotive product lifecycles. A fuller summary is given in (Rivett 2012).

Although it is not currently referenced in any of the regulations, vehicle manufacturers and suppliers are adopting its use as it is seen as a definition of best practice and the normal policy of automotive companies is to follow best practice where it is defined. In some markets the need to follow best practice has legal force and in those situations it might be considered a legal requirement. If it were to be referenced in any regulation it would become *de facto* a legal requirement.

Some of the risk assessment concepts used in ISO 26262 were first developed during the creation of the ADAS CoP, but whereas ADAS addresses the driver-vehicle interaction this is out of the scope of ISO 26262. The relationship between the ADAS CoP and ISO 26262 is shown in Figure 1.

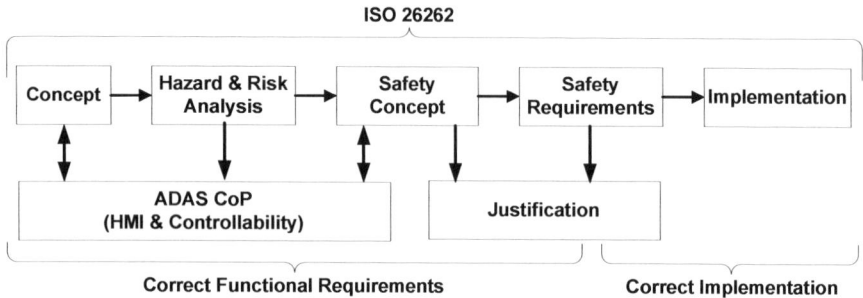

Fig. 1. Relationship between ADAS CoP and ISO 26262

7.3 SAE

Formed in 1905 as The Society of Automobile Engineers, it was renamed to the Society of Automotive Engineers in 1916 so that its scope could include the fledgling aeronautic industry. It publishes many standards some of which are referenced in FMVSS regulations. In 2011 a committee started work on providing guidance for the application of the ISO 26262 risk assessment scheme.

7.4 MISRA publications

Since 1994 MISRA (MISRA 2012), a UK automotive association, has been publishing guidelines addressing both software development and functional safety. Current publications include:

- development guidelines for vehicle based software
- guidelines for the use of the C language in critical systems
- guidelines for safety analysis of vehicle based programmable systems

- modelling design and style guidelines for the application of Simulink and Stateflow
- modelling style guidelines for the application of TargetLink in the context of automatic code generation
- guidelines for the application of MISRA-C in the context of automatic code generation
- guidelines for the use of the C++ language in critical systems.

Although not a legal requirement, these guidelines are much used throughout the automotive industry, and other industries, as they are seen as a definition of best practice. ISO 26262 references some of the MISRA publications as examples of coding guidelines.

7.5 ISO/TS 16949

Many automotive companies adopt ISO/TS 16949 as their base quality standard. It is based on ISO 9001 and other national quality standards and was first published in 2002. This is a process standard based around customer, supporting and management processes and includes relationships with suppliers and customers. It focuses on understanding the whole process.

Companies can be certified to this standard, but again this is not a requirement of any of the regulations; however certification can help support the conformity of production requirement of type approval.

8 Other pressures

Although all the regulations for a market must be met before a vehicle can be sold, there are many other pressures on an OEM to take every necessary step to ensure that their product is fit to be sold. These include the consumer protection laws in many countries which require a product sold to the public to be safe. Also product liability law may hold manufacturers responsible for injuries caused to the public by their products

The insurance industry also exerts an influence in that a vehicle performance can affect the cost of insuring it. One example of this is the New Car Assessment Programme (NCAP) in which independent organisations assess how well a vehicle protects its occupants in the event of a collision by performing their own tests and then publishing the results as a position in a five star rating. The first such scheme was introduced in 1979 by NHSTA in the US, Euro NCAP (Euro NCAP 1997) was established in 1997 and several other markets have similar schemes. The Euro NCAP frontal and side impact crash tests are based on those used in European legislation but with higher performance requirements, for example the frontal impact speed used by Euro NCAP is 64 km/h compared 56 km/h for legislation. Some see the NCAP schemes as having encouraged safety improvements to new car design.

In the UK the Thatcham motor insurance repair research centre (Thatcham 2012) conducts its own assessments of crash performance, including Euro NCAP tests and vehicle security systems, and publishes the results. It also provides data used by insurers to define a car's insurance grouping.

9 Challenges for the future

9.1 Autonomous vehicles

The trend is to fit more and more ADAS features and bring in more and more automation, an example is the automated parking of the vehicle in a tight space with the driver outside of the vehicle.

The EU project, Safe Road Trains for the Environment (SARTRE 2012), is developing technology for vehicle platoons, also known as 'road trains', where vehicles autonomously follow the vehicle in front with the lead vehicle being driven manually by a professional driver. Changes to the legislation are necessary for these to be legal in European countries and it is debateable whether the current 'black box' style of performance criteria around which the current regulations are based will be appropriate for such systems.

The US states of Nevada, Florida and California have already passed laws permitting driverless cars and Google are developing technology for such vehicles.

9.2 Safety and security

Another trend is to connect the vehicle to the Internet. This allows the customer to enjoy the same features in the vehicle that they have in their home. It also opens up the possibility for the manufacturer to collect data from the vehicle and upgrade software in the vehicle without the need for the driver to take the vehicle to a garage. Clearly such facilities have both safety and security implications; currently there are no regulations that address either issue.

9.3 Driver distraction

The information provided to the driver is increasing due to the increased ability of the electronic systems to report their status, the growing presence of ADAS features and the increase of the infotainment features (radio, satellite navigation, phone connectivity, internet connectivity). All this additional information has the potential to distract the driver from the driving task. This has led the US to propose legislation for driver distraction; there are also driver distraction guidelines published by the EU Commission, the Japanese Motor Manufacturers Association (JAMA) and the US Auto Alliance.

10 Concluding remarks

The regulations pertaining to the automotive industry are significantly different from those for civil aviation. This may be because much of the automotive industry still sees what it does as primarily mechanical engineering with some electrical parts added on.

The view of the industry is that it is very heavily regulated and under much public scrutiny and as such will always adopt best practice as it develops, driven as much by the need to take account of product liability as much as anything else.

As increasing use of software-based technology changes the nature of the vehicle, will the regulations that apply to it need to change from the 'black box' performance criteria to include scrutiny of how the systems were designed, implemented and validated?

References

ADAS (2009) A code of practice for developing advance driver assistance systems. http://www.trl.co.uk/online_store/reports_publications/trl_reports/cat_intelligent_transport_systems/report_a_code_of_practice_for_developing_advance_driver_assistance_systems.htm. Accessed 30 September 2012
Euro NCAP (1997) http://www.euroncap.com. Accessed 30 September 2012
IEC (2010) Functional safety of electrical/electronic/programmable electronic safety-related systems. IEC 61508 edn 2.0. International Electrotechnical Commission
ISO (2011) Road vehicles – functional safety. ISO 26262. International Organization for Standardization
MISRA (2012) http://www.misra.org.uk/. Accessed 30 September 2012
NHTSA (2012) National Highways Traffic Safety Agency. http://www.nhtsa.gov/. Accessed 30 September 2012
Rivett RS (1997) Is there a role for third party software assessment in the automotive industry? Safety-critical System Symposium
Rivett RS (2012) The challenge of technological change in the automotive industry. Safety-critical System Symposium
NHTSA (2004) Lives saved by the FMVSS and other vehicle safety technologies, 1960-2002
NTSB (2012) National Transportation Safety Board. http://www.ntsb.gov. Accessed 30 September 2012
SARTRE (2012) The SARTRE project. http://www.sartre-project.eu/en/Sidor/default.aspx. Accessed 30 September 2012
Thatcham (2012) Thatcham motor insurance repair research centre. http://www.thatcham.org Accessed 30 September 2012

UNECE (2012) United Nations Economic Commission for Europe. http://www.unece.org/. Accessed 30 September 2012

VCA (2012) Vehicle Certification Agency. http://www.dft.gov.uk/vca/index.asp. Accessed 30 September 2012

Vienna (1968) Convention on road traffic. http://treaties.un.org/pages/ViewDetailsIII.aspx?&src=TREATY&mtdsg_no=XI~B~19&chapter=11&Temp=mtdsg3&lang=en. Accessed 30 September 2012

VOSA (2012) Vehicle and Operations Services Agency. http://www.dft.gov.uk/vosa/index.htm. Accessed 30 September 2012

Getting Accepted in the UK Rail Industry

Peter Sheppard[1]

Bombardier Transportation RCS

Reading, UK

Abstract   In this paper I intend to share with you the evolution of the railway acceptance process (mainly in the UK, but there will be forays into other countries), and the changes in processes, methods and techniques that have had to be made by suppliers as a result of this evolution leading up to where the UK acceptance process is in the current day.

1 Background

I have been fortunate to have been involved in the UK acceptance process for nearly 30 years. I have also been very privileged to have been involved in a significant number of projects, that for the UK railway industry were either leading edge in technology, leading edge in safety processes and in some cases both! These projects include:

- first application of an electronic interlocking on London Underground (Vital Processor Interlocking (VPI) at Northolt)
- amending Automatic Train Operation and Automatic Train Protection (ATP) profiles on Birmingham Maglev
- safety audit prior to the opening of the Docklands Light Railway
- safety engineering of the Docklands Light Railway extension to Bank
- application of Enhanced Radio Electronic Token Block in Zimbabwe
- dissemination of Solid State Interlocking (SSI) validation process to StateRail (now Railcorp) for first application of SSI to Liverpool in New South Wales
- first significant application of axle counters in the UK (220 sections in the Stafford/Stoke-on-Trent area).

I shall be referring to the lessons learnt in some of these projects throughout the paper.

---

[1] This paper reflects the views of the author and not necessarily those of his employer.

I have found that this is not an easy paper to write in chronological order, so I apologise that the text tends to 'jump around a bit' as I have used brief case studies where possible to exemplify the point.

2 History of UK acceptance and approvals

Well no paper on railway safety can be considered to be complete unless it includes a reference to the Armagh (12 June 1889) accident and the subsequent legislation that colloquially became known as 'Lock, Block and Brake'.

The UK government had been trying to persuade the railway companies that safety on the railways needed to be improved and this was primarily in a move away from the crude 'time interval working' used to protect trains travelling in the same direction, to have a better form of interlocking between the points and signals and finally to have some form of automatic continuous braking between the coaches.

In the Armagh accident a combination of an overloaded train, inexperienced drivers, no system of block signalling and no automatic continuous brakes lead to 9 coaches and a brake van running away down a hill to collide with a second train that had been permitted to proceed on the time interval system. This collision led to a loss of 80 lives and 260 injuries.

Following this accident, questions in Parliament revealed the dire state of the railway industry at that time, namely in England 18% of the passenger rolling stock had no continuous brake, and a further 22% had non-automatic brakes and in Northern Ireland only 23 of 518 miles of railway were operated on a signalling block system.

As a result of the seriousness of this accident (and the perceived reluctance of the railway companies to voluntarily improve safety), less than two months following the Armagh accident Parliament had completed the enactment of the Regulation of Railways Act 1889, which authorised the Board of Trade to require railway operators to use:

- interlocking between points and signals
- a block system of signalling
- the use of continuous automatic brakes on passenger railways.

The only other time that I can think that a UK government body has implemented such measures on the UK railway industry was with the implementation of Train Protection and Warning System and again this following a number of high profile railway accidents and the lack of implementation of ATP except as two trial schemes.

2.1 Early approvals

A very good book by Stanley Hall, 'Railway Detectives' (Hall 1990) charts the history of the Railway Inspectorate from their inception in 1840 'to provide for the due supervision of railways, for the safety of the public', and in that role they can be seen as the first overseers of railway safety. Their purpose was to inspect (mainly new) lines to make sure that they were safe to operate but more importantly, when there was an incident to investigate the root cause of that incident and put controls in place to ensure that there was no repeat of that incident. These controls could be anything from improved rules and regulations (human prevention) through to changes in circuit design (technological prevention) and railways, like a lot of other safety critical industries can (unfortunately) chart its improvements in safety through accidents and incidents. It is only (and in my view relatively recently) that we have moved from a reactive approach to safety to a pro-active approach to safety.

I will come back to peer review later in the paper.

2.2 Recent history

This paper is largely based on my experience with the UK railway industry (metro and mainline) over the last 30 years where I have been involved in the approval of safety critical and safety related products and systems. Indeed when I first became involved with the signalling of the London Underground it was very black and white (or vital and non-vital). It was described to me at the time that from the contacts on the back of the relay interlocking to the route request circuitry (all relays with metal to metal contacts) was considered 'non-vital' and from the contacts on the lever locks forward was 'safety' these relays being gravity drop and dissimilar (non-welding) contacts. Safety Integrity Levels (SIL) had not been heard of yet and an intermediate level of safety (e.g. SIL 2 or 'safety related') had not been considered.

It was also the case that in the early days (and I'm talking about the early 1980s) that the principles of needing to provide any form of safety argument (in the railway industry) was relatively rare as the signalling designs followed standard principles and only used 'type approved' equipment[2].

---

[2] Type approved: a piece of equipment that has been designed to a specification and tested against that specification. It is considered that 'type approved' equipment does not require further safety evidence as long as it is applied in a prescribed way. The equivalent in the CENELEC standards is the Generic Product Safety Case.

2.2.1 London Transport

My earliest experience of 'safety approvals' was with London Transport in the Signals Drawing Office. At that time very little electronics was in use on the underground and where it was used it was in what was called 'non-vital' applications, either in the train operations side (for example requesting routes for trains), or providing train information (train running number used to drive the platform indicators). In all cases these systems either had no direct effect on the safety systems, or an incorrect action was protected by the vital systems, although at the time I was there an electronic timer was under development as was the first application of a digital track circuit.

In the drawing office signalling circuits were developed using 'standard practice' that was taught to the designers through an internal 'Drawing Office Course'. These circuits used standard, type approved equipment, even to the point that standard contacts were used on each relay. Like a significant part of the railway industry these circuits had evolved over the years to become 'standard practice' and if a deviation from the standard practice was required then it was subject to close scrutiny.

The principal specification document used in any signalling scheme is the 'Signalling Control Table'; this defines the conditions for the operation of the signalling system and no design work can be performed until this has been approved by the senior people in the design office.

From this point, the signalling circuits can be designed and every circuit design followed a very clear hierarchy of approvals, including independence for the 'Prepared', 'Checked' and 'Approved' for each sheet. However for some re-signalling schemes there may have been hundreds of these sheets where potentially there was interaction between the circuits and this was subject to review by the Principal Engineer of the drawing office. It would not be unusual at this stage to find that there were undesirable interactions between some circuits either due to a race condition or because nobody else had the 'bigger picture' of how all the circuits interacted with each other.

When these circuits were approved they were then installed on site and a further, separate team would be involved in the installation. To prevent errors in installation, again standard cables were used that ended in a plastic 'paddle' with fixed connections, so it was very difficult (although not impossible) to get that fitted incorrectly, either initially or during a failure! Finally the system was thoroughly tested by an engineer separate from the design office both to the control table (effectively validation) but also by 'Principles Checking' where the control tables are put to one side and the tester's experience is used to check whether any untoward interactions occur. This to me highlights the difference between verification (showing that the design meets the specification) and validation (principles testing) which will ultimately show that the system is 'fit for purpose in its intended environment'.

Her Majesty's Railway Inspectorate (HMRI) would not necessarily be involved in looking at the detailed design, but would focus on 'the inspection and approval, from a safety point of view, of new physical works, including signalling, on railways carrying passengers'. They would however look at the overall scheme plans and undertake site visits to satisfy themselves that the system as installed was a safe as practicable and that lessons learned from any recent accidents or incidents had been taken into account. It should be noted that the system could not be taken into use unless there had been approval from HMRI.

So to summarise the experience of the 1908s:

- control tables for signalling design specification
- peer review at many levels in the design phase (from control tables to relay circuits)
- use of standard circuits and relay allocations
- use of standard, type approved equipment in vital circuits
- competence based on experience
- independence between design, installation and test
- final approval given by HMRI.

Thus the safety of any new signalling system was very much based on the competence of the designers and peer reviewers but did include the use of standard, type approved proven equipment. At that time I had not come across the term 'safety case', 'case for safety' or 'safety argument' in connection with any of the sites that I was involved in. Until VPI came along!

2.2.2 Later trends

This works very well as long as standard circuits and standard equipment is used. Specifications that were prevalent in the British Railways era were very prescriptive. The following is an extract from a lamp unit for level crossings:

3. Lamp and Lamp Holder
3.1 The lamp used in the optical system shall be 24 volt, 50 watt, long life, tungsten halogen with its quartz envelope clear and un-coloured, and meet the following requirements:-

Nominal luminous flux	900 lumens at 24 volts
Nominal life	2000 hours continuous burning at 24 volts
Nominal colour temperature	2850K at 24 volts input
Overall length	44mm maximum
Overall diameter	12mm maximum
Light centre length	30 ± 0.25mm from end of pins
Type	L.I.F. reference M89 with single lateral coiled coil filament
Base	Single-ended bi-pin to international designation GY6.35-13

In all respects, space could have been saved in the specification if you just included a catalogue number! With this level of detail, there isn't exactly a lot of choice!

However this leads to the problem that when you are so specific (and the above example is relatively trivial) but it also applies to specifications for vital signalling equipment, that the safety requirements are actually buried with the requirements and are not explicitly defined. So whilst the equipment may be 'type approved' and safety is assured through the tight control of the product, innovation is effectively stifled as when you want to make a change to an item of equipment, it is difficult to know whether or not you are affecting any of the safety functions or not. This has led to some interesting problems in the creation of safety arguments to existing equipment, in particular how far do you go?

This came to a head some years later when a company I was working for was looking to bring a new piece of railway signalling equipment into the UK (these days called 'Cross Acceptance' and covered by standard TR 50506-1 (CENELEC 2007)). At that time, bringing equipment that had been previously used in another country to the UK was a relatively novel exercise and in this case the equipment in the UK had a very prescriptive specification that whilst the equipment had similar 'fail to safe' functions the way they were applied was very different and it was not possible to identify the relevant safety requirements. I was informed by the safety acceptance panel that the only way forward was to start from first principles and through standard safety techniques (hazard identification, risk assessment, etc.) and identify the safety requirements. So effectively to bring the equipment into the UK I had to identify the safety requirements and re-write the product specification!

3 The move towards safety arguments and safety cases

3.1 Network South East work instructions

Although not appreciated at the time, I think the Network South East work instructions have probably now been recognised as a pivotal event in the way that the railways approached the approval of electronic safety systems. International standards (e.g. IEC 61508 (IEC 2002)) were still in their infancy, RIA 23 Software for Railway Signalling Systems (RIA 1991) was still being debated in the UK and the (now well known) EN 50126, EN 50128 and EN 50129 standards (CENELEC 1999, 2011 and 2003) were in very early stages of development.

Network South East Signalling and Telecommunications had recognised that there were more electronic systems appearing on the railway both on the signalling side and as electronic drives on the rolling stock, and that a better form of managing the introduction of both was required – although, this was not without its difficulties!

Thus the Network South East work instructions were developed that provided a systematic approach to the approval and acceptance of software based systems. Around the same time the tripartite agreement between Westinghouse Brake and Signal, GEC General Signal and BR Research at Derby had been set up and the

British Rail SSI was being developed. This was 'state of the art' of the time and utilised a 1MHz 8 bit processor.

At the inception of Railtrack the Network South East work instructions were packaged together and became Issue 1 of what is known today as the Yellow Book. In the railway industry the Yellow Book brought together the first concept of a systematic approach to safety including peer review at two levels; these being an acceptance panel for the railway authority and the now ubiquitous Independent Safety Assessor (ISA).

3.2 Acceptance panels

This is now a common way of accepting equipment onto the railway infrastructure. These are primarily operated by Network Rail and London Underground and have their own remits and methods of working, but essentially follow the same basic principles. It should be noted that sub-panels may be set up for specific projects, for example there were ones on Network Rail for axle counters, West Coast Main Line and Manchester South; London Underground has had panels focussing on Jubilee Line, Victoria Line, etc. The following are the broad principles that the panels will follow for a signalling scheme:

Initial Agreement. No introduction can (should be) contemplated without the full support of the acceptance panel. It is important that this is achieved as an output from the acceptance panel will be the details of what standards you are expected to follow and the SIL(s) you may be expected to demonstrate you have achieved.

Acceptance Remit. – As above, this will contain details of what standards that you are expected to follow and any SIL(s) you are expected to achieve.

Safety Plan. A key document, this may be submitted as a preliminary document for a complicated or novel project and then resubmitted as a 'Full' safety plan when the early hazard identification and risk assessment work has been completed.

Safety Case. The final document that presents the safety argument is invariably incomplete at the time of submission, yet conditional acceptance will probably be given to allow the works to proceed with the final evidence being provided at or during the commissioning.

Now when considering vehicles, the broad principles used are very similar however the safety cases for vehicles were treated slightly differently and they have a number of different safety cases that incrementally allows more access to the railway. Initially trains need to be assessed by the Vehicle Acceptance Body which shows it meets the relevant standards. Tests may then take place on the railway, but under very controlled conditions (normally out of service hours and with no other trains present), this then moves to testing in traffic, followed by in traffic with passengers and finally a route specific safety case. It should be noted that only one train, the Class 323 electric multiple unit powered by a Holec traction system has a nationwide safety case.

3.3 Independent Safety Assessment (ISA)

One activity that was brought into more focus through the Yellow Book was the principle of independent review. This had of course been performed in the past, however whilst the review was performed by competent individuals, they were not considered sufficiently independent.

The ISA is normally employed and paid for by the party who was trying to gain acceptance, however they must be approved/acceptable to the acceptance panel of the railway authority. There is of course a trade off in the selection of the ISA. They need to be independent of the design, but then must have domain knowledge to be able to make intelligent (or what you hope is intelligent) observations. These two are slightly contradictory requirements in that if you are familiar with the domain, how independent can you be?

3.4 Independence

How is this related to acceptance? Well, the various railway standards from the international generic IEC61508 to the railway specific EN50126, EN50128 and EN50129 all require levels of 'independence', but as stated in the previous section, is true independence actually beneficial or if we had a true 100% level of independence, would if actually give a benefit, or more probably a dis-benefit. This was discussed at an IRSE lecture 'Is Independence an Overrated Virtue' in 2008 by Rod Muttram (Muttram 2008) and with his permission I repeat parts of his paper below.

An independent person has to be considered to have three main qualities, this is their:

- accountability and governance
- independence
- competence.

However, to be exclusive in one at the expense of the other two, serves no purpose; see Figure 1.

It must be noted that contradictions exist in each area, as discussed below.

Accountability & Governance

Stay out of the corners!

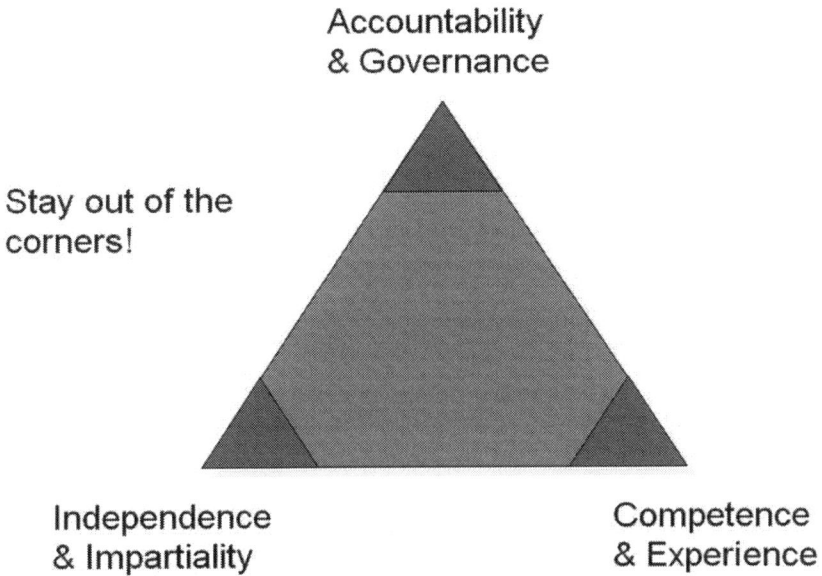

Independence & Impartiality

Competence & Experience

Fig. 1. Independence triangle

3.4.1 Competence and experience

- Competence requires both theoretical knowledge and experience.
- Experience requires involvement.
- Once someone has been involved in a process, organisation or industry, how independent can they ever really be?

Therefore, to what degree are independence and competence incompatible?

3.4.2 Impartiality

Impartiality is a difficult thing to judge, it is not just about direct financial benefit.

3.4.3 Governance

- For organisations or responsible individuals 'independent' cannot or should not mean 'unaccountable'.
- Therefore, some kind of governance is required.

But governance and accountability means a degree of control, anything controlled cannot be wholly independent.

Once again we need a compromise.

Therefore, true independence can never be achieved; pragmatism must be applied when considering independence at all levels.

4 Changes in UK (plc) safety governance

As was stated in the introductory paragraphs, in the beginning was HMRI with a dual role of approving railway systems for use and a second function to hold inquisitorial (i.e. no blame to be attached) investigations when things went wrong and then promote the suggested improvements to the railway industry. Whilst 'type approved' equipment was used and a standard approach to the signalling of the railways (mainline and metro), this approach was fine. The contractors and railway infrastructure owners were effectively self regulating and no additional internal or external independent reviews were generally considered necessary (above that what was normally performed). Two events occurred that brought a major change to the status quo. Firstly there was the rapid introduction of electronic and more importantly software based systems on the railway infrastructure and more importantly, these new software products were involved in controlling vital systems; secondly and latterly there was the Ladbroke Grove accident.

The former affected the approach taken to how electronic systems were approved and recognised that the biggest change you could make to a signalling system was to introduce some new rolling stock! This has been discussed previously. The latter affected how the safety governance of the UK railways was managed and will be discussed in the following sections.

4.1 Railtrack

When Railtrack was formed it was recognised that there needed to be a distinction between the 'production' side of the organisation and the safety and standards part, thus Railtrack Safety and Standards Directorate was formed as a quasi independent body within Railtrack. However following the Ladbroke Grove accident it was decided that the body needed to be further independent and Railway Safety was born.

4.2 Railway Safety

Railway Safety was a company limited by guarantee with a specific constitution aimed at 'securing railway safety in the public interest'. It was still a subsidiary of the Railtrack organisation, however steps were taken to ensure independence, for example the executive directors of Railway Safety were obliged to have no financial interest in any railway company. Ultimately this was still considered not to be sufficiently independent and the independent standards setting organisation, the Railway Safety and Standards Board was created.

4.3 Railway Safety and Standards Board (RSSB)

RSSB was established in 2003 is a not-for-profit company owned and funded by major stakeholders in the railway industry, but is independent of any one party. The RSSB is funded by levies on its members and grants for research from the Department for Transport. It is a not-for-profit company operating as a centre of excellence for all matters relating to railway safety. RSSB manages the rail group standards for the mainline railway and it should be noted that compliance with these standards is mandatory through the operating licence conditions. RSSB facilitates the development of these standards through standards committees to get consensus across the industry. Following the enactment of the European directives on safety and interoperability into UK law, RSSB is now also involved in supporting the UK rail industry in satisfying the Technical Specifications for Interoperability (TSI) and providing input to the content of these TSIs.

5 The European effect

Interoperability has been a desire of the European railway organisation since the 1990s. It is interesting to note that if you type 'interoperability', the Word spell checker will suggest a correction of 'inoperability'. Not only is Europe looking to harmonise how products are to be accepted on certain high speed routes (the Trans European Networks or TENS routes), but there is an effect on the overall safety governance (see ROTS and ROGS below). The enactment of the interoperability legislation has meant that any significant changes made to a TENS route (in the UK that is HS1&2, West Coast Main Line, East Coast Main Line and Western Main Line) requires the employment of a notified body to assess the compliance to the TSIs as well as an assessor to assess that the integration of these products together with other items on the project satisfies the overarching UK legal requirements embodied in the 1974 Health and Safety at Work etc. Act (HSW 1974).

The enactment of the various EU legislation has been progressive over the years and the ultimate aim is to harmonise not only the approach to how products are accepted in the EU (currently several different principles are used in different countries, for example the UK uses ALARP, Germany has MEM (Minimum Endogenous Mortality) quoted in the CENELEC standards although the German Eisenbahnbau und Betriebsordnung (EBO) defines 'minimum same safety' as the principle to be adopted, France uses GAMAB (Globalement au Moins Aussi Bon) etc.) the overall safety targets to be achieved will be pan European (although that is still some way off).

5.1 UK railway specific legislation

5.1.1 Railways and Other Transport Systems (approval of works, plant and equipment) regulations 1994 (ROTS)

The ROTS regulations were created at the privatisation of the UK railway industry in 1994. The ROTS regulations required operators of 'railways and other transport systems' to gain approval from HMRI before bringing into use any new or altered plant, works and equipment. The ROTS regulations were very wide ranging in terms of the transport groups they covered (everything from mainline railway to metros, heritage railways, trams, trolley buses and even included guided buses and monorails. Additionally the scope of the scheme required to be submitted through ROTS could be from a major re-signalling project (e.g. West Coast Main Line) to a newspaper stall on a station.

As a result of progressive EU legislation (initially The Railways (Interoperability) (High-speed) Regulations 2002) which whilst only relevant to the TENS network would have taken them out of the need to meet the ROTS regulations, then the similar EU legislation which applied to the conventional lines (non TENS routes) meant that ROTS would ultimately not be applicable to any of the main lines in the UK and would thus only be relevant to a few local railways, together with trams, metros (including London Underground Limited), heritage railways (that operate in excess of 25mph), trolley buses and guided transport systems.

This meant that a new regulation was introduced to meet these new European requirements. This happened in 2006 and was the Railway and Other Guided Transport System Regulations (ROGS).

5.1.2 The Railways and Other Guided transport systems (Safety) regulations 2006 (ROGS)

The ROGS came into force in 2006 and they provide the requirements for the regulatory regimes for railway safety and cover (in the same way as the ROTS used to) the following transport modes including mainline railways, metros (including London Underground), tramways, light rail and heritage railways. The ROGS are designed to implement the European Railway Safety Directive (2004/49/EC).

The significant difference between ROTS and ROGS is that the new ROGS regulations require most railway operators to maintain a Safety Management System (SMS) and hold a safety certificate or authorisation indicating the SMS has been accepted by the Office of Rail Regulation (ORR). This means that no longer is an 'Operating Safety Case' required for the various operators, just evidence of an acceptable SMS (which is audited by HMRI (now part of ORR) to ensure the SMS as approved is being correctly applied.

This is captured in the section of safety verification where operators must show that they have procedures in place to introduce new or altered vehicles or infrastructure safely. Where previously under ROTS, the HSE had responsibility for this, under ROGS, the railway operators are now responsible for this. Therefore where a new or significantly increased risk is involved, they must appoint an Independent Competent Person, either an internal person from the organisation, or someone externally, to help them make sure they go through the right processes. This person is additional to any form of acceptance panel or ISA.

5.1.3 UK External Governance

Her Majesty's Railway Inspectorate (HMRI). The HMRI was formed in 1840 and was a non-departmental government within the Department of Transport. It remained in that form until 1990 when the HMRI was transferred to the Health and Safety Executive (HSE). At this time the HMRI expanded its scope and recruited additional staff, railway employment officers. It was their job to monitor the workplace safety and health of railway employees.

One of the main roles of the HMRI was to investigate incidents and accidents, but purely in an inquisitorial approach where no blame was to be attached. However following a number of high profile accidents (Southall, Ladbroke Grove) these accident/incident investigations were held as public inquiries presided over by a High Court Judge; and the findings published.

These inquiries were intended to be inquisitorial, but because of the parties involved and the usually high profile of the accident/incident tended to be more adversarial; with the aim of identifying the guilty parties. In some of these accidents criminal prosecution of some parties has occurred in parallel with the public inquiry, which has had the unfortunate result of delaying the inquiry until the criminal prosecutions have been completed.

As part of its rail review in 2004 the government announced that HMRI would be transferred from the HSE to merge with the ORR. This move actually took place in April 2006.

As stated earlier HMRI had responsibilities in monitoring both operational safety and the initial integrity of new and modified works. However, as a result of the move to the ORR, the scope of HMRI activities was significantly reduced and in fact no longer covered guided bus, trolleybus and most cable-hauled transport systems.

The final change occurred in May 2009 when the legal entity known as HMRI ceased to exist and when a single rail regulatory body covering both safety and economic issues, called the 'Safety Directorate', was created. However the individual inspectors are still known as 'Her Majesty's Railway Inspectors'.

Railway Accident Investigation Branch (RAIB). The RAIB came into existence in 2005 and met an EU railway safety requirement embodied in European Railway Safety Directive 2004/49/EC which required the UK to have an independent rail investigation body.

The RAIB is the railway equivalent of the Air Accident Investigation Branch and with the same ethos as the HMRI investigation, the RAIB are looking for the root causes and what can be done to prevent a repeat. The RAIB will not bring prosecutions as a result of any of its investigations.

The RAIB has its remit laid down in law by The Railways (Accident Investigation and reporting) Regulations 2005, which principally require the branch to investigate any accident or dangerous occurrence that results in:

- the death of at least one person
- serious injury to five or more people
- extensive damage to rolling stock, the infrastructure or the environment.

The RAIB produces reports, all of which are available on their website at www.raib.gov.uk.

6 The future

In recent months it has been announced that as far as main line railways are concerned the Yellow Book is now discontinued and The European Commission Common Safety Method (CSM) on Risk Evaluation and Assessment Regulation 352/2009 is to be applied in the EU member states and be followed by the respective railway authorities and suppliers.

The principle behind CSM is to give a common framework across the EU for the hazard identification, risk analysis and thus risk assessment. The regulation is non-prescriptive, so allows countries to continue to use existing methods and codes of practice, but to provide an overarching structure to ease the process of cross acceptance between EU railway authorities.

This is a very recent change and the UK is still considering what effect it will have on the approach to safety acceptance.

7 Conclusions

So I suppose the question I should ask is – have any (or all) of these changes improved safety? Well, we have an enviable safety record from the passengers' point of view: on the main line (and ignoring trespassers/suicides and level crossing accidents) the last passenger fatality was at Greyrigg in 2007 and on London Underground (ignoring trespassers/suicides, terrorism and the King's Cross fire) it was actually the Moorgate accident in 1975. Is this because of, or despite the raft of changes we have seen to the way safety is managed on the railway over the years?

The answer is maybe!

We have seen prescriptive specifications move towards a performance based specification, the effect from Europe has had a significant effect on how we operate the UK acceptance process, yet at the end of the day, regardless of the overarching safety management systems we are ultimately relying on the competence of the acceptance panels and peer reviewers (whether they are an ISA or ICP) and the professionalism of those producing the design. It is my view that whilst we have the acceptance panels and other peer reviewers, they are not a fall back to the designers making an error; it is up to the designer to produce the best possible design and be able to satisfy themselves that the safety case produced is robust. In a similar way it needs to be the acceptance panel's and ISAs responsibility to be constructive with the criticisms made and have a positive view in helping the supplier to achieve approval, not looking at ways to refuse approval.

In my experience acceptance panels can be like a curate's egg, in fact the attitude of the panel (and sometimes the ISA) can actually dictate whether or not some companies decide to take innovation forward. This means that in some cases the decision is made by the supplier to use older, but previously approved equipment (that may not be ideal) as against the risk to timescale and not insignificant cost associated with the approval of a new or novel piece of equipment.

The Yellow Book, which has been a cornerstone of most SMSs has been discontinued for main line railways and replaced with the CSM, where some areas are still to be fully developed in each country.

I shall be interested to see how this change affects the acceptance process in the coming years.

References

CENELEC (1999) EN 50126 Railway applications – the specification and demonstration of Reliability, Availability, Maintainability and Safety (RAMS)
CENELEC (2003) EN 50129 Railway applications – communication, signalling and processing systems – safety related electronic systems for signalling.
CENELEC (2007) TR 50506-1 Railway applications – communication, signalling and processing systems – application guide for EN 50129 – Part 1: Cross-acceptance
CENELEC (2011) EN 50128 Railway applications – communication, signalling and processing systems – software for railway control and protection systems
Hall S (1990) Railway detectives. Ian Allen Ltd, Shepperton

HSW (1974) Health & Safety at Work etc. Act 1974

IEC (2002) IEC 61508 Functional safety of electrical/electronic/programmable electronic safety-related systems, Parts 1 to 7. International Electrotechnical Commission

Muttram R (2008) Is independence an overrated virtue? IRSE lecture

RIA (1991) RIA 23 Safety related software for railway signalling. Railway Industries Association

Generating Formal Model-Based Safety Requirements for Complex, Software- and Human-Intensive Systems

John Thomas and Nancy Leveson

Complex Systems Research Laboratory, MIT

Cambridge, MA USA

Abstract   Systems Theoretic Process Analysis (STPA) is a powerful new hazard analysis method designed to go beyond traditional safety techniques – such as Fault Tree Analysis (FTA) – that overlook important causes of accidents like flawed requirements, dysfunctional component interactions, and software errors. While proving to be very effective on real systems, no formal structure has been defined for STPA and its application has been ad hoc with no rigorous procedures or model-based design tools. This paper defines a formal mathematical structure underlying STPA that can be used to rigorously identify potentially hazardous control actions in a system. A method for using these unsafe control actions to generate formal safety-critical, model-based system and software requirements is presented based on the underlying formal structure, as well as a way to detect conflicts between safety and other functional requirements during early development of the system.

1 Introduction

The introduction of new technology, such as computers and software, is changing the types of accidents we see today. The level of complexity in many of our new systems is leading to accidents in which no components failed but instead unsafe interactions among non-failed components lead to the loss. At the same time, traditional hazard analysis techniques assume accidents are caused by component failures or faults (Vesely and Roberts 1987) and oversimplify the role of humans (Dekker 2005, 2006). Attempts have been made to extend these traditional hazard analysis techniques to include software and cognitively complex human errors, but the underlying assumptions remain the same and do not match the fundamental nature of systems we are building today. For example, most software-related accidents can be traced to incomplete or flawed software requirements (Leveson 1995, Lutz 1992); however, traditional hazard analysis methods like Fault Tree Analysis

(FTA) emphasize component failures and overlook unsafe requirements. More powerful hazard analysis techniques are needed.

Formal verification techniques have been useful in ensuring that given requirements are satisfied by an implementation, but do not assist in generating the requirements – i.e. they verify that given requirements are implemented correctly but do not validate that the given requirements are sufficient to enforce safe behaviour of the system. Model checking is one such approach used to ensure that specific software properties or safety requirements are met (Clarke et al. 1999). By developing a formal model of the software and specifying the desired requirements as formal logic statements, automated algorithms can be used to check the software model and either verify that the stated requirements are upheld in the assumed environment or provide a counterexample or scenario in which the requirements are violated. However model checking requires a detailed model of the software implementation to be checked, and it does not validate that the requirements to be checked are adequate to enforce safe behaviour from an encompassing system perspective.

Formal methods have also been developed to refine high-level goals and requirements into more precise specifications of software behaviour (Darimont and Lamsweerde 1996, Lamsweerde et al. 1998). However, these methods do not interface with the system hazard analysis outputs. Other work has developed criteria for software requirements completeness (Heimdahl and Leveson 1996, Leveson 2000). This approach provides some basic guidance by identifying common ways in which a requirements specification can be incomplete or inconsistent. However, this effort focuses on desirable criteria for all software requirements in general; additional work is necessary to verify that software requirements are not only complete and consistent, but *safe*. It also does not necessarily identify requirements that are related to the specific application involved, such as when the throttle on an aircraft needs to be advanced to prevent a stall.

While all of these techniques are useful for their intended goals, they do not solve the problem of identifying or generating the safety requirements. This paper presents a method for generating and validating safety-critical requirements using a new hazard analysis method, STPA (System-Theoretic Process Analysis) that is based on a new accident causation model called STAMP (System-Theoretic Accident Model and Processes).

1.1 STAMP and STPA

STAMP is a model of accident causation that treats safety as a control problem rather than as a failure problem (Leveson 2012). While unsafe control includes inadequate handling of failures, it also includes system and software design errors and erroneous human decision making. In STAMP, accidents are viewed as the result of inadequate enforcement of constraints on system behaviour. The reason behind the inadequate enforcement may involve classic component failures, but it may also result from unsafe interactions among components operating as designed and consistent with their specified requirements – or from erroneous control actions by software or humans.

STAMP is based on the observation that there are four types of hazardous control actions that can lead to accidents:

- A control action required for safety is not provided or is not followed.
- An unsafe control action is provided that leads to a hazard.
- A potentially safe control action is provided too late, too early, or out of sequence.
- A safe control action is stopped too soon or applied too long.

One potential cause of a hazardous control action is an inadequate process model used by human or automated controllers. The process model contains the controller's understanding of:

1. the current state of the controlled process
2. the desired state of the controlled process
3. the ways the process can change state.

It is used by the controller to determine what control actions are needed. In software, this process model is usually implemented in variables and may be embedded in the algorithms used. For humans, the process model is often called the 'mental model'. Software and human errors frequently result from incorrect process models, e.g., the software thinks the spacecraft has landed and shuts off the descent engines. Accidents can therefore occur when an incorrect or incomplete process model causes a controller to provide control actions that are hazardous. While process model flaws are not the only cause of accidents involving software and human errors, they are a major contributor.

STPA is a hazard analysis technique built on STAMP. Identifying the hazardous control actions for the specific system being considered is the first step in STPA. These unsafe control actions can be used to identify basic constraints (requirements) on the behaviour of the controller in order to ensure that unsafe behaviour does not result. Additional analysis can then be performed to identify the detailed scenarios leading to the violation of these safety constraints, potentially identifying the need for even more requirements. As in any hazard analysis, the detailed scenarios are then used to alter the design to eliminate or control the hazards in the system design. Additional design features to control hazards, in turn, may generate new hazards or new paths to hazards and lead to additional safety-critical requirements.

This paper presents a formal technique based on STPA that can be used to identify hazardous control actions and generate formal, model-based specifications that enforce safe behaviour in the system.

1.2 Overview of the STPA process

Before beginning an STPA hazard analysis, potential accidents and corresponding system-level hazards are identified. As an illustrative example, consider a simple automated door control system for a train. The accidents to be considered are: injury to a person caused by falling out of the train, a person is hit by a closing door, or people are trapped inside a train during an emergency. The system-level hazards relevant to this definition of an accident include:

H-1. Doors close on a person in the doorway.

H-2. Doors open when the train is moving or not aligned with a station platform.

H-3. Passengers/staff are unable to exit during an emergency.

STPA is performed on a functional control diagram of the system, shown in Figure 1 for the train door controller. STPA has two main steps.

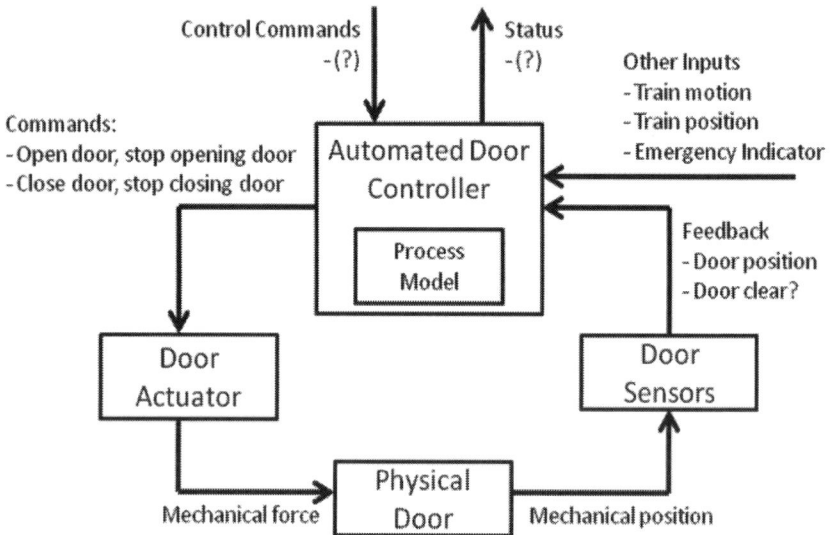

Fig. 1. Simplified control diagram for an automated door controller

STPA Step One. The first step of STPA identifies control actions for each component that can lead to one or more of the defined system hazards. The four general types of hazardous control actions shown above can be used to guide the engineering team as they perform this step. For example, one hazardous control action would be a *close door* command that is issued while a person is in the doorway.

STPA Step Two. The second step of STPA examines each control loop in the safety control structure to identify potential causal factors for each hazardous control action, i.e., the behaviours that can lead to the hazardous control actions identified in Step One. 0shows a generic control loop that can be used to guide this step. While STPA Step One focused on the provided control actions (the upper left corner of 0), STPA Step Two expands the analysis to consider causal factors along the rest of the control loop.

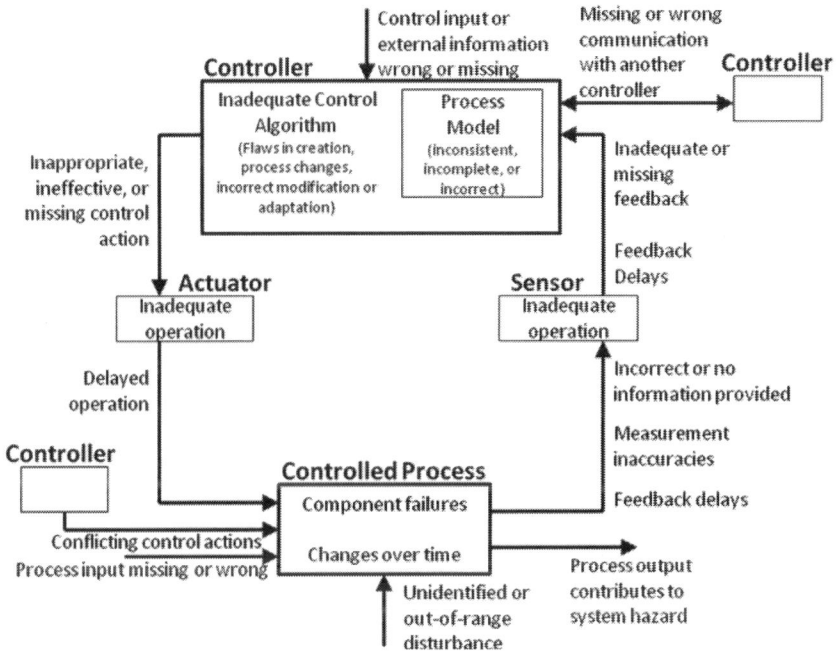

Fig. 2. General control loop with causal factors

Consider the example above where the hazardous control action is to command the doors closed on a person in the doorway. STPA Step Two would identify one potential cause of that action as an incorrect belief that the doorway is clear (an incorrect process model). The incorrect process model, in turn, may be the result of inadequate feedback provided by a failed sensor or the feedback may be delayed or corrupted. Alternatively, the designers may have omitted a feedback signal.

Once the second step of STPA has been applied to determine potential causes for each hazardous control action identified in STPA Step One, the causes should be eliminated or controlled in the design.

STPA has been described in other places (Leveson 2012) and is not described in further detail here due to space limitations. The goal of this paper is to formalize the process and identify tools that can be used to perform it.

2 Formal syntax for hazardous control actions

A hazardous control action in the STAMP accident model is a critical output of STPA Step One and forms the basis for STPA Step Two. In this section a formal syntax is defined for hazardous control actions. Sections 3 and 4 describe how STPA hazard analysis can be partially automated based on this syntax and how model-based safety requirements can be generated.

Hazardous control actions can be expressed formally as a four-tuple (S, T, CA, C) where:

- S is a controller in the system that can issue control actions. The controller may be automated or a human.
- T is the type of control action. There are two possible types: *Provided* describes a control action that is issued by the controller while *Not Provided* describes a control action that is not issued.
- CA is the specific control action or command that is (or is not) output by the controller.
- C is the context in which the control action is (or is not) provided.

For example, in the case of the automated train door controller from Section 1.2, consider the following hazardous control action: the train door controller provides the open door command while the train is moving. This control command can be expressed as (S, T, CA, C) where:

S = Train door controller.
T = Provided.
CA = Open door command.
C = Train is moving.

Each element of a hazardous control action is a member of a larger set, i.e. the following properties must hold:

1. S ∈ $\mathcal{S}$, where $\mathcal{S}$ is the set of controllers in the system.
2. T ∈ $\mathcal{T}$, where $\mathcal{T}$ = {Provided, Not Provided}.
3. CA ∈ $\mathcal{CA}$(S), where $\mathcal{CA}$(S) is the set of control actions that can be provided by controller S.
4. C ∈ $\mathcal{C}$(S), where $\mathcal{C}$(S) is the set of potential contexts for controller S.

To assist in enumerating or aggregating individual contexts, the context C can be further decomposed into variables, values, and conditions:

- V is a variable or attribute in the system or environment that may take on two or more values. For example, *train motion* and *train position* are two potential variables for a train.
- VL is a value that can be assumed by a variable. For example, *stopped* is a value that can be assumed by the variable *train motion*.

- CO is a condition expressed as a single variable/value pair. For example, *train motion is stopped* is a condition.
- The context C is the combination of one or more conditions and defines a unique state of the system or environment in which a control action may be given.

The following additional properties related to the context of a hazardous control action can therefore be defined:

5. V ∈ $\mathcal{V}$(S), where $\mathcal{V}$(S) is the set of variables referenced in the system hazards $\mathcal{H}$.
6. VL ∈ $\mathcal{VL}$(V), where $\mathcal{VL}$(V) is the set of values that can be assumed by variable V.
7. CO = (V, VL) ∈ $\mathcal{CO}$(S), where $\mathcal{CO}$(S) is the set of conditions for controller S.
8. C = (CO_1, CO_2, ...), where each CO_i is independent. That is, no two CO_i refer to the same variable V.

Finally, each hazardous control action must be linked to a system-level hazard:

9. To qualify as a hazardous control action, the event (S, T, CA, C) must cause a hazard H ∈ $\mathcal{H}$, where $\mathcal{H}$ is the set of system level hazards.

A hazardous control action expressed as a four-tuple (S, T, CA, C) must satisfy the above properties 1-9.

3 Identifying hazardous control actions

An informal procedure for identifying hazardous control actions has previously been described in (Thomas and Leveson 2011). This section defines a formal method that can be used to automate much of that manual process.

Using the formal definitions in Section 2, a set of potentially hazardous control actions can be enumerated once certain information about the system is known. The information needed is:

$\mathcal{H}$: the set of system-level hazards
$\mathcal{S}$: the set of controllers in the system
$\mathcal{CA}$(S): the set of control actions for each controller S
$\mathcal{V}$: the set of variables referenced in the hazards $\mathcal{H}$
$\mathcal{VL}$(V): the set of potential values for each variable V.

Most, if not all, of this information can be determined well in advance of the detailed design of a system. The set $\mathcal{H}$ is typically determined during the Preliminary Hazard Analysis (PHA) of the system. The sets $\mathcal{S}$ and $\mathcal{CA}$(S) can be extracted from a preliminary control structure of the system. The set $\mathcal{V}$ is identical to the process model variables in the control structure, and can be extracted from the set of hazards $\mathcal{H}$. The potential values $\mathcal{VL}$(V) are also found in the process model, and can be defined once $\mathcal{V}$ is known.

Given this basic information about the system, properties 1-8 from Section 2 can be applied to automatically generate a list of potential hazardous control actions in the form of combinations of (S, T, CA, C). First, a controller S is selected from the set $\mathcal{S}$. Then the set of conditions $\mathcal{CO}$(S) is generated by pairing each variable in $\mathcal{V}$ with each value in $\mathcal{VL}$(V). Then the set of contexts $\mathcal{C}$ is generated by combining each independent condition from $\mathcal{CO}$(S). Finally, the list of potentially hazardous control actions for the selected controller S is generated by combining each element of $\mathcal{T}$, $\mathcal{CA}$(S), and $\mathcal{C}$(S). This process can be repeated for each controller S in the set $\mathcal{S}$.

This process generates a set of potential hazardous control actions in which properties 1-8 from Section 2 are guaranteed to be satisfied. Because a detailed behavioural model of the system typically does not exist during the earliest phases of development, it may not be possible to automatically apply property 9. However, this final step can be performed by the engineering team. Because the algorithm above generates combinations that satisfy all other criteria, the generated list is a superset of the actual hazardous control actions. Therefore the remaining part of the task that is not automated is a trimming exercise: the engineering team does not need to propose any new hazardous control actions, they only need to remove non-hazardous control actions from the generated list based on their knowledge of the physics and other engineering properties of the overall system.

For example, in Tables 1 and 2 the engineering team would need to fill in the columns on the far right:

Table 1. Example hazardous control action table for door open command NOT provided

Control action	Train motion	Emergency	Door obstruction	Hazardous?
Door open command NOT provided while...	(doesn't matter)	Yes	(doesn't matter)	Yes (see H-3)
Door open command NOT provided while...	(doesn't matter)	(doesn't matter)	Closing on obstruction	Yes (see H-1)[1]
Door open command NOT provided while...	(all others)	(all others)	(all others)	No

For each potential hazardous control action in Table 1 (T = Provided), timing information such as potentially hazardous delays within a given context should also be considered. For example, suppose it is not hazardous to provide a door open command while the train is stopped and there is an emergency. In fact, this behaviour may be exactly what is expected of the system. However, providing the door open command *too late* in that context could certainly be hazardous even if the control action is eventually provided. This condition can be addressed by adding

---

[1] Of course, the system should be designed so the doors never close on a person. However, in the event that the doors do close on a person, the system must be designed to immediately open the doors (i.e. minimize H-1).

the columns *hazardous if provided too early* and *hazardous if provided too late* as illustrated in the second row of Table 3.

Table 2. Example hazardous control action table for door open command provided

Control action	Train motion	Emergency	Train position	Hazardous?
Door open command provided while...	Moving	(doesn't matter)	(doesn't matter)	Yes (see H-2)
Door open command provided while...	Stopped	Yes	(doesn't matter)	No
Door open command provided while...	Stopped	No	Not at platform	Yes (see H-2)
Door open command provided while...	Stopped	No	At platform	No

Table 3. Example hazardous control action table including timing information

Control action	Train motion	Emergency	Train position	Hazardous?	Hazardous if provided too early?	Hazardous if provided too late?
Door open command provided while...	Moving	(doesn't matter)	(doesn't matter)	Yes (see H-2)	Yes (see H-2)	Yes (see H-2)
Door open command provided while...	Stopped	Yes	(doesn't matter)	No	No	Yes (see H-3)
Door open command provided while...	Stopped	No	Not at platform	Yes (see H-2)	Yes (see H-2)	Yes (see H-2)
Door open command provided while...	Stopped	No	At platform	No	No	No

Once the hazardous control actions have been identified, each action can be examined to define a safety constraint for the system. For example, consider the hazardous control action from the first row of Table 1:

Hazardous control action. Train door controller provides the open door command while the train is moving.

Safety constraint. Train door controller must not provide the open door command while the train is moving.

While this simple example is fairly obvious and would probably not require the use of a formal method, our experience using STPA on real systems such as spacecraft (Ishimatsu et al. 2010), the air transportation system (Fleming et al.

2011, Laracy 2007), and missile defence systems (Pereira et al. 2006) has led to the identification of safety-critical requirements that were never considered during the normal development of these systems.

4 Generating model-based specifications

Because hazardous control actions have been defined with a formal representation, it is possible to compare these actions against an existing formal model-based specification (e.g. SpecTRM-RL) to determine whether the hazardous control actions can occur in an existing design. Furthermore, if no formal specification exists, it is possible to automatically generate the parts of the specification necessary to ensure hazardous behaviour is prevented.

The following functions can be defined from the set of hazardous control actions:

HP(H, S, CA, C). This function is *True* if and only if hazard H results from controller S providing command CA in context C. This function is defined for all H $\in$ $\mathcal{H}$, S $\in$ $\mathcal{S}$, CA $\in$ $\mathcal{CA}$(S), C $\in$ $\mathcal{C}$(S).

HNP(H, S, CA, C). This function is *True* if and only if hazard H results from controller S not providing command CA in context C. This function is defined for all H $\in$ $\mathcal{H}$, S $\in$ $\mathcal{S}$, CA $\in$ $\mathcal{CA}$(S), C $\in$ $\mathcal{C}$(S).

The formal requirement specification or control algorithm to be generated can be expressed as the following function:

R(S, CA, C). This function is *True* if and only if controller S is required to provide command CA in context C. This function must be defined for all S $\in$ $\mathcal{S}$, CA $\in$ $\mathcal{CA}$(S), C $\in$ $\mathcal{C}$(S).

The goal, then, is to compute the function R such that hazardous behaviour is prevented. Namely, any control action that is hazardous in a given context must not be provided by the control algorithm in that context:

$$\forall \; H \in \mathcal{H}, S \in \mathcal{S}, CA \in \mathcal{CA}(S), C \in \mathcal{C}(S): HP(H, S, CA, C) \Rightarrow \neg R(S, CA, C)$$

In addition, if a control action that is absent in a given context will produce a hazard, then the control action must be provided by the control algorithm in that context:

$$\forall \; H \in \mathcal{H}, S \in \mathcal{S}, CA \in \mathcal{CA}(S), C \in \mathcal{C}(S): HNP(H, S, CA, C) \Rightarrow R(S, CA, C)$$

The required behaviour R can then be generated to satisfy these two criteria. Any behaviour appearing in HNP must appear in R, and any behaviour that appears in HP must be absent from R.

The resulting controller requirements (R) can be converted into a formal model-based requirements specification language such as SpecTRM-RL (Leveson et al. 1999). For example, Figure 3 contains a formal SpecTRM-RL specification for the train door example. The three columns on the right specify three contexts in which the open doors command must be provided: when the train is aligned and stopped, or when the train is stopped and an emergency exists, or when the doors are closing on a person and the train is stopped. The right two columns specify behaviour that is required to prevent the system hazards, and were automatically generated by a software tool that implements the procedure above. The first column specifies behaviour that is necessary for the intended function of the system, not to avoid hazards, and therefore is not automatically generated by the procedure above.

		Behavior required for function	Behavior required for safety	
Door State =	Doors not closing on person			
	Doors closing on person			T
Train Position =	Aligned with platform	T		
	Not aligned with platform			
Train Motion =	Stopped	T	T	T
	Train is moving			
Emergency =	No emergency			
	Emergency exists		T	

Provide 'Open Doors' command

Fig. 3. Generated SpecTRM-RL table for the door open command

4.1 Automated consistency checking

If the same behaviour appears in HNP and HP, then no R can satisfy both criteria. The following additional criterion can be defined to detect these conflicts and ensure that a solution R exists:

$$\forall \ H_1 \in \mathcal{H}, \ H_2 \in \mathcal{H}, \ S \in \mathcal{S}, \ CA \in \mathcal{CA}(S), \ C \in \mathcal{C}(S): HP(H_1, S, CA, C) \Rightarrow \neg HNP(H_2, S, CA, C)$$

The third criterion above is a consistency check that can be applied to the hazardous control actions even before the formal specification R is generated. If the third criterion does not hold, there is a design or requirements flaw in the system. Both action and inaction by controller S will lead to a hazard and violate a safety constraint. Although the conflict cannot be automatically resolved, it can be automatically detected and flagged for review by the engineering team.

For example, suppose the train from Section 3 is moving and there is an onboard emergency such as a fire. HNP will state that not opening the door in this situation is hazardous due to H-3. However, HP states that opening the door in this situation is hazardous due to H-1. This is an example of a conflict that can be automatically detected by the formal criterion above.

In general, the system design may need to be reviewed or revised to ensure that conflicts are handled appropriately. Ideally, the conflict would be eliminated by a design change. If elimination is not possible, hazard mitigation or reduction may be performed by placing constraints on other control actions in the system (constraints on HP and HNP for other S and CA). For example, if the train is moving and there is an emergency then a constraint can be defined for the braking system controller such that the brakes are always applied in this situation. The *Train Motion* variable will soon transition from *moving* to *stopped,* thereby resolving the conflict for the train door controller.

If hazard mitigation or reduction is not possible, the conflict could alternatively be handled based on hazard severity or priority.

4.2 Extending hazard analysis to non-safety goals

One of the columns in Figure 3 specifies behaviour that is necessary for the intended function of the system, not to avoid safety hazards. However, this column is clearly important; without it, the whole train system could not achieve its purpose of transporting people.

Although the procedures thus far have focused on safety-related behaviour, the functional behaviour of the system can be defined in the same way and functional specifications can be generated along with the safety-related specifications by following a similar method. More specifically, in addition to HP and HNP – which capture hazardous control actions – a new function FP can be introduced to capture control actions that are needed to achieve functional goals:

FP(F, S, CA, C). This function is *True* if and only if system-level function F must be achieved by controller S providing command CA in context C to achieve a system-level function F.

The function FP can be defined by identifying which control actions in each context are necessary to achieve the system-level functions $\mathcal{F}$. The same process used in Section 3 to identify hazardous control actions can be applied to the system-level functions $\mathcal{F}$ as opposed to the system-level hazards $\mathcal{H}$. The required behaviour R can then be computed as in Section 4, but with an additional criterion to capture the functional behaviour:

$$\forall\, F \in \mathcal{F},\, S \in \mathcal{S},\, CA \in \mathcal{CA}(S),\, C \in \mathcal{C}(S)\colon FP(F, S, CA, C) \Rightarrow R(S, CA, C)$$

Applying this criterion, any behaviour appearing in FP must also appear in R. Note that if the same behaviour appears in FP and HP, then there is a design or requirements flaw in the system because the same control action is both necessary to achieve a system-level function and prohibited because it presents a system-level hazard. In that case, no R would exist that prevents the hazards while achieving the system functions. The following additional criterion can therefore be defined:

$$\forall\ H \in \mathcal{H},\ F \in \mathcal{F},\ S \in \mathcal{S},\ CA \in \mathcal{CA}(S),\ C \in \mathcal{C}(S):\ HP(H,\ S,\ CA,\ C) \Rightarrow \neg FP(F,\ S, CA, C)$$

This final criterion is a consistency check to detect conflicts between hazardous and functional behaviour. As before, these conflicts cannot be automatically resolved, but they can be automatically detected and flagged for review by the engineering team. The full SpecTRM-RL model in Figure 3 was generated automatically by a software tool that implements the five criteria from this section.

5 Conclusions

This paper presents a formal structure underlying STPA hazard analysis and a corresponding method to systematically identify hazardous control actions in a system. A set of formal criteria have been defined to automate much of the hazard analysis process even when a detailed model of the system or software components has not yet been developed. A method for using the STPA hazard analysis results to generate formal safety-critical, model-based system and software requirements is also presented. The generated formal requirements are executable and can be imported into the SpecTRM toolset (Leveson et al. 1999) for simulation if needed.

The ability to formally translate between the hazard analysis and model-based requirements also permits the automatic detection of requirements flaws or conflicts in which not all hazards are prevented. The criteria necessary to detect such conflicts are defined in Section 4 and a prototype tool has been developed to automatically identify such conflicts in a set of formal requirements. The same approach can be applied to generate functional requirements in parallel with the safety requirements. As a result, conflicts between safety and functional goals can also be detected by evaluating the additional criteria defined in Section 4 above.

Acknowledgements This work was partially supported by NASA Contract NNL10AA13C, a JAXA research grant, and a fellowship provided by Sandia National Laboratory.

References

Clarke EM, Grumberg O, Peled D (1999) Model checking. MIT Press
Darimont R, Lamsweerde Av (1996) Formal refinement patterns for goal-driven requirements elaboration. Proc 4th ACM SIGSOFT symposium on Foundations of software engineering, San Francisco, California, United States
Dekker S (2005) Ten questions about human error: a new view of human factors and system safety. Lawrence Erlbaum Associates, Mahwah NJ
Dekker S (2006) The field guide to understanding human error. Ashgate, Aldershot, UK; Burlington, VT

Fleming C, Spencer M, Leveson N, Wilkinson C (2011) Safety assurance in Nextgen. NASA Technical Report

Heimdahl MPE, Leveson NG (1996) Completeness and consistency in hierarchical state-based requirements. IEEE Trans Softw Eng, 22(6):363-377

Ishimatsu T, Leveson N, Thomas J, Katahira M, Miyamoto Y, Nakao H (2010) Modeling and hazard analysis using STPA. Paper presented at the Conference of the International Association for the Advancement of Space Safety, Huntsville, Alabama

Lamsweerde Av, Letier E, Darimont R (1998) Managing conflicts in goal-driven requirements engineering. IEEE Trans Softw Eng 24(11):908-926

Laracy JR (2007) A systems-theoretic security model for large scale, complex systems applied to the US air transportation system. MIT, Engineering Systems Division

Leveson N (1995) SafeWare: system safety and computers. Addison-Wesley, Reading, Mass..

Leveson N (2000) Completeness in formal specification language design for process-control systems. Proc 3rd workshop on Formal methods in software practice, Portland, Oregon, USA

Leveson N (2012) Engineering a safer world: systems thinking applied to safety. MIT Press, Cambridge, Mass.

Leveson NG, Heimdahl MPE, Reese JD (1999) Designing specification languages for process control systems: lessons learned and steps to the future. Paper presented at the Proceedings of the 7th European software engineering conference held jointly with the 7th ACM SIGSOFT international symposium on Foundations of software engineering, Toulouse, France

Lutz RR (1992) Analyzing software requirements errors in safety-critical, embedded systems. Paper presented at the International Conference on Software Requirements

Pereira S, Lee G, Howard J (2006) A system-theoretic hazard analysis methodology for a non-advocate safety assessment of the ballistic missile defense system. Paper presented at the AIAA Missile Sciences Conference, Monterey, CA

Thomas J, Leveson N (2011) Performing hazard analysis on complex, software- and human-intensive systems. International System Safety Conference, Las Vegas, NV

Vesely WE, Roberts NH (1987) Fault tree handbook. US Independent Agencies and Commissions

Safety Case for the Airborne Collision Avoidance System

Stephen Thomas[1] and Derek Fowler[2]

[1]Entity Systems Ltd, Cheltenham, UK

[2]JDF Consultancy LLP, Chichester, UK

Abstract   The Airborne Collision Avoidance System (ACAS) has been in use worldwide for many years as a 'last resort' means of preventing aircraft mid-air collision. Although its efficacy was predicted via extensive simulation studies, measurement of actual collision risk reduction in the airspace is impractical. Furthermore, ACAS had not been subjected to contemporary safety assessment practices. Upon its mandated deployment in European airspace, ACAS therefore presented a unique opportunity to apply state-of-the-art thinking on air traffic management safety cases (the so-called 'success and failure' approach) to a mature operational system. The paper describes the background to the safety case, the safety assessment process that underpinned it by synthesising hitherto missing evidence, and some of the safety issues it has revealed.

1 Introduction

1.1 Background

The Airborne Collision Avoidance System, ACAS II (hereafter simply ACAS) is an airborne safety net which has been in use worldwide for many years as a 'last resort' means of preventing aircraft mid-air collision.

Its progressive introduction into European airspace was completed in 2006 as a result of mandate, managed by EUROCONTROL – the European organisation for the safety of air navigation, which prescribed the use of ACAS for all civil fixed-wing turbine-engined aircraft having a maximum take-off mass exceeding 5,700 kg or a maximum approved seating configuration of more than 19. As part of its remit, EUROCONTROL decided that it should prepare an ACAS Post-implementation Safety Case (APOSC) (EUROCONTROL 2011) in line with its normal practice of developing safety cases for other Air Traffic Management (ATM) programmes under its control.

The purpose of the safety case was to demonstrate that the safety of aircraft operations is substantially improved by ACAS. Airworthiness of equipment (including the associated maintenance aspects) was not considered because it is deemed to be adequately covered by standard avionics-development and aircraft-certification practices.

This paper does not present the safety case itself; rather it describes the process by which the safety case and its supporting safety assessment came into being, and the rationale behind that process. Some specific issues that emerged from safety case development are also described.

1.2 ACAS description

ACAS (ICAO 2006b) makes use of an aircraft's Secondary Surveillance Radar (SSR) transponder to provide advice to pilots on potentially conflicting traffic, by interpreting the signals received from aircraft that are equipped with compatible transponders.

Each reply from a nearby aircraft's transponder provides ACAS with the necessary information to calculate that aircraft's range, bearing, and, if suitably equipped, its altitude. From this, ACAS provides a flight deck display of traffic in the vicinity and, if appropriate, alerts the pilot that an aircraft presents a *potential* threat by generating a Traffic Advisory (TA). The pilot may use the TA as a prompt to acquire the intruder visually and prepare for subsequent action. Furthermore, if the system calculates an actual risk of collision with an intruder aircraft it will recommend avoidance manoeuvres, in the vertical dimension, to the pilot by generating a Resolution Advisory (RA), which the pilot is expected to follow immediately.

ACAS operates independently of ground-based equipment; at all traffic levels; in all classes of airspace; during those phases of flight in which it is capable of reliably detecting and safely resolving mid-air collisions; at all operational altitudes (except when the aircraft is close to, or on, the ground); and irrespective of the type/performance characteristics of aircraft involved.

1.3 Rationale

Many years of successful operational experience with ACAS has been complemented by several safety studies (EUROCONTROL 2002a, 2002b, 2006b) aimed at predicting its collision avoidance efficacy, and led to the conviction that it provides the expected safety benefit. However, the nature of ACAS operations makes it impracticable to obtain direct evidence of its actual risk reduction capability because the fact that ACAS was involved in a particular conflict with a successful outcome would not necessarily mean that the outcome would have been a mid-air collision had ACAS not been involved. Moreover, as acknowledged in (EURO-CONTROL 2011), and discussed later in this paper, there have, in the past 11 years, been at least one mid-air collision and one *very* near miss which ACAS operations not only failed to prevent, but actually made a major adverse contribution to the outcome.

Furthermore, since ACAS development generally pre-dated contemporary approaches to ATM safety assessment, it had not been subjected to systematic hazard and risk assessment to ensure that all its hazards and causes had been identified and mitigated. Such an *a priori* analysis is of course extremely important in providing safety assurance for systems, such as protection systems, which are brought into use relatively infrequently.

All of these were motivations for taking a more holistic view of safety assessment when developing the safety case. At the time that APOSC was being developed, EUROCONTROL was expanding its ATM safety assessment methodology (EUROCONTROL 2006d) to include guidance on the construction of ATM safety cases, using its own flavour of Goal Structuring Notation, and based on a whole-lifecycle model which included the so-called 'success and failure' viewpoints described later. The most recent advances on this topic, including the systems engineering context into which safety reasoning fits, were reported in (Fowler and Pierce 2012a). For a protection system like ACAS, consideration of the success viewpoint must take precedence over consideration of its failure because it provides the justification for introducing the protection system in the first place – i.e. that the positive safety benefits of the protection system greatly exceed any negative safety consequences arising from its possible failure[1].

The concepts and safety argument structure that was emerging from EURO-CONTROL's work on safety cases were therefore appropriate and timely for adoption by APOSC. Furthermore, due to the lack of in-service data on *actual* risk reduction from ACAS operations, and the ever-present concern that there are latent problems in the design not yet revealed by operational experience, it was deemed appropriate to apply this 'whole lifecycle' argument structure in order to yield assurance progressively from each lifecycle step. A recognised drawback, however, was that ACAS, as a fully developed operational system, might have a paucity of evidence necessary to support all the strands of the argument because it had not followed a contemporary systems engineering lifecycle.

Nevertheless, ACAS provided a unique opportunity to adopt EUROCON-TROL's innovations in ATM safety cases for the construction of a safety case for a mature operational system. The challenge would be to fit, or adapt, the available evidence on ACAS to the strands of the generic argument without compromising the argument structure, and ideally without placing demands on ACAS stakeholders for the production of new evidence.

---

[1] In European ATM there is no absolute safety target relating to safety nets – indeed, satisfaction of the quantified tolerable level of risk prescribed by EUROCONTROL Safety Regulatory Requirement 4 (ESARR 4) (EUROCONTROL 2001) has to be demonstrated without counting the benefit from safety nets such as ACAS.

2 Safety concepts

2.1 Conflict management

The starting point for explaining how ACAS contributes to aviation safety is ICAO Doc 9854 (ICAO 2005b). It includes a description of conflict management which can be thought of as comprising three layers or barriers: strategic conflict management, separation provision, and collision avoidance, as shown in Figure 1. The input to this simple model is the air traffic, the existence of which represents hazards to, *inter alia*, other aircraft within it and the barriers prevent these hazards from leading to an accident.

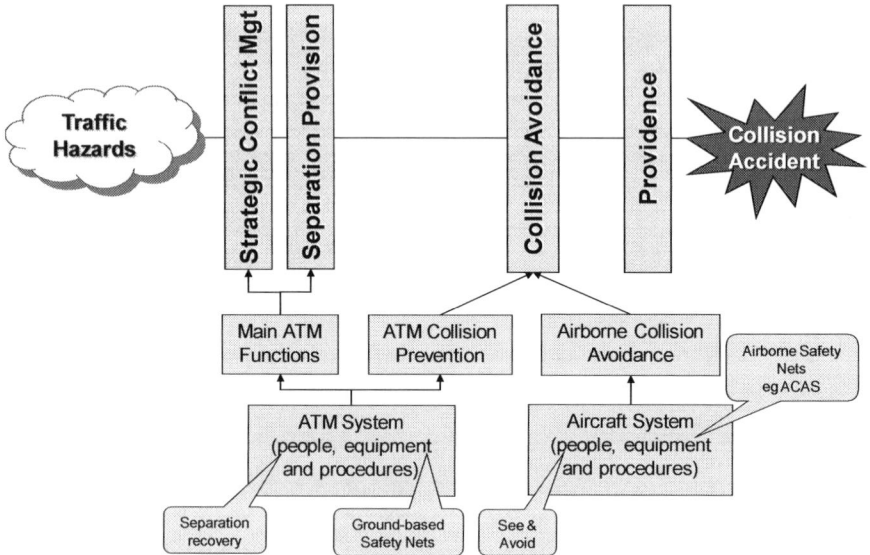

Fig. 1. Conflict management model

The strategic conflict management and separation provision barriers are provided by ATM functions such as airspace design, flow management, traffic synchronisation, and tactical intervention by air traffic controllers.

The collision avoidance barrier is intended to recover the situation only when the previous two barriers have failed to address conflicts sufficiently and there remains risk of collision. It can be initiated by either air traffic controllers, often supported by ground-based safety nets, or collision-avoidance action by flight crew, often supported by airborne safety nets such as ACAS.

Providence is the final barrier and simply represents the probability that aircraft involved in a given encounter, albeit in close proximity with another aircraft or obstacle, would not actually collide. Therefore, each barrier contributes to safety (i.e. reduces collision risk) by removing a *percentage* of the conflicts which exist in the operational environment.

The barriers operate from left to right in sequence, but they are not 100% effective either individually or collectively because of limitations of functionality/performance and (occasional) failure. Consequently, a residual risk of collision exists even after the provision of multiple barriers.

2.2 Success and failure viewpoints

The degree and extent to which the *man-made* barriers are able to reduce risk (by eliminating conflicts) depends, in the first place, on the functionality and performance of the various physical elements that underlie each barrier. However, acting against this *intrinsic* risk reduction capability there can be unwanted factors which erode the safety benefit provided by the barrier, such as loss of the underlying system components, hazards from insidious modes of failure and even hazards from normal operation of the barrier. As a result, the adequacy of the *net* risk reduction afforded by each barrier needs to be argued via both a 'success viewpoint' concerned with intrinsic risk reduction, and a 'failure viewpoint' concerned with the factors that erode it, as depicted in Figure 2.

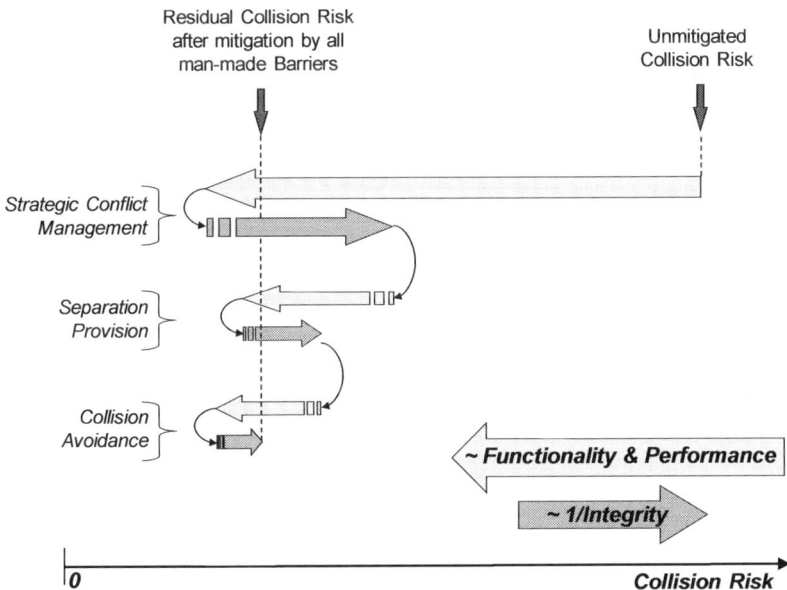

Fig. 2. Barrier success and failure components

2.3 ACAS risks

It can be seen that ACAS is a part of the collision avoidance barrier implemented entirely within the aircraft system. It could be argued that operations with ACAS are 'safe' if ACAS provides a net safety benefit with respect to pre-ACAS operations. Primarily, this means demonstrating that the functionality and performance of ACAS are sufficient to reduce the residual risk of collision[2] that remains as a result of the inherent limitations (or failure) of the preceding barriers *and* the other collision avoidance functions. However, ACAS also carries with it the possibility of behaviours which have the potential to erode its benefit to aviation safety because they constitute risk-bearing hazards in their own right. These hazards could either diminish the collision avoidance capability of ACAS (as part of the 'failure viewpoint') or induce harmful outcomes other than mid-air collision. The safety argument must therefore embrace the effect of ACAS on the risk of *all* types of aircraft accident, not just Mid-Air Collision (MAC).

3 Safety argument

These ACAS safety concepts were used to tailor EUROCONTROL's generic safety argument and associated safety criteria. The argument structure used in APOSC was a prototype of the refined structure that subsequently appeared in (EUROCONTROL 2010) and (Fowler and Pierce 2012a). However, the basic principles are unchanged and therefore the latter will be used for illustration herein. In EUROCONTROL terminology, the term 'argument' is used for the whole structure as well as for the individual goals of which the structure consists.

As suggested in Section 2.3, the safety criteria address accident risk and not simply the mid-air collision risk. Furthermore, it is important to argue a substantial risk reduction because of the uncertainty inherent in quantifying and comparing its safety benefit with any risk-increasing side-effects. The criteria also include the general regulatory requirement under ESARR 3 (EUROCONTROL 2000) to reduce risk as far as reasonably practicable (AFARP). These two criteria are shown as Cr001 in Figure 3 and are referred to as Safety Criterion #1 and Safety Criterion #2, respectively.

The top-level claim (Arg 0), and its five supporting principal arguments, are also shown in Figure 3.

The first two principal arguments (Arg 1 and Arg 2) are wholly concerned with higher levels of definition of ACAS operations, whereas Arg 3 and the term 'implementation' encompass the lower levels of definition, and the realisation of these definitions in physical equipment, people and procedures.

---

[2] Unless otherwise stated, the term 'collision' used herein refers only to the mid-air collision component of the collision avoidance barrier by default.

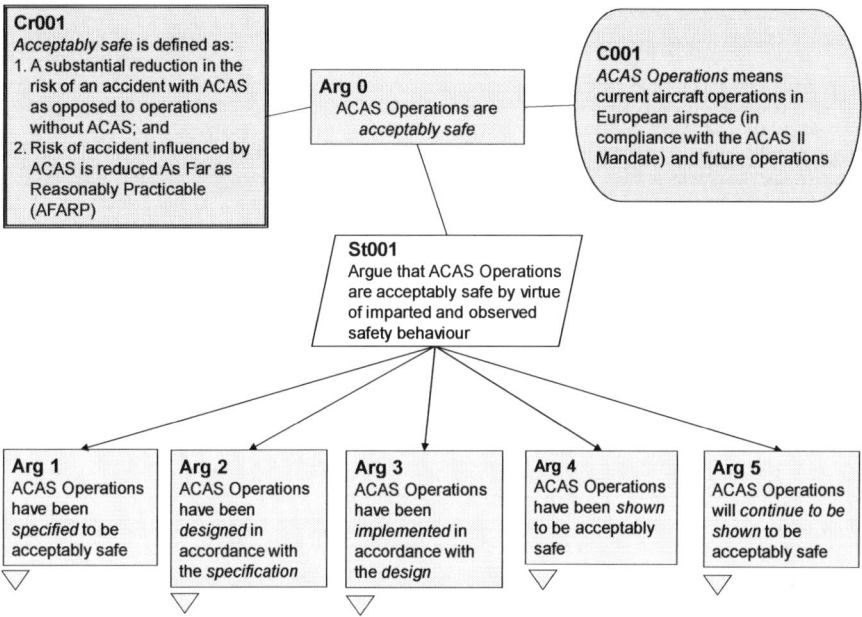

Cr001
Acceptably safe is defined as:
1. A substantial reduction in the risk of an accident with ACAS as opposed to operations without ACAS; and
2. Risk of accident influenced by ACAS is reduced As Far as Reasonably Practicable (AFARP)

Arg 0
ACAS Operations are *acceptably safe*

C001
ACAS Operations means current aircraft operations in European airspace (in compliance with the ACAS II Mandate) and future operations

St001
Argue that ACAS Operations are acceptably safe by virtue of imparted and observed safety behaviour

Arg 1
ACAS Operations have been *specified* to be acceptably safe

Arg 2
ACAS Operations have been *designed* in accordance with the *specification*

Arg 3
ACAS Operations have been *implemented* in accordance with the *design*

Arg 4
ACAS Operations have been *shown* to be acceptably safe

Arg 5
ACAS Operations will *continue to be shown* to be acceptably safe

Fig. 3. Top-level argument structure

The safety of ACAS operations stems from the system properties (functional and non-functional) that are embedded in the various levels of definition. Consequently, the sub-arguments under Arg 1, Arg 2 and Arg 3 are concerned with addressing the 'designed-in' safety properties of ACAS operations from the success and failure viewpoints. Satisfaction of these three arguments therefore relies heavily on the *existence* of evidence related to definition of behaviour, together with evidence of associated *analyses* that show that the required behaviour would be safe if the defined behaviour were implemented.

For brevity, the breakdown of these principal arguments, and the linkage of the lowest levels with individual evidence items is not further described herein, as these are fully explained in (Fowler and Pierce 2012b). Instead, the paper will describe how the safety assessment exploited pre-existing evidence, and created new evidence, in order to support Arg 1, Arg 2 and Arg 3.

4 ACAS safety assessment

4.1 High-level specification of ACAS

ACAS operations are defined in a disparate set of documents promulgated by ICAO[3] (ICAO 2001a, 2001b, 2001c, 2002, 2005a, 2006a), other international/ national regulatory and standards bodies, ATM service providers, aircraft operators, and manufacturers.

The problem is that, even at the highest level of definition, each of these documents captures only an individual aspect of ACAS operations. Consequently, there exists no abstract conceptual description of ACAS operations as a whole which can be used as a starting point for supporting Arg 1, for assuring that the detailed provisions are correct, coherent and consistent with each other, or for verifying that any future changes to ACAS operations would be compatible with the original intent of the system.

Therefore, it was necessary to produce a conceptual description of ACAS operations as an integral part of its safety case; in other words, a definition of the basic principles behind ACAS-based collision avoidance that is independent of a design solution, because arguing the safety of any system has to be based on an understanding of what the system was originally intended to do. This conceptual description was produced by abstraction (or 'reverse engineering') of the information in ICAO and other existing ACAS documentation and was termed 'ACAS fundamentals' in order not to imply that it constituted a formal concept of operations.

The ACAS fundamentals comprise statements that describe the principles of ACAS operations, covering the following:

- environment – the attributes of the airspace in which ACAS operates
- collision avoidance – the basic mechanism by which ACAS operations avert collision
- segregation – the independence of ACAS operations from the rest of ATM
- prioritisation – the relative importance of ACAS operations with respect to other accident-prevention functions
- universality – the ACAS global interoperability features
- deployment – the progressive introduction of ACAS operations to the airspace.

In line with the more recent approach of (Fowler and Pierce 2012a), these free-text narratives could then be captured in a concise requirements form as safety objectives[4]. Some examples are shown in Table 1.

---

[3] The cited versions are those applicable to APOSC.

[4] This step was not conducted in APOSC – thus the safety requirements for the design (see Section 4.2) were traced straight back to the ACAS fundamentals rather than to the safety objectives, as being suggested here.

Table 1. Examples of ACAS safety objectives

Ref	Safety objective
SO_1	In the event of an imminent mid-air collision, one or both of the aircraft involved shall initiate a vertical manoeuvre such that the collision is avoided.
SO_2	Collision-avoidance manoeuvres shall be initiated in a timely manner and in a way that does not generate positive or negative 'g' forces that would over-stress the airframe or injure the aircraft occupants.
SO_8	Collision-avoidance action shall be unaffected by interference from air traffic services.
SO_9	Collision-avoidance action shall not interfere with the provision of air traffic services to non-involved aircraft.
SO_10	Collision-avoidance action shall take priority over the need to resolve situations that present a lower risk to the aircraft.

Like the ACAS fundamentals, these safety objectives represent the required behaviour of ACAS in a form that is independent of their subsequent implementation in the ACAS equipment and associated operating procedures. In order to satisfy Arg 1, evidence would, of course, have to be provided to show that the safety objectives are sufficient – i.e. correct, complete and consistent such that, if satisfied in their entirety, would result in ACAS operations satisfying the specified safety criteria, in the stated operational environment.

4.2 ACAS high-level design

The ACAS high-level design on the other hand is a logical architectural model that reflects the established solution to satisfying the safety objectives (or in the case of the APOSC, the ACAS fundamentals themselves) using the elements of the aviation system. The scope of the ACAS design is considered to encompass all those elements that collectively produce the required collision-avoidance function, as shown in Figure 4.

The roles played by the elements within the design, and the environment and elements external to the design, where they affect, or are affected by, the operation of ACAS were analysed. From this analysis, a set of Functional Safety Requirements (FSRs) were derived that were deemed to be applicable to the elements of the logical model. This initial set was progressively expanded and refined as the subsequent steps in the safety assessment were conducted. Some examples are shown in Table 2.

Hierarchically, the ACAS high-level specification and design sit above the level of the ICAO and other documents mentioned in Section 4.1. However, it should be emphasised that they were devised for the purpose of constructing the safety case and do not purport to be official representations of ACAS in any other context.

Returning to the safety argument in Figure 3, the term 'specified' relates to the definition of ACAS operations via the fundamentals/safety objectives, whereas *'designed'* relates to the ACAS logical model and its associated FSRs. It follows that Arg 3 considers any definition of ACAS operations below the level of ACAS design, including the level of the current ICAO and other documents, as being part of the *implementation* of the design.

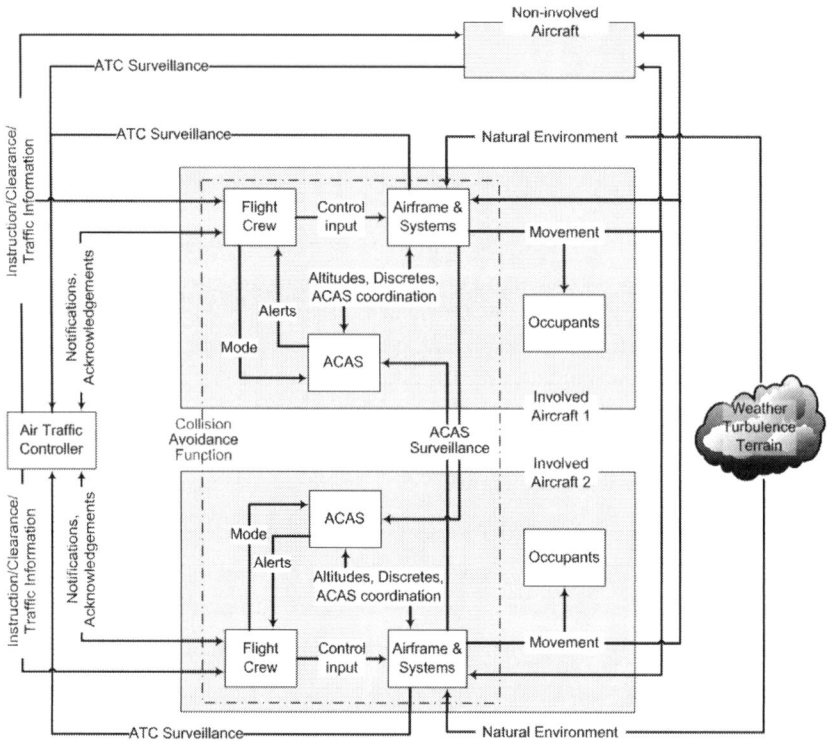

Fig. 4. Collision avoidance logical model

However, as ACAS is a worldwide system, it is impractical to obtain direct evidence that every organisation responsible for ACAS implementation has complied precisely with the ICAO provisions. The safety assessment was therefore curtailed at the ICAO level, and the argument about lower level specifications being compliant with ICAO and then correctly realised in physical form, was dealt with by an assumption that established aviation practices enforce the correct adoption of ICAO provisions. On the other hand, asserting that compliance with the ICAO provisions would yield safe ACAS operations presupposes those provisions to be complete, correct and unambiguous in the first place. Therefore, the safety assessment paid particular attention to determining whether this was in fact the case. It will be seen later that the consistency between the (coherent) FSRs and the ICAO documents was assessed as a means of arguing that the ICAO regulations are internally and mutually coherent.

Table 2. Examples of ACAS functional safety requirements

Ref	Safety requirement
SR_A6	ACAS shall provide collision avoidance indications (RA) which are compatible with all types of equipped aircraft in the environment and all points in their flight envelope relevant to the environment.
SR_A7	ACAS shall provide collision avoidance indications (RA) which correspond to the minimum manoeuvring necessary to avoid collision.
SR_A8	ACAS shall not produce collision avoidance indications (RA) which would cause the aircraft to descend when close to the ground.
SR_F1	Flight frew shall prepare themselves to act immediately in accordance with any subsequent collision avoidance indications (RA), in response to potential collision warning (TA) from ACAS.
SR_F3	Flight crew shall act in accordance with collision avoidance indications (RA) from ACAS by using control inputs similar in strength to those used for routine aircraft manoeuvres.
SR_F5	Flight crew shall switch ACAS to TA-only mode when there exists an aircraft-related failure which would preclude an ACAS-initiated manoeuvre should it be necessary.
SR_C1	Air traffic controller shall cease to issue clearances or instructions to an aircraft that has notified its execution of an ACAS-initiated collision avoidance action.

The fundamentals/safety objectives, design and FSRs therefore provide the bases for arguing that there is a coherent definition of ACAS at the ICAO level, even though they have been created by abstraction partly from those lower level definitions. While this might seem to be circular logic, the exercise in fact it serves two important purposes:

- The abstraction process means that a description of ACAS operations is produced that is by definition unfettered with the implementation details that are prevalent in all existing documentation. This facilitates a proper understanding of ACAS fundamental behaviour that can be scrutinised and validated via peer review.
- If it proves impossible to devise a conceptual behavioural description, the implication is that either the required behaviour of ACAS-based collision avoidance is inherently ill-defined (and therefore potentially unsafe), or there are irreconcilable inconsistencies in its detailed definitions.

4.3 Success properties in design

The decomposition of Arg 2 in Figure 3 is concerned with asserting that all the safety properties required to fully support the success and failure viewpoints have been included in the ACAS high-level design. These properties comprise risk reduction performance, design completeness, correctness, coherence and robustness, correct dynamic behaviour, inter-system compatibility[5] and mitigation of system-generated hazards.

However, with the exception of the last one (covered in Section 4.5 later), the evidence that the ACAS design has these properties mainly arises from pre-existing ACAS documentation covering specifications, simulations, testing, trials and operations. They cannot be inferred directly from the logical model and initial FSRs.

These pre-existing evidence items were therefore analysed and the information was extracted, partitioned according to the strands of the sub-arguments, and summarised within APOSC. Any documented properties that could not be reconciled with the initial list of FSRs, but were consistent with the fundamentals, were abstracted as additional FSRs. A consequence of this approach was that, strictly, most of the *direct* evidence to support Arg 2 came from the *implementation* evidence that would appear under Arg 3, which is then argued in reverse to assert that the ACAS design is correct.

4.4 Risk reduction performance

Being a static model supported by *functional* statements, the ACAS design and FSRs do not in themselves provide assurance that an implementation solution exists that can provide a substantial reduction in the risk of a MAC (ignoring for the moment any potential ACAS influences on non-MAC accidents), because this is a *performance* issue.

Additionally, therefore, as part of Arg 2 it is necessary to show that a design solution exists which will produce effective collision resolution in the majority of encounter scenarios in the ACAS operating environment. The ACAS equipment detects conflicts and issues RAs using algorithms applied to aircraft relative-position information. It effects collision avoidance via the flight crew, which implies the need for human functionality and performance (i.e. timely and appropriate response to ACAS) in addition to that provided by equipment.

The evidence for such functionality came from simulations that had been conducted extensively and reported in the many ACAS safety studies such as (EUROCONTROL 2002a, 2002b, 2006b) performed prior to APOSC development.

Within the modelling studies, the theoretical effectiveness of ACAS in reducing the risk of collision is expressed using a metric known as Risk Ratio, which is defined as:

$$Risk\ Ratio = \frac{Risk\ of\ collision\ with\ ACAS}{Risk\ of\ collision\ without\ ACAS}$$

---

[5] Meaning compatibility with other airborne accident avoidance systems, air traffic management and proximate non-involved aircraft.

A variant of this parameter, known as Logic Risk Ratio (LRR), is calculated based upon the behaviour in simulated encounters purely of the ACAS algorithms and a pilot-response model. The most recent study containing an estimate for LRR for the whole of European airspace (EUROCONTROL 2006b) has predicted an LRR of 19.6%, which represents a substantial reduction in the risk of collision, consistent with Safety Criterion #1.

As these simulations were based on the algorithms prescribed for TCAS II Version 7 in DO-185A (RTCA 1997), any assertion in APOSC about ACAS-related risk reduction was only valid in the context of using algorithms of equivalent performance and this was therefore captured as an FSR. This link was crucial in arguing that the risk reduction capability demonstrated by the simulated system would find its way into the airborne equipment.

The LRR does not, however, take into account the wide range of 'real-world' factors that can influence ACAS efficacy. Hence, the results from dynamic modelling are also used, in conjunction with a combinatorial logic model known as contingency tree (EUROCONTROL 2006c), to predict the collision risk reduction achievable by ACAS in the presence of factors beyond the mere operation of its algorithms. These factors represent the variables affecting ACAS operations, categorised as follows:

- ACAS logic performance
- ACAS tracking
- aircraft equipage
- altitude reporting
- controller involvement
- encounter geometry
- pilot response
- see-and-avoid
- traffic display
- visual acquisition.

Each factor has an associated set of events, as shown in the example for altitude reporting in Table 3.

Table 3. Altitude reporting events

Factor	Event description	Event code
Altitude reporting	Mode C aircraft does not report altitude .	EACX
Altitude reporting	Mode C aircraft reports altitude .	EACY
Altitude reporting	non-ACAS Mode S aircraft does not report altitude.	EASX
Altitude reporting	non-ACAS Mode S aircraft reports altitude .	EASY

The probabilities assigned to the events influence the overall collision-risk reduction and since the factors are intended to represent effects in the real world, the result obtained is a metric known as System Risk Ratio (SRR), whose risk ratio formula is the same as LRR.

Each probability represents the likelihood of occurrence of the event within the sample of simulated encounters used to calculate SRR. Importantly, the contingency tree events are not categorised as either normal or abnormal states; rather this discrimination is implied by the relative event probabilities. Nor does it explicitly represent failures, although failure of the elements of the design (or the environment) could in principle contribute to some of the event probabilities. The meaning of these events was therefore significant not only in the context of them supporting the success viewpoint as part of SRR, but also in representing certain unwanted behaviours that were relevant to the failure viewpoint, as described later.

The SRR is more representative of actual operations than LRR and also shows (EUROCONTROL 2002a) that ACAS is capable of producing substantial collision-risk reduction (by approximately a factor of 5) commensurate with Safety Criterion #1. In the absence of evidence from actual collision risk reduction in the airspace, satisfaction of the safety claim was to rely heavily on evidence from these modelling studies. Hence, APOSC included backing arguments and evidence about the validity of the system and encounter models used, the completeness of the contingency tree events, and the validity of their allocated probabilities.

4.5 Construction of accident-causation model

The ACAS design or its environment needs to mitigate sufficiently the risk increase from any hazards that originate within the design in order not to erode the safety benefit of ACAS to the point where it cannot provide a substantial net reduction in the risk of an aircraft accident. This is the classical failure viewpoint to which many system safety assessments confine themselves.

In the context of ACAS, hazards are considered to be events with potential to contribute to an accident; i.e. they produce a risk increase. Hence, loss of ACAS is considered to be a hazard even though it will not result in a collision by itself.

Hazardous behaviour of the system could therefore arise from loss of functionality reducing the collision avoidance effectiveness of ACAS, or from anomalous behaviour inducing a risk that would otherwise not have arisen. The anomalous behaviour in turn could arise as a by-product of the normal operation of the system as well as from failure of its elements. In all cases the hazard is considered as belonging to the failure viewpoint because it is risk-increasing. Furthermore, the risk associated with system hazards need not necessarily be confined to mid-air collision. All behaviours which could contribute to an aircraft accident must be considered in accordance with the safety criteria.

Since the development of ACAS pre-dated contemporary approaches to safety assessment, no formal hazard-identification workshops were ever conducted. To circumvent the need to conduct such workshops on a mature operational system, an accident-causation model was instead developed primarily using ACAS-generic information that had been produced by the safety assessment workshops for the EUROCONTROL project on feasibility of RA downlink (EUROCON-TROL 2007). This was used to populate an accident-causation model represented as a fault tree whose top-level structure was based upon the integrated risk picture developed by EUROCONTROL EEC (EUROCONTROL 2006a) according to the conflict management model. The ACAS accident-causation model included both MAC, and 'non-MAC' accidents such as controlled flight into terrain or accidents due to stall, windshear and wake vortex.

The top level of the model is shown in Figure 5, in which the alignment with the conflict management model of Figure 1 can be seen. The model identifies five hazards (H1-H5) related to ACAS operations, their immediate consequences, and (via the AND gates) the mitigations that prevent each hazard from producing an accident.

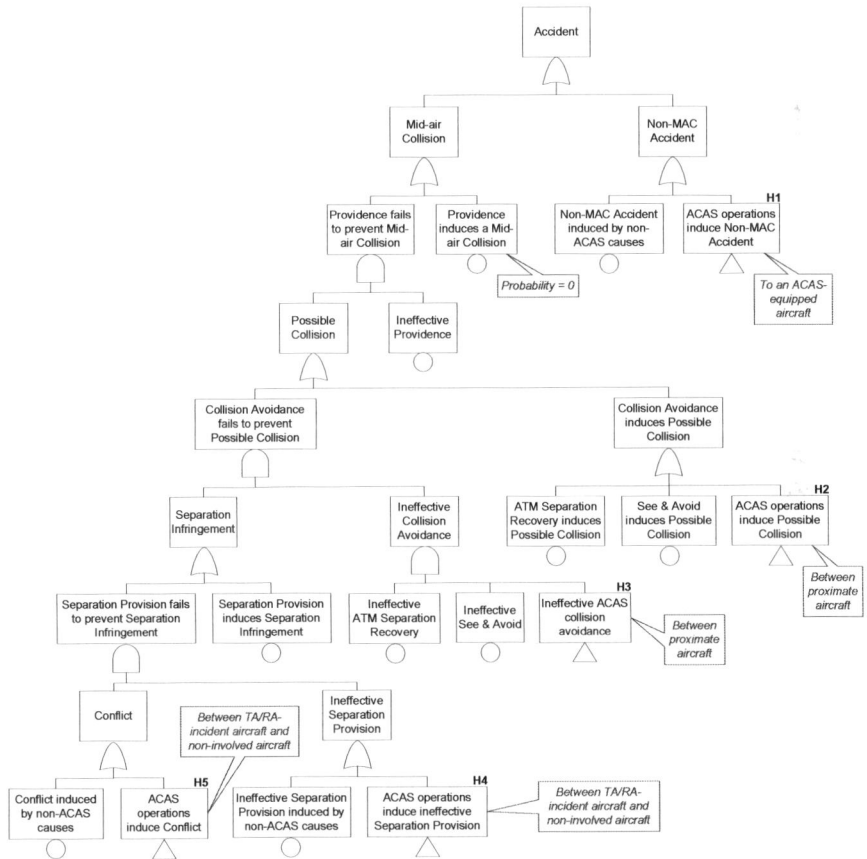

Fig. 5. ACAS hazards

The external mitigations for the ACAS hazards all correspond to existing functions within the conflict management model. As these functions are established parts of civil aviation, it was not necessary (with the exception of ACAS itself) to capture FSRs or assumptions for these mitigations as part of the safety case.

The model was also used to elaborate the hazard causes arising from the elements of the design or the environment, some of which include normal events as well as abnormal conditions and failures. Further reduction on collision risk might be possible as a result of re-examining the rules that permit these events, and this was captured as a safety issue in APOSC.

4.6 Correlation of causes with FSRs

The model was used as an aid to completing the set of FSRs by revealing causes for which there was no corresponding functionality already defined as part of the design or its environment. Any causes that could not be equated to non-compliance with an FSR or permitted normal ACAS operation, could point to an omission in the set of FSRs.

Example results from the analysis of hazard causes against (non-compliance with) the FSRs are shown in Table 4. Column 5 identifies whether there are any contingency tree event(s) which are equivalent to the hazard causes.

Table 4. Examples of hazard causes

Hazard ref	Hazard cause	Cause ref	Non-compliance with SR	Included in contingency tree?
H3	ACAS inadequately resolves encounter.	C_A3	SR_A4	✓
H3	ACAS passive failure (ACAS fails to produce RA).	C_A5	SR_A3 or SR_A4	✓
H3	Flight crew incorrectly operates ACAS.	C_F4	SR_F7	NO
H3	Flight crew prioritises ATC instruction/clearance over RA.	C_F5	SR_F2, SR_F8	✓
H3	Flight crew prioritises reaction to traffic information over RA.	C_F6	SR_F2	NO
H3	Flight crew doesn't notice RA.	C_F10	SR_F2	NO
H3	Flight crew performs inadequate manoeuvre.	C_F11	SR_F2	✓

4.7 Correlation of causes with contingency tree

Having derived a set of hazard causes related to failures within the system, it was necessary to demonstrate that the risk they represent is commensurate with the safety criteria.

In order to determine the risk from system-generated hazards, any overlap between the hazard causes and the contingency tree events first needs to be identified because the contribution to risk from the latter is already accounted for as a component of ACAS MAC net risk reduction within the SRR, as illustrated in Figure 6.

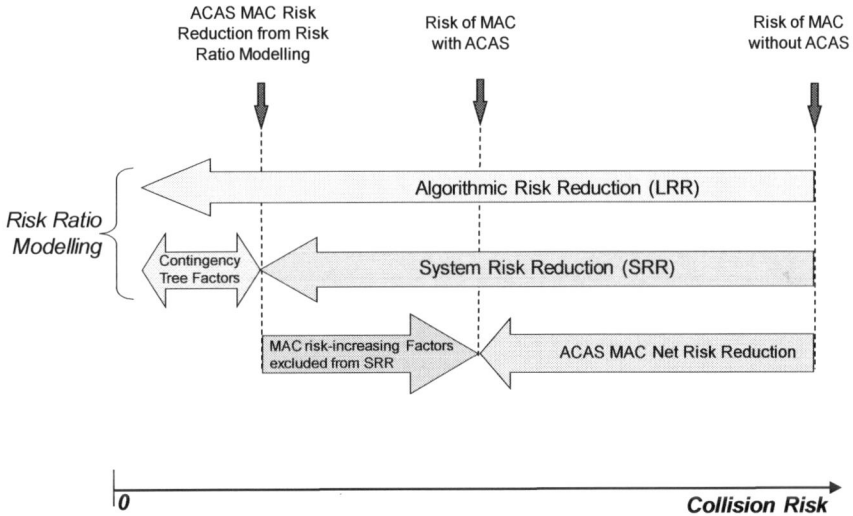

Fig. 6. ACAS MAC risk reduction components

It can be seen that ACAS MAC net risk reduction comprises the SRR minus the risk increase due to any hazard causes which are not covered by the contingency tree factors. In order to satisfy the safety criteria, it is therefore necessary to demonstrate that the risk from MAC hazard causes which are not covered by the contingency tree events is sufficiently small that ACAS MAC net risk reduction remains substantial.

In addition, the risk from ACAS-induced non-MAC accident causes should be sufficiently small compared to ACAS MAC net risk reduction, thus yielding substantial ACAS *accident* risk reduction.

This is accomplished by first identifying those hazard causes which have equivalent contingency tree event(s). Any hazard causes *without* an equivalent contingency tree event were then verified as having mitigations defined via FSRs as part of the ACAS design or its environment. This supports an assertion that the functionality within the design is sufficient to reduce the risk of an ACAS-induced accident AFARP.

However, the qualitative model does not quantify the risk increase represented by failure to comply with these FSRs due to the finite reliability of the design elements. Therefore, the satisfaction of Safety Criterion #1 was not supported by the available evidence. APOSC dealt with this deficiency by asserting that standard aviation practices will have imparted sufficiently low probability of such failures, but also captured it as a safety issue whose resolution would produce the necessary quantified risk evidence.

4.8 Assessment of ICAO specifications

Assurance of completeness is an omnipresent problem in any safety assessment as it is much harder to identify a missing hazard, cause or safety requirement than one which is ambiguous or contradictory. The ACAS safety assessment had the benefit of being able to draw from, and correlate, the following three diverse and independently produced sources of information in order to assure that the final set of FSRs was complete:

- abstract logical model derived from ACAS documentation
- accident-causation model primarily derived from FARADS safety assessment workshops
- contingency tree events derived from ACAS safety studies.

Recall that Arg 3 considers the ICAO specification level and below as being part of the implementation of the design, and that assessing direct evidence of the implementation of ICAO specifications was deemed outside the scope of APOSC. Consequently, the majority of the evidence to support Arg 3 was related to an assertion that ACAS internationally applicable operational and system requirements conform to the ACAS design; in other words the ICAO specifications were shown to be consistent with the ACAS FSRs (that had been assured complete via the preceding safety assessment steps).

This assertion was supported by evidence from a systematic assessment of each line of the ICAO specifications against the FSRs in which each ICAO clause was first mapped to the corresponding FSRs for that element and then a determination made about the degree of compliance. This assessment also addresses the degree and extent of the consistency within and between the ICAO ACAS provisions themselves.

The results from the complete assessment revealed the following weaknesses in the ICAO specifications:

- some ambiguities and inconsistencies within ICAO flight crew provisions, some of which can be equated to non-compliances with the associated ACAS safety requirements
- some ambiguities and inconsistencies within ICAO air traffic controller provisions

- no ICAO provisions dealing with independence between ATM separation provision and separation recovery, and ACAS.

Any ambiguity in the operational requirements could in principle lead to their potentially hazardous misapplication. However, the ICAO provisions, like the ACAS equipment itself, have arisen from many years of experience with ACAS operations and are not considered serious enough to undermine the safety claim. Even the presence of non-conformity with a particular FSR does not imply that ACAS operations are *unsafe*, rather it means that ACAS might not be as fully effective as it would otherwise be. Nevertheless, existence of these discrepancies was raised as a safety issue.

4.9 Analysis of ACAS-implicated accidents

The final consideration in the safety case was to take four aircraft accidents in which ACAS was a significant factor and rationalise what had occurred in the context of the analyses and conclusions in APOSC. Although such accidents do not in themselves indicate that ACAS operations are unsafe according to the risk-based criteria used in APOSC, these real events should nevertheless not undermine the safety case in other respects, and ideally should vindicate it. Of interest to the safety assessment part of APOSC was whether the causes of these accidents could actually be explained in terms of non-compliance with ACAS FSRs.

The accidents were:

- Yaizu accident, 31 January 2001 (JTSB 2002)
- Überlingen accident, 2 July 2002 (BFU 2004)
- Jeju Island, Korea accident, 16 November 2006 (ASC 2008)
- Brazil mid-air collision, 29 September 2006 (CENIPA 2008).

The second and fourth accidents are well known since they resulted in a mid-air collision with multiple fatalities. The others are less well known; although one resulted in a very close approach between the involved aircraft, with structural damage and serious injuries to persons on board, both aircraft were able to make a safe landing without fatalities.

The safety case includes a short summary of the accident sequences showing how and why ACAS as a 'socio-technical system' did not prevent the accidents (despite the fact that the technical functioning of the ACAS *equipment* was correct) and linking the accident to the failure modes/hazards, mitigations and safety issues identified in the safety case. In all cases, non-conformity with at least one ACAS safety requirement was evident. Perhaps more importantly, it brought into focus the inherent difficulty in formulating procedures that allow the flexibility to deal with the unexpected, yet remain unambiguous during foreseeable scenarios.

5 Conclusions

As there is little direct statistical evidence of the collision risk reduction achieved by ACAS in operation, the safety case for ACAS operations relied heavily on a new safety assessment to provide the evidence necessary to support a safety argument based on success and failure viewpoints.

As an established system that pre-dated contemporary approaches to systems and safety engineering, the ACAS safety assessment process included abstraction and reverse-engineering to yield a coherent definition of ACAS operations starting from its fundamental concepts in order to assert that ACAS operations are fully defined, understood, and coherent.

An important output from the safety assessment was a complete set of ACAS functional safety requirements that could be used to identify suspected weaknesses in the ICAO specifications that have hitherto been the starting point for the formal definition of ACAS.

The results from pre-existing analytical risk reduction studies were positioned within this part of the assessment to provide assurance that ACAS predicted behaviour manifests itself in the airborne equipment.

The other main strand of the safety assessment was the construction of an accident-causal model to demonstrate how ACAS operations can lead to various accident types due to normal and abnormal behaviour of the elements of a logical model. Its casual events were correlated with the safety requirements and factors used in the analytical risk reduction studies in order to assure that sufficient functionality had been defined to mitigate ACAS hazards, and to identify which risk-increasing events had not already been accounted for in predicting ACAS risk reduction.

Limitations in the scope of the safety assessment and the weaknesses it revealed in the ICAO specifications were raised as safety issues. However, they were deemed insufficient to render ACAS operations unsafe by contravening Safety Criterion #1; rather ACAS might not produce as much collision risk reduction as it otherwise could, in contravention of Safety Criterion #2.

Acknowledgments   Figures 1, 2, 4, 5 ,6 and Tables 2, 3, 4 herein are reproduced from the ACAS II Post-implementation Safety Case © EUROCONTROL 2011 in accordance with the authorisation at http://www.eurocontrol.int/articles/copyright. Accessed 30 September 2012.

References

ASC (2008) Aviation Safety Council, Taiwan. Far Eastern Air Transport EF306, Boeing 757-200/Thai Airways (…) Flight TG659, Boeing 757/300. A TCAS event in narrow collision avoidance at an altitude of 34,000 ft and 99nm south of Jeju Island, Korea on November 16 2006. Final Report
BFU (2004) Bundestelle fur Flügunfallundersuchung (German Federal Bureau of Aircraft Accident Investigation), Investigation Report AX001-1-2/02
CENIPA (2008) Aeronautical Accident Investigation and Prevention Center, Command of Aeronautics, General Staff of the Aeronautics, Final Report A-00X/CENIPA/2008 on the mid-air

collision between Boeing B-737 8EH and Embraer EMB-135 BJ Legacy aircraft over Brazil on 29 September 2006

EUROCONTROL (2000) ESARR 3, use of safety management systems by ATM service providers, edn 1.0

EUROCONTROL (2001) ESARR 4 – Risk assessment and mitigation in ATM, Edn 1.0

EUROCONTROL (2002a) ACAS programme, ACAS safety study, safety benefit of ACAS II phase 1 and phase 2 in the new European airspace environment, ACAS/02-022, edn 1

EUROCONTROL (2002b) ACAS programme, ACASA project, work package 1, final report on studies on the safety of ACAS II in Europe, ACAS/ACASA/02-014, edn 1

EUROCONTROL (2006a) Main report for the 2005/2012 integrated risk picture for air traffic management in Europe, EEC Note No. 05/06

EUROCONTROL (2006b) ASARP project, work package 9: final report on the safety of ACAS II in the European RVSM environment, ASARP/WP9/72/D, Version 1.1

EUROCONTROL (2006c) ASARP project, work package 6: final report on post-RVSM ACAS full-system safety study, ASARP/WP6/58/D, Version 1.0

EUROCONTROL (2006d) Air navigation system safety assessment methodology, SAF.ET1. ST03.1000-MAN-01-00, edn 2.1

EUROCONTROL (2007) ACAS RA downlink combined FHA and PSSA Report, edn 1.2

EUROCONTROL (2010) Safety assessment made easier, part 1, safety principles and an introduction to safety assessment, edn 1

EUROCONTROL (2011) ACAS II post-implementation safety case, edn 2.3. http://www. eurocontrol.int/msa/public/standard_page/ACAS_APOSC.html. Accessed 30 September 2012

Fowler D, Pierce RH (2012a) Safety engineering – a perspective on systems engineering. In: Dale C, Anderson T (eds), Achieving Systems Safety. Springer

Fowler D, Pierce RH (2012b) A safety engineering perspective. In: Cogan B (ed) Systems Engineering – Practice and Theory, InTech. http://www.intechopen.com/articles/show/title/a-safety-engineering-perspective. Accessed 30 September 2012

ICAO (2001a) Operation of aircraft, annex 6 to the convention on international civil aviation, part 1 – international commercial air transport – aeroplanes, 8th edn

ICAO (2001b) Air traffic services, annex 11 to the convention on international civil aviation, 13th edn

ICAO (2001c) Procedures for air navigation services, air traffic management, PANS-ATM Doc 4444, ATM/501, 14th edn

ICAO (2002) Aeronautical telecommunications Volume IV, surveillance radar and collision avoidance systems, annex 10 to the convention on international civil aviation, 3rd edn

ICAO (2005a) Rules of the air, annex 2 to the convention on international civil aviation, 10th edn

ICAO (2005b) Global air traffic management operational concept, Doc 9854, 1st edn

ICAO (2006a) Aircraft operations Volume I, flight procedures, Doc 8168 OPS/611, 5th edn

ICAO (2006b) Airborne Collision Avoidance System (ACAS) Manual, Document 9863 AN/461, 1st edn

JTSB (2002) Aircraft and railway accident investigation commission of Japan (now Japan transportation safety board), accident report number 02-5-JA8904. (summarised in http://www. asasi.org/papers/2005/Hiroaki%20Tomita%20-%20near%20collision%20in%20Japan.pdf). Accessed 30 September 2012

RTCA (1997) Minimum operational performance standards for traffic alert and collision avoidance system II airborne equipment. RTCA DO-185A

Elaborating the Concept of Evidence in Safety Cases

Linling Sun and Tim Kelly

University of York

York, UK

Abstract   Unlike argumentation in safety cases, evidence (also an important component), has received less attention in the literature. In this paper, we compare the concept of evidence in different disciplines and analyze the characteristics of evidence in the safety domain. A model of evidence is proposed for a better understanding of evidence and its evaluation. Evidence assertions, the minimal assertions that are drawn out of the source data of evidence, are explained with the model. The model will provide clarity to the interface between evidence and argument that is useful for confidence establishment in safety cases.

1 Introduction

Both valid argument structure and sound evidence are important components of compelling safety cases. However, the study of safety evidence is not as well developed as the argumentation part of safety cases. The understanding and usage of the concept of evidence is diverse in safety practice.

In recent years, the importance of evidence has been highlighted in the development of dependable software systems (Jackson et al. 2007) and more people are concerned about the inspection, analysis, and requirements on evidence presented in safety cases (Hamilton 2006; Jackson et al. 2007; Hawkins and Kelly 2010; Reinhardt and McDermid 2010). From the published literature, standards and guidance, we observe the following two issues. Firstly, various existing definitions focus on different aspects of evidence, e.g. its source data, its documentation or its role in supporting a claim. This, unsurprisingly, can result in diverse understanding and sometimes misconceptions of safety evidence in safety engineering practice. Secondly, the existing view of evidence-argument interface is too simplified. The interface between evidence and argument is usually presented as references to source data that are associated with *domain* safety claims only. However, the reasoning between what we can obtain from evidence and the domain safety claims being supported by the evidence is unclear. It is difficult, with current documentation and representation of evidence in safety cases, to determine how, and to what extent, the items of evidence fit for their role in a specific application context. Hence, the justification of safety evidence can be difficult and the confidence in the system safety demonstrated by a safety case may be insufficiently established.

In this paper, we define the concept of evidence in the context of safety cases on the basis of comparison of definitions of evidence in several disciplines. We also define a model of evidence (EviM) in order to have a clear view of the grounds on which established confidence associated with safety cases is based. Within this model, the notion of *evidence assertion* is introduced as the interface element to help integrate safety evidence and argument effectively.

2 The concept of evidence

A commonly-cited definition of a safety case is from DS 00-56 (MoD 2007).

> A structured argument, supported by a body of evidence that provides a compelling, comprehensible and valid case that a system is safe for a given application in a given operating environment.

It is clear from the definition that 'a body of evidence' is a part of a safety case. However, DS 00-56 does not provide a definition of 'evidence'. This, sometimes, leads to inconsistent and arbitrary usage of this notion by practitioners. Evidence has been viewed as artefacts, documents, facts, or statements of facts in different situations.

The connotation of a concept (Mill 1879), which is also referred to as intension, essence or nature of a concept, depicts the abstract meaning of a term, which serves as shared principles and characteristics that apply to *all* objects of that concept. In this section, we probe the essential meaning of evidence in different disciplines and explore the common understanding of this concept within the domain of safety cases. This is the foundation for proper comprehension, interpretation, usage and documentation of evidence in safety.

2.1 Evidence in other domains

In order to gain an initial understanding of the concept, we refer to different definitions of evidence in three other domains for insights – from the fields of philosophy, law and medicine, in which evidence has been studied for a considerable time.

> **Definition 1.** That which tends to prove the existence or nonexistence of some fact. It may consist of testimony, documentary evidence, real evidence, and, when admissible, hearsay evidence. (Law and Martin 2009)

Definition 2. The assembled information and facts on which rational, logical decisions are based in the diverse forums of human discourse, including courts of law, and in the practice of evidence-based medicine among many others. (Last 2006)

Definition 3. That which raises or lowers the probability of a proposition. The central question of epistemology is the structure of this process and its ultimate rationale. (Blackburn 2005)

The rigour and the function of evidence in the three disciplines are not the same. In the realm of law, evidence is presented to help establish (to a court) that something existed or happened in the past. This view of evidence cannot be viewed as interchangeable with the definition of a *fact*. Once admitted as relevant, evidence tends to work as a foundational proof that substantiates subsequent reasoning or tests hypotheses towards a truth or fact. In medicine, especially in evidence-based medical decision-making, evidence is collected from various sources and evaluated for its applicability and validity in order to determine whether it is suitable for supporting the treatment decision of a patient at hand (Gross 2001). Matching the available evidence and the specific application scenario to confirm the 'fitness of usage' is a primary task of evidence-based medicine. The user of evidence needs the information concerning how the evidence is generated, but is not responsible for the generation of such evidence. In philosophy, the definition has not constrained the form or content of evidence, but places emphasis fully on the intent of presenting evidence. The power of evidence in philosophy is of some *degree*; it confirms or refutes a proposition, but not in an absolute sense, instead changing the probability of the proposition only.

Even though it is not reflected in aforementioned definitions, literature in law, philosophy and medicine unanimously highlight the importance of evidence evaluation or appraisal of significance. Because evidence can be fallible, trust in evidence must be settled by rigorous scrutiny or examination of evidence in the context of its usage. We should not attach more responsibility on an item of evidence than that which goes beyond its capability or use it in an unsuitable or inapplicable context.

2.2 Evidence in safety domain

There are several guidance materials (Adelard 1998; EUROCONTROL 2006; OMG 2010b) that provide definitions of evidence in the safety domain. But each of them is presented in a particular context and has its limitations.

Definition 4. Which is used as the basis of the safety argument. This can be either facts, assumptions, or subclaims derived from a lower-level sub-argument. (Adelard 1998; Bishop and Bloomfield 1998)

Definition 5. Safety evidence is information, based on established fact or expert judgement, which is presented to show that the safety argument to which it relates is valid. (EUROCONTROL 2006)

Definition 6. A document or other exhibit that provides justification to a certain claim. (OMG 2010b)

Definition 4 addresses the concept of evidence from the perspective of its role in safety cases. This definition, which is proposed in context of the CAE notation (Adelard 2012), however, does not address clearly the interface between the source data of evidence and an argument. The examples of evidence presented in this definition, e.g. facts, assumptions and subclaims, are debatable. For instance, treating subclaims as evidence may lead to confusion in safety case development.

Definition 5 clarifies both the nature and function of safety evidence clearly. Information is the core. However, it leaves out the possibility of counter-evidence which can challenge claims in safety arguments. It also does not imply that justification of evidence is necessary to understand the level of truth expressed by a safety argument.

Definition 6 focuses on the documentation aspect of evidence. It is convenient for data management of items of evidence. But the nature of evidence as an information element and its role as the grounds of argument are underspecified in the definition.

2.3 Common basis

From the discussion presented in the previous two sections, we can see that evidence is defined in various ways and it is difficult to achieve a general definition with all features presented for all types of evidence. Nevertheless, we argue that the following aspects need to be agreed as common bases of evidence in safety.

Evidence is information, but usually more than simply just the actual source data of evidence. The source data of evidence may come from a mixture of different sources, e.g. established facts, expert judgment, outcomes of engineering activities, or field service. The source data of evidence can only properly be termed 'evidence' when it is in use for a specific purpose, e.g. supporting or challenging a specific safety claim, which may or may not be different from the initial intent of generating the source data. The information associated with the use of evidence source data should be addressed as part of evidence.

Evidence is not the same as truth. It is something that we produce and adopt to represent some degree of truth (as depicted by Definition 3 in Section 2.1) or merely understanding of potential truth (in the past or in the future) from a specific perspective in a certain scope, in order to justify various safety goals. The degree of truth represented by an item of evidence is uncertain and must be subjected to rigorous evaluation within any application context.

Evidence does not simply equate to documents or artefacts. It is more about the information that we can draw out and use as grounds for arguments, rather than the physical instantiation.

Evidence is the grounds and starting-point of arguments. It serves (either supports or challenges) claims within a safety argument.

Evidence should be examined in context of safety arguments. Whilst it is possible to perform some evaluation of evidence outside the context of a specific safety case (e.g. examining the rigour of a safety assessment method) it should be recognised that this is only part of the justification of evidence that is required in the context of a safety case. Other issues to be addressed include evidence relevance, coverage, and consistency.

The association between evidence and safety claims is a multiplicity relationship. One item of evidence can support more than one claim; one claim can be supported by multiple items of evidence.

The association between items of evidence and physical artefacts being cited is a multiplicity relationship. One physical artefact may provide two items of evidence. For example, a fault tree report may contain both the quantitative analysis result of a fault tree and the human review results of that fault tree. The partition and organization of information into artefacts is dependent on particular practice in the systems engineering life cycle.

The working definition of evidence proposed in this paper is:

> Evidence is information that serves as the grounds and starting-point of (safety) arguments, based on which the degree of the truth of the claims in arguments can be established, challenged, and contextualised.

3 A model of evidence in safety

Based on the definition of evidence in safety cases in Section 2, we claim that the model of evidence in safety cases should integrate views of evidence from three distinct perspectives.

- the content perspective
- the utilisation perspective
- the evaluation perspective.

It is inappropriate to interpret evidence merely as the content of an evidence entity (the source data) that embodies the information to be used as evidence, because the information that is used in a specific application scenario of the source data of evidence is insufficiently clarified. First of all, different observations can be made of the source data of evidence depending on viewpoint. If we observe the evidence source data from the viewpoint of being an item of evidence for a particular domain safety claim, the content of our concern is quite specific. Secondly, an assertion or proposition is a different concept from a data item. The evidence source data may contain a variety of data items. An item of evidence, for its intended role within a safety case, should clearly define assertions in order to connect it with proper argument elements (in addition to the source data of evidence or references to the source data). A proposition should be clearly separated from the concepts of individuals, objects, and properties etc. that are deemed as data items in the evidence source data. These propositions based on evidence source data are often implicit in existing practice.

The utilisation perspective is primarily concerned with the linkage of an item of evidence with its source data and its argumentation context, which must be elicited and documented clearly during safety case development. From the utilisation perspective, we aim at answering the following two questions, 'Where is the evidence from?', and, 'Where is the evidence used?'. During the development stage of a safety case lifecycle, an item of evidence must be connected with a piece of evidence source data planned at the beginning of the stage, or released at the end of the stage. Additionally, the connections between items of evidence with argument elements (claims or links between argument elements) within a safety case should be explicitly presented. Otherwise, an item of evidence is not yet actually adopted as a part in a safety case.

The evaluation of evidence includes the evaluation of the source data of evidence and the evaluation of its usage within the context of an argument. The evaluation of the usage of evidence places emphasis on the capability and sufficiency of evidence items individually and collectively in terms of its function of supporting or challenging claims. We should carry out the evaluation with consideration of the specific application scenario, whereas the evaluation of the source data of evidence (e.g. a fault tree or a software testing result) can be considered without associating it with a domain claim.

The following sub-section introduces a model of evidence (EviM) that integrates relevant information of evidence from the three perspectives.

3.1 EviM overview

Figure 1 depicts in UML a conceptual model of evidence (EviM) in the context of safety cases, along with its relationships with arguments. The data elements of EviM, which place emphasis on the evidential content and properties of evidence in safety cases, have been established based on the analysis of the concepts of evidence performed in Section 2. EviM consists of five key elements: *EvidenceItem*, *EvidenceSet*, *EvidenceAssertion*, *EvItemProperty* and *EvSetProperty*.

EvidenceItem describes the items of evidence adopted or referenced in safety cases. This element is basically a container class of evidence-related information, including references to safety analysis artefacts, evidential properties for a single item of evidence, and assertions made for the information embodied within an evidence entity. *EvidenceItem* references the source data of evidence, but does not *contain* the source data. Although evidence should not equate to documents or analysis artefacts, it is popular for safety assessment artefacts to be termed 'evidence' by practitioners, because we have some prior knowledge of their intended usage as evidence for safety claims. But we must understand that, in fact, safety assessment artefacts are *source data* of evidence without explicitly stated evidential roles and evidential properties.

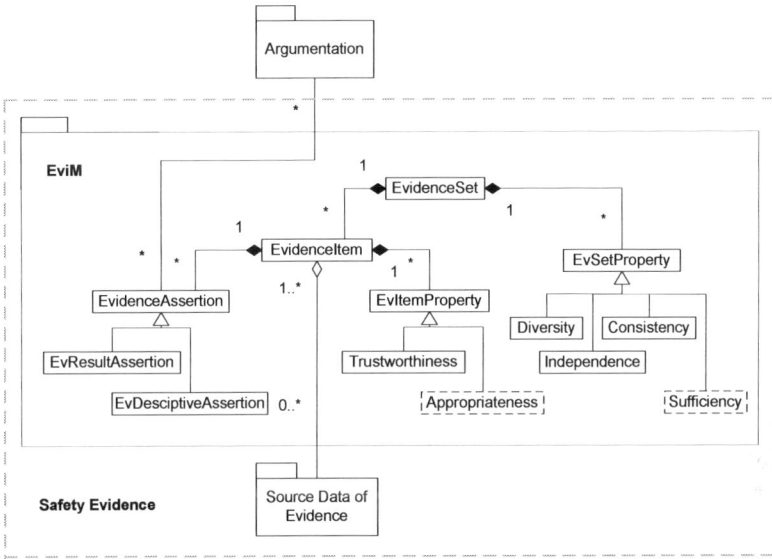

Fig. 1. A model of evidence (EviM)

A collection of evidence items for a safety claim or an argument module (Kelly 2001) can be packed up as a set of evidence items, depicted as *EvidenceSet* in Figure 1. The objects of *EvidenceSet* can possess a different set of evidential properties to be considered from the ones under concern for objects of *EvidenceItem*.

EvidenceAssertion in Figure 1 represents the core propositional content of an item of evidence that is obtained from the source data of evidence. *EvidenceAssertion* is a subtype of *Claim* in ARM (OMG 2010a). It is proposed specifically to clarify the usage of information embodied by an evidence entity in argumentation. *EvidenceAssertion* is further subtyped as *EvResultAssertion* and *EvDescriptiveAssertion*. We will explain this notion and its sub-types in detail in Section 4.

The properties of evidence (*EvItemProperty* and *EvSetProperty* in Figure 1) should be obtained through the evaluation of the usage of *EvidenceItem* and *EvidenceSet* rather than the evaluation of the source data of evidence by themselves without the context of argumentation. In a compelling safety case, each individual item of evidence and its relationship with the argument presented should possess two properties – *Trustworthiness* and *Appropriateness*. Moreover, a set of evidence items should also exhibit some special properties, such as sufficiency (or coverage), independence, diversity, and consistency. These properties are concerned more with the interrelationships between items of evidence and the factors influencing their collective supportive capability. All these evidential properties, if achieved, help ensure the level of confidence we can have in the grounds of a safety argument. Two of the properties presented in Figure 1 are depicted with dashed-line rectangles, because they are in fact properties of the relationships between an item of evidence and an argument element, typically, a domain safety claim. We present them in EviM primarily for a comprehensive view of various evidential properties that are relevant to items of evidence.

EvidenceAssertion presented in Figure 1 is associated with elements in an argumentation model (e.g. a domain safety claim, or a relationship between two argumentation elements in ARM (OMG 2010a). The source data of an object of *EvidenceItem*, comes from system development and operation, e.g. safety assessment models.

We have not presented metadata about evidence as part of *EvidenceItem* in EviM, because EviM is a conceptual model. During safety argument construction, we are concerned more about the metadata of the source data of evidence, such as who performed the analysis and the method that was used in generating the source data of evidence, rather than the metadata associated with the application of specific items of evidence (such as who linked the source data of evidence with the claims in safety arguments, or when the source data was designated as an item of evidence). For evidence data management at the implementation level, metadata elements associated with items of evidence could be added to EviM.

4 Evidence assertions

The notion of 'evidence assertion' has been suggested in the OMG ARM (OMG 2010a) and GSN community standard Version 1(GSN Working Group 2011). However, the explanation of this notion is not yet sufficient for practical application. The following sub-sections explain this concept further.

4.1 Definition

An evidence assertion is a statement that we can take as a *true* proposition according to the content of the source data of evidence. Representing evidence assertions drawn from source data explicitly can provide us a clear view of what is apparent from an item of evidence. Evidence assertions are not intended to record *judgments* about the source data of evidence, but instead to document propositions that can be established directly from the information embodied by the source data of evidence. The truth value of an evidence assertion is not intended to be debatable. However, *true* evidence assertions do not directly mean that the corresponding *domain claims* are true, unless the trustworthiness of items of evidence and the appropriateness of claim-evidence relationships are justified.

The description of evidence assertion in ARM includes the following key points (OMG 2010a):

- The nature of an evidence assertion is a claim.
- An evidence assertion is minimal and does not need supporting argumentation.
- An evidence assertion is the interface element to integrate argument and evidence.

Based on these key points, we propose the definition of evidence assertion as follows:

An evidence assertion is a minimal proposition that describes 'factual information' concerning an item of evidence. It does not need support from further arguments or evidence and it directly concerns the source data of an item of evidence without involving subjective judgment.

As a specific type of claim, an evidence assertion is unique in its source and function. An evidence assertion is drawn directly from the content of the source data of evidence. An evidence assertion can be used as grounds for a domain safety claim.

Evidence assertions should be distinguished from domain safety claims in arguments. A domain safety claim is what we want to state in the problem 'application' domain; it is a statement concerning the subjects (or concerns) in a real problem domain. Unlike an evidence assertion, the truth of a domain claim is uncertain unless supporting argument and evidence are provided. Domain safety claims may form a hierarchy of claims which represent how higher level safety goals are decomposed into more concrete ones; they can be supported by either claims or evidence. By contrast, an evidence assertion is a propositional statement on the subjects in an item of evidence that model or represent subjects in the real problem domain; it does not need any further support, neither from claims or evidence.

An evidence assertion differs from the data items contained in the source data. It is a claim that is *about* what is embodied by those data items. The true value of an evidence assertion is not determined by the facts of a problem domain in reality, but endowed by the facts of presence or absence of specific data items in the source data of evidence.

There are two subtypes of evidence assertions: *evidence result assertion* and *evidence descriptive assertion*.

4.2 Evidence result assertion

An *evidence result assertion* is a proposition that can be made from the source data of evidence and can be used to support domain claims in safety arguments. It answers the question, 'What does an item of evidence say?'. For example, we may use a fault tree as an item of evidence. Then the *evidence result assertion* encapsulated in this item of evidence could be 'the probability of the modelled EventX is 1.0×10^{-4}'.

Formulating evidence result assertions from items of evidence directly has two advantages.

- It may help to clarify the role or function of potential items of evidence as early as possible.
- It may also ease the management of items of evidence in parallel to the management of safety cases.

EvResultAssertion can serve as the 'data' element in Toulmin's model directly (Toulmin 1958). It is the starting-point of a line of safety argument. The subject of an *EvResultAssertion* addresses some aspects of the source data of evidence, which represents the subject in the problem domain (e.g. a modelled subject in a model). For example, the principal noun of a domain claim may be 'the probability of an undesired event E_x'; E_x is the undesired event in the problem domain. By contrast, the principal noun of a corresponding evidence result assertion of an item of evidence (e.g. a fault tree) may be 'the probability of a modelled undesired event E_m'; E_m is the top event in that fault tree that *models* or *represents* E_x. In reality, an *EvResultAssertion* of safety evidence may have features or styles determined by the types of safety evidence (e.g. the substantial analysis outputs of a safety analysis technique or a specific type of software testing results). Table 1 presents three examples of evidence result assertions.

Table 1. Examples of evidence result assertion

Types of safety evidence	Example of evidence result assertion
FTA (Fault Tree Analysis)	• The probability of failure condition FC_x modelled in FT_x is P_x. • Failure condition FCx modelled in FTx was caused by more than one failure event in FTx. (according to a fault tree model – FT_x)
Software performance test	• The output arrival timing T_o is within the range of $T_a \pm \Delta t$ through the software test STT_x. (according to a software timing test – STT_x) (T_a is the ideal arrival timing in software specification; Δt is the user-defined tolerable difference.)

4.3 Evidence descriptive assertion

Alongside evidence result assertions, there are also other assertions we can make according to (and about) the content of the source data of an item of evidence. *Evidence descriptive assertions* are propositions that describe an item of evidence but that cannot be directly observed *from* the source data. They are not used to support domain safety claims, but for providing support for the confidence argument associated with primary safety argument elements (e.g. the backing argument that supports the applicability of a fault tree that is used as direct evidence in a safety case).

Evidence descriptive assertions are statements about the source data of evidence or the process of which the source data of evidence is generated. These evidence descriptive assertions can help present factual information that is necessary for the evaluation of the trustworthiness of an item of evidence and the appropriateness of the usage of that item of evidence in a safety case. While evaluating an item of evidence in its application context, evidence descriptive assertions can introduce clues and facts that help us to make decisions. For example, consider again a fault tree (FT_x) as an item of evidence. Two examples of evidence descriptive assertions concerning the fault tree (FT_x) are: 'Repair events are not considered in FT_x' or 'Operator errors have been considered in FT_x'. The normal metadata from the source data of an item of evidence can be addressed by evidence descriptive assertions if needed, e.g. 'FT_x is constructed by Engineer Y' or 'FT_x is constructed with FaultTree+ Tool'.

An item of evidence may have many evidence descriptive assertions. The subject of an evidence descriptive assertion can be a wide variety of things, such as the scope of the source data, the creator of the source data, and the limitations of the source data. In practice, it is impossible and unnecessary to try to elicit them completely. Instead, they should be formulated according to the need of the backing arguments of the safety case. Table 2 presents several examples of evidence descriptive assertions.

Table 2. Examples of evidence descriptive assertion

Types of safety evidence	Examples of evidence descriptive assertion
FTA	• System component C_x is considered in Evidence FT_x
	• Evidence FT_x is created by Engineer E_x.
	• Timing issues are not considered in Evidence FT_x
Software performance test	• Evidence STT_x uses 20 test scenarios.
	• Evidence STT_x is performed by Engineer E_y.

4.3 Utilising evidence assertions

Evidence assertion is a core component of EviM. It is useful for facilitating the application and justification of evidence in safety case development. Three questions should be considered in the process of evidence selection and justification (Hawkins and Kelly 2010):

1. Is the *type* of evidence capable of supporting the safety claim?
2. Is the particular *instance* of that type of evidence capable of supporting the safety claim?

3. Can the instance of that type of evidence be *trusted* to deliver the expected capability?

The two subtypes of evidence assertion can help in determining the answers to these questions. The form of the evidence result assertion of an instance of a type of evidence should meet the need of a domain safety claim. The content of the evidence result assertion of an instance of a specific type of evidence determines whether the instance of evidence is supportive. The evidence descriptive assertions (e.g. one associated with assumptions of a model) of that instance of the specific type of evidence constrains whether the supportive relationship holds for the domain safety claim. Furthermore, the evidence descriptive assertions associated with the generation of the source data of the evidence are useful for determining the trustworthiness of the specific item of evidence.

Figure 2 depicts the common view of evidence-claim interfaces (expressed using GSN terms) in existing practice. It shows a *Solution* being used to cite '*Evidence ItemX*' for the '*Safety Claim*'. The argument link L_a connects the '*Evidence ItemX*' and the '*Safety Claim*'. A confidence argument (Hawkins et al. 2011) is needed for justification of the asserted evidence relationship between the '*Evidence ItemX*' and the '*Safety Claim*'.

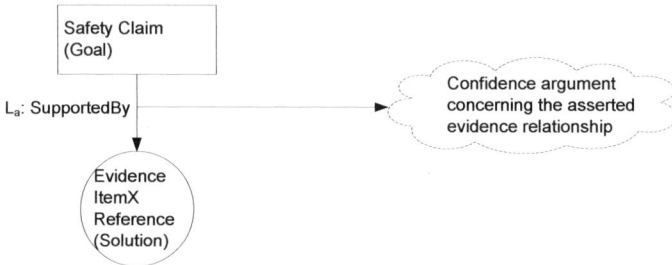

Fig. 2. A common view of evidence-claim interface

Figure 3 illustrates the usage of the two types of evidence assertions in structured safety cases (in GSN terms). The argument link L_a presented in Figure 2 is broken down into three new elements, L_{b1}, a goal depicting a result assertion of *EvidenceItemX*, and L_{b2}. It can be clearer to examine the relationship between a claim and an item of evidence in two steps: 'Does the item of evidence contain the expected form of evidence result assertions required for support of the claim?' and 'Could the evidence result assertion of the item of evidence infer the truth or falsity of the claim?'

The confidence argument that is not developed in Figure 2 is also illustrated in Figure 3. We can see that evidence descriptive assertions can provide support for claims on the trustworthiness of *EvidenceItemX* or the appropriateness of L_a. Besides evidence descriptive assertions, confidence claims may have other supporting evidence items and other supporting claims. For example, the trustworthiness claim of a Fault Tree FT_x can be supported by an evidence descriptive assertion

('Evidence FT$_x$ is created by Engineer E$_x$') in conjunction of an undeveloped confidence claim ('Engineer E$_x$ is competent in fault tree analysis of System X').

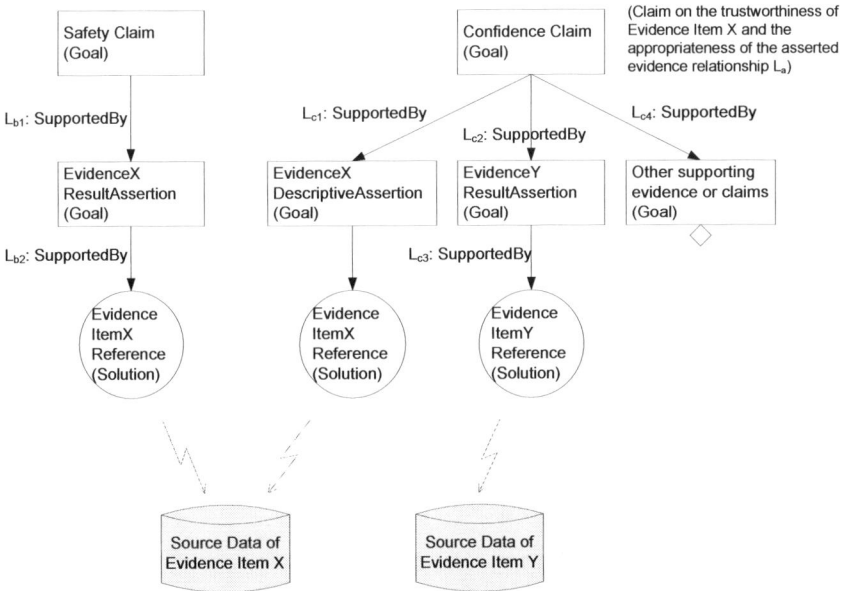

Fig. 3. An elaborated view of evidence-claim interface

The source data of evidence items are not graphically presented in existing structured safety cases. The shaded blocks presented in Figure 3 are the targets of the evidence references presented in *Solutions*, but not part of a structured safety case. *EvidenceItemY* is indirect evidence in a safety case; *EvidenceItemX* is direct evidence for a domain safety claim.

Eliciting, matching, and examining evidence assertions is a necessary step during the construction of structured safety cases (including both the primary safety argument and the confidence argument), even though they may increase the workload during safety case development. Using evidence result assertions is helpful for accumulating both existing and expected usage of the evidence source data, which can provide a better understanding of the evidence-argument relationship and help facilitate the potential reuse of evidence items in new context. Using evidence descriptive assertions is helpful for providing the foundation claims for evidence justification that form part of establishing confidence in safety cases. It may be difficult to enumerate all potential descriptive assertions completely and it is unreasonable to ask for all details without a focus. Typically, we are concerned of the evidence descriptive assertions that address factors that may influence the confidence in the usage of direct safety evidence. For example, the modeller, the tool, the method associated with an item of safety assessment evidence (e.g. a fault tree model) should have corresponding evidence descriptive assertions.

5 Related work

Existing literature on evidence in safety can be classified with four themes:

1. the classification of evidence according to different principles
2. the required or desired features of evidence in general
3. justification of the appropriateness of evidence in context of argumentation
4. modelling evidence for more structured representation in order to support evidence information collection and exchange.

The classification of evidence concerns the denotation of the concept of evidence. Different from the connotation of a concept, the denotation of a concept (Mill 1879) addresses the features of a group of individuals of a concept that are not possessed by other objects of the concept. Evidence can be classified in a variety of ways. The organizing principles of the classification can be the sources or features of evidence (MoD 2007; Sun and Kelly 2009), the requirement type supported by evidence (Weaver 2004), or the relationships of evidence and argument (EUROCONTROL 2006; CAA 2012).

Safety experts (Hamilton 2006) and regulators (EUROCONTROL 2006; MoD 2007) are concerned about the desired features of evidence, but there is no common acceptance criteria of evidence yet in reality. Hamilton identifies two types of evidence properties: objective properties such as existence, completeness and correctness, and subjective properties such as relevance and sufficiency. However, most of the objective properties suggested cannot be 'objectively' evaluated and the suitability and means of evaluation of these properties are dependent on the nature of the evidence presented. Some researchers recommend managing safety evidence with qualitative requirements (Bishop et al. 2001) or assessing the strength of evidence, e.g. AELs (Assurance Evidence Levels) (CAA 2012) and SEAL (Safety Evidence Assurance Level) (Fenn and Jepson 2005). The levels in AELs and SEAL are a qualitative tag that defines the breadth and strength of evidence, or even the specific types of analysis or forms of artefacts required. Grouping evidence with such requirements is informative for planning safety activities and resources. But users still need to interpret and select an appropriate evidence assurance level according to the features of their products or service to be assured.

Another theme under study focuses on clarifying the level of assurance of the evidence can provide through justifying the evidence. A structured software evidence selection and justification process is proposed for evaluating software evidence in context of arguments (Hawkins and Kelly 2010). ESALs (Evidence Safety Assurance Level) (Reinhardt and McDermid 2010) are suggested as a means of setting requirements for the level of rigour of the justification of the soundness of evidence in the context of safety arguments.

Some existing research work (Panesar-Walawege et al. 2010; Zoughbi et al. 2011) concerns extracting items of required evidence and their relations with system design and recommended processes from standards in order to help the practitioners to plan their safety activities and deliverables for certification. They are primarily process-oriented and constrained by the forms of evidence required or recommended by specific standards and guidance. The role and nature of safety evidence, therefore, is not explored and elicited in these models. SAEM (OMG 2010b) provides a common vocabulary and structure of information elements associated with evidence in assurance cases. However, SAEM is complex, due to its motivation of supporting automation in the generation, exchange and management of assurance evidence. The high level understanding of the essence of evidence is obstructed by the details of implementation-level information elements in SAEM.

6 Conclusion

'What is safety evidence?' is an intriguing and difficult question. Even though there is no single and definitive answer to this question, domain-specific understanding of the content, purpose, and feature of the concept of 'evidence' is essential. Existing views and understanding of safety evidence and its interface with safety argument lack detail. It is dangerous to support a domain safety claim with an item of evidence that is less capable and effective than that which is needed. The gap between what we can say according to the source data of evidence and a domain safety claim can significantly undermine the confidence in safety cases.

In this paper, we have studied some relevant definitions and elaborated the concept of evidence in the context of safety cases. A conceptual model of evidence is proposed for the purpose of explicit integration of the source data of evidence and safety argument. The notion of evidence assertion is described and illustrated with examples. The EviM presented in this paper will help in explicitly considering the content, utilisation and evaluation of evidence and will facilitate more rigorous application and justification of safety evidence in safety cases.

In the future, we will explore more about the implementation level issues of the proposed evidence model. Further work can also be undertaken to investigate the nature of results and descriptive evidence assertions that can be associated with different evidence types.

References

Adelard (1998) Adelard safety case development manual v1.1. http://www.adelard.com/resources/ascad. Accessed 26 February 2012
Adelard (2012) CAE Notation Description. http://www.adelard.com/asce/choosing-asce/cae.html. Accessed 20 April,2012
Bishop P, Bloomfield R (1998) A methodology for safety case development. Safety-critical Systems Symposium. Birmingham, UK
Bishop PG, Bloomfield RE, Froome PKD (2001) Justifying the use of software of uncertain pedigree (SOUP) in safety-related applications. HSE Books, Her Majesty's Stationery Office
Blackburn S (2005).The Oxford dictionary of philosophy. Oxford University Press
CAA (2012) CAP 670 air traffic services safety requirements. Civil Aviation Authority Safety Regulation Group. http://www.caa.co.uk/docs/33/CAP670.PDF. Accessed 3 March 2012

EUROCONTROL (2006) Safety case development manual. 2.2. http://www.eurocontrol.int/ link2000/gallery/content/public/files/documents/Safety%20Case%20Development%20Manu al%20V2.2_RI_13Nov06.pdf. Accessed 3 March 2012

Fenn J, Jepson B (2005) Putting trust into safety arguments. In: Redmill F, Anderson T (eds) Constituents of modern system-safety thinking. Springer, London

Gross R (2001) Decisions and evidence in medical practice: applying evidence-based medicine to clinical decision making. Harcourt

GSN Working Group (2011) GSN community standard version 1. GSN Working Group, Origin Consulting (York) Limited

Hamilton V (2006). Criteria for safety evidence. The Safety-Critical Systems Club Newsletter - Safety Systems 16(1)

Hawkins R, Kelly T (2010) A structured approach to selecting and justifying software safety evidence. 5th IET International Conference on System Safety 2010

Hawkins R, Kelly T, Knight J et al (2011) A new approach to creating clear safety arguments. In:: Dale C, Anderson T (eds) Advances in systems safety. Springer, London

Jackson D, Thomas M, Millett LI (2007) Software for dependable systems: sufficient evidence?, National Academies Press

Kelly T (2001) Concepts and principles of compositional safety cases. COMSA/2001/1/1 – research report commissioned by QinetiQ

Last J (2006) A dictionary of public health. Oxford University Press

Law J and Martin EA (2009) A dictionary of law. Oxford University Press

Mill JS (1879) A system of logic, ratiocinative and inductive: being a connected view of the principles of evidence and the methods of scientific investigation. Longmans, Green and Co,. London

MoD (2007) Defence Standard 00-56 Safety management requirements for defence systems Part 2: Issue 4. Guidance on establishing a means of complying with Part 1, Ministry of Defence

OMG (2010a) Argumentation metamodel. ARM Working Document 1.0 Beta 1

OMG (2010b) Software Assurance Evidence Metamodel. SAEM Working Document 1.0 Beta 1

Panesar-Walawege RK, Sabetzadeh M, Briand L et al. (2010) Characterizing the chain of evidence for software safety cases: a conceptual model based on the IEC 61508 standard. 3rd International Conference on Software Testing, Verification and Validation (ICST)

Reinhardt DW, McDermid JA (2010) Assurance of claims and evidence for aviation systems. 5th IET International Conference on System Safety 2010

Sun L, Kelly T (2009) Safety arguments in aircraft certification. 4th IET International Conference on Systems Safety 2009, incorporating the SaRS Annual Conference

Toulmin SE (1958) The use of arguments. Cambridge University Press

Weaver R (2004) The safety of software - constructing and assuring arguments. University of York, UK

Zoughbi G, Briand L, Labiche Y (2011) Modeling safety and airworthiness (RTCA DO-178B) information: conceptual model and UML profile. Software & Systems Modeling 10:337-367

Assessing the Overall Sufficiency of Safety Arguments

Anaheed Ayoub, Jian Chang, Oleg Sokolsky and Insup Lee

Computer and Information Science Department, University of Pennsylvania

Philadelphia, PA, USA

Abstract Safety cases offer a means for communicating information about the system safety among the system stakeholders. Recently, the requirement for a safety case has been considered by regulators for safety-critical systems. Adopting safety cases is necessarily dependent on the value added for regulatory authorities. In this work, we outline a structured approach for assessing the level of sufficiency of safety arguments. We use the notion of basic probability assignment to provide a measure of sufficiency and insufficiency for each argument node. We use the concept of belief combination to calculate the overall sufficiency and insufficiency of a safety argument based on the sufficiency and insufficiency of its nodes. The application of the proposed approach is illustrated by examples.

1 Introduction

A safety assurance case presents an argument, supported by a body of evidence, that a system is acceptably safe to be used in the given context (Menon et al. 2009). Recently, the U.S. Food and Drug Administration (FDA) has been highlighting the upcoming call for certain 510(k) medical device submissions to include safety assurance cases (FDA 2010). Adopting safety cases necessarily requires the existence of proper reviewing mechanisms.

Safety cases are, by their nature, often subjective (Kelly 2007). The objective of safety case development, therefore, is to facilitate mutual acceptance of this subjective position. The goal of safety case evaluation, therefore, is to assess if there is a mutual acceptance of the subjective position. We define the safety argument assessment as answering a question about the overall sufficiency of the argument, i.e., are the premises of the argument 'strong enough' to support the conclusions being drawn. The simplest way to assess a safety argument is to ask an expert reviewer to evaluate the overall sufficiency of the argument. Although this is a commonly accepted practice, most probably the final decision is not accurate enough. Research in experimental psychology shows that the human mind does not deal properly with complex inferences based on uncertain sources of knowledge (Cyra and Gorski 2008a), which is common in safety arguments. Therefore, reviewers should only be required to express their opinions about the basic elements in the safety argument. Then a mechanism should provide a way to aggregate the reviewer opinions to communicate a message about the overall sufficiency of the safety argument. A potential problem with evaluating the safety arguments lies in psychology and the notion of a *mindset*. A mindset is a set of assumptions, methods or notations held by one or more people or groups of people which is so established that it creates a powerful incentive within these people or groups to continue to adopt or accept prior behaviours, choices, or tools (Wikipedia 2012b). An important component of mindset is the concept of *confirmation bias*. Confirmation bias is a tendency for people to favour information that confirms their preconceptions or hypotheses regardless of whether the information is true (Leveson 2011). Confirmation bias is a prime example of a mindset that can produce defective decision making. The problem of the confirmation bias is not easy to eliminate. But it can be reduced by changing the goal. In other words, the reviewer should take the opposite goal: try to show that the provided safety argument is insufficient to support the system safety conclusion. We propose assessing the safety argument insufficiency as well as its sufficiency.

In this paper, we outline a structured method for assessing the level of sufficiency and insufficiency of safety arguments (Section 4). The reviewer assessments and the results of their aggregation are represented in the Dempster-Shafer model (Sentz and Ferson 2002). We use the notion of *basic probability assignment* (also referred to as a *degree of belief* or a *mass*) to provide a measure of the degree of belief in the sufficiency and insufficiency of each argument node to do its role. For example, a mass of the sufficiency and insufficiency of an evidence node Ev, which is directly addressing a conclusion node n, is a measure of the degree of belief in the sufficiency and insufficiency of Ev to support n.

We propose *aggregation rules* (Section 3) to calculate the mass of the overall sufficiency and insufficiency of a safety argument by aggregating the mass of the sufficiency and insufficiency of the safety argument nodes. The selection of the appropriate aggregation rule is discussed in Section 4.1. The assessing of the missing support (if any) and its impact on the degree of beliefs is given in Section 4.2. The application of the proposed method is illustrated by a complete example in Section 5. The related work is discussed in Section 6, and Section 7 concludes the paper.

2 Safety cases

Recently, safety cases are being explored as ways for communicating ideas and information about the safety-critical systems among the system stakeholders. The manufactures submit safety cases (to present a clear, comprehensive and defensible argument supported by evidence) to the regulators to show that their products are acceptably safe to operate in the intended context (Kelly 1999). There are different approaches to structure and present safety cases. The Goal Structuring Notation (GSN) is one of the description techniques that have been proven to be useful for constructing safety cases (Kelly and Weaver 2004). In this work, we use the GSN notation in presenting safety cases. In GSN a top-level goal (i.e., conclusion) is decomposed into sub-goals through implicit or explicit strategy, and eventually supported by evidence. In this paper, we use the term *conclusion* to describe the relation between any goal, sub-goal or strategy and its child nodes. Also we use the term *supporting node* to describe how any sub-goal, strategy or evidence node is related to its parent node. For example, Strategy S1 in Figure 7 is a conclusion for G2 and G3, and a supporting node for G1.

A new approach for creating clear safety cases is introduced in (Hawkins et al. 2011). This new approach basically separates the major components of the safety cases into safety argument and confidence argument. A safety argument is limited to give arguments and evidence that directly target the system safety. A confidence argument is given separately to justify the sufficiency of confidence in this safety argument. The separation between safety and confidence related aspects facilitates the development and reviewing processes for safety cases. In this paper, we introduce a structured mechanism to assess the overall sufficiency and insufficiency of safety arguments. Confidence arguments should be used by the reviewer to make his/her assessments on the sufficiency and insufficiency of the evidence nodes.

3 Aggregation rules

We define the safety argument assessment as answering the question about the overall sufficiency of the argument, i.e., are the premises of the argument 'strong enough' to support the conclusions being drawn. The first step of the proposed assessment procedure is to ask the reviewer to express his/her opinion about the basic elements in the safety argument. Then a systematic mechanism is used to aggregate the reviewer opinions to communicate a message about the overall sufficiency of the safety argument. The process of assessing the argument basic elements is nothing but a *decision-making* process. Decision making can be regarded as the mental processes resulting in the selection of a course of action among several alternative scenarios (Wikipedia 2012a). Every decision making process produces a final choice. In the case of evaluating the safety argument node, the output would be a choice either the node under evaluation is sufficient or not. According to psychologists, a natural phenomenon known as *confirmation bias* contaminates the mental process of the decision-making. Confirmation bias is a tendency for people to favour information that confirms their preconceptions or hypotheses regardless of whether the information is true (Leveson 2011). For example, in the case of evaluating the safety argument nodes, the reviewer may have an existing belief that the submitter of the safety argument is trusted based on his reputation, and probably the system is safe based on past success. In this case, the reviewer will choose to focus on the facts that conform to his/her existing belief. If the reviewer is not careful, his/her mind that is biased toward confirming the safety argument sufficiency would prevent him/her from seeing any contrary evidence that is actually there. Consequently, the reviewer decision would be that the node is sufficient; however this may not be the truth. This is one of the main problems of the Nimrod safety case (NSC) (Haddon-Cave 2009), the safety case was built and reviewed with the mindset that the system is safe based on past success. Consequently, NSC failed to identify the design flaws that led to the total loss of the Nimrod. The case of NSC shows how the consequences of confirmation bias to decision making are serious. In order to fight the confirmation bias the reviewer should do the opposite; assess the safety argument insufficiency. Although assessing the insufficiency fights the confirmation bias, it increases the vulnerability to negative confirmation bias. The existing belief in case of negative confirmation bias would be that the node is insufficient. To fight confirmation bias and negative confirmation bias, we propose that the reviewer assesses his/her belief in the sufficiency and insufficiency of the argument nodes. This forces the reviewer to evaluate the node from two different perspectives; the positive one (the node is sufficient) and the negative one (it is insufficient). In addition, the reviewer may not be able to precisely determine if the node is sufficient or insufficient, meaning that he/she has a belief that this node could either be sufficient or insufficient. In other words, the reviewer describes his/her belief in the node sufficiency and insufficiency, and then the gap between these two beliefs presents the uncertainty.

3.1 Dempster-Shafer theory

Dempster-Shafer Theory (DST) is a mathematical theory of evidence (Sentz and Ferson 2002). It offers an alternative to traditional probabilistic theory for the mathematical representation for uncertainty, which is required for the safety arguments assessment. DST is a potentially valuable tool when knowledge is obtained from expert's elicitation, which is the case of safety arguments assessment. We use the Dempster-Shafer model to present the reviewer assessments and the results of their aggregation. The most important part of DST is *basic probability assignment (BPA)*, also referred to as a *degree of belief* or a *mass*. Let x be a finite set known as frame of discernment. In the safety argument assessment, $x = \{Sufficient, Insufficient\}$. The power set $P(x)$ is the set of all subsets of x including itself and null set ϕ. For $x = \{Sufficient, Insufficient\}$ then $P(x) = \{\phi, \{Sufficient\}, \{Insufficient\}, \{Sufficient, Insufficient\}\}$. The *BPA*, represented by m, defines a mapping from every subset of the power set to interval between 0 and 1. Formally, $m:P(x) \rightarrow [0, 1]$. The *BPA* satisfies the following two conditions:

- The *BPA* of the null set is 0. Formally, $m(\phi) = 0$.
- The summation of the *BPA's* of all the subsets of the power set is 1. That is, $\sum_{A \in P(x)} m(A) = 1$, where A is a set in the power set ($A \in P(x)$).

Every set in the power set of the frame of discernment which has mass > 0 is a focal element (i.e., hypotheses). For the safety argument assessment, $P(x)$ has three focal elements: hypothesis S = *{Sufficient}* that the node is sufficient, hypothesis I = *{Insufficient}* that it is insufficient, and (universe) hypothesis U = *{Sufficient, Inefficient}* that the node is either sufficient or insufficient. For each argument node n, $m_n(S)$ and $m_n(I)$ represent the degree of belief in the sufficiency and insufficiency of n. And $m_n(U)$ represents the uncertainty; n is either sufficient or insufficient, where $m_n(S) + m_n(I) + m_n(U) = 1$.

Example 1. Suppose the reviewer checked the confidence argument/measure provided for node n, and got a belief of 0.5 that n is sufficient ($m_n(S) = 0.5$). However, he/she got a belief in n insufficiency with a degree 0.2 ($m_n(I) = 0.2$). The remaining mass of 0.3, which is the gap between the 0.5 supporting n sufficiency on one hand and the 0.2 for n insufficiency on the other hand is 'indeterminate'. Which means that n could either be sufficiency or insufficient ($m_n(U) = 0.3$).

One of the main attractions of DST is the availability of a rule to combine the data obtained from multiple sources. It allows one to combine evidence from different sources and arrive at a degree of belief. This is the case of addressing a conclusion supported by different nodes, where each supporting node arrives with a degree of belief. DST is based on the assumption that these supporting nodes are independent. The original combination rule of multiple *BPA's* is known as Dempster's rule of combination (Voorbraak 2012).

Definition 1. Given two *BPA's* m_1 and m_2, the combination (called joint m) is calculated from the aggregation of m_1 and m_2 as:

$$m(\phi) = 0$$

$$m(C) = m_1(C) \oplus m_2(C) = \frac{\sum_{A \cap B = C} m_1(A) * m_2(B)}{1 - K} \text{ where } C \neq \phi$$

$$K = \sum_{A \cap B = \phi} m_1(A) * m_2(B).$$

The denominator, $1 - K$, is a normalization factor, which is a measure of the amount of conflict between the two supporting nodes. For the safety argument assessment, C is S, I, or U. The Dempster's rule of combination is commutative and associative. For the simple case shown in Figure 1, a conclusion node n1 (i.e., GSN goal, sub-goal, or strategy node) is addressed by two supporting nodes n2 and n3 (i.e., GSN sub-goal, strategy, or evidence nodes). The pairs for A and B sets for which $A \cap B = S$ are (S and S), (S and U), and (U and S). The pairs for A and B sets for which $A \cap B = I$ are (I and I), (I and U), and (U and I). The pairs for A and B sets for which $A \cap B = \phi$ are (S and I), and (I and S).

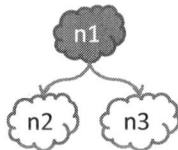

Fig. 1. A simple case

The following definition, which we will frequently use in the rest of the paper, is the application of Definition 1 to the simple case given in Figure 1.

Definition 2.

$$m_{n1}(S) = m_{n2}(S) \oplus m_{n3}(S)$$

$$= \frac{m_{n2}(S) * m_{n3}(S) + m_{n2}(S) * m_{n3}(U) + m_{n2}(U) * m_{n3}(S)}{1 - K}$$

$$m_{n1}(I) = m_{n2}(I) \oplus m_{n3}(I)$$

$$= \frac{m_{n2}(I) * m_{n3}(I) + m_{n2}(I) * m_{n3}(U) + m_{n2}(U) * m_{n3}(I)}{1 - K}$$

$$K = m_{n2}(S) * m_{n3}(I) + m_{n2}(I) * m_{n3}(S).$$

There is a known problem with the normalization of Dempster's rule of combination as explained in (Zadeh 84). We avoid this issue because the elements of our sets (S, I and U) are not independent.

3.2 Mixing

In addition to using Dempster's rule of combination, we also use a mixing (i.e., weighted averaging) rule.

Definition 3. The mixing rule: $m(C) = \dfrac{w_1 * m_1(C) + w_2 * m_2(C)}{w_1 + w_2}$, where w_1 and w_2 are the weights assigned to the supporting nodes. These weights represent the coverage of the conclusion by each supporting node. The weighted averaging rule of combination is commutative and associative. The following definition, which we will frequently use in the rest of the paper, is the application of Definition 3 to the simple case given in Figure 1.

Definition 4. $m_{n1}(C) = \dfrac{w_1 * m_{n2}(C) + w_2 * m_{n3}(C)}{w_1 + w_2}$, where w_1 and w_2 represent the coverage of n1 by n2 and n3 respectively. The use of mixing rules with Dempster-Shafer structures is justified in (Sentz and Ferson 2002).

Definitions 1 and 3 give the general form of the aggregation rules. Definitions 2 and 4 are the case of instantiation to the safety argument assessment settings for two supporting nodes. Discussions for the criteria to select between the aggregation rules (Definition 2 and Definition 4), and how to apply these rules to aggregate the degree of belief in the sufficiency and insufficiency of the argument nodes, are given in Section 4.1.

4 Assessment mechanism

The move toward using safety cases in certification and regulation requires a way to review them. Safety cases are, by their nature, often subjective (Kelly 2007). The goal of safety case evaluation, therefore, is to assess if there is a mutual acceptance of the subjective position.

We propose an assessment method to assess the overall sufficiency and insufficiency of safety arguments. This method consists of the two steps shown in Algorithm 1. The sufficiency and insufficiency of the top goal is the overall sufficiency and insufficiency of the safety argument.

Algorithm 1. Assessment procedure

Step 1. Evidence assessment

- Estimate the 'sufficiency' and 'insufficiency' of each evidence node to address the goal it is used to support. These estimations express the degree of the reviewer belief in the sufficiency and insufficiency of the evidence (e.g., Ev) to support its goal. We use the notion of the BPA to represent these estimations. Formally, $m_{Ev}(C)$, where $C \in \{S, I, U\}$.

Step 2. Automatic aggregation

- Starting from the leaves of the safety argument, apply the next steps for each conclusion node.

  - *Aggregate* the estimates of the supporting nodes to obtain the degree of belief in the sufficiency and insufficiency of the conclusion (Section 4.1).
  - *Recalculate* the degree of belief in the sufficiency and insufficiency of the conclusion, in case of identifying missing supports (Section 4.2).

- Repeat the process until the top goal has been reached.

Confidence. The reviewer should use the confidence arguments (Ayoub et al. 2012, Hawkins et al. 2011) or any confidence measure (Bloomfield et al. 2007, Denney et al. 2011) in the evidence assessment.

Assumptions. We assume that the safety argument is understandable, free from structural errors (e.g., no circular arguments), fully connected (i.e., no dangling evidence or unsupported goal), sufficiently expressed (e.g., no missing context), and contains no conflicts (e.g., assumptions attached to *all* the argument nodes are consistent). These assumptions can be satisfied by applying the step-by-step reviewing mechanism (Kelly 2007) before running the proposed assessment method. More discussion of the complementary use of these two methods is given in Section 6.

4.1 Argument types

Note that the degree of belief in the support given to a conclusion by its supporting nodes depends on the kind of inference used to derive the conclusion. We therefore begin by characterizing inference types (i.e., argument types). We use the case shown in Figure 1 to define the main argument types. Let n1 be a goal node claiming that {*the system satisfies 10 safety requirements; SRs 1-10*}. Table 1 shows examples of different argument types for the same conclusion. For the case shown in Figure 1, we distinguish four argument types (see Figure 2).

Table 1: Argument types example

	Description	Argument Type
n2	the system is formally verified against SRs 1-10	Alternative
n3	the system is tested against SRs 1-10	
n2	the system is formally verified against SRs 1-3	Disjoint, $w_1 = 3$ and $w_2 = 7$
n3	the system is tested against SRs 4-10	
n2	the system is formally verified against SRs 1-4	Overlap, $w_1 = 3$, $w_{Overlap} = 1$, and $w_2 = 6$
n3	the system is tested against SRs 4-10	
n2	the system is formally verified against SRs 1-4	Containment, $w_1 = 4$ and $w_{Containment} = 6$
n3	the system is tested against SRs 1-10	

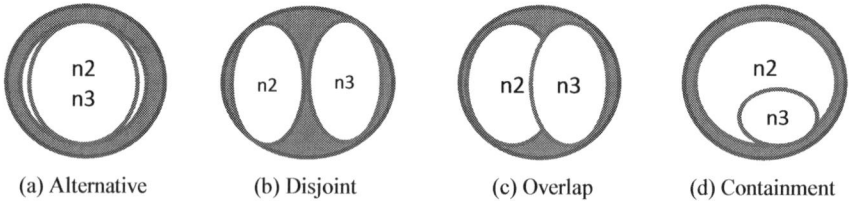

(a) Alternative   (b) Disjoint   (c) Overlap   (d) Containment

Fig. 2. Argument types

Alternative relates to a situation where more than one independent support of the common conclusion is provided. In other words, each of the supporting nodes supports the whole conclusion (e.g., the first row in Table 1). In this case, the rule given in Definition 2 is used to aggregate the mass of the sufficiency and insufficiency of n2 and n3 to obtain the mass of the sufficiency and insufficiency of n1.

Disjoint relates to a situation where the supporting nodes provide complementary support for the conclusion. This means, each of the supporting nodes covers part of the conclusion (e.g., the second row in Table 1). In such a case, not only the assessments of the supporting nodes but also the weights, representing the coverage, associated with each supporting node are taken into account. The final assessment of the conclusion is a sort of weighed average (i.e., Definition 4) of the contribution of all the supporting nodes.

Overlap relates to a situation where the supporting nodes support overlap parts of the conclusion. So each of the supporting nodes covers 'not disjoint' part of the conclusion (e.g., the third row in Table 1). In such a case, the weights associated with each supporting node and the weight of the overlap are taken into account. For the simple example given in Figure 2c, first the two overlapped nodes are restructured into three disjoint parts as shown in Figure 3a. This restructuring is valid under the assumption that the degree of belief in a node equals the degree of belief in its pieces. E.g., the degree of belief in an evidence node referring to *the testing results for 3 safety requirements SR1, SR2, and SR3* is the same as the degree of belief in the testing results for each single safety requirement *SR1, SR2,* and *SR3*. In other words, this combined evidence can be seen as three smaller evidence nodes each of which points to the testing results for one safety requirement. In this case, the degree of belief in each small piece of evidence equals the degree of belief in the combined evidence as the same testing mechanism and settings are used for the three safety requirements. The middle part in Figure 3a is covered by both evidence nodes, so Definition 2 is applied for hypothesis $C \in \{S, I, U\}$

$$m_{Overlap}(C) = m_{n2}(C) \oplus m_{n3}(C).$$

The result is three disjoint nodes as shown in Figure 3a, so Definition 4 is applied twice. We can compute this by combining any pair of m_{n2}, $m_{Overlap}$, and m_{n3} with the corresponding weights, and then combine the result with the remaining third mass. Let's first combine m_{n2} and $m_{Overlap}$

$$m_{int\,ermediate}(C) = \frac{w_1 * m_{n2}(C) + w_{Overlap} * m_{Overlap}(C)}{w_1 + w_{Overlap}}.$$

Then combine the result with m_{n3}

$$m_{n1}(C) = \frac{(w_1 + w_{Overlap}) * m_{int\,ermediate}(C) + w_2 * m_{n3}(C)}{(w_1 + w_{Overlap}) + w_2}.$$

The result would be

$$m_{n1}(C) = \frac{w_1 * m_{n2}(C) + w_{Overlap} * m_{Overlap}(C) + w_2 * m_{n3}(C)}{w_1 + w_{Overlap} + w_2},$$

where w_1, $w_{Overlap}$ and w_2 represent the coverage of n1 by n2 only, the overlap, and n3 only respectively.

Containment relates to a situation where one supporting node coverage is included in a bigger supporting node coverage. In other words, each of the supporting nodes covers part of the conclusion; this part is covered also by the next larger support (e.g., the last row in Table 1). In such a case, the weights associated with each supporting node are taken into account. For the simple example given in Figure 2d, first the two nodes are restructured into two disjoint parts as shown in Figure 3b. This restructure is valid under the same assumption given for the overlap case. In Figure 3b, the degree of belief in the part covered by both supporting nodes is calculated by applying the rule given in Definition 2.

$$m_{Containment}(C) = m_{n2}(C) \oplus m_{n3}(C)$$

The result is two disjoint nodes, so Definition 4 is used:

$$m_{n1}(C) = \frac{w_1 * m_{n2}(C) + w_{Containment} * m_{Containment}(C)}{w_1 + w_{Containment}}$$

where w_1, and $w_{Containment}$ represent the coverage of n1 by n2 only and the containment respectively.

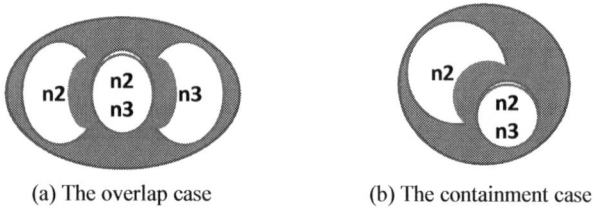

(a) The overlap case   (b) The containment case

Figure 3. Argument types restructure

Example 2. Table 2 shows the results of applying the aggregation rules for each argument type with different weights for each supporting node.

Table 2. Example of different argument type aggregation results

	Alternative	Disjoint $\{w_1, w_2\}$	Overlap $\{w_1, w_{Overlap}, w_2\}$			Containment $\{w_1, w_{Containment}\}$		
weights		{6, 4}	{6,1,3}	{5,3,2}	{4,5,1}	{8, 2}	{5, 5}	{2, 8}
$m_{n1}(S)$	0.8148	0.58	0.592	0.6344	0.7185	0.563	0.657	0.752
$m_{n1}(I)$	0.1111	0.16	0.161	0.1533	0.1343	0.182	0.156	0.129

We can see that for the overlap case, when the overlapping is significant then the results are close to the alternative case, and when the overlapping is insignificant then the results are close to the disjoint case (using the same weights). For the containment case, when one of the supports is very small, then its contribution is negligible, and the results are determined by the significant support. But when the coverage of the smaller support increases, the results become closer to the alternative case. These observations are useful in practice, because it is not always obvious how to characterize the overlapping part. In such cases, the overlap is approximated to either alternative or disjoint case based on the reviewer assessment for the overlapping significance. In the same way, the containment can be approximated to either alternative case or the significant evidence numbers based on the reviewer assessment for the small evidence coverage.

It is assumed that the reviewer is an expert with sufficient competence to assess the argument nodes and express his/her opinion (as required for Step 1 in Algorithm 1), and to determine the argument type of each decomposition in the safety argument. The expert defines the argument type based on his/her understanding to the conclusion and its basis, and the supporting nodes and their basis. Where the node basis is defined by *all* context, justification, and assumption nodes attached to this node.

Example 3. Figure 4 is an example to show how the node basis is important in identifying the argument type. By checking the supporting nodes G1 and G2, it is clear that the argument type is alternative as both G1 and G2 cover the whole G0 conclusion. However, by checking A1 the expert may believe that testing reveals only 80% of the cases but there is 20% of the cases will not be covered by testing. That means G1 covers only 80% of G0, but G2 covers the whole conclusion. So the argument type is not alternative but containment where G1 is the small support, its weight is 0.8.

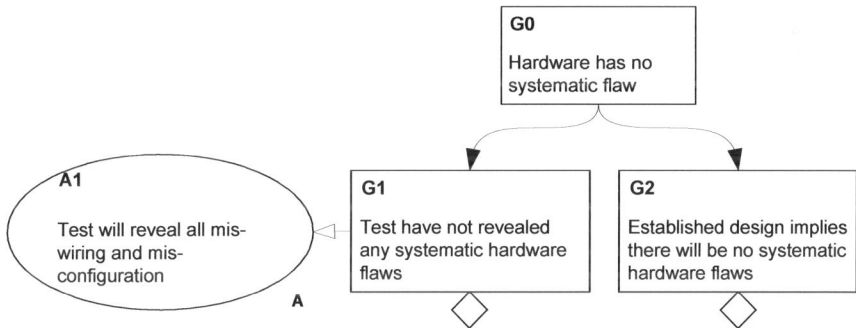

Fig. 4. Identify the argument type

In the general case, i.e., when more than two nodes support the conclusion, the four argument types are still valid. In addition, a general argument type, called *arbitrary*, can be found. The arbitrary argument type corresponds to the situation where there is no common part to *all* supporting nodes, though some supporting nodes may cover a common part. Figure 5 shows an example of such case. The arbitrary argument type can be structured as a combination of alternative and disjoint cases. Although Dempster's rule of combination and the mixing rule are associative and commutative, they do not have the same precedence and so when both rules are applied the order matters. It is the same as the case of the multiplication and addition operators, both are associative and commutative but that does not mean that $a + b + c = (a + b) * c = a + (b * c)$. The precedence of the aggregation rules impacts significantly the calculations for the arbitrary argument type. For this paper, we focus on the basic four argument types (alternative, disjoint, overlap, and containment). Elaborating the impact of the aggregation rule precedence on the degree of belief calculations for the arbitrary case is one of the directions for future work.

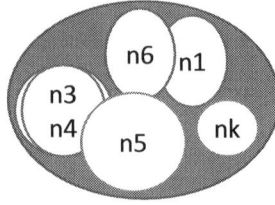

Fig. 5. Arbitrary argument type

4.2 Missing support

The first step in the aggregation process (Step 2 in Algorithm 1) is applying the corresponding aggregation rules (i.e., Definition 2 and/or Definition 4) based on the argument type. Then independently from the argument type, there may be part of the conclusion that is not covered by any of the supporting nodes. This uncovered part is represented by the shading in Figures 2, 3 and 5. For *all* the argument types, the uncovered part of the conclusion can be presented as a missing supporting node; node nm in Figure 6, where ns represents the part of n1 that is covered by the provided supporting nodes. As nm is missing then we know nothing about it. Which means, unless the reviewer has a different opinion, the degree of belief in the sufficiency and insufficiency of nm are set to 0; $m_{nm}(S) = m_{nm}(I) = 0$. In this case, nm is defined with the missing coverage weight w_m and the weight of the part of n1 that is covered by ns is w_s. In this case, the relation between n1 as a conclusion and ns and nm can be seen as the disjoint case. For n1, the mass for hypothesis $D \in \{S, I\}$ is recalculated using Definition 4 as:

$$m_{n1}(D) = \frac{w_s * m_{ns}(D) + w_m * m_{nm}(D)}{w_s + w_m} = \frac{w_s * m_{ns}(D)}{w_s + w_m} \tag{1}$$

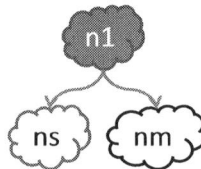

Fig. 6. Representing the missing coverage

If the missing coverage is significant, then this recalculation will significantly decrease the mass of the conclusion sufficiency and insufficiency. On the other hand, the uncertainty about the conclusion increases.

Worth notice is that based on the discussion given in Section 4.1 regarding the different precedence for the aggregation rules, the order of applying the rules matters. And as m_{ns} can be calculated by applying any aggregation rule based on the argument type, then to get consistent results the recalculation because of the missing support would be the last step to be done for any conclusion node (as shown in Algorithm 1).

There are three possible sources of missing supports. We use Figure 7 as an example to show these sources.

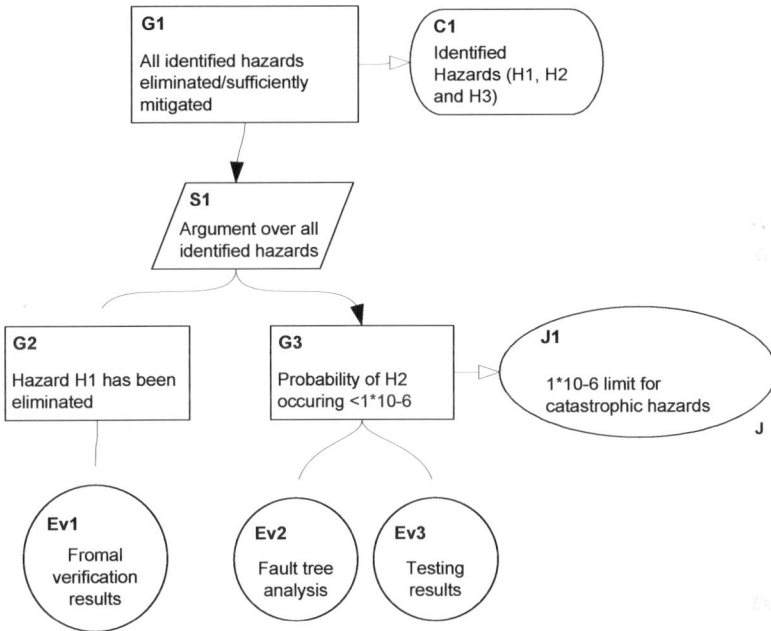

Fig. 7. A simple safety argument example

Case 1. The expert assesses the uncovered part of the conclusion by *checking the conclusion, the supporting nodes, and their basis including the inherited basis* (i.e., the context, justification, and assumption nodes attached to the conclusion, the supporting nodes, and any node higher in the argument tree). For example, S1 inherits context C1 form G1 (Kelly 1999). For S1, C1 identifies three hazards, but only two hazards are covered by G2 and G3, so only 2/3 of S1 is covered. In this case, using Equation 1, $m_{S1}(D) = \dfrac{2 * m_{S1}(D)}{3}$.

Case 2. In case of explicit or implicit strategy node, the expert assesses the uncovered part by *evaluating the used inference*. For example, for G1, the inference rule given in the explicit strategy **S1** states {*argument by hazards mitigation*}. This inference supports **G1** by showing that each individual hazard is adequately mitigated, but nothing is given to cover the situation of accumulated hazards. If the probability of getting accumulated hazards is 30%, then there is a missing support to **G1** with a weight of 0.3. In this case, $m_{G1}(D) = 0.7 * m_{G1}(D)$.

Case 3. Another source of the missing support is a *defective definition for the conclusion basis*. For example, for **G1**, the sufficiency of the identified hazards list should be taken into consideration. In other words, if the hazards are not sufficiently identified then a missing support is identified. For example, the expert would believe that only three hazards are identified in **C1**, while there are three other hazards that were not mentioned. In this case, $m_{G1}(D)$ is recalculated as

$$m_{G1}(D) = \frac{3 * m_{G1}(D)}{6}.$$

As shown, more than one source of missing supports can be found for the same conclusion. E.g., Case 2 and Case 3 define missing supports to **G1** in Figure 7. It is clear that the missing mitigation for *H3* is already impacted the calculations for **S1**. And so for **G1**, Case 1 does not define missing supports.

It is also clear that it is not important which source of missing supports is assessed first as the multiplication operator is associative and commutative. But the important thing is to check *all* sources (e.g., for the given example, the resultant calculations for **G1** would be $m_{G1}(D) = \frac{0.7 * 3 * m_{G1}(D)}{6}$).

Note that, we assume the expert is certain about his/her opinion about the node basis, so that the expert is certain about his/her opinion that **C1** in Figure 7 is missing three hazards. This may not always be the case. The expert may be uncertain about his/her opinion in many different ways. For example, the expert may have a belief that some hazards are not defined but cannot certainly tell how many hazards are missing. This uncertainty should be considered in the calculations; this is one of the directions for the future work to extend the proposed mechanism.

5 Illustrated example

We use the complete simple example given in Figure 7, inspired by the example given in (Weaver et al. 2003), to illustrate how to apply the proposed procedure given in Algorithm 1.

Step 1. Evidence assessment

- Assume the expert estimates as: $m_{Ev1}(S) = 0.8$, $m_{Ev1}(I) = 0.1$, $m_{E21}(S) = 0.7$, $m_{Ev2}(I) = 0.1$, $m_{Ev3}(S) = 0.5$ and $m_{Ev3}(I) = 0.2$.

Step 2. Automatic aggregation

- Starting from the leaves

  - For G2

    o Only one evidence Ev1 supports G2, so $m_{G2}(S) = m_{Ev1}(S) = 0.8$ and $m_{G2}(I) = m_{Ev1}(I) = 0.1$.

    o Missing support

      o **Case 1.** Assume the expert opinion is that Ev1 covers the whole G2 conclusion.

      o **Case 2.** Not applicable as there is no implicit or explicit strategy between G2 and Ev1.

      o **Case 3.** The conclusion node G2 has no basis and so no dimensioning is required.

  - For G2

    o Assume the expert opinion is that both Ev2 and Ev3 cover the whole G3 conclusion so the rule given in Definition 2 is applied. $m_{G3}(S) = 0.815$ and $m_{G3}(I) = 0.111$.

    o Missing support

      o **Case 1.** Assume the expert opinion is that conclusion G3 is totally covered by Ev2 and Ev3.

      o **Case 2.** Not applicable as there is no implicit or explicit strategy.

      o **Case 3.** Assume the expert opinion is that the justification J1 covers only 80% of the cases. By applying equation 1, $m_{G3}(S) = 0.652$ and $m_{G3}(I) = 0.089$.

- Repeat the process

  - For S1

    o It is clear that the argument type is disjoint. Assume all hazards have the same importance; the weights of all hazards are equal. Using Definition 4, $m_{S1}(S) = 0.726$ and $m_{S1}(I) = 0.094$.

    o Missing support: this is given as example in Section 4.2. The recalculation result: $m_{S1}(S) = 0.484$ and $m_{S1}(I) = 0.063$.

  - For G1

    o Strategy S1 is the only support to G1, so $m_{G1}(S) = m_{S1}(S) = 0.484$ and $m_{G1}(I) = m_{S1}(I) = 0.063$.

    o Missing support: this is the example discussed in Section 4.2. The result is that $m_{G1}(S) = 0.169$ and $m_{G1}(I) = 0.022$.

The calculations are summarized in Figure 8. In this case, the mass of the overall sufficiency and insufficiency of the safety argument given in Figure 7 equal 0.169 and 0.022 respectively, and the uncertainty equals 0.809. Using these numbers the expert can decide if this safety argument should be rejected or not. In the given example, most probably the expert would reject this safety argument as the degree of uncertainty is very high relative to the degree of belief of the argument sufficiency which is quite low. In addition, the expert can provide aclear feedback to the submitter guiding where enhancements are required. For the given argument, it is clear that the first effective weakness of this argument is missing mitigation for *H3*. The inappropriate identification for the hazards has a significant negative impact as well.

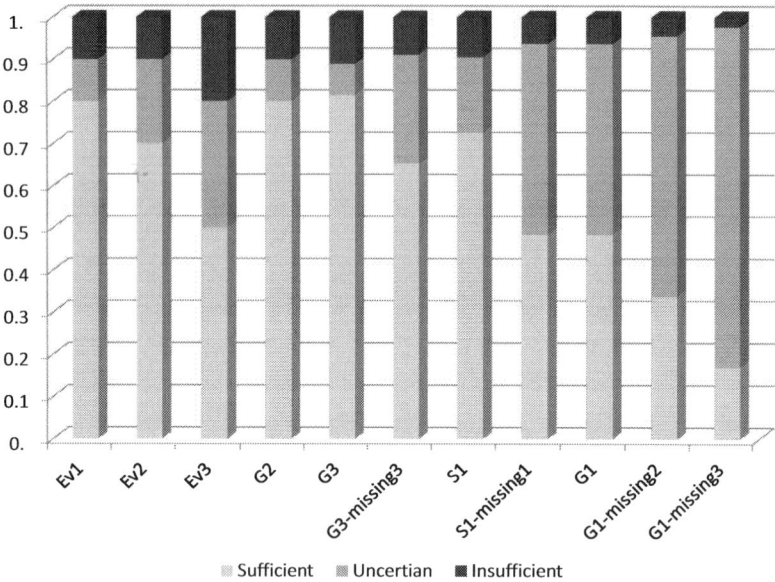

Fig. 8. The example numbers

6 Related work

The proposed assessing mechanism can be used in conjunction with the step-by-step review mechanism proposed in (Kelly 2007) to answer the question given in the last step of this reviewing mechanism, which is of the overall sufficiency of the safety argument. At the same time, applying the step-by-step reviewing mechanism guarantees the assumptions of the proposed mechanism as given in Section 4. In other words, the step-by-step review mechanism provides a skeleton for a systematic review process; however the proposed assessment mechanism provides a systematic procedure to measure the sufficiency and insufficiency of the safety arguments.

An appraisal mechanism is proposed in (Cyra and Gorski 2008a) to assess the trust cases. Although this mechanism targets trust cases and the proposed mechanism targets safety cases, both mechanisms use the Dempster-Shaffer model. Both mechanisms propose different aggregation rules based on the argument types. However, the argument types are not identical. The proposed argument types cover the case when the falsification of one of the premises decreases, but not nullifies, the support for the conclusion. This case is also covered for the trust cases appraisal mechanism, however only two argument types are defined; alternative and complementary (i.e., disjoint). The additional argument types we defined (i.e., overlap and containment) are treated as an alternative or a complementary type based on the overlap significance. Another case defined for the appraisal mechanism is when the falsification of a single premise leads to the rebuttal of the conclusion or to the rejection of the whole argument because nothing can be inferred about the conclusion. Two argument types are defined for this case; necessary and sufficient condition list (NSC-argument) and sufficient condition list (SC-argument). These two argument types are not considered in the proposed mechanism because we believe that for safety cases, each premise should have a contribution in supporting the conclusion. So no single premise has such a huge impact that it may lead to the rejection of the whole argument. And in case of a single premise that is sufficient to reject the whole argument then it is a simple process to check that premise and decide about the argument rejection without any aggregation.

The linguistic scales given in (Cyra and Gorski 2008b) to express the expert opinions and the aggregation results are appealing. In their work, the linguistic values are mapped into the interval [0, 1] and then quantitative rules are used for the aggregation (Cyra and Gorski 2008a). Although linguistic scales are more appropriate for human decisions than numbers, the mapping has a significant impact on the computed results and there is no evidence that the used mapping is proper.

5 Conclusion

In this paper, we propose an assessment method to assess the overall sufficiency and insufficiency of safety arguments. For the proposed mechanism, there are various parts that require interaction with the reviewer. The reviewer has to assess the evidence hypotheses, the argument types, the existence and the weight of missing supports, and the inference deficits. In other words, the proposed method does not replace the reviewer; instead it provides a framework to lead the reviewer through the evaluation process and to combine the reviewer estimates.

One of the main limitations of the proposed method is that the evidence nodes have to be independent as required by Dempster-Shafer Theory. However in many safety arguments, evidence nodes are not independent. Extending the proposed mechanism to cover this dependency is one of the directions for future work. Our preliminary experience of applying the proposed method has revealed that the assessing mechanism yields the expected benefits in guiding the safety argument reviewer and helping him/her to reduce the effect of the confirmation bias mindset.

Acknowledgments   This work is supported in part by the NSF CPS grant CNS-1035715 and the NSF/FDA Scholar-in-Residence grant CNS-1042829.

References

Ayoub A, Kim B, Lee I, Sokolsky O (2012) A systematic approach to justifying sufficient confidence in software safety arguments. In: SAFECOMP

Bloomfield R, Littlewood B, Wright D (2007) Confidence: its role in dependability cases for risk assessment. In: DSN

Cyra L, Gorski J (2008a) Supporting expert assessment of argument structures in trust cases. In: PSAM

Cyra L, Gorski J (2008b) Expert assessment of arguments: a method and its experimental evaluation. In: SAFECOMP

Denney E, Pai G, Habli I (2011) Towards measurement of confidence in safety cases. In: ESEM'11

FDA (2010) Guidance for industry and FDA staff – total product life cycle: infusion pump – premarket notification [510(k)] submissions. US Food and Drug Administration Center for Devices and Radiological Health

Haddon-Cave C (2009) The Nimrod review: an independent review into the broader issues surrounding the loss of the RAF Nimrod MR2 aircraft XV230 in Afghanistan in 2006. Technical report, The Stationery Office (TSO)

Hawkins R, Kelly T, Knight J, Graydon P (2011) A new approach to creating clear safety arguments. In: Dale C, Anderson T (eds) Advances in systems safety. Springer

Kelly T (1999) Arguing safety. A systematic approach to managing safety cases. PhD thesis, Department of Computer Science, University of York

Kelly T (2007) Reviewing assurance arguments - a step-by-step approach. In Proceedings of Workshop on Assurance Cases for Security – The Metrics Challenge, DSN '07.

Kelly T, Weaver R (2004) The goal structuring notation – a safety argument notation. In: DSN 2004 Workshop on Assurance Cases

Leveson N (2011) The use of safety cases in certification and assurance. Working paper

Menon C, Hawkins R, McDermid J (2009) Defense standard 00-56 issue 4: towards evidence-based safety standards. In: Dale C, Anderson T (eds) Safety-critical systems: problems, process and practice. Springer

Sentz K, Ferson S (2002) Combination of evidence in Dempster-Shafer theory. Technical report, Sandia National Laboratories, SAND 2002-0835

Voorbraak F (2012) Dempster-Shafer theory. www.blutner.de/uncert/DSTh.pdf. Accessed 30 September 2012

Weaver R, Fenn J, Kelly T (2003) A pragmatic approach to reasoning about the assurance of safety arguments. In the Australian workshop on Safety critical systems and software

Wikipedia (2012a) Decision making. http://en.wikipedia.org/wiki/Decision_making. Accessed 30 September 2012

Wikipedia (2012b) Mindset. http://en.wikipedia.org/wiki/Mindset. Accessed 30 Sept 2012

Zadeh L (1984) Book review: A mathematical theory of evidence. AI Magazine, 5(3):81-83

A Preliminary Study towards a Quantitative Approach for Compositional Safety Assurance

Alejandra Ruiz[1], Huáscar Espinoza[1], Fulvio Tagliablò[2], Sandra Torchiaro[2] and Alberto Melzi[2]

[1]TECNALIA Research and Innovation, Zamudio, Spain

[2]Centro Ricerche FIAT, Turin, Italy

Abstract   Modern engineering and business practices in the automotive domain use massive subcontracting of SW/HW components and subsystems. We present a preliminary research towards applying a quantitative, compositional safety assurance approach based on the ISO 26262 concept of SEooC (Safety Element out of Context). In this approach a component must be evaluated against 'assumed' operational context conditions in a quantitative manner (based on compatibility/gap analysis), instead of using inspections. Once the component becomes part of a specific system in an actual operational context, the evaluation is optimised by comparing assumed context conditions against actual context conditions. We propose a classification to organize information about assumptions and guarantees and outline a procedure to systematically manage their specification, validation and gap analysis.

1 Introduction

Safety assurance is amongst the most expensive and time-consuming tasks in the development of safety-critical embedded systems. The increasing complexity and size of this kind of system combined with the growing market demand requires the industry to implement a coherent reuse strategy (Espinoza et al. 2011). The concept of reuse is not limited to the reuse of software and hardware components. It is also applicable to the reuse of safety assurance artefacts, including safety argumentation used for conformity assessment. A major problem in safety assurance arises as typically a safety-critical product and accompanying safety evidence is monolithic, based on the whole product, and evolutions to/reuse of the product become costly and time consuming because they entail regenerating the entire evidence-set (Ruiz et al. 2012).

In the automotive domain, the evolution is towards adopting functional safety standards such as ISO 26262 (ISO 2011) to reach a competitive advantage in the market. ISO 26262 has introduced the concept of SEooC (Safety Element out of Context) where a component is evaluated against 'assumed' or 'presumed' operational context conditions. This is in the right direction though it deserves to be investigated further by harmonizing the way assumptions and the operation context are specified and compared in order to increase the reuse opportunities.

In this paper, we present a preliminary research of applying a quantitative, compositional safety assurance approach based on the ISO 26262 SEooC concept. In our approach, we use SEooC modules as basic composable specifications. Each SEooC module in an integrated system and the associated system architecture produces and consumes a set of commitments. A commitment is an assumption, configuration, functional feature, or limitation (performance or behavioural), which is provided by a SEooC module. An element is evaluated against 'assumed' operational context conditions in a quantitative manner (based on compatibility/gap analysis), instead of using inspections. Once the element becomes part of a specific system in an actual operational context, the evaluation is optimised by comparing assumed context conditions against actual context conditions.

The means to transfer a common frame for functional and design characteristics of an element or component from provider to integrator for the compatibility/gap analysis would bring a big benefit to the embedded system community for sharing components and increasing the safety by the broad service history. We illustrate the proposed approach by using a case study concerning the development of an ePARK system, as SEooC, for electric vehicles. The ePARK element is the device that controls and manages the parking of the electric vehicle.

This paper is organised as follows. Section 2 describes the domain background and related work. Section 3 provides details on the proposed approach as well as the challenges of using the SEooC for compositional safety assurance and conformity assessment. Last but not least, Section 4 presents our conclusions.

2 Background and related work

Most automotive companies already have mature practices in place for engineering electrical and mechanical equipment, but rather evolving practices for software and hardware development. With the ever growing use of automated tools (e.g. model-based development and AUTOSAR tools (AUTOSAR 2012)), what is needed are advancements on expressing precise safety criteria, safety information management, and on safety assessment, so that the maturity of safety assurance approaches can be brought up to that of the rest of the components of a complex vehicle. As we describe below, the adoption of standards such as ISO 26262 and the definition of more structured guidance to use this standard will lead to substantial improvements over the state-of-the-art.

2.1 Prescriptive scenario in the automotive domain

In the automotive domain several technical standards define the guidelines for the top level design and development of vehicles. For instance, for hybrid/electric vehicles the consumptions, performances and testing constraints are prescribed in terms of achieving the best technological state of the art and practice, where emissions are severely bounded by the thermal engine standard requirements. In this context, the ISO 26262 standard aligns for the first time the best state of the art and practices related to the functional safety, describing the requirements for the deployment of functional safety applied to the development of the electrical/electronic systems of the vehicles and their reciprocal relationships.

This standard extends the IEC 61508 standard (IEC 2011), applied to functional safety of electrical/electronic/programmable safety-related systems, to comply with needs specific to the application sector of electrical and electronic systems within road vehicles. Actually, ISO 26262 has to be applied to all of the activities during the safety lifecycle of safety-related systems comprised of electrical, electronic, and software components.

Furthermore, while there are more and more risks from systematic failures and random hardware failures, because of the trend of increasing technological complexity, software content and mechatronic implementation, ISO 26262 includes guidance to avoid these risks, by providing appropriate requirements and processes in a more general, complete, articulated and self-consistent framework than in IEC 61508. Indeed, ISO 26262 supports the entire automotive safety lifecycle (management, development, production, operation, service, decommissioning) and contains an automotive scheme for hazards classification. The key aspect of ISO 26262 is the definition of the objectives that a component/system must achieve for assuring its compliance with the established safety requirements, depending on the scenario (the vehicle integration, the vehicle characteristics and intended behaviour and performance, with related environmental conditions).

Additionally, its formal and structural completeness, from design until to the decommissioning of a vehicle, assures the level of responsibility (liability) of the car maker with respect to the safety compliance of its products. The application of ISO 26262 in the automotive domain aims to produce the necessary 'evidence' that confirm the effectiveness of the safety behaviour of the vehicle and its components. This result could be recognized in law as best practice, but (until now) is not yet certified in an official way by any organizational bodies external to the stakeholders.

Therefore, ISO 26262 does not prescribe any certification process, but instead a conformity assessment in terms of its reference safety lifecycle. The conformity assessment defines the extent to which a safety-critical product has been developed in accordance to the phases and sub-phases prescribed in the standard. This assessment must also include the verification of compliance with a set of work products (plans, design artefacts, V&V results, etc.), a set of confirmation measures to be performed during the product lifecycle, and data management mechanisms such as change and configuration management.

2.2 Business practice in the automotive industry supply chain

The automotive industries and the related suppliers develop generic elements, not integrated into the context of an actual vehicle, which can consist of:

- parts/subparts for multi-platform vehicles
- elementary HW components for different applications
- elementary SW components for different applications.

These generic elements can be treated as a safety related element, developed outside of a specific item or developed concurrently as a distributed development. According to ISO 26262 (Part 10 – Clause 9), these elements (system, subsystem, software component, hardware component or part) can be classified as SEooC.

From the supply chain point of view, the ISO 26262 SEooC concept defines a procedural aspect to tailor the safety cycle workflow, that allows a specific functional safety management for the development of the vehicle components so called 'on the shelf', ready for new functionalities in existent vehicles or for the development of new vehicles. These are all the elements, typically the innovative ones, which are developed without an actual reference vehicle on the background, but according to hypothetical assumptions about a family of target vehicles.

To develop a SEooC it is necessary to make some assumptions to provide consistency to the application of the reference standard (ISO 26262) on developing the generic element(s). The assumptions are made in such a way that the requirements (including safety requirements) are placed on the element by the higher levels of the development flow (concept, design, development, integration) and on all the implications of the design external to the element itself.

The integration of a SEooC into a specific vehicle is allowed once the consistency of the assumptions with respect to the specific interfaces of the actual vehicle is established. In the case that the SEooC does not fulfil the actual vehicle requirements, a change(s) to the SEooC or a change(s) at the vehicle level is necessary.

The SEooC can be developed 'off line' and put 'on the shelf' for future usage. During the development of a specific vehicle this approach constitutes an important way of cost reduction, since it reduces:

- the 'time to market', because a component can be used off the shelf that is already verified and evaluated in terms of conformity assessment
- the 'effort', because the SEooC can be used for many applications on different models and types of vehicles.

3 Outlining the SEooC-based approach

The objective of this work is to lay the groundwork to define a compositional, quantitative approach for using SEooC in the automotive industry. The key point is to understand how to capture each SEooC's assumptions and guarantees and how to validate this information for acceptance in the integration phase. Also, mismatches and unexpected interactions which may arise during integration must be assessed using a quantitative approach. This is the basic principle of a SEooC compositional approach, which is outlined in this section.

3.1 Problem description

As an example for the SEooC-based approach, we present an ePARK system for an electric vehicle.

This system is in charge of the management of the park pawl (mechanical engagement/disengagement) actuation. The ePARK system provides mechanical locking or unlocking of the transmission when the parking mode is selected (by the driver or automatically), avoiding unwanted movement of the vehicle when stopped. The selection of the parking mode is actuated by a gear selector equipped with switches dedicated to the modes of operation of the vehicle:

- *parking* (for the actuation of the ePARK functionality and for setting the electric motor torque to zero)
- *drive* (for driving forward)
- *rear* (for driving backward)
- *neutral* (idle status and transitions: electric motor torque set to zero).

The ePARK system can be considered as composed of the following elements:

ePARK control unit, implementing the high level management logic

'PRND' switches (gear selector module), implementing the low level software and physically driving the motor which moves the park pawl

parking lock system, including mainly the park pawl, the motor for the actuation, the motor position sensor and the park pawl position sensor.

The man-machine interface of the vehicle dashboard communicates continuously to the driver the status of the gear shift last selected and, then, also the parking state, if this is the case. The communication is transmitted by the Vehicle Control Unit (VCU), which is an electronic board in charge of monitoring the complete status of the vehicle and, in particular for this case, the status of the gear shift.

The parking actuation consists of a mechanical lock on the vehicle gear. When the vehicle is switched off, the only way to alert the driver of the parking actuation (mechanical) is an acoustic alarm (the electrical supply is assured by a direct connection to the 12V auxiliary battery of the vehicle), whose intervention is triggered when the vehicle door is opened without a parking actuation.

3.2 SEooC conformity assessment

The ePARK system is our SEooC, including its whole mechanical, electronic, and software parts, and as such its development must comply with ISO 26262. The latter implies a set of rules that has been disaggregated through the different parts of the document and, therefore, the interpretation of concepts such as the SEooC are difficult, in particular in determining how to measure the degree of compliance of products developed under this concept.

In Figure 1, we summarize our interpretation of being compliant with the SEooC related activities.

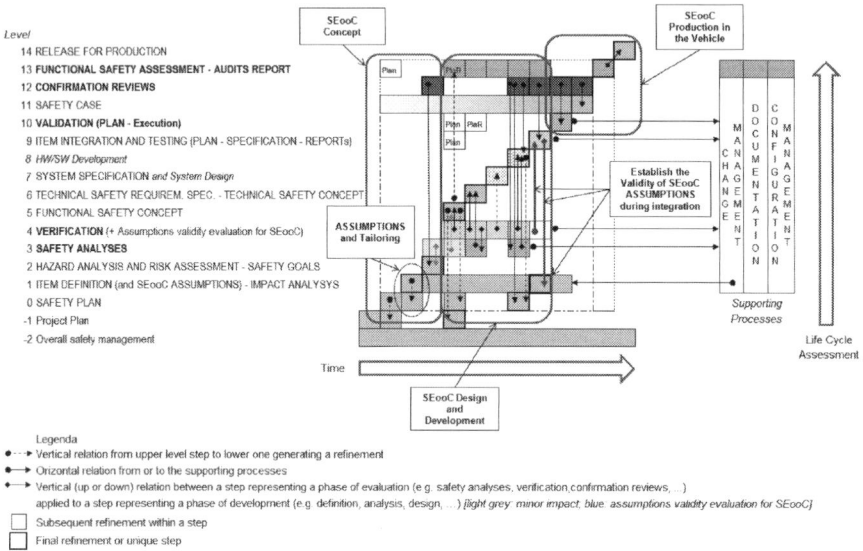

Fig. 1. An interpretation of being compliant with SEooC topics within a view of the progressing steps in a typical ISO 26262 workflow

The 'level' label is a degree of evolution in the lifecycle assessment towards the whole set of required evidence, where its value represents a baseline for implementation. Each degree of evolution is built based on its previous baseline; but in some cases the requirement in some higher baseline can cause a revision (refinement) of a requirement in a lower baseline (e.g. item definition versus safety plan). Some requirements that are recursive or are simple 'refinements' belong to the same level, even if they are performed subsequently (e.g. refinements of the safety plan belong to the same level: the safety plan level).

The main aspects to consider in such levels are:

hazard analysis and risk assessment: producing requirements for safety design specifications at hardware, software and system level

verification reviews: supporting processes requiring a plan and producing reports

validity check of assumptions for SEooC while integrating into the application context (reference vehicle); an activity with a report as an output

validation at vehicle level: the main process, requiring a plan and producing a report

confirmation measures: confirmation reviews and functional safety audits, including external reviews and producing reports

functional safety assessment: final audit compiling all the safety arguments, collected as the 'safety case', and the verification reviews, the validation and the confirmation measures;. a core process requiring a plan and producing a report.

Additionally, during the safety cycle the following actions/processes are performed when necessary, impacting and managing the arguments for safety:

impact analysis: an activity with a report as output

change management: a supporting process requiring a plan at the input

configuration management: a supporting process providing 'work products' traceability and requiring a plan

documentation (management): a supporting process requiring a plan.

One important aspect from this view is that the development of a SEooC involves making assumptions on requirements of its corresponding phase in the ISO 26262 vehicle safety lifecycle. These assumptions are related to SEooC use with respect to a reference vehicle context and the corresponding external interfaces and are verified during integration of the system (ePARK in our case) into the actual vehicle. A SEooC is thus developed based on assumptions on an intended functionality and use context, including external interfaces. These assumptions are set up in a way that addresses a superset of vehicles, so that the SEooC can be used in multiple different but similar vehicles later.

Finally, during the actual vehicle development, the validity check of SEooC requires that:

- the validity of the assumed requirements and the other assumptions, e.g. assumptions on the design external to the SEooC, are established
- examination and tests demonstrate that the developed SEooC is consistent with the requirements in the context where it is intended to be used.

3.3 Applying SEooC

To develop the ePARK system as a SEooC, it has been necessary to define a set of assumptions to which the system itself aims. Table 1 provides some typical examples of assumptions for the ePARK SEooC.

Table 1. Examples of typical assumptions

Aspect	Examples of assumptions
ePRND system: vehicle gear selection system (possible gear positions are driving, reverse, neutral and park)	Assumption (A) → functional requirement: override to park when vehicle is in charge mode
	Assumption (B) → ePRND function acquires the recharge plug-in status
	…
	Assumption (N)
Park system: engage/disengage park pawl	Assumption (C) → architecture assumption: the parking actuator node communicates with the electric vehicle controller via high-speed network
	…
	Assumption (M)

Starting from the assumptions, defined in the preliminary system development phase, the safety analysis has been performed. In particular the hazard analysis and risk assessment (HARA) is articulated in the following steps:

1. analysis of the operating conditions of the item in order to identify the most relevant scenarios for the safety
2. analysis and identification of the possible malfunctions (using FMEA and FTA)
3. list of the hazards derived from the identified malfunctions (using FMEA and FTA)
4. analysis of the potentially hazardous events by ranking the relative 'controllability', 'severity', 'exposure' parameters
5. risk assessment (ASIL definition for each hazardous event)
6. formulation of the safety goal for each hazard considered as safety relevant.

To assess the level of risk associated to the ePARK function we identified all the hazards related to ePARK. Each hazard has been analyzed in each reasonable scenario to define the hazardous event and for each of them we determined the ASIL level. Due to space limitation, we will describe only some excerpts of the analysis.

The main function of the ePARK system is to maintain the transmission of the electric vehicle blocked, avoiding any undesired motion of the wheels when it is stopped for parking. This function of the system is achieved by the management of the park pawl (mechanical engagement) actuation when the parking state is entered or exited by the gear selector module logic, respectively when parking mode has been selected or deselected by the driver.

When the parking mode is enabled, the torque request sent from the electronic VCU to the power inverter module of the drive train (power inverter plus electric motor) is set to zero and the latter is required to remain in torque disabled mode, thus the electric motor cannot receive any electric current able to make it rotate. When this mode is selected, a request is sent to the logic of the ePARK system to engage the park pawl, thus providing the mechanical locking of the transmission.

Table 2 summarizes the results of the analysis for the hazardous event related to the abovementioned ePARK function.

Table 2. Hazardous event example

Hazardous event	Persons at risk	ASIL	Safety goal (example)
Sudden displacement of vehicle when vehicle is in recharge mode and driver is out of board	People around the vehicle	The level of ASIL assigned to this hazardous event can be reasonably assumed to be ≥ B. As a safe margin, we can assign ASIL C to the SEooC, in order to ensure the integration with the most critical items possible.	To be sure that P (parking) is engaged before the driver leaves the vehicle and that system remains in P, when the vehicle is in charge mode.

In the case of the ePark system, a further deployment of the safety goals related to hazardous events has to be performed. In particular, even if for each safety goal and applicable safe state at least one safety requirement has been specified, nevertheless in order to develop a complete set of effective functional safety requirements and a complete functional safety concept, an ASIL decomposition has to be performed, going through the elements of the system for the identification and analysis of all common causes of failure and single points of failure where necessary. Moreover the architectural elements of the ePARK system are sufficiently independent to allow this kind of decomposition, fulfilling also the conditions to apply redundantly the safety requirements, by the analysis of the functional redundancies (according to ISO 26262, Part 9, Clause 5) and the analysis of the faults and failures propagation through the elements for each hazardous event.

The ASIL decomposition has been performed by keeping in mind the defined assumption, in terms of functional and architectural requirements, and the risk assessment outcomes.

The hazard we are considering (see Table 2) is classified as ASIL C. Hence, at a first stage all the involved components inherit the safety classification as 'starting ASIL'. By applying the ISO 26262 ASIL decomposition rules, we can decompose the ASIL C as shown in Figure 2.

To establish the validity of the assumptions it is necessary to demonstrate that the ePARK developed on the shelf as SEooC is consistent with the requirements in the context (vehicle) where it is intended to be used, with reference to its previous definition. The ePARK is a complex system and the validity verification of its assumptions applies at the end of its complete hardware and software development and integration (see Figure 3). In some other cases of simple SEooC, like hardware single components, e.g. microcontroller, or software modules, the validity verification applies before the level of system integration and is performed at the hardware or software level correspondingly.

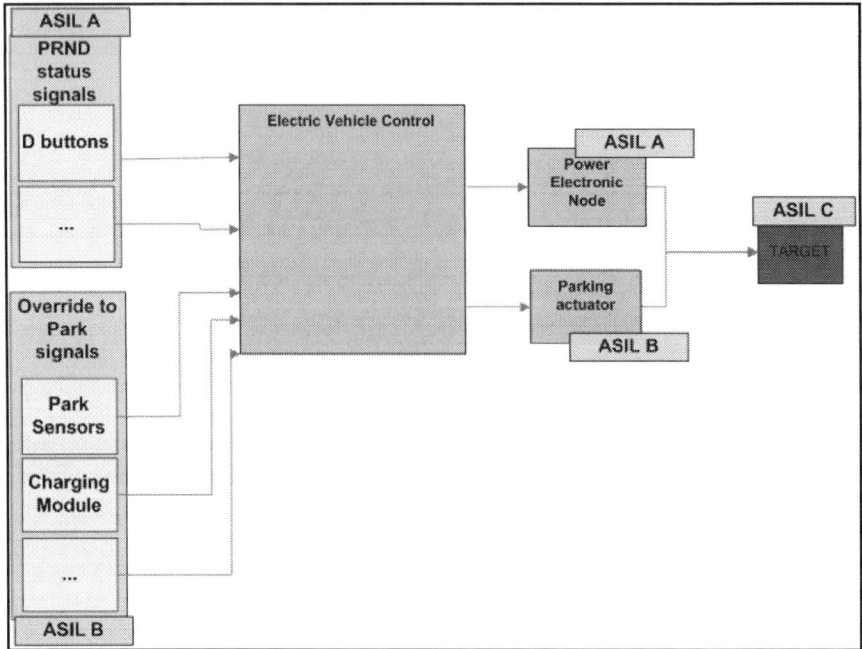

Fig. 2. ASIL decomposition for the SEooC (ePARK)

If the validity of the assumptions made during the SEooC development cannot be established during its integration into the vehicle, a change to the SEooC is made (ISO 26262, Part 8, Clause 8: Change Management). The validity of the assumptions is established producing a report.

The ePark system is an example of an SEooC application, for which the safety is assured by a closed loop in ISO 26262: a list of assumptions to be used for the application of the system in new contexts is outlined as a part of the item definition and this list will be verified during the integration of the system in the vehicle.

3.4 Formalizing and validating assumptions

The ePARK system is assumed to be compliant to certain characteristics of an electric vehicle for its application. These characteristics are related to the vehicle maximum speed, weight and available sensors signals, and with respect to the electric/electronic basic interface of the dashboard and to the mechanical interface of the transmission. All the vehicles which have the suitable characteristics within a certain limited range (e.g. vehicle speed and weight under a certain maximum value, some standard interfaces for sensor signals and communication data, value of mechanical strength of parking pawl) can integrate this system after the verification of assumptions.

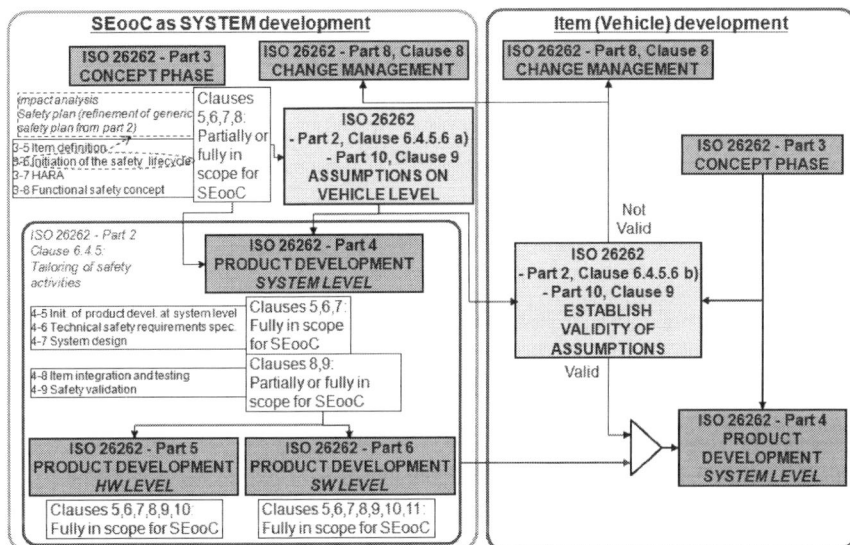

Fig. 3. SEooC system development from ISO 26262 – Part 10

To develop a SEooC, it is necessary to define a set of assumptions to which the SEooC aims:

- *external:* related to the reference target (E/E architecture, system(s), environment, etc.)
- *internal:* requirements and safety requirements, related to the application that are placed on the element by higher levels of design.

If we look carefully to ISO 26262, we can identify the set of assumptions shown in Table 3.

This is a high level classification that is useful for organizing coarse-grained activities. However, this does not provide a sufficient baseline to perform an automated, quantitative approach on SEooC. One of the problems found in the industry is that generally the assumptions are done in an informal way with ambiguities and lacks which makes it difficult for a team to use an element developed by another team. In some cases the time and resources needed for the reuse can exceed the developing from scratch efforts. Hence, any further approach for formalization of specification assumptions must ensure a trade-off between detail level and completeness.

Typical assumptions can be also found in other standards such as IEC 61508 and AUTOSAR. For instance, Annex D in Part 2 of IEC 61508 (safety manual for compliant items) defines a set of technical assumptions that provide additional examples. As a result of a preliminary study of assumptions both from standard documents and from practice, we have defined a more low-level assumptions classification. In Table 4, we show an excerpt of assumptions at HW and SW level.

Table 3. Assumptions classification according to ISO 26262

Assumptions classification	Example	Source
Scope	The system has interfaces with other external systems to get the required vehicle information.	ISO 26262-10 Section 9.2.2
Functional requirements	The system activates the function when requested by the driver in certain vehicle condition.	ISO 26262-10 Section 9.2.2
Functional safety requirements	The system does not activate the function at high vehicle speeds (ASIL x).	ISO 26262-10 Section 9.2.2
Hardware related	Failures of the CPU instruction memory are mitigated by safety mechanism(s) in hardware with at least the target value (e.g. 90 %) assigned for the single-point fault metric at the HW part level (might also be expressed in terms of required DC).	ISO 26262-10 Section 9.2.3.3
Software related	The software component is integrated into a given software layered architecture.	ISO 26262-10 Section 9.2.4.2

Table 4. Some technical assumptions at HW and SW level

Assumptions	Example
Timing	The time base is provided in a dependable way and faults are detected and handled.
Communication	There are means to send a message on different communication links and to detect 'corrupted' messages and eventually recover from this failure mode.
Sharing resources	RTE provides communication between software modules belonging to different memory partitions; i.e. between SW-C and SW-C and between SW-C and base software. RTE can use IOC, it can alternatively use OS trusted functions.
Fault modes	Failure modes of the compliant item (in terms of behaviour of its outputs), due to random hardware failures, that result in a failure of the function and that are detected or not by diagnostics internal to the complaint item.
Maintenance	Any periodic proof test and/or maintenance requirements.
Configuration	The configuration of the software element, the software and hardware run-time environment and if necessary the configuration of the compilation/link system shall be documented.

To define a more quantitative approach for assumptions validation, we propose to use the previous classification of assumptions together with a 'contract-based' approach. A similar 'contract-based' approach has been defined in (Kelly 2001), where a contract allows 'safety case' modules to be integrated if assumptions match with contextual characteristics. In our approach, we define a contract with three types of data:

1. assumption classification

2. SEooC assumption
3. item characteristics.

The validation of assumptions will be done by comparing the SEooC assumptions with item characteristics in the context of the assumption classification. Some of the assumption validations can be done easily by using a Boolean assertion of comparison (e.g. match, less than, greater than, etc.), however the matching and consistency checks for the general case are non-trivial due to the complexity and diversity of the kinds of assumptions.

In Table 5, we provide some examples identified for the specification and validation of assumptions.

Table 5. Assumption validation examples

Assumptions classification	SEooC assumptions (examples)	Item characteristics (examples)	Validation needed
Scope	The SEooC includes mechanical, electric and electronic systems.	The item is prepared to integrate mechanical and electronic systems.	A more detailed analysis should be done as electric systems were not identified on the item.
Functional requirements	Override to park when vehicle is in charge mode.	Override to neutral when vehicle is in charge mode.	Logic true/false sentence: FALSE
Functional safety requirements	Failure mode: it permits a degraded use of the element.	Failure mode: a degraded use is not accepted.	Logic true/false sentence: FALSE
Hardware related	The parking actuator node communicates with the electric vehicle controller via high-speed network. As a result the Fault Tolerant Time Interval (FTTI) = diagnosis time + recovery time + safe state time = 200ms + 600ms + 200ms = 1s.	The parking actuator node communicates with the electric vehicle controller via different high-speed network. As a result FTTI = 400ms + 600ms + 500ms = 1.5s.	Quantitative validation: 1s < 1.5s → NOT VALID
Software related	ePRND function acquires the recharge plug-in status.	The recharge plug-in status is sent as a message broadcast to the bus.	A detailed analysis should be done in order to validate this integration.

The problem of validating assumptions can be partly addressed by disciplined recording of assumptions during analysis. It is expected that appropriate format for recording of this information will be defined in our future work. To this purpose, we propose the creation of a 'language' to be used for the contract specifications (assumptions, context, and validation assertions). The rationale to create a language is because the proposed contract need be tested and validated not only inside one organization but should also include various companies in the supply chain.

Whilst full automation and formalization is difficult, our aim is to provide some support to the tasks of contract matching and SEoCC composition. It is expected that the use of the mentioned language within the statements of assumptions and contracts could be beneficial for parsing of the structures and would provide the basis for development of some assistance tools.

Figure 4 summarizes the proposed approach in terms of the general SEoCC procedure. The ePark system is an example of an SEooC application, for which the safety is assured by a closed loop in ISO 26262. A list of assumptions to be used for the application of the system in new contexts is outlined as a part of the item definition and this list will be verified during the integration of the system in the vehicle. If the assumptions are shown to be invalid, the impact analysis and the related configuration management and change management workflows will support the further modifications of the various safety work products for the envisioned aims.

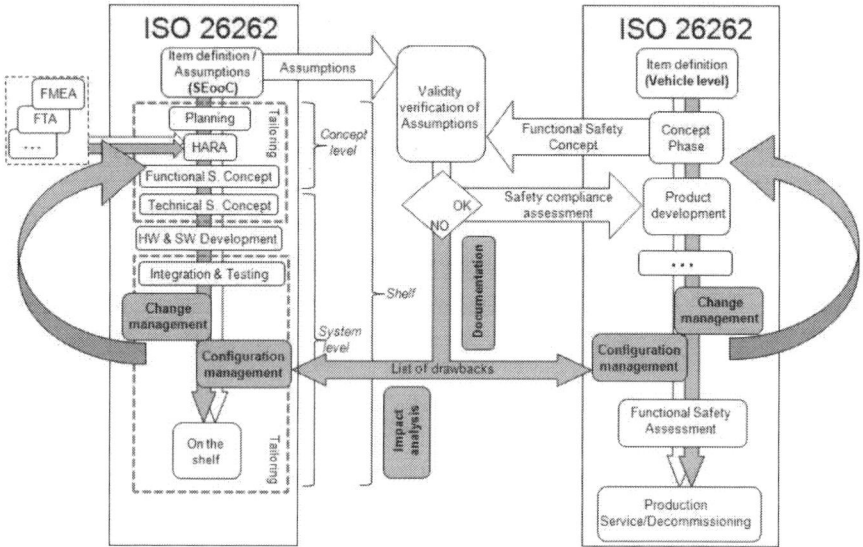

Fig. 4. General approach of SEooC assumption development, validation and change management

4 Conclusions

The ISO 26262 standard is a very new standard that includes the state of art in functional safety aspects. One of the concepts supporting reuse in ISO 26262 is the SEooC. The SEooC helps to:

- take into account the distribution of roles in the supply chain when developing ISO 26262-compliant products (systems, hardware components or software components)
- reduce the reuse of conformity assessment effort and costs for elements reused across many items.

In this paper, we present a description of SEooC in terms of the product lifecycle and the functional safety assurance activities. Industrial practice with respect to ISO 26262-compliance may vary to great extent between different organisations. Required work products are captured by means of mainly textual reports with reconciliation of artefacts typically performed in fully manual manner and through informal manual inspections. This often results in lengthy and labour intensive process.

In this paper, we have explored some initial solutions to deal with a more quantitative management of the SEooC development and integration process. This approach is based on a contract-based specification of assumptions, item characteristics related to the SEooC context, and validation assertions.

Whilst a contract-based solution is reasonably useful, there should be a strong support from standardised system architectures. A standardised well-defined software and system architecture is AUTOSAR. Future work will consider specific architectures to specify sound assumptions and validations assertion.

The SEooC can be viewed as a complementary way with respect to that of the proven in use argument: the second is a new element derived from a known and tested context (vehicle) and has to be integrated in a different context (vehicle), while SEooC is a known system (on the shelf) for an assumed context (vehicle) in which it should be integrated, once the initial assumptions would be shown to be valid.

Acknowledgments   The research leading to these results has received funding from the FP7 programme under grant agreement n° 289011 (OPENCOSS).

References

IEC (2011) IEC 61508 Functional safety of electrical/electronic/programmable electronic safety-related systems. International Electrotechnical Commission
ISO (2011) ISO 26262 Road vehicles – functional safety. International Organization for Standardization
Espinoza H, Ruiz A, Sabetzadeh M, Panaroni P (2011) Challenges for an open and evolutionary approach to safety assurance and certification of safety-critical systems. WOSOCER 2011: 1-6
Ruiz A, Habli I, Espinoza H (2012) Towards a case-based reasoning approach for safety assurance reuse. SASSUR 2012, to appear in October 2012
AUTOSAR (2012) AUTOSAR project. http://www.autosar.org/. Accessed 25 October 2012
Kelly TP (2001) Concepts and principles of compositional safety case construction. COMSA/2001/1/1

Safety Case Approach for the Victoria Line Re-signalling Project

Jonathan Storey

INVENSYS Rail Systems Ltd

Chippenham, UK

Abstract The re-signalling of the Victoria line and introduction of distance-to-go automatic train operation was a major London Underground (LU) project completed in time for the 2012 Olympics. The development and re-signalling was carried out by Invensys Rail Limited (IRL) in collaboration with the train builder (Bombardier) and LU, and was unique in both its design and implementation. The upgrade aims were to deliver a complete re-signalling replacement whilst minimising service disruption. This was achieved via a staged overlay system which was implemented as a hybrid signalling system, controlling both existing and new rolling stock simultaneously. This provided considerable assurance challenges in both managing the system hazards and system approvals. This paper focuses on the management of the staged project delivery whist tracking and maintaining a robust safety argument.

1 Introduction to the Victoria Line project

The first metro was opened in London in 1863 and there are more than 160 worldwide with more being built each year. The aim of a metro or rapid transit rail system is to enable the transportation of large numbers of people, at high frequency, through urban areas, with minimum land use and at low cost. As technology has improved the capability and efficiency of metros have increased and the safety argument to support their continued operation has become more complex.

The Victoria Line in London is an automated line which is completely underground and represents one of the deep-level 'tube' tunnel systems. It has 16 stations on two lines (north and south) with 36 trains running during the rush hour; this gives a two minute gap between trains at each station equating to a 30 trains per hour service. Ultimately, with the next timetable, the service will increase to 39 trains in peak to support a 33 trains per hour operation. Passenger trains run from 5 am through to 1 am. Any disruption to the service on any part of the line can bring the whole service to a stand, a situation that needs to be resolved in minutes as there are more trains than platforms on the line. This limitation means it is only possible to conduct track based engineering works and maintenance during engineering hours, i.e. between 1 am and 5 am, a total of four hours each night or, in the case of extensive works, by closing the whole of the Victoria Line for a period during passenger hours. This is sometimes done, but normally confined to weekends; such closures need to be strictly controlled and extremely well planned.

Part of the upgrade works to the Victoria Line was to increase train capacity for the whole of the line by re-signalling and re-controlling to allow trains to operate closer together. This was supported by an improvement in train performance and optimising the Automatic Train Control (ATC). Due to the restrictions of access for engineering works the Victoria Line re-signalling and re-control asset replacement had to be conducted in stages.

This paper seeks to present the safety management of the staged project delivery whist implementing and maintaining a robust safety argument. It also describes how the approach to safety met the requirements of a staged renewal to ensure that all aspects were addressed and all hazards reduced to an acceptable level.

2 Definition of the system

The renewal of the Victoria Line was a major London Underground (LU) project completed early in time for the 2012 Olympics. Bombardier Transportation (UK) were contracted originally by Metronet (a supplier to LU as part of the public-private partnership contract and subsequently as part of LU post administration), to replace the Victoria Line's existing tube stock with new 2009 tube stock and replace the legacy signalling infrastructure that was first installed in 1967. Invensys Rail Limited (IRL) was then sub-contracted by Bombardier Transportation (UK) to upgrade the signalling, control centre and ATC on their behalf.

The proposed design solution for the re-signalling of the Victoria Line included the introduction of distance-to-go (DTG-R) a radio based automatic train operation system. The DTG-R system development and re-signalling was carried out by IRL in collaboration with Bombardier and LU. The upgrade aims were to deliver a complete replacement of the signalling and control systems whilst minimising service disruption. This was achieved via a staged overlay system which was implemented as a hybrid of old and new signalling systems, controlling both existing and new rolling stock simultaneously. This provided considerable assurance challenges in both managing the system hazards and system approvals.

In order to facilitate the introduction of the 2009 tube stock in advance of the new Signalling Train Control System (STCS) being fully implemented, an overlay system was installed throughout the line. During this overlay phase the existing interlocking system continued to provide all signalling functions and transmit permitted train movement authority to the existing tube stock, itself fitted with Automatic Train Operation (ATO) by IRL in 1967. The overlay system 'listened in' to the legacy system and transmitted data to the 2009 stock, to enable the on-board DTG-R system to calculate its permitted movement authority. Within this overlay phase, it was necessary to transfer the control of the operational railway to the new Service Control System (SCS) whilst also introducing the 2009 tube stock.

To complete the system migration to the end signalling solution an Asset Replacement (AR) phase was conducted as part of the Victoria Line Upgrade (VLU). This AR phase commenced once sufficient 2009 tube stock was introduced to allow a service to be run without the need for 1967 tube stock. In the AR phase, the previous legacy trackside detection and interlocking assets were replaced and the new WESTRACE interlocking system and trackside detection took over all signalling functions.

This final asset replacement process was carried out over eight weekend possessions (railway closed to traffic) over the course of a year. These seven stages replaced all existing trackside equipment with new trackside equipment controlled by the WESTRACE interlocking system housed in the Signalling Equipment Rooms (SERs).

At this point, the increased performance provided by the new STCS could be realised.

The system level overview of the design solution that IRL has provided for the Victoria Line STCS is shown in Figure 1. It provides a view of the overall system, reflecting the main equipment items associated with performing the core functions and shows both final and overlay versions of the system.

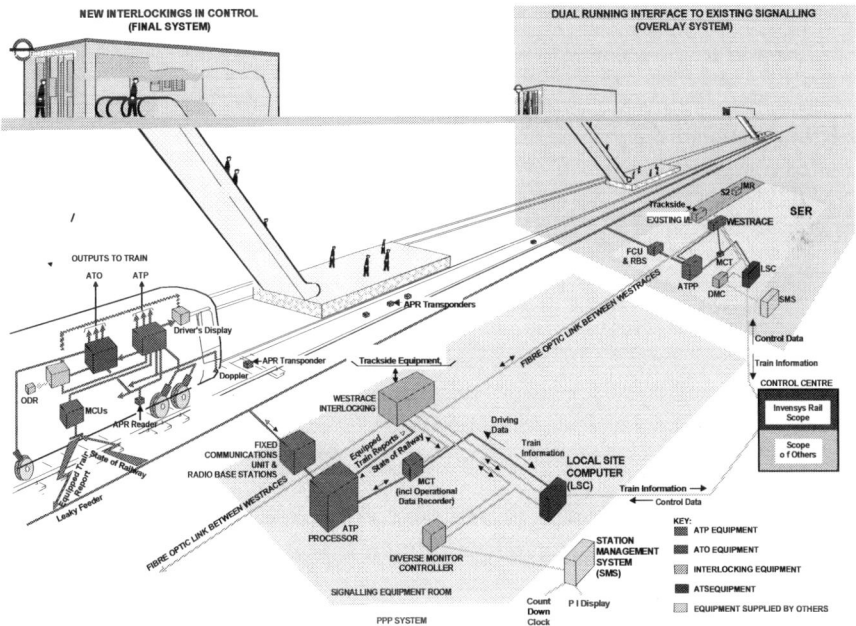

Fig. 1. Location and interaction of products

2.1 Overview of the system

The overall functions of the IRL STCS are to control the movement of trains around the railway network in accordance with the timetable and to provide protection to prevent hazards from resulting in potential train collisions or overspeeds, whilst achieving the required performance. During overlay, the existing signalling principles, locking and functionality were retained; the overlay system functionality being the means of providing the trains with movement authorities that enforce the existing limits of authority. The 2009 tube stock ATC prime functions are:

Determination of the correct speed and location of the train: a computation of the actual and predicted speed and location of the train

Target speed determination: calculation of allowable speed with respect to the current geography and location of other trains

Movement authority function: calculation of the permitted areas of movement authority for each train across the railway

Driving limit enforcement: activation of emergency brake demands and other control mechanisms if the train should attempt to exceed its permitted speed and location

Auto driving: use of correct brake and traction demands to drive the train between platform stopping points

Provision of information for autodriving and manual driving.

Each of these functions was assessed in the system safety case and the prime safety considerations associated with each area are discussed. This was achieved through the identification of core safety principles or safety constraints for the DTG-R product. The assessment focused on ensuring that these safety constraints were not compromised.

2.1.1 Migration strategy

The technical solution for the renewal of the signalling and train control systems was defined by IRL and encompassed the DTG-R transmission based STCS, WESTRACE interlocking and a service control system. The migration strategy for the introduction of this system architecture followed a generic signalling migration method, the major phases being summarised in Table 1.

The full details of each migration phases are provided in Tables 2 and 3.

Table 1. Generic migration phases

Phase	Main purpose	Description/comments
1	Enabling works	Work in Phase 1 covered work that was needed before the implementation of some or all of Phase 2.
2	Overlay	At the end of Phase 2 the DTG-R ATC system was overlaid on the existing signalling, supporting operation of DTG-R equipped trains in DTG-R mode. The existing signalling remains operational to support operation of existing trains under its protection.
3	Signalling and control renewal	At the end of this phase the existing signalling and control systems were renewed and replaced. Wherever possible the design and much of the installation and testing for this phase was performed during earlier phases, so as to minimise the site access requirements. Thus the work of this phase was mainly about changing over to the new equipment.
4	Recoveries	This phase addresses the removal and recovery of redundant equipment, following completion of the relevant elements of Phase 3.

Table 2. Victoria Line migration Phase 2 overview

Phase	Description/comments	Output	Applies to
2A	**SER and trackside overlay.** The SER and trackside equipment was designed, installed and tested, covering all elements of the system. The existing legacy interlocking circuits were modified to feed relevant status information to the new SER equipment, this included indications needed to support Phase 2D. The test train (an existing Victoria Line train) was used to test the operation of ATP and ATO track to train communications systems and the geographic data. The SER and track side design that was installed included all equipment and wiring required for Phase 3 but not required for this phase. This was plate racked or not connected until Phase 3.	Site commissioned for DTG-R ATC operation with pre-production trains. Existing stock was unaffected. The whole of the SER had commissioned status in respect of access for work.	Signalling system, train system and SCS
2C	**ATC pre production trains.** The main work was the verification and validation of the operation of the system using the pre-production trains. The work in this phase started at the test track, then moved to engineering hours running on the Victoria Line and ending with traffic hours running on the Victoria Line.	System commissioned for DTG-R ATC service operation with production trains.	Train system
2D	**SCS overlay.** The new SCS took control of the existing interlockings. The new SCS was tested and commissioned in respect of the functionality associated with the production trains. The introduction of the new SCS was such that it progressively took control of the whole line for longer and longer periods of time, until it became the primary system of control.	SCS system commissioned line wide for service operation with existing interlockings in control.	SCS

Table 3. Victoria Line migration Phases 3 and 4 overview

Phase	Description/comments	Output	Applies to
3A	**Production trains.** Rolling programme of testing and delivery of new trains.	Production trains delivered.	Train system
3B	**Signalling renewal.** This was the commissioning of the part of the SER and trackside signalling which was installed at Phase 2A but not commissioned. It was inclusive of the new signalling being controlled by the new SCS. It only commenced after the last old train has been removed. This work took place in stages, working from one end of the line to the other and included block layout changes necessary to achieve the full improved performance.	Site commissioned with new interlocking (WESTRACE) controlling the railway, all old track circuits replaced. New SCS system controlling the train movements.	Signalling system, train system and SCS
4A	**Signalling and ATC recovery.** This stage was the recovery of all redundant signalling and ATC equipment. This took place after Phase 3B was completed.	All redundant signalling and ATC equipment removed from site.	Signalling system and train system
4B	**SCS recovery.** This stage was the recovery of all redundant ATS equipment. This happened after phase 3B was completed.	All redundant SCS equipment removed from site.	SCS

3 Safety assurance processes for a multistage project

The lifecycle for the system assurance aspects of the VLU signalling project was based on CENELEC 50126 and covered all lifecycle stages from conception through to decommissioning. The Victoria Line System Assurance Plan (SAP) provided the details of the IRL safety and reliability analysis activities performed at each lifecycle phase. The SAP also considered the assurance of core system and R&D generic products that were developed under the remit of the VLU signalling project. The approach to the management of safety and acceptance required IRL to:

- use staged acceptance related to lifecycle activities
- submit specific documents for acceptance with the necessary independent safety assessment reports written by independent bodies, with respect to the completeness and correctness of each document pack.

The safety management process applied also required IRL to show that the necessary qualitative safety targets/SIL targets were derived and mapped for each subsystem and function. Where no contractual quantitative safety targets were provided by the customer via the customer requirements specification, then the necessary deterministic risk assessment was made against a defined risk criterion. The safety requirements of the project were:

1. to ensure that the signalling system achieved an acceptable level of safety, as required for the intended project application, in a timely and cost-effective manner, and in all phases of its lifecycle
2. minimisation of the frequency of an accident occurring and, where reasonably practicable, reduced severity of the effects of hazardous events for the whole IRL signalling system to either a negligible level or a level that is both tolerable and As Low As Reasonably Practicable (ALARP), these being defined as necessary by the client for each identified risk
3. to operate the safety programme in line with the IRL safety engineering handbook and project SAP
4. to identify, evaluate and record all hazards of the system in a hazard log, to be maintained throughout the contract lifecycle
5. to provide the necessary safety criteria to arrive at a reasonable and acceptable balance between the reduction of the risk to safety and the cost of that risk reduction (i.e. ALARP)
6. to ensure the systematic application of analysis and assessment techniques, as outlined later, in such a way that the results are both comprehensible and in accordance with the client's requirements and to satisfy safety case regulations.

The project specific activities were allocated to each lifecycle phase. These activities were grouped into the two main traditional phases:

- Preliminary Hazard Analysis (PHA)
- System Hazard Analysis (SHA).

4 Migration based assessment

One of the key areas in ensuring that the system remained acceptably safe during the migration phases was the system safety analysis. The establishment of a quantified risk assessment criterion early within the system assurance plan gave clear guidance to enable comparisons against the existing systems. Another key factor was the mapping of all system level analysis into both the system hazard log and the system safety requirements. This traceability mapping was crucial as it provided a mechanism to show the changes in hazard risk by the implementation of each of the migration phases. The focus of the analysis specifically targeted areas of expected risk to ensure that the effort in the system modelling was not wasted on just completing models for modelling sake. This principle also helped to ensure that areas that could not be quantified easily were considered via alternative appropriate analysis techniques. The development of key safety constraints and safety principles against which the system could be assessed provided the acceptance criteria for the more complex and dynamic systems. The following sections describe two of the more commonly used techniques that were applied to assess the system safety during the migration phases.

4.1 Fault Tree Analysis

An initial system level hazard analysis was conducted via a fault tree model for the Victoria Line final asset replacement. This model was then regressed back through the migration stages gradually reducing the IRL system contribution and replacement with the existing LU equipment. This was achieved by the use of an adaptive fault tree model that allowed the switching off and on of different system elements. This model provided a quantified system level Fault Tree Analysis (FTA) and was used to demonstrate how the hardware architecture met its primary quantitative safety targets for each passenger accident classification. An FTA report was produced for each migration phase of the project based on this adaptive model. The analysis was carried out to the lowest level in a structured top-down approach, and considered:

- environmental conditions, including electromagnetic interference
- all operational modes
- independent, dependent and simultaneous hazardous events including failure of safety devices and common mode failure
- effects of defined human errors including operator and maintenance errors
- degradation in the overall performance of the system or sub-systems or safety systems from the normal operation condition.

The results of the system Functional Failure Analysis (FFA), zonal analysis and the product level fault trees were fed into the top-level system fault trees and used to verify their base event data. The top-event failure occurrence rate figures were directly compared with the Victoria Line targets specified from LU's own Quantified Risk Assessment (QRA).

The Victoria Line STCS system level fault tree hazard analysis was used to demonstrate compliance with the safety targets for each migration phase of the project. This quantitative evidence supported the ALARP justification made for the system.

The FTA was also used to identify each functional hazard of the system and provided a valuable cross check that all the system hazards had been identified. Results were transferred into the system hazard log, which demonstrated that all the functional system hazards (non-dynamic) had been quantified or suitable alternative analysis provided.

4.2 Functional Failure Analysis

A system Functional Failure Analysis (FFA) was conducted on the Victoria Line STCS configuration at each major phase of the project. The FFA performed the role of a functional Failure Modes and Effects Analysis (FMEA) and considered the effects of single faults upon the system, how the system mitigated the faults, and the means of detection and the resultant state of the system. The analysis was based on the system functionality covering products and interfaces, and included the DTG-R system.

The first system FFA was conducted on the Victoria Line STCS final asset replacement model; this was again regressed to cover the overlay system. The system FFA was used to identify the credible system hazards, levels of severity and mitigation measures incorporated into the STCS to reduce the risk. In most cases the analysis served to independently substantiate the safety arguments and related mitigations already assessed during the STCS safety lifecycle.

Several undetected functional failures including systematic failures and common cause failures were revealed which required further assessment. The report suggested possible additional mitigations to control the effects of systematic failure and reduce the risk. These actions were assessed for effectiveness and possible improvement and completed as part of the system design process.

The system FFA was also used to define a series of negative test cases for the demonstration that the system functionality and behaviour was correct as specified. This was successful in identifying the product level failure modes that may have affected system safety or service performance. The FFA provided an in-depth safety related failure analysis in key functional areas of the system to identify and assess:

* The credible system hazards, levels of severity and mitigation measures incorporated into the STCS to reduce the risk. In most cases the analysis served to independently substantiate the safety arguments and related mitigations already assessed during the STCS safety lifecycle.
* The revealed undetected systematic failures and common cause failures which could have had a major impact on system safety, and additional design and diverse protection measures needed to be incorporated into the system to adequately mitigate and control the failure effects. In particular the ATP undetected systematic failures that have potential to result in a hazard are either 'signalling states' related, 'speed and location' related, or 'emergency brake' related. These functions are fundamental to system safety, being directly concerned with train safe protection and operation within a safe driving profile and have been extensively analysed in the FFA and mitigated.
* The derivation of negative test verification requirements which serve to verify the vital areas of architecture, communications and train protection relative to critical safety parameters which determine the system fault tolerance, mitigations and failure to a safe state.

5 Hazard management

A strong hazard management process needed to be applied to ensure that the system hazards could all be tracked and monitored throughout the system migrations.

This was achieved by maintaining a rigid control over the system configurations and product baselines. Without these controls the infrastructure assessments would have blended into each other and design and functionality misaligned. A clear understanding of each migration phase configuration enabled the hazards applicable to the functionality and behaviour being implemented to be segregated and compartmentalised. Once the scope of each migration phase or system baseline was clearly defined, the impact of moving from one system to another could be clearly defined. Understanding the baselines and the changes being made was vital for the assessment of the impact on the system hazards. For each phase of the project a separate baseline of the hazard log was created each with its own subset of top level hazards, respective causes and ultimately mitigation, requirements and closure. This was maintained via a specifically developed Microsoft Access database which was used throughout the life of the project. The following sections define the processes used throughout the migration process.

5.1 Hazard identification

IRL used a range of techniques to elicit potential hazards in the system. A variety of suitable techniques was chosen to ensure the completeness of the hazard identification process. The range of specified techniques was agreed and verified by peer review, based upon an assessment of the risks associated with the scope of works, and considered factors including:

- Specified techniques to assess the effects of: single faults, multiple independent faults and common-cause systematic faults (e.g. Fault Tree, Functional Failure and Interface Hazard Analysis). All identified hazards were recorded and monitored through the system hazard log.
- The identified hazards generated a set of safety requirements that were recorded in the RAMS (Reliability, Availability, Maintainability and Safety) specification and traced into the design through the appropriate system design module.

Hazard identification was undertaken through the preliminary analysis phase. The aim of the preliminary analyses was to identify the system functional requirements as early as possible. The following processes were undertaken to ensure adequate hazard identification:

- Historical data hazards review – assessment of previous similar projects.
- Brainstorming hazard identification (HAZID) meetings. The results from which were assessed as hazards, hazard causes and threats, and incorporated into the relevant documentation.
- Fault tree analysis (FTA).

The initial preliminary hazard identification process was developed further through the system hazard analysis phase, by both the update of the Preliminary

Hazard Analysis documentation supplemented by system safety and reliability analysis.

The hazards identified in the IRL system hazard log were assessed against the results of the LU HAZIDs, and the necessary mapping established between the IRL hazard log entries and the IRL owned hazards in the Bombardier and LU hazard logs. This provided additional validation of the completeness of the hazard identification process.

Later once the top level system hazards were well established safety assessment workshops or HAZID style meetings were held specifically to assess the impact on the system by the proposed migration phase. These sessions were also used to assess any site specific hazards that needed to flow into the specification application safety cases.

5.2 VLU hazard log

The hazard log and the system hazard report for the Victoria Line signalling and train control system contains the hazards identified during the PHA and SHA phases. It was used in conjunction with the system analysis to derive targets for products, functions and interfaces for the system. Compliance with the defined hazard targets ensured that the system meets its top level safety targets. Evidence of the compliance with the safety targets for each product, function and interface was provided in the system safety case. The IRL approach to the classification of risk was based upon the following:

1. Risks were classified into three zones: intolerable; tolerable; acceptable.

   – Risks were not accepted if in the intolerable zone.
   – If the risk was in the tolerable zone, it was mitigated to ALARP, having regard to cost and other penalties.
   – If the risk was in the acceptable zone, no further reduction was necessary.

2. Boundaries between zones were determined from standards/guidelines and the contractually defined specifications.

All IRL STCS system safety hazards were assessed both qualitatively and quantitatively and closed with satisfactory mitigation and closure statements to a negligible level of risk. The Occupational, Health and Safety (OHS) hazards were assessed on a qualitative basis and closed with satisfactory mitigation and closure statements to a level of risk that was deemed acceptable. It should be noted that a specific hazard was introduced to map to service disruption or service affecting failures to allow for the reliability contribution to be assessed in the same model as safety related hazards.

6 Safety requirements management

The project requirements for safety, reliability and maintainability were initially derived from the customer requirements specification. RAMS requirements were then defined as requirements on the system which provided mitigation for an identified hazard or cause. RAMS requirements were identified during hazard analysis, with the aim of defining a set of requirements which, when implemented, reduced the risk of the hazard(s) to an acceptable level. The main RAMS requirements were initially identified during the PHA phase. Hazard analysis continued as the project progressed (during the SHA phase) and these requirements were refined (and new ones identified) as appropriate throughout the project. The requirements for each phase of the system were baselined and mapped to a unique configuration baseline and compliance statement for every commissioned stage and phase.

The RAMS requirements were included in the appropriate (system) requirements specification and traceability added from the hazard log to the design requirements specification, in order to identify the requirements to be implemented to reduce the risk of each hazard or cause. The hazard log also recorded evidence that the requirements were correctly implemented; without this evidence it would have been difficult or impossible to justify that the related hazard could be closed.

IRL's safety case demonstrated that the STCS complied with all the relevant product Safety Related Application Conditions (SRACs), originated either from the product safety cases or from the acceptance certificates for the products. This demonstration formed part of the phased generic application safety case. The system was also developed to the agreed set of LU standards. Any derogation required against standards was managed via a concession request and required acceptance by LU.

An area that proved to be essential to monitor and track was the list of open test logs and outstanding issues logs. Through dedicated tracker tools and monitors the status and impact of any open item or issue could be realised and any justification required was presented within a single log. This tracking process became even more beneficial when it came to the project closure and acceptance as full visibility of these items was crucial for client acceptance. By tracing these trackers into the system analysis and hazard log the impact of the items could clearly be understood.

7 Safety case structure

Prior to the first commissioning several of the systems safety principles were covered by separate individual safety cases. These safety cases covering items, such as signalling prinicples and installation, sought to gain the acceptance of the whole system by acceptance by parts of the system prior to the commissioning. However this approach struggled to pull together a consistent argument for the entire system. So to permit the first major commissioning of the overlay stage under DTG-R control and protection, a single generic application safety case (Phase 2A) was produced. This placed a reliance on the other lower level safety cases for evidence and supporting arguments and was successfully accepted into service. This case was superseded by the generic application safety case for the VLU STCS for Phases 2C and 2D and the safety argument for overlay contained within the supporting documentation, which was summarised using Goal Structured Notation (GSN). This generic application safety case was updated to remove the reliance on previous system safety cases by the inclusion of the full safety justification and incorporation of the elements of the updated GSN for overlay. The final version of the generic applcation safety case for the VLU STCS was an update to support the final asset replacement (phase 3B).

The migration phases that had a staged delivery, such as asset replacement, were covered by site specific safety cases to ensure that the boundary states and system transition risks were suitably assessed on a site-by-site basis.

The objectives of these safety cases was to provide the safety argument to allow the introduction of the VLU STCS functionality under the control and protection of the DTG-R system for each phase of operational hours (passenger service hours i.e. 5 am through to 1 am) with the 'STCS Total' architecture. The high level objectives of the safety cases were to:

• provide the necessary safety argument that the VLU STCS configuration met its top level numerical safety targets and that the level of residual system risk associated with the operation was reduced to an acceptable level
• assess the residual system risk associated with the VLU STCS, such that the residual risk associated with all system hazards were demonstrated to be negligible or both tolerable and ALARP
• confirm that the Victoria Line STCS configuration was designed, built, installed and tested to demonstrate the system met its functional, safety and reliability requirements to an acceptable level
• confirm that the introduction of DTG-R with the 'STCS Total' architecture provided a benefit to the Victoria Line STCS wider safety argument and did not degrade the safety of the assured system.

The safety case objectives were met by demonstation of an agreed set of top level goals. A summary of the top level goals as defined in the GSN used on the VLU Project is provided below:

G1 IRL shall demonstrate through VLU STCS SC that the system and stageworks system is acceptably safe subject to compliance with restrictions.

The context that surrounds this goal includes the identification of the operational envelope of the system and identification of what constitutes 'acceptably safe'. In order to demonstrate that Goal 1 is met, a number main goals have to be satisfied; these are discussed further in the sub-goals detailed below:

G2 An acceptably safe and integrated technical solution is provided (technical design and build).

G3 Effective safety management must have been applied throughout the project.

G4 Effective quality management must have been applied throughout the project.

G5 The system must have been adequately tested, and the result of that testing must show that any residual risks are acceptably low.

G6 There must be an effective operation and maintenance regime in place.

G7 The safety case must have completed the required reviews; this includes the reviews that have been undertaken throughout the lifecycle of the project.

G8 An effective safety management of the stageworks commissioning and decommissioning schedule must have been completed

Under each of the GSN main goals a number of sub-goals were identified, broken down into lower event goals and traced into appropriate sections in the safety case. The asset replacement works were assured under the final system safety case. The strategy for the delivery of the asset replacement commissionings is shown in Figure 2.

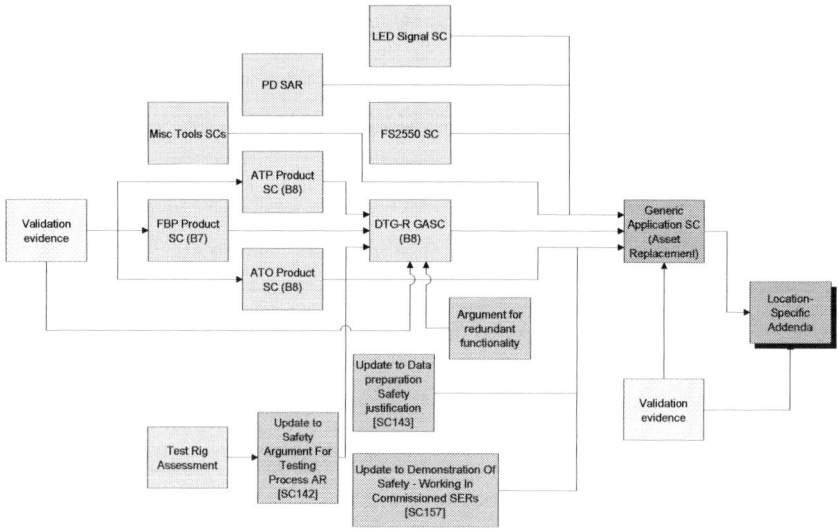

Fig. 2. Asset replacement STCS Generic Application Safety Case (GASC) delivery strategy.

8 Conclusion

The VLU project RAMS programme achieved the difficult task of integrating a migrating system though the delivery stages, whilst tracking and assessing the impact on the system at each phase. This was not without its challenges; notable issues arising from the system assurance approach described in the above document were:

- The various migration phases required a quantified risk assessment to be applied, such that it could then be demonstrated that the necessary LU system level QRA safety targets had been met for each migration phase. The use of a quantified risk acceptance criterion, rather than qualitative risk assessment alternatives proposed by the common safety method, resulted in the system modelling having to extend beyond the corporate scope in order to make like for like comparisons. This quantified risk assessment method was often difficult to apply for all system failure scenarios, particularly for complex software behaviour scenarios. However, the acceptance criteria had been clearly defined; so once quantified a risk assessment could easily be made.
- Introduction of new trains resulted in train regulation complications as the driving characteristic of the new trains, which were faster with more efficient braking capability, meant that during the overlay phase the new trains were catching up to the legacy 67 tube stock and an extended dwell time had to be used in the station areas to allow a manageable timetable. This reduced the service benefits in terms of performance, as final targets could not be fully realised until all the legacy trains were removed from the system.
- Managing converging systems integration issues with tight programme constraints was difficult, as changes on one subsystem often impacted on adjoining systems over their shared interfaces. This was tracked via detailed configuration management processes which ensured the interfacing systems were both defined and compatible. Each change was reviewed and suitably assessed but this often resulted in multiple change cycles.
- Assessment of complex system changes on the system was both time consuming and complex. Improved behaviour and functionality modelling of lower level software algorithms that were fully integrated into the system models would have significantly reduced the effort of these assessments. The use of safety constraints at the lower level however worked well.
- The management of interfaces with existing legacy equipment required considerable effort. The interface hazard analysis process was used to effectively manage the assurance of the interfaces between the IRL scope of supply and both the train (BT) and LU legacy signalling. Additionally extensive over and back exercises were carried out to provide measurable demonstrations that the equipment would perform as intended and the signalling and safety principles remained valid. Additional safety requirements were added to ensure that the overlay system, including the legacy equipment, met modern requirements.
- Technology constraints meant that some of the proposed system mitigation could not always be implemented such that the system impact on lower level products had to be reassessed.

Where the system management approach worked well:

- Each phase and change to the operational railway was assessed on a case by case basis with its impact on the overall system modelled and any impact on existing or new hazards agreed.
- The use of high level GSN in the safety case significantly reduced the time spent undertaking review cycles, when assessing the changes to system safety cases both internally and by the client.
- The use of GSN provided a clearly defined structure for the safety case which was complemented by strongly defined roles and responsibilities of the acceptance panel which ensured that the system was thoroughly reviewed prior to acceptance.
- The use of adaptive FTA modelling reduced the number of system models that needed to be developed and maintained.
- The change control process worked in ensuring that all parties reviewed the system changes up front and enabled the impact to be assessed in good time before any design or safety submissions were made. This early design review process therefore ensured that all parties were aware of any pending changes.

Ultimately, the Victoria Line Upgrade programme has been regarded as a great success. It has delivered enormous changes to the railway through controlled and detail planned migration stages. This approach has enabled the system to continually meet safety targets with minimal disruption to the operating service. The programme delivery and reliability performance has also successfully supported the 2012 Olympics, whilst the enhanced system performance will support the future increases in operational service capacity demands.

Four Principles of Product Safety

Nick Sibley[1], Chris Elliott[2] and Bill Walby[1]

[1]BAE Systems, Newcastle, UK

[2]Pitchill Consulting Ltd, Cranleigh, UK

Abstract   In 2010 BAE Systems conducted a review of the management of product safety across all its sectors. The review examined many issues associated with the safety of the company's products and consulted widely with its businesses around the world. The outcome of the review was a set of four principles:

1. accountability
2. level of safety
3. conforming products
4. learning and sharing information.

The principles were tested by examining how six other sectors (automotive, civil aviation, construction, health, offshore, and rail) address their equivalent challenge. This paper explains the four principles and provides detail of the associated research and findings.

1 Introduction

As a large international company in the global market place, BAE Systems works across a number of continents and countries with vastly different cultures. BAE Systems' product range is vast and varies greatly across the globe, and, given its international footprint, it operates under a number of regulatory and legislative environments, and established practices. The differing legal and regulatory requirements and established practices, when considered alongside recent world events relating to safety, and the ever increasing public interest and expectations, have resulted in the company's approach to product safety evolving around a set of 'principles' rather than taking a 'rules' based approach.

In January 2010 BAE Systems set up a holistic review of product safety to examine the company's existing practices and procedures and to consider whether they met the appropriate standards.

The review examined many issues associated with the safety of the company's products and consulted widely within BAE Systems' home markets[1].

The review focused on what the product safety standard for BAE Systems should be and both concluded and summarised this as four principles for the safety of products. The principles address:

- accountability
- level of safety
- conforming products
- learning and sharing information.

These four principles:

1. describe BAE Systems' approach to the safety of itsproducts
2. are a goal for BAE Systems' governance system
3. align with BAE Systems' values of being trusted, innovative and bold. The BAE Systems Code of Conduct expands on these values:

> 'To be *trusted* we must deliver on our commitments. We must be honest and take responsibility for our actions and respect that everyone's contribution matters. If we are to be *innovative*, we must embrace openness and candour on all issues. We must value the imagination and experience within our organisation and work together to turn our ideas and technologies into leading-edge solutions. In being *bold* we should constructively challenge our own behaviours and practices with tenacity and resolve. Acting with integrity, we will accept challenges, manage risk and set ourselves stretching goals.'

Together the principles recognise that the safety of BAE Systems' products can only be assured if the integrity of the product is also assured. Product integrity means that:

- *We say what our products are and what they do.*
- *We deliver products that are and do what we say.*

This paper sets out and explains BAE Systems' Product Safety Principles and some of the evidence and thinking that led to them being adopted and implemented across the company.

2 Principle 1: accountability

We shall work with our customers and others to ensure that there is, at all times through the life of every product, accountability for its unintended effects on the safety of people:

- *We are and remain accountable for those aspects of our products that are under our control or for which we are legally responsible.*

---

[1] Details of BAE Systems' home markets can be found at www.baesystems.com.

- *We shall make reasonable efforts to maintain accountability when we no longer have control of, or responsibility for, our products.*

The company's accountability will be delegated to individuals.

2.1 Purpose

This principle implicitly requires that BAE Systems identifies all products under its control or for which it retains some liability (for example in relation to legacy products) and has two purposes:

1. The first is that BAE Systems establishes a hierarchy of accountabilities for the safety of each product. Ideally this flows up to the customer and flows down into all levels of the business and supply chain, through the life of the product. This accountability is personal and should be understood and accepted by those with such responsibility.
2. The second purpose is to encompass the somewhat confused concept of 'design authority' and the more well-defined and recent concept of 'maintenance authority'. Design authority and the related term 'design intent' have different meanings in different contexts. Accountability provides the underlying rationale for all of those concepts and can be developed in different ways to suit each sector and type of product. Where an 'authority' exists, this accountability should be coherent with its responsibilities.

2.2 Guidance

The Oxford Dictionary defines 'accountable' as 'required or expected to be able to justify actions or decisions'. BAE Systems adopts that in its definition of accountability:

Accountability is hierarchical. From each element of the product the line reaches up through the supply chain to the person in the customer organisation who is personally accountable for the safety of the people rather than the product. For example:

- In a civilian airline it is the accountable manager.
- In the UK Ministry of Defence (MoD) this person is called the duty holder (see Def Stan 00-56).

Accountability is the 'golden thread' that runs through the contractual, commercial and operational structures to ensure that in any organisation someone is always personally accountable for every decision that affects safety. It allows everyone to know to what he or she is accountable for and to whom. In principle it extends all the way from head of state to the lowest level in the supply chain. It is personal in that the person who is accountable for a decision or action remains accountable; it is not the current holder of that office but the person who was in office at the time the decision or action was taken. Of course, when subsequent accountable people carry out their duties as they arise, they may need to revisit the earlier decisions or actions of their predecessors.

All products exist within a system, or increasingly within a system of systems. Good systems engineering should ensure that the boundaries within those systems, and the flow of accountability across them, are clear, complete, understood, and accepted. Ideally any contractual or commercial interfaces would align with the natural physical interfaces, reflecting a rational decomposition into sub-systems with boundaries where the flow of interactions is minimised.

2.2.1 'unintended effects on the safety of people'

All products can have unintended effects on the safety of people; this is particularly relevant for weapon systems which are designed to inflict harm if used in earnest. Companies therefore seek to prevent *unintended* harm. This may be to the users of a company's products, to third parties such as civilians or bystanders, and even to the intended victims if the harm is greater than or different from that which was intended.

BAE Systems seek to do this in a manner that is consistent with reasonable expectations when the product is used in an intended or reasonably foreseeable manner.

2.2.2 'delegated to individuals'

BAE Systems appoints individual employees to exercise its accountability, in some cases with formal letters of delegation and with the approval of the customer.

This principle embodies the concept of stewardship. Individuals whom BAE Systems nominates discharge those elements of accountability that lie with BAE Systems. The accountable individuals are, perhaps only temporarily, the stewards of the product, responsible for looking after it for the future. As a steward of another person's property BAE Systems has either to take care of it, or ensure that it has delegated that responsibility to another, or has been relieved of the responsibility by the person who delegated it to us.

This includes responsibility for keeping records; the product is defined by a suite of information that starts with the concept and grows to include test results, jigs, test rigs, operating instructions and limitations. This suite of information defines the product and is considered more with Principle 3: conforming product. The role of maintaining the suite of information could be formalised as a design or maintenance authority or similar title, which can be an enduring role throughout the life of the product until disposal.

The accountable person may be responsible for changing the product, by developing further its design or construction or for maintenance or operation. Accountability brings clarity and boundaries. For example, the person accountable for maintenance should know how far he or she may deviate from the standard maintenance procedure. Minor modifications, to procedure or the product, may be within the accountability of the maintainer but significant changes may need to be referred back to a different accountable person who has access to the information and the expertise to assess the impact of those changes.

The person responsible for any element of a product is likely to change during its life. The customer may be accountable for the initial concept, drawing on advice from suppliers, consultants and the product's intended users. The concept may then be passed to a manufacturer for outline design, then to the design office, then to a procurement office to obtain sub-systems and to production for manufacture. The functions will have different names for a non-physical product such as software, a study or maintenance but the structure remains the same. Accountability may be transferred as the product moves through this sequence.

When the product moves into test, acceptance, commissioning and use, the customer may assume a greater accountability.

The critical feature is that, at every stage, the person who is accountable knows the scope of the accountability and that there are no gaps between accountabilities. Any transfer of accountability needs to be absolutely clear.

2.2.3 'no longer have control of, or responsibility for,'

The person who is accountable need not be the owner of the product – this fits with the concept of stewardship. Even where the contractual framework is complex, for example when incorporating Government Furnished Equipment (GFE), the line of accountability should remain clear. At all times someone must be accountable for every element of the product and there must be an unambiguous hierarchy of accountability.

Accountability is different from legal responsibility and hence potential liability. The accountable person is answerable for the execution of assigned responsibilities, whether directly or by delegation.

3 Principle 2: level of safety

We shall work with each customer to agree the level of safety that is to be achieved by each product through its life.

We shall seek the highest level of safety of those who might be unintentionally harmed by the product that is compatible with the product's required performance, cost and schedule and the way that it will be used.

3.1 Purpose

The purpose of this principle is to make it clear that the level of safety is finite and that BAE Systems will try explicitly to define the acceptable level of safety of a product, in collaboration with its customers, as part of the trade-offs that are always necessary when reconciling conflicting demands.

If the highest level of safety that can be achieved within the other constraints appears to be lower than that demanded by law, or by BAE Systems' own ethical standards, the company will refuse to supply the product.

3.2 Guidance

3.2.1 'agree'

There is no single level of safety that is appropriate to all products at all times in all circumstances. Ideally BAE Systems will agree with its customer the level of safety that is appropriate, as part of the trade-off process by which all conflicting requirements are reconciled. This ensures that the customer is aware of, and agrees to, the level of safety that is required, recognising the realities of what is practicably achievable.

The level of safety that is to be achieved should not just be agreed, it should be communicated to all those whose actions affect product safety. The designers, builders, operators and maintainers of the product should be aware of their role. Where the product is supplied to another organisation to be integrated into a system, that organisation will usually be the customer so will have agreed the contribution of BAE Systems' product to the safety of the system.

Similarly, where BAE Systems is the integrator of one or more sub-systems, it will seek sufficient information from the suppliers to ensure that the agreed level of safety can be achieved and demonstrated.

3.2.2 'level of safety'

The minimum level of safety of most civilian products is defined by compliance with standards, by the demands of consumer or criminal law, or by regulators. For military products, it is unusual to have that clarity and the level of safety emerges from system trade-offs.

Ideally the agreed level of safety is an explicit feature of the specification of the product. This might be expressed in many different ways:

- quantitative, for example by developing a quantitative risk model that shows the probability that the product will fail in service and that this meets or exceeds the agreed target
- qualitative, for example:

    - at least as safe as the product that this one will replace
    - at least as safe as a reference product

- compliance, for example with a standard, regulation or established good practice.

Exceptionally, it may be possible to require that the risk due to the product is small compared to the risk arising from the context in which it is to be used – for example, if it is to be used under circumstances where there are other, much greater, risks present – but this is a poor basis for setting the level of the safety because it relies on extrinsic considerations outside the control of the supplier.

Whichever approach is taken, BAE Systems has to be able to provide evidence that the way that the product is designed, built and is intended to be operated, maintained and decommissioned will achieve the agreed level of safety. This is no different from agreeing and demonstrating the achievement of any other parameter that defines the product's qualities, like speed or mean time to repair.

3.2.3 'through its life'

BAE Systems intends that the principles should apply to products throughout their lives. For civilian products, life includes the initial 'shake-down' period, in-service operations and maintenance, and the end of the product's life when it may be wearing out or needs disposal. Military products have a similar cycle but also have to reflect all phases of national defence, from peacetime training through preparations for combat and use in a war zone. BAE Systems will help its customers to make operational decisions, for example by proposing limitations to the range of a product's use when it is new or when a safety issue emerges which, if adopted, will allow the customer to continue to meet the safety objective. Principle 4: learning and sharing information complements Principle 1: accountability by setting out how BAE Systems will seek to exchange information with its customers.

Customers and BAE Systems also have to recognise that the acceptable level of safety for a product that is still operating long after it entered service may be based on assumptions or standards that are no longer valid.

3.2.4 'the highest level of safety ... that is compatible with the product's required performance, cost and schedule and the way that it will be used.'

The level should be as high as is reasonably practicable. As well as being ethical, this reflects the legal requirement in several of BAE Systems' home markets to reduce risk wherever reasonably practicable. It should also be consistent with reasonable expectations when the product is used in an intended or reasonably foreseeable manner, while avoiding dangers inherent in the design that outweigh the design's benefits.

Trade-off might be needed: the performance required may necessarily restrict the level of safety that can be achieved. The level of safety of a product is one of the parameters that define the product, not an absolute value. It is therefore subject to trade-offs with all of the other parameters that define capability and cost.

3.2.5 'those who might be unintentionally harmed by the product'

Given that some military systems will not be able to achieve the level of safety that would be expected of civilian systems, it is essential that the effect on those who will bear the consequences are taken into account. The interests of the users (crew, operators, and maintainers) are best taken into account through the customer. Third parties (civilians, non-combatants) have to be represented through a combination of the actions of a regulator (where applicable), agreement with the customer and the supplying company's ethical behaviour.

All products can have unintended effects on the safety of people; this is particularly relevant for weapon systems which are designed to inflict harm if used in earnest. We therefore seek to prevent unintended harm. This may be to the users of our products, to third parties such as civilians or bystanders, and even to the intended victims if the harm is greater than or different from that which was intended The business will take reasonable care to ensure that the harm inflicted on the intended targets will not be greater than intended, e.g. in case of non-lethal weapons.

4 Principle 3: conforming product

We shall ensure that our products conform to their definition:

- *with internal and, where necessary, external approvals for the organisation and product*
- *by deploying suitably qualified and experienced people*
- *by applying independent assurance.*

4.1 Purpose

There is little value of a set of principles for the safety of products unless the company which adopts them can also ensure that its products are and do what they say – that is the essence of product integrity. This principle demands that BAE Systems establishes procedures to define each product and to ensure that it conforms.

4.2 Guidance

4.2.1 'ensure'

BAE Systems' capability to deliver conforming products should include all aspects that can affect how the product performs. This includes ensuring that the definition of the product is consistent from concept through design and build through to commission, use and maintenance.

BAE Systems recognises that it cannot ensure that products will conform to their definition without input from third party organisations. Suppliers have a crucial role and the customers may have two roles, always as the people who specify at the highest level what is needed and accept from us the final product, and sometimes because they are themselves part of the supply chain.

Consequently BAE Systems has processes in place which ensure that we obtain and, where necessary, require, all relevant input from suppliers and customers to ensure that it can deliver a conforming product.

4.2.2 'definition'

In order to assure the safety of a product, there must be at all times through its life a suite of information that defines a product and its features and that:

- may define many versions of the product over its history – as conceived, as designed, as built, as maintained, as modified
- reflects the current state of product
- may include jigs, test rigs, operating instructions and limitations.

This requires, at all times through the life of a product:

- an organisation responsible for the suite of information that defines the product
- a mechanism for ensuring that the suite of information and the product remain aligned
- a procedure for transferring responsibility for the suite of information to any successor organisation.

Customers or third parties are likely to contribute to these.

4.2.3 'internal and, where necessary, external approvals'

In some cases BAE Systems is subject to appropriately independent internal or external approval to provide control, for example when handling nuclear plant or materials. In other cases there are no external regulators with power to regulate BAE Systems' capability to deliver conforming products and we will use an appropriately independent internal approval to provide control.

4.2.4 'deploying suitably qualified'

Not all of the people responsible for the safety of BAE Systems' products will be in its direct employment so the principle refers to 'deploying' and not 'employing'. Whether people are employees, employees of its suppliers, or contractors working in BAE Systems facilities, the company will always ensure that they have the capability necessary to ensure the safety of BAE Systems' products.

4.2.5 'independent assurance'

BAE Systems' internal quality assurance processes must be sufficiently independent of the design and build of products to provide an effective challenge and confirmation that all of its activities result in a product that conforms to its definition. BAE Systems' assurance processes must confirm that, through concept, design, manufacture and support, our products conform to their definition.

5 Principle 4: learning and sharing information

We shall work with our customers and suppliers through the life of each product to:

- *provide topical information on safety so that each customer may determine how the product is used*
- *obtain information on the use and performance of the product to assess the consequences for safety*
- *understand the cause of significant accidents and incidents involving our products, where appropriate with independent accident investigators, to reduce the probability of recurrence.*

We shall seek to learn from other parts of the company, organisations and domains.

5.1 Purpose

This principle consists of two parts, both of which are concerned with information about BAE Systems' products.

1. The first part allows BAE Systems to fulfil its commitment under Principle 1 throughout the life of the product, by informing the customer of anything BAE Systems learns that might affect safety, and by learning from customers about how the product performs and is used, including from incidents and accidents.
2. The second part commits BAE Systems to learning widely, wherever it can find information that helps it to manage the safety of its products.

5.2 Guidance

5.2.1 'provide topical information'

Over time BAE Systems might acquire information that is relevant to the safety of one of its products. For example, it might have discovered that ordnance is deteriorating with age and that there is an increased risk of unintended detonation, or that a material that it thought to be inert can be toxic. In those circumstances, BAE Systems might conclude that the product in question is less safe than the level of safety that was agreed with the customer when the product was delivered.

If this happens, BAE Systems will seek to notify its customer(s) promptly, accurately and comprehensively of the new information and its implications for safety.

5.2.2 'customer may determine'

BAE Systems is not in a position to determine whether a military product should be withdrawn from service. The customer, or probably the political and military authorities in the customer's country, needs to make an assessment of the relative risks of continuing to use the product versus leaving the country less well defended if it is withdrawn. Any such decision will need to take account of the customer's perception of the current threats to the country and of its capacity to defend itself by other means. BAE Systems does not have the authority or information to make that assessment; however, it can and will cooperate fully with the customer to make sure that the customer can make an informed assessment.

5.2.3 'information'

Ideally a company would have access to all information on how its products perform and a continuing contractual relationship to analyse and interpret that information. If a company's customers do not provide that information, that company will not be able to ensure the product's level of safety. As such it may want to consider informing its customer(s) that it considers them subsequently responsible for the safety of the product.

The way in which the product is operated and maintained has a major impact on its through-life safety. No company can fully discharge its commitment or duty to provide relevant and topical information to its customers unless it is aware of all of the factors that might influence safety. BAE Systems therefore considers that it is vital that its customer provides it as much information on its products as is possible within the constraints of security and operational confidentiality.

Information on products which are being used in an operational environment is also vital to inform the development of future products, whether development of the current ones or wholly new. Failure modes and rates, accident inquiry reports, unscheduled maintenance and spares requirements all contribute to constantly improving product safety as well as helping BAE Systems to advise the our customers on the current level of safety.

5.2.4 'understand the cause'

Investigation of incidents and accidents must be directed towards finding out why the event occurred in order to prevent recurrence and not towards attributing blame. This fits with a culture in which people are not afraid to speak out and share information without fear of punishment – a 'fair and just culture'.

5.2.5 'significant accidents and incidents'

These include incidents and accidents that occur wholly within BAE Systems' premises or control and those that occur on other sites or after handover of the products to customers. They may also include similar products that share components, designs, ways of working or other elements with BAE Systems products. Significant incidents are not necessarily big incidents and, maybe on the surface, seem trivial – it is their potential for serious accidents that makes them important.

5.2.6 'independent accident investigators'

The degree of independence should reflect the possible severity of the event and the roles and seniority of the persons or organisations that might have contributed to the cause. Independent investigation is held in high regard, especially in transport where it is routine for aviation, rail and marine accidents. The following was written by Professor Andrew Lo, of Massachusetts Institute of Technology Sloan School, in the Financial Times on 1 March 2010:

> 'The National Transportation Safety Board (NTSB) is a compelling model for financial reform. A fiercely independent government agency with no regulatory authority and whose primary mission is to investigate accidents, the NTSB provides careful and conclusive forensic analysis, making recommendations for avoiding such accidents in the future. ... This process has been one of the key factors underlying the remarkable safety record of commercial air travel.'

5.2.7 'learn from other'

BAE Systems aims to learn from any sources of useful information. This includes seeking to share information between different the types of platform that it builds and also with other companies, in as far as that is reasonable and compatible with commercial sensitivity and national security.

6 Sharing the outcome

Having spent time considering and evolving the product safety principles, BAE Systems is keen to 'share' them with others. Sharing them also provides the opportunity to further test them and to check their relevance with other companies with a different construct who may also be working in a different market or market sector. Doing this provides extended endorsement that the principles are correct.

Whilst the company was evolving its product safety principles it shared its thinking with the UK MoD Defence Equipment and Support (DE&S) organisation which has resulted in further extended sharing across the UK defence sector. The discussions with MoD DE&S covered a series of activities, including product safety, with the aim of better understanding each other's perspective and short, medium and long term objectives therein. Work on the company's product safety principles was shared and subsequently DE&S have adopted a similar set of principles, including a fifth principle of 'leadership'. These five principles were endorsed by the DE&S Safety Board in November 2011 and are now accepted as their own philosophy of approach to product safety.

Further work with UK MoD and the wider UK defence sector followed the introduction of a twelfth question to the DE&S performance review process; performance review being a process which allows both the MoD project team and a contractor's project team to annually assess performance against set criteria. The aim of the activity is to better inform each other on performance, highlighting areas of potential improvement in all aspects of a project. The introduction of the new question, titled 'culture of safety', and based around the five DE&S princi-

ples led to a cross-industry group of key defence contractors being brought together to discuss the new question and how it might best be implemented.

Having a cross-industry group of major defence contractors together provided
the opportunity to consider all aspects of product safety. As part of these discussions BAE Systems shared its principles with the group and initially sought further involvement from those with a keen interest to consider further research based
around them. The group has now been reconstituted and has agreed to undertake
work, focusing on three areas with the aim of shared learning and a consolidated
position for all involved.

The work has initially been focused toward:

- principles
- guidance
- training.

The first working group is considering product safety principles from a range of
sources with the aim of producing a consolidated set of principles which could be
used across the defence sector.

The second working group is considering the UK MoD 'White Book' and
'Green Book', and other similar guidance and handbooks existing within and
across those companies participating in the work. Early comparisons based solely
upon the chapter headings of these documents suggest a large proportion of common ground. As a result the group are considering whether some of these documents could be consolidated and adopted by the defence sector as a 'core' document which can then be tailored by individual companies as they consider necessary. Figure 1 summarises the current and future positions.

Current position where both UK MoD and industry sector may have
independent guidance documents with different language and Business
interpretation of the same or similar intent.

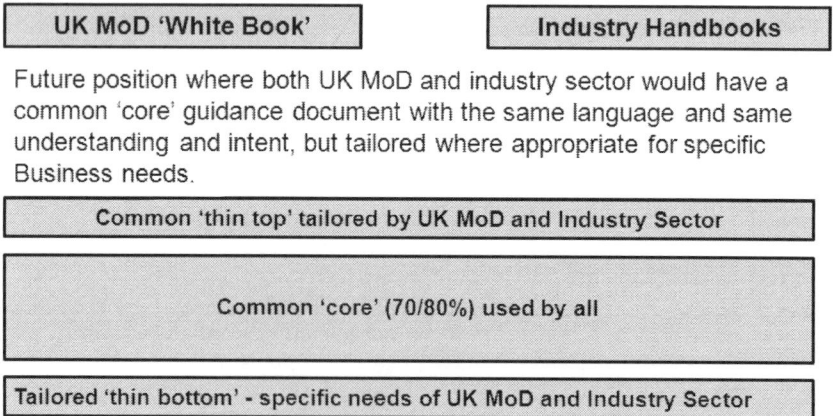

UK MoD 'White Book'	Industry Handbooks

Future position where both UK MoD and industry sector would have a
common 'core' guidance document with the same language and same
understanding and intent, but tailored where appropriate for specific
Business needs.

Common 'thin top' tailored by UK MoD and Industry Sector

Common 'core' (70/80%) used by all

Tailored 'thin bottom' - specific needs of UK MoD and Industry Sector

Fig. 1. Guidance restructure

The final working group is reviewing the mass of training material that participant companies have produced to support the training and awareness of their own employees in product safety. The process has begun by understanding what each of the organisations has available and where that material sits in regard to 'basic' to 'expert' training material on a matrix. The aim is that over a period of time requirements from each can be distilled out and used to form the basis of one consolidated set of training material usable by all.

Opportunities for further shared working are vast. For example, the work which has commenced looking at training material can naturally be extended to consider competency frameworks and professional body requirements. Further opportunities exist for sharing best practice in the area of 'conforming product' and the related subjects of product quality, legacy products and counterfeit issues. Further working groups looking at legislation, standards and regulators, and product environmental, sustainability and associated procurement aspects also have relevance; see Figure 2.

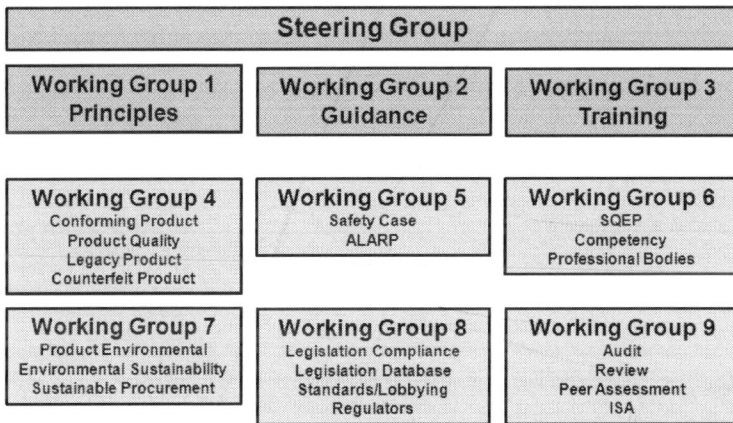

Steering Group		
Working Group 1 **Principles**	**Working Group 2** **Guidance**	**Working Group 3** **Training**
Working Group 4 Conforming Product Product Quality Legacy Product Counterfeit Product	**Working Group 5** Safety Case ALARP	**Working Group 6** SQEP Competency Professional Bodies
Working Group 7 Product Environmental Environmental Sustainability Sustainable Procurement	**Working Group 8** Legislation Compliance Legislation Database Standards/Lobbying Regulators	**Working Group 9** Audit Review Peer Assessment ISA

Working Groups 1, 2 and 3 have agreed subjects and launch dates planned. Groups 4 to 9 are suggested groupings of related subjects for future activity.

Fig. 2. Steering group/working group structure

7 Why do it?

In moving to a position where all those in the defence sector are working from a consolidated set of product safety principles framing their philosophy of approach – a set of 'core' guidance and training material, based upon wide learning and sharing, and adopting best/good practice, used by all but still allowing individual company 'tailoring' where required – must surely put us all in a stronger position. Further, the cost of maintaining a number of assets disappears as all those involved share the burden of managing and maintaining one set of core data.

The Military Aviation Authority's Approach to Defence Aviation Risk Management

John Allan and James Carr

Military Aviation Authority

Bristol, UK

Abstract   The Military Aviation Authority was formed in April 2010 in response to a review into the loss of Nimrod XV230 in September 2006. It was tasked with the rewriting of the defence aviation regulations and to reassess the defence air environment's approach to risk management. Two years on a new suite of aviation regulations have been published and defence aviation Risk-to-Life is now clearly owned by those responsible for the people at risk.

1 Introduction

Risk management was not new to defence aviation; however, it took the tragic loss of Nimrod XV230 on 2 September 2006 and the death of 14 military personnel as a catalyst for change. In 2007 the UK Government instigated an independent review into the broader issues surrounding its loss led by Charles Haddon-Cave QC; the Nimrod Review (Haddon-Cave QC 2009) was presented to the Secretary of State (SofS) for Defence with 84 recommendations.

Pre-Haddon-Cave the MOD's defence aviation risk management system had largely evolved rather than been designed. Individuals had multiple responsibilities – some of them conflicting; airworthiness, and consequently risk management, is a full-time 24/7 job.

2 The Nimrod Review

In the Nimrod Review, Charles Haddon-Cave QC heavily criticised MOD's approach to the regulation of aviation safety. He focused on the complexity of regulation, the regulator's lack of authority, the lack of accountability and the disparate regulatory structure. He also criticised the regulator's lack of oversight of the front line commands and Defence Equipment and Support (DE&S), inconsistencies in the way risk was assessed and managed, and the demise of the flight safety inspectorate role in the RAF. He assessed the 'virtual' Military Aviation Authority (MAA) as too ethereal, recommending that it should be collocated and made wholly independent from the front line commands and the DE&S to enhance its authority.

Charles Haddon-Cave QC presented the SofS for Defence with 84 recommendations; 80 of these were accepted by the SofS and, subsequently, implemented. A key recommendation was the establishment of a new independent MAA to govern all aspects of military aviation.

3 Responding to the Haddon-Cave recommendations

The recommendations accepted by the SofS were grouped into 17 workstreams, ten aviation specific and seven with wider implications. The specific requirements for the defence air environment were addressed in Workstreams 1-10 and were implemented by the MAA. Workstreams 1, 2, 3 and 10 dealt specifically with the formation of the MAA, the establishment of the Duty Holder (DH) framework, the management of defence aviation risk and the rewriting of the aviation regulations respectively. These workstreams were tackled as follows:

Workstream 1 – establishing the Military Aviation Authority. Workstream 1 developed the protocols, governance, organisation and functional aspects of the MAA resulting in a regulator that is a self-standing, separate and independent entity reporting directly to the then 2nd Permanent Under-Secretary[1] at the MOD. The project teams and aircraft operators retained their responsibility to make airworthiness decisions and to manage their own activity, but under the governance and watchful eye of the MAA which has the authority and duty to provide direction, oversight and assurance.

Workstream 2 – establishing duty holders. The airworthiness regime operating in the MOD was manifestly unsatisfactory: there was no clearly recognisable DH structure within which those who carried risk fully understood the nature and extent of their responsibility. Moreover, those who were accountable did not necessarily have the authority or resources needed to properly exercise their duties and mitigate the risks they owned. The Nimrod Review recommended the establishment of a defence aviation risk holder model that specified responsibility and accountability at the key senior operating positions that control the conditions of work in terms of equipment, resources and task; Workstream 2 established the DH framework. Now, within each aircraft operator there is a clearly identified accountable DH, at three senior levels: Service Chief (Senior Duty Holder – SDH), Chief of Staff (Operational Duty Holder – ODH) and Unit Commander (Delivery Duty Holder – DDH). These DHs have the legal responsibility for: the safety of

---

[1] These responsibilities are now carried out by the Permanent Under-Secretary (PUS).

their people; the equipment they provide them with; the environments in which they work; and the tasks they give them. The current ODHs are:

Royal Air Force: AOC 1 Group, AOC 2 Group and AOC 22 Group.

Royal Navy: ACNS(A&C).

Army: Commander Joint Helicopter Command.

Workstream 3 – rewrite aviation safety regulations. The aviation safety regulations within the defence air environment were impenetrable and not fit-for-purpose for both the regulatory and user community. This was due to their complexity, repetition and overlapping nature, as they contained a mixture of policy, regulation and guidance that was open to interpretation and used to justify action already taken or in place. Workstream 3 produced a new aviation safety regulatory framework focussed on Risk-to-Life (RtL) that is easy to read, teach, assimilate and apply, and which clearly articulates how aviation safety is governed within the MOD. These regulations were named the MAA Regulatory Publications (MRP)[2]; they were split into three layers:

MAA Overarching Documents containing information on the MAA's regulatory policy (MAA01), master glossary (MAA02) and regulatory processes (MAA03).

Regulatory Articles for general aspects (1000 Series), flying (2000 Series), air traffic management (3000 Series), continuing airworthiness engineering (4000 Series) and design and modification engineering (5000 Series).

MAA Manuals providing enhanced guidance to the regulatory articles. These include manuals on post-crash management, maintenance and airworthiness processes, and aerodrome design and safeguarding etc.

Workstream 10 – develop the approach for MOD defence aviation risk management. The Nimrod Review identified a number of problems with the management of Safety Management Systems (SMS) citing varying maturities and effectiveness across the aviation domain. To support the DH construct developed in Workstream 2, a comprehensive approach to defence aviation risk management was required to focus on RtL and to ensure that there was a common method of assessing risks within the DH chain and also across the defence air environment. To emphasize the importance placed on this, a previous SofS had stated that 'the MAA will be configured to focus on RtL, a core role of the new MAA'. It was recognised that there are many other risks to be managed, including business, finance and operational risk but Workstream 10 was focused on the delivery of a system that was specifically to manage 'Risk to Life'.

Audit. One of the recommendations from the Nimrod Review was that two years after its publication an independent auditor be appointed to report to the SofS and 2nd PUS on the progress made in implementing the recommendations. In April

---

[2] http://www.maa.mod.uk/regulation/index.htm

and May 2012 a team of six, comprising members of the UK Health and Safety Executive (HSE), US Navy, UK Civil Aviation Authority and the Royal Netherlands MAA led by Dr David Snowball of the HSE, carried out a review of the MAA. Their remit was to examine and report on the progress made into the implementation of the Nimrod Review recommendations, the effect being created in the defence air environment and areas of risk. They reported that: the MAA had rapidly and purposefully started to recalibrate the defence air safety regime in its first two years of activity; there was strong evidence that the key DH concept was well understood; and the building blocks to address and eliminate the frailties in the system for air safety were being progressively established. It was noted that there was significant work still to do further to embed the changes but the right direction and tempo had been set.

4 The principles of defence aviation risk management

It was clear that in order to ensure a consistent approach to risk management a number of key principles needed to be developed. It was known that consistency in the defence air environment was important to enable risks to be compared, ranked and scarce mitigation resources targeted accordingly. A regulatory notice[3] was published articulating the six principles that would underpin both the management of defence aviation risks and the corporate understanding of RtL, thereby enabling effective, prioritised risk management:

Principle 1: Defence aviation risks are owned by the relevant DH, who is legally accountable and responsible for all air safety risks within their area of responsibility.

ODHs should maintain a single, unified risk register for all RtL within their area of responsibility; this risk register should include both type-specific risks and pan-Defence Lines of Development[4] (DLoD) elements. A DH can transfer the management of a risk to another party by agreement, but they will always retain ownership and remain accountable for that risk.

---

[3] DG/RN/04/10 – Aviation risk management – Principles, dated 01 Nov 10.

[4] DLoD: a 'checklist' to ensure all key factors relevant to the capability have been considered. Within MOD, the DLoDs provide a mechanism for coordinating the parallel development of different aspects of capability that need to be brought together to create a real military capability: Training, Equipment, Personnel, Information, concepts and Doctrine, Organisation, Infrastructure and Logistics (i.e. sustainability). Interoperability is regarded as an overarching theme. The co-ordination of the DLoDs is sometimes referred to as capability integration.

Principle 2: A discrete approach to the management of aviation RtL is to be adopted that will drive a clear focus on effective mitigation, the residual risk and the probability of occurrence.

The risk assessment should consider the worst credible[5] outcomes from known RtL and those risks that can be reasonably considered to cause a RtL; the scope of assessment should include the full range of injuries, including fatality. The risk assessment should not consider materiel loss in isolation, or any environmental impacts other than those that put life at risk. Societal impacts from RtL should also be considered.

Principle 3: Formal air safety risk management is to form an integral component of a DH's aviation safety management system.

A common approach to air safety risk management should be adopted across the defence air environment. Individual air safety risks should be identified, evaluated and articulated in a consistent format to enable them to be prioritized against and/or aggregated with other air safety risks, including pan-domain. As part of its assurance role, the MAA will routinely audit DHs' air safety management systems and their identification, assessment and management of air safety risks.

Principle 4: Risks are to be mitigated to at least tolerable and As Low As is Reasonably Practicable (ALARP).

DHs have a legal responsibility to cease routine aviation operations if RtL are identified that are not demonstrably at least tolerable and ALARP. DHs should consider the impact of the aggregate RtL when deciding whether risks associated with an activity are at least tolerable and ALARP. Tolerability judgements are the preserve of the DH and should be based on all available evidence. In any assessment as to whether risks have been reduced to ALARP, a DH should only exclude options to reduce risk if the sacrifice, whether in time, money or trouble, would be grossly disproportionate to the benefit of the risk reduction.

In assessing whether or not a risk is ALARP, the ability to afford a potential mitigation measure is not a legitimate factor in isolation – the consequences of making a potential measure affordable must also be considered. Priority should be

---

[5] It is necessary to consider the full range of credible risks and safety consequences, up to and including the worst credible. Usually, there will be a spectrum of risk scenarios, with the worst-credible outcome occurring only rarely and a range of less severe outcomes occurring more frequently.

given to those mitigation actions that provide greatest gain in overall safety; hence, initially mitigating several lower level risks quickly may be more beneficial than focussing time and resource on dealing with a more intractable, single, higher risk.

If the operational imperative dictates, operational commanders are at liberty to accept air safety risks worse than tolerable; however, any such decisions should be captured within an appropriate and auditable operational command governance process that clearly identifies risk ownership.

Principle 5: A clear and effective risk escalation/referral protocol should be implemented.

The protocol should ensure positive control of risks throughout the escalation process. Risk ownership should sit at the lowest level unless, and until, formally escalated. Once escalated, the superior DH should provide formal and expeditious feedback to the subordinate DH on the treatment of the subject risk. The MAA is to be advised formally of mitigation strategies and actions for any air safety risks elevated to and held at the SDH level.

Principle 6: Risk decisions must only be taken by authorized and accountable individuals and be auditable.

For decisions taken outside the DH chain that have the potential to communicate air safety risks to DHs, particularly resource decisions, there is a personal obligation on the decision-maker to be answerable and to notify the affected ODH(s) without undue delay. Air safety risk decision making will be subject to MAA assurance.

5 Management of operating risk

Prior to the issue of new regulation an interim regulatory instruction[6] was issued mandating a risk management framework to support DH decision making, developed from the principles of risk management mandated in the earlier regulatory notice. The regulatory instruction and regulatory notice have subsequently been replaced by Regulatory Article (RA) 1210[7] which is part of the MAA regulatory publications established under Workstream 3.

---

[6] MAA RI/02/11 (DG) – Air safety: risk management, dated 28 Jan 11.
[7] RA 1210 – Management of operating risk (Risk to Life).

RA 1210 mandated a standardized approach to risk with detailed minimum requirements of a standardized risk register, hazard risk matrix and referral/escalation protocols. It reinforced that DHs were legally accountable for the safe operation of systems in their area of responsibility and for ensuring that RtL are at least tolerable and ALARP. In the execution of their specific DH responsibilities, DHs were accountable and answerable to the SofS via their superior DH chain.

RA 1210 mandated that risk management should consider both the single risks and overall risk[8] exposure, i.e. aggregated risk. It was noted that single risks provide a clear focus for the effective management of issues at lower levels, but a superior DH should understand the overall risk exposure. Where an individual or group of people was exposed to more than one risk, the superior DH should make an assessment that the overall risk exposure to these personnel is at least tolerable and ALARP. One of the tenets of defence aviation risk management is that people should only be exposed to a risk of harm where a defined benefit is expected and where the risks are adequately controlled.

Societal concern was a recognized factor in risk management when there is potential for public condemnation arising from accidents, particularly those involving significant numbers of people and/or vulnerable groups[9]. This factor was generally significant in the context of the management of RtL in UK military aviation. Measures introduced to mitigate this class of risk needed to be considered on a case-by-case basis and take into account the political dimension.

Risk Boundaries. Notwithstanding the unique nature of, and unavoidable risks associated with routine[10] defence aviation activity, wherever possible the aim must be to define risk of death boundaries comparable to those applicable in wider society, informed by HSE guidance for relevant civilian activities (HSE 1992). Historical evidence indicates that these are achievable in practice and, therefore, they are the levels mandated at Table 1.

These risk boundaries for risk of death per annum are used by the ODH and SDH to judge the relative RtL from the routine operation of aircraft within their area of responsibility. These boundaries reflect the risk of death from all causes for the population at risk on a per annum basis and must include consideration of safety trends across the DH area of responsibility and a prediction of future performance.

---

[8] Overall risk is sometimes referred to as 'aggregated risk'. Aggregated risk is defined within the ISO risk management vocabulary as: 'the process of combining individual risks to obtain a more complete understanding of risk'. The purpose of risk aggregation is to provide a more complete picture of the risks posed by a system, or risks faced by an individual or group of people, than is given by considering possible risk outcomes one at a time.

[9] HSE publication Reducing Risks, Protecting People (R2P2) paragraph 25/26 – ISBN 0 7176 2151 0, first published 2001.

[10] That is, activity out with operations governed by Chief of the Defence Staff (CDS) Directive, where operational pressures and/or enemy action may introduce additional risks that, in particular circumstances, might be accepted by operational commanders in the field.

Table 1. Risk boundaries for risk of death

Boundary	Aircraft types	Risk of death per annum for population at risk		
		1st party	2nd party	3rd party
Intolerable	All	> 1 in 1000[11]	> 1 in 1000	> 1 in 10,000
Tolerable	All	≤ 1 in 1000	≤ 1 in 1000	≤ 1 in 10,000
Broadly acceptable	All	≤1 in 1,000,000	≤ 1 in 1,000,000	≤ 1 in 1,000,000

DHs must ensure that the overall risk of death from operating aircraft is below the intolerable/tolerable boundary at all times and should strive towards the broadly acceptable region, commensurate with delivering operational capability.

Hazard risk matrix. A hazard risk matrix enables classification according to each single risk's assessed severity and likelihood. The Nimrod Review noted that there were a myriad of different hazard risk matrices used to determine risk categorisations, this was confusing, potentially dangerous, and made it more difficult to compare risks across platforms. It was recommended that there should be a simple, common hazard risk matrix which: comprised no more than a 4 x 4 matrix grid; provided a system for pro-actively managing all risks that fall under the 'catastrophic' heading where assessments on likelihood are often based on small samples; and provided for meaningful comparative assessments to be made between platforms. The defence aviation hazard risk matrix at Table 2 was designed to determine the appropriate levels of DH risk ownership and to assist with assessing the risks on a like-for-like basis. It should be noted that the position of a risk in the hazard risk matrix is not an indication of its ALARP status.

Table 2. The defence aviation hazard risk matrix

		Severity			
		Minor	Major	Critical	Catastrophic
Likelihood	Frequent	M	H	VH	VH
	Occasional	L	M	H	VH
	Remote	L	L	M	H
	Improbable	L	L	L	M

The severity of a single risk is an assessment of the worst credible[12] event that could result from the hazard. The severity categories listed below are used:

Catastrophic. Three or more fatalities of MOD employees[13] engaged in the activity in question or a single fatality of a member of the public.

[11] Defined in HSE guidance as 'just tolerable for any substantial category of workers for any large part of a working life' – HSE Reducing Risks, Protecting People (R2P2) paragraph 132 – ISBN 0 7176 2151 0, First published 2001.

[12] Although the HRM is calibrated on worst credible outcome, care should be taken to ensure that DHs are aware of the full range of outcomes when considering appropriate mitigations.

[13] Including MOD contractors engaged in MOD-supervised activity.

Critical. One or two fatalities of MOD employees engaged in the activity in question. A large number of major injuries must also be included in this category.

Major. Major injuries[14] to any person. A large number of reportable injuries[15] must also be included in this category.

Minor. Reportable injuries of any person.

Likelihood is assessed with respect to the likelihood of the assessed consequence of a hazard. This is based on the likelihood of a single accident resulting in harm for a particular fleet. The appropriate categories listed below are used:

Frequent. Likely to occur at least several times a year.

Occasional. Likely to occur one or more times per year.

Remote. Likely to occur one or more times in ten years.

Improbable. Unlikely to occur in ten years.

Risk Ownership. In order to ensure there is management attention commensurate with the levels of risk, ownership of and the authority to accept post-mitigation single risks are as follows:

- Very High (VH) risks – SDH
- High (H) and Medium (M) risks – ODH
- Low (L) risks – DDH.

All risks must have a DH owner and this is indicated in the risk register. DHs can delegate the management of risks to other suitably qualified and experienced individuals as and when appropriate; however, as the risk owners, the DH must always remain accountable for RtL within their area of responsibility.

ALARP. It was clear that guidance was required to assist DHs determine whether risks were ALARP. The following three approaches were developed from the HSE R2P2 (HSE 2001) document:

Good practice. Good practice justification is based upon the argument that compliance with a recognised code of practice/MAA approved process/guidance/defence standards is acceptable. However, DHs must understand that practices change over time and that 'good practice' is only the minimum initial standard to achieve.

Qualitative. Qualitative judgements are founded upon evidence of professional and military judgement, common sense and experience from suitably qualified and experienced personnel.

---

[14] Including injuries such as fractures (other than to fingers, thumbs and toes), amputation, dislocation of the shoulder, hip, knee or spine or loss of sight (temporary or permanent).

[15] In accordance with Reporting of Injuries, Diseases and Dangerous Occurrences Regulations (RIDDOR) 1995.

Quantitative. Quantitative assessment is based upon practicable methods of risk reduction and control. A quantitative ALARP argument/judgement must consider aggregated risk and is normally based upon a Cost Benefit Analysis (CBA) and a gross disproportion test, the results of which may be used as evidence to support the ALARP claim[16].

As previously stated, in order to exercise their legal duty of care to employees and 3rd parties, DHs are bound by MOD regulation to reduce the RtL within their area of responsibility to at least tolerable and ALARP. A CBA can inform ALARP decisions by assigning monetary values to the costs and benefits associated with risk mitigation measures, enabling a comparison of like quantities and a perspective on proportionality. Also, amongst other things, consistency of approach enables proposed mitigations to be compared and ranked, allowing finite resources to be prioritized accordingly.

Additionally, in the context of managing RtL, a CBA can help establish whether potential expenditure to reduce risk is 'proportionate' to the level of risk. However, it is no more than a tool to assist in the selection of the most appropriate risk reduction option. HSE guidance in R2P2 (HSE 2001) and convention dictates that the results of CBA cannot be the sole determinant of an ALARP decision, and cannot in any circumstances be used as justification for removing existing control measures, or overriding applicable legal constraints or good practice. It is emphasized that quantitative methods supplement and inform, but do not replace, qualitative assessments of risk and mitigation founded upon professional and military judgement, experience and common sense. A regulatory notice[17] was issued in 2011 to provide additional guidance on how to conduct CBA quantitative evaluations of potential air safety risk mitigation measures to inform ALARP assessments.

6 The future of defence aviation risk management

In the independent audit report it was noted that there was strong evidence of positive behavioural changes and an improving defence air safety culture in many significant areas of the defence air environment. However, it was recognised that there was further work to do to at all levels to firmly embed and sustain these improvements.

---

[16] Although quantitative ALARP arguments are rarely required, they can be emotive and challenging: monetary values are placed on harm to people, and decisions are made about when possible further risk reduction measures are not required. Great care is therefore required to ensure that disproportion factors are correctly considered and that the conclusion is explored for its sensitivity to assumptions.

[17] MAA/RN/12/11 (DG) – Cost benefit analysis of potential air safety measures – Principles, dated 8 Nov 11.

It is too simplistic to rely solely on historic occurrence rates, factors such as changes in the operating environment and 'near misses' should also be taken into account, to underpin as true a representation of the risk as possible – i.e. a low level of occurrence historically does not necessarily equate to there being low risk; consequently, there is now a greater sharing of information across the defence air environment with, amongst many things, the ODHs' risk register being readily available for others to learn from. The MAA is using such information to develop a total system risk picture from which a proactive approach to risk can be taken.

Work continues on the development of the pan-DLoD Air System Safety Case (ASSC). Prior to the Nimrod Review most safety cases were equipment centric, owned by the release to service authority and maintained by the equipment project team; however, most accidents are not equipment failures. The new ASSC is owned by the ODH – the owner of the risk, and each DLoD element is maintained by the relevant specialist who reports to the ODH.

References

Haddon-Cave QC, C (2009) The Nimrod Review – an independent review into the broader issues surrounding the loss of the RAF Nimrod MR2 Aircraft XV230 in Afghanistan in 2006. HMSO

HSE (1992) The tolerability of risk from nuclear power stations. HMSO

HSE (2001) Reducing Risks, Protecting People (R2P2). HSE's decision making process. HSE Books

Assurance Case as a Proof in a Theory: towards Formulation of Rebuttals

Yoshiki Kinoshita and Makoto Takeyama

National Institute of Advanced Industrial Science and Technology (AIST)

Amagasaki, Japan

Abstract   A framework is given to formulate an assurance case as a pair of a formal theory (vocabulary and basic assumptions; a formal model) and a proof in it, thus objectifying ontological presumptions separately from reasoning based on it. Our formulation is given in Agda, a programming and proof description language based on constructive type theory. Emphasis on explicit presumptions improves upon currently prevailing structured-argument notations such as GSN and CAE. Changes and vagueness in modern complex systems must be reflected by rebuttals to their assurance cases. We sketch our approach to formulate rebuttals to that end, where objectification of ontological presumptions works effectively.

1 Introduction

In their pioneering paper, Bishop and Bloomfield defined a safety case to be 'a documented body of evidence that provides a convincing and valid argument that a system is adequately safe for a given application in a given environment' (Bishop and Bloomfield 1998). Since around 2003, the notion has been generalised to that of assurance case for other attributes of systems such as reliability, maintainability, security and dependability. Following Bishop and Bloomfield, we may define an assurance case to be 'a documented body of evidence that provides a convincing and valid argument that given attributes of a system adequately satisfy given requirements for a given application in a given environment'. Assurance cases are considered useful for assurance communication among stakeholders of the systems, and may be required to be submitted for evaluation and certification of systems.

The current practice for clearly presenting assurance cases, and thus helping their validation, includes the use of graphical notations to make explicit the structure of arguments in assurance cases, such as Goal Structuring Notation (GSN) (Kelly and Weaver 2004, Origin Consulting Limited 2011), Claims-Argument-Evidence (CAE) (Bishop and Bloomfield 1998) and Toulmin model (Toulmin 2003). They all can be considered as semi-formal formulation of the reasoning aspect of assurance cases.

However, reasoning cannot stand on its own without its basis, i.e., the ontology it presumes. What we mean here by the ontology includes that of concepts necessary to formulate claims of assurance cases, that of objects such as systems and environments being reasoned about, basic assumptions and relationship among them, as well as reasoning principles to be admitted.

A limitation of the current formulations such as GSN is that they do not provide a way to present the ontology explicitly, leaving its explanation to natural language descriptions scattered over various parts of assurance cases and external documents referred therein. What is the agreed basis of reasoning is subject to interpretation. Checking whether the reasoning conforms to the basis, including very mundane kinds, must solely rely on manual review. The distinction between defining the basis and using it can be obscured, as in 'since the system is claimed to be safe with this reasoning, probably the term "safe" here should be understood in this way'.

We propose a notion of formal assurance cases that avoids those shortcomings by making explicit the ontology and its relationship to the reasoning. The basic idea is to formalise the ontological aspect of an assurance case as a formal theory (formal model) in a formal logic, the reasoning aspect as a formal proof in the theory, and let a formal assurance case to be this pair. We further propose to describe such formal assurance cases in a programming language that supports the correspondence 'propositions as types, proofs as programs'. We use the Agda language (Agda Team 2012) for concreteness of exposition, but the idea is applicable in other languages with similar features.

Another related motivation for a formal assurance case is to account for its dynamic and evolving aspects and manage its changes. A formal assurance case captures more details of elements of arguments and relationship among them than an informal assurance case. It represents them as data, enabling their identification and manipulation. Such ability is a prerequisite for change management.

Our interest in evolution of assurance cases comes from that in Open Systems Dependability (Tokoro 2012). Complex information systems are 'open systems' in that their functions, structures and boundaries keep changing over time to accommodate changes in requirements and environments. Because of this and their sheer complexity, our understanding of their behaviour is inherently incomplete, uncertain and subject to change. Open Systems Dependability focuses on these open aspects not addressed by conventional dependability means. By explicitly codifying the systems and our understanding thereof, formal assurance cases provide a solid foundation for systematic management of these changes.

One of the significant evolution processes of an assurance case is a rebuttal to it and a subsequent amendment. Our work in progress attempts to formulate this process with formal assurance cases.

This paper is organised as follows. Section 2 gives further motivations for formalisation of assurance cases; we emphasise that the formality is not for absolute truth or for detailed precision, but it is for definiteness that enables better communication among both humans and machines. Section 3 explains the concept of formal assurance cases and shows its concrete realisation in the Agda language.

Section 4 presents our current formulation of a rebuttal to an assurance case in the framework of formal assurance cases and Section 5 concludes. Appendix A introduces the idea of Open Systems Dependability, which gives the background of our study of assurance cases. Appendix B and Appendix C give examples of Agda code used in Sections 3 and 4, Appendix D gives further details of formal assurance cases in Agda, and Appendix E is a table comparing terms used here and in related literature.

2 Why formal assurance cases?

Advantages of a formal assurance case as a formal theory and a proof in it include better assurance communication, machine-checking and machine-processing.

2.1 Assurance communication

A formal assurance case provides a firmer ground for assurance communication than an informal one. Its mathematical meaning is determined; the proposition proved is true under whatever interpretation of the primitive notions of the theory so long as it validates the axioms.

Readers can argue whether the interpretation of the proposition proved matches his or her intention, whether the interpretation of an axiom holds in reality, or more generally whether the theory and proof adequately capture the system of interest. The acceptability of the formal assurance case remains open in that sense, but the readers are in a much better position to discuss matters than with an informal assurance case.

In the informal assurance case, the distinction between what is the common basis and what are subject to interpretation may be left vague in 'expert domain knowledge', 'familiarity with the operation', etc. When a decomposition of a certain claim into subclaims in the reasoning is not immediately clear to a reader, the reader must consider many possibilities:

1. The reader is missing some implicit domain knowledge.
2. The writer is stipulating that the claim and subclaims should be understood in a way that makes the decomposition correct.
3. The reader must try harder to connect the decomposition and explicitly given information.
4. The writer erred in applying the decomposition.

With the formal assurance case, the reader need not worry for the cases 1, 2 and 4, since the common basis, i.e., the theory, is given explicitly and separated from the reasoning and since the reasoning is 'correct' with respect to the theory. The formal assurance case gives the detail of how the decomposition is derived from the theory. The reader can look into the detail and either convince oneself or identify the part of the theory to which the reader cannot agree. We quickly note that whether the reasoning and its basis are given formally or not has nothing to do with how detailed they are, and that the details need not be presented from the beginning but can be gradually revealed as necessary.

2.2 Machine-checking

A formal assurance case can be mechanically checked for various kinds of integrity. Much of the checking done in a documentation review can be replaced by mechanical checking of whether a given purported proof is indeed a well-formed formal proof in the given theory. This is practically the most significant benefit for a large assurance case consisting of many files that are updated frequently and independently.

The role of formal languages in assurance cases is analogous to that of strongly typed programming languages in programming. Type checking frees programmers from worrying about type-errors that can be subtle and burdensome to check manually. Although avoiding type-errors is only a part of problems in programming, many desirable properties of programs can be established through type checking.

Various integrity checking can be done in general. There are already many assurance case tools that check, for instance, if a given graph structure of an argument conforms to a specified graphical notation. Formal assurance cases, however, have possibilities of more powerful checking. Examples include the following.

- The contents of argument elements can be checked to the degree of explicitness in which they are formalised; in particular, arguments may be checked as derivations in a formal system.
- Consistency between arguments, contextual information, the model and references to external assurance cases may be checked.
- Whether patterns and modules etc. are properly defined and correctly used can be checked.

A formal assurance case is not meant for guaranteeing absolute veracity of its claims. Even when its argument is checked to be a correct formal proof in a formal theory, the truth of its claims depends on whether the formal theory adequately models the real world.

What a formal assurance case enables is to let expert reviewers concentrate on judging the appropriateness of its contents rather than checking the integrity of its form such as internal consistency of various parts of the documentation.

2.3 Machine-processing

A formal assurance case can not only be machine-checked but also be machine-processed. Automated change management is an example. Automation in version control, traceability analysis, cause and effect analysis and impact analysis, etc. is vital for assurance cases of ever-changing, complex open systems. A formal assurance case makes possible more systematic and principled automation since the meaning of its components and relationship among them is made explicit to machines. For another example, it may be electronically connected to the systems in operation. The system can interpret its formal assurance case to react to its changing environment in accordance with the agreement written in the formal assurance case (Tokoro et. al. 2012).

3 Formal assurance cases

A formal assurance case consists of the *theory part* and the *reasoning part*. The theory part presents a formal theory in a formal logic as the basis of argument in the assurance case. The reasoning part presents a formal proof in the formal theory as the argument itself.

We first explain the basic idea using a familiar formal logic. A concrete realisation of the idea is then explained using the Agda language and its constructive type theory as the formal logic.

3.1 The basic idea

3.1.1 Reasoning part

Our starting point is the simple observation that the structure of an argument made explicit by a graphical notation is essentially the same as the structure of a formal proof in the natural deduction style. Roughly stated, the correspondence is as follows (elements of arguments are variously named in different communities; see Appendix E for a comparison and our usage of 'claim', 'strategy' and 'evidence').

- A claim is a proposition.
- A strategy is an inference rule.
- A piece of evidence is an axiom rule.
- To decompose a claim by a strategy into subclaims is to infer a conclusion by an inference rule from premises.
- To support a claim by evidence is to show that a proposition is an axiom by an axiom rule.

A formal proof of a proposition is either

- an application of an inference rule whose conclusion is the proposition to formal proofs of its premises, or
- an application of an axiom rule that shows the proposition is an axiom.

Thus, a formal proof in the reasoning part is an argument in which all claim decompositions and supports by evidence are 'correct' applications of inference and axiom rules that match a premise of one rule with a conclusion of another rule.

This analogy might have been too narrow for Toulmin, but it is reflected in his diagrammatic notation, GSN, and CAE. The precise correspondence to formal proofs, however, was made explicit much later, for instance, in (Hall et al. 2007), (Basir et al. 2009), and (Takeyama et al. 2012) in terms of sequent calculus, natural deduction, and constructive type theory, respectively.

3.1.2 Theory part

The role of the theory part is to specify those inference and axiom rules available to the reasoning part. This cannot be done without specifying what propositions are there, what predicates are available to construct them, what objects are there to be predicated. In all, the theory part specifies the ontology presumed by the reasoning part.

The specification is given as a choice of a formal logic and a formal theory in it. The former need not be fixed by our framework, but our intention is to choose a well-established one and let the choice be understood from the context. For this section, we take the many-sorted first order logic. A formal theory then consists of

- sort symbols to name a sort (type) of objects
- constant- and function-symbols with sort information to construct a term to denote an object
- proposition and predicate symbols with sort information to name a primitive concept or relation applicable to objects of specified sorts
- axioms (axiom rules) specifying relationship among all of the above (by restricting interpretations of symbols to those which make axioms true).

A formal theory does not add a new inference rule, but axioms in the form of implications can be used to that effect. We now consider 'inference rules' (strategies) available in the reasoning part to include derived inference rules of the given theory.

We emphasise again that the formality of the theory part and the reasoning part has nothing to do with the depth of analysis. In fact, any informal structured argument is trivially a formal proof in the formal theory that has every claim in the argument as a proposition symbol and every strategy and evidence as axiom rules. What is gained by the formality is the definiteness of the analysis of whatever depth, which makes it clear to humans and amenable to mechanical manipulation.

3.1.3 Problems

The framework of 'formal assurance case' as explained so far is not sufficient for realising the merits given in the previous section.

- It does not have a notion of definitions. In order to organise our analysis and express abstractions on top of primitive symbols and axioms, we must be able to make and use parameterised definitions that name complex terms, propositions and derived inferences. Some of that can be encoded in terms of symbols and axioms but are not practical.
- Declaring symbols and axiom rules of a formal theory is not a notion formalised within a formal logic.

In textbooks on formal logics, they are done at the level of running text in whatever way mathematically acceptable. Our framework must contain their formulation that is clear to humans and amenable to machine processing. Note that we have not discussed context nodes appearing in a structured argument yet. Those nodes are references to parts of declarations and definitions; hence the latter must be formulated first.

3.2 Agda language and the 'propositions as types' principle

Agda is a general purpose, dependently typed, functional programming language based on constructive type theory. It contains a variant of higher order intuitionistic logic through the principle of 'propositions as types, proofs as programs'. Roughly stated, the correspondence is as follows.

- Evidence is a piece of data. It is also called a direct proof.
- A proposition is a data type. The type specifies what data counts as a verification that the proposition holds, i.e., what data counts as evidence.
- An inference rule is a function that constructs evidence of its conclusion from evidence of its premises.
- A theory corresponds to a collection of library modules that declare and/or define types, functions and constants used to construct such programs-as-proofs.
- A program-as-proof is a correct formal proof if it passes type checking as a program.
- A context for a part of a proof is references to some of library modules that import declarations and definitions in them and make them available to that part of the proof.

Combined with the observations in Section 3.1, we immediately have the correspondence 'claims as types, arguments as programs'.

We use Agda for concreteness of exposition, but the idea is applicable in any language with similar features including a rich type system to express propositions: static type checking that guarantee termination without runtime exceptions, modern conveniences of programming language for abstraction, modularisation, and user-extendable syntax by infix, mixfix and binding operators.

3.3 Theory as formal theory written in Agda

Our running example for this section is a simplified version of the example assurance case for a control system in GSN Community Standard, Figure 6 (Origin Consulting Limited 2011) (see Figure 1).

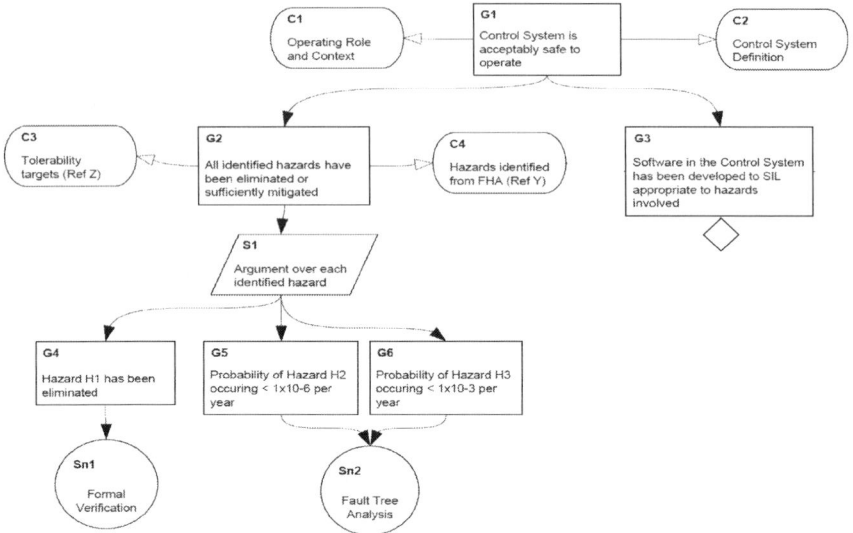

Fig. 1. Example assurance case for a control system

The corresponding formal assurance case written in Agda is given in Appendix B.

The reasoning part corresponds to the GSN diagram. Its top-level goal claims that the control system of interest is acceptably safe, and the safety is demonstrated by showing that the identified hazards of the system are treated and that the software is developed according to the appropriate SIL.

The theory part determines the vocabulary for concepts and objects used in the reasoning part, including the following.

3.3.1 Specific objects and their types mentioned in the assurance case

Example. The following introduces the type `Control-System-Type` of control systems in general and the particular object `Control-System` of that type, which is the subject of the assurance case. They are postulated, meaning that nothing is presumed yet besides so-named object of so-named type exist.

```
postulate
  Control-System-Type : Set
  Control-System : Control-System-Type
```

Example. The set `Identified-Hazards` is defined as the one consisting of exactly three references H1, H2, H3 to identified hazards.

```
data Identified-Hazards : Set where
  H1 H2 H3 : Identified-Hazards
```

3.3.2 Specific properties necessary to state the claims and basic assumptions

Example. The following introduces a primitive proposition `software-has-been-developed-to-appropriate-SIL`. Its type is `Set` because a proposition is a set as explained in Section 3.2.

```
postulate
  Software-has-been-developed-to-appropriate-SIL : Set
```

`Acceptably-safe-to-operate` is introduced as a predicate on `Control-System-Type`, i.e., a function that maps an object of that type to a proposition.

```
postulate
  Acceptably-safe-to-operate : Control-System-Type → Set
```

The proposition `Acceptably-safe-to-operate Control-System` obtained by applying this predicate to `Control-System` is the top-level claim G1 of Figure 1. We can write this as `Control-System is Acceptably-safe-to-operate`, using the auxiliary binary application operator `is` for readability.

Example. A basic assumption on the predicate `Acceptably-safe-to-operate` is that it can be shown to hold on `Control-System` from sub claims G2 and G3 of Figure 1. The following states this, introducing the primitive strategy `argument-over-product-and-process-aspects`.

```
postulate
  argument-over-product-and-process-aspects :
    (∀ h → h is Eliminated Or Sufficiently-mitigated) →
    Software-has-been-developed-to-appropriate-SIL →
    Control-System is Acceptably-safe-to-operate
```

Of course, most reviewers would reject making this an outright assumption. The point here is that formalisation forces us to be explicit about our presumptions.

Example. The predicate `Sufficiently-mitigated` on `Identified-Hazards` is defined using more primitive notions such as `Probability-of-Hazard`, `mitigation-target` and the binary predicate `<`.

```
Sufficiently-mitigated : Identified-Hazards → Set
Sufficiently-mitigated h =
  Probability-of-Hazard h < mitigation-target of h
```

3.3.4 References to evidence

Formally speaking, making a reference to external evidence of a claim is the same as making the claim a basic assumption.

```
postulate
  Formal-Verification   : H1 is Eliminated
```

However, reviewing evidence of a claim is much different from reviewing appropriateness of making an assumption, so references to evidence are introduced separately from other assumptions.

3.3.5 Context definitions

Those declarations and definitions of vocabulary for concepts and objects are grouped into several named modules. Context nodes appearing in the reasoning part correspond to references to modules.

Modules are used to group together related declarations and definitions, and to control access to them from outside modules. Identifiers declared or defined in a module named *module* are not directly visible outside the module. Outside the module, they must appear within the scope of an explicit 'open *module*' declaration that brings them into the current scope of visibility[1]. The same common name can be defined differently in different modules, and an open declaration sets 'context' for a use of the name by specifying to which definition it refers.

3.4 Reasoning as a proof in formal theory in Agda

As explained in Section 3.2, for the type representing a proposition, any well-typed Agda expression of the type is a formal proof of the proposition (in the theory given by the declarations and definitions accessible in the expression). However, we use the following specific style to represent the reasoning part in order to make explicit the correspondence with graphical notations such as GSN. The style is given by the following mutually recursive clauses.

A *case* has one of the following forms:

- *claim* by *argument*
- let open *module* in *case*

These are argument structures whose roots are claims. The second form corresponds to those with context nodes attached to roots.

---

[1] They can be used without opening the module by qualifying them with the module name.

Here, *claim* is a proposition, so it is a type, i.e., an expression of type `Set`. The infix binary function `by` takes a type and a value of that type as arguments and returns the second as the result. So if *claim* `by` *argument* is well-typed, *argument* is a formal proof of *claim*.

The expression `let open` *module* `in` *case* is well-typed if case is well-typed after opening the module named *module* for *case*, i.e., after making identifiers declared or defined in *module* visible in *case* (in addition to those identifiers that were already visible to the whole `let` expression). This corresponds to the situation where under-determined terms appearing in, say, a goal node in a GSN argument is explained by a reference given in a context node.

An *argument* has the one of the following forms:

- *strategy* • *case* ... • *case*
- *evidence*
- `let open` *module* `in` *argument*

These are argument structures whose roots are strategy (inference) nodes and evidence nodes. The third form has context nodes attached to roots.

Here *strategy* is a function that constructs an evidence of a parent claim from those of sub-claims. The infix binary function • is the (left associative) application. So if *strategy* • *case* ... • *case* is well-typed then we know that those sub-*cases* are indeed proofs of expected sub-claims. *evidence* is evidence data of a parent claim. That the *strategy* or *evidence* indeed gives evidence of the expected parent claim is checked when application of `by` in the previous clause is type-checked.

A further explanation can be found in Appendix D.

4 Rebuttal and evolution of assurance cases

Rebuttal to an assurance case is a central topic in our study of evolution of assurance cases. It is a driving force of its change; a rebuttal to an assurance case gives its writer an opportunity to remedy it by producing a new version that withstands the rebuttal. The process of such rebuttal and remedy strengthens the assurance case.

Any part of assurance case can be variously attacked. This section concentrates on the kind of attacks where a claim of an assurance case is attacked by showing a proposition contradicting the claim.

A theory in which both a claim and its negation is proved is inconsistent in general, and useless as a basis of further arguments because any claim can be proved in an inconsistent theory. If the theory of the rebutter proves both the original claim as well, then we must conclude that the thesis is presented in an inconsistent and useless theory.

On the other hand, a rebuttal typically occurs when our knowledge grows with newly established facts and rules. The theory on which rebuttal is based should be considered more up to date and preferable than the theory of the original assurance case. We address this problem in the following.

Solutions to this problem, typically found in the area of argumentation in AI, involve replacing ordinary logic with certain kinds of unorthodox logic. Paraconsistent logic allows for meaningful arguments in the presence of inconsistency by denying that anything can be inferred from inconsistency. Non-monotonic logic denies that the claim shown in the original theory can always be shown in the theory extended with newly established facts and rules, thus possibly avoiding inconsistency in the latter.

The rest of this section presents our work in progress on rebuttals, which avoids the need for such special logics by formulating rebuttals in our framework of formal assurance cases. We use the dialectic formula of 'thesis, antithesis and synthesis' in exposition.

4.1 Thesis, antithesis and synthesis

Intuitively, the thesis is any proposition, the antithesis is another proposition contradictory to the thesis, and the synthesis resolves the conflict by reconciling the truth underlying both the thesis and the antithesis. These three entities are formulated as follows in our formulation of rebuttal. (See Figure 2 for the well-known example of 'The penguin Tweety does not fly'.)

A *thesis* consists of (T, A), where T is the theory part of some assurance case and A is its top-level claim. We know A has a proof in T because A is its top-level claim; we write $T \vdash A$ for this fact. In our example, A is taken to be $(\forall x)\ Bird(x) \rightarrow Flies(x)$.

An *antithesis* (T_R, T_C) to the thesis (T, A) consists of two theories T_R, T_C such that T_C is a subtheory of both T and T_R, A is well-formed in T_C, and there is a proof of the claim $\neg A$ in the theory T_R (i.e., $T_R \vdash \neg A$). T_C gives the common grounds to the thesis and the antithesis; the symbols in A must be common in the thesis and antithesis, for instance.

The *synthesis* of a thesis (T, A) and its antithesis (T_R, T_C) is a pair (T_S, A') of a consistent extension T_S of T_R for which $T_S \vdash A'$. Note that A must have no proofs in T_S ($T_S \nvdash A$) for T_S to be consistent. The synthesis is meant to be the arbitration in the following sense: it resolves the contradiction by working in the theory T_S where A is not provable but $\neg A$ is. The intention is that the arbitration retains as much part of A as possible.

postulate
$(\forall x) \neg Penguin(x) \rightarrow (Bird(x) \rightarrow Flies(x))$
$\vdash \neg ((\forall x) Bird(x) \rightarrow Flies(x))$
$\nvdash (\forall x) Bird(x) \rightarrow Flies(x)$

$\vdash \neg ((\forall x) Bird(x) \rightarrow Flies(x))$
$\vdash (\forall x) Bird(x) \rightarrow Flies(x)$

SYNTHESIS T_S

$T_R + T$ contra-
diction

ANTITHESIS   THESIS

Tweety: Obj
Penguin: Obj → Set
postulate
$(\forall x) Penguin(x) \rightarrow \neg Flies(x)$
$(\forall x) Penguin(x) \rightarrow Bird(x)$
Penguin(Tweety)
$\vdash \neg ((\forall x) Bird(x) \rightarrow Flies(x))$

T_R T

postulate
$(\forall x) Bird(x) \rightarrow Flies(x)$

T_C

Bird : Obj → Set
Flies : Obj → Set

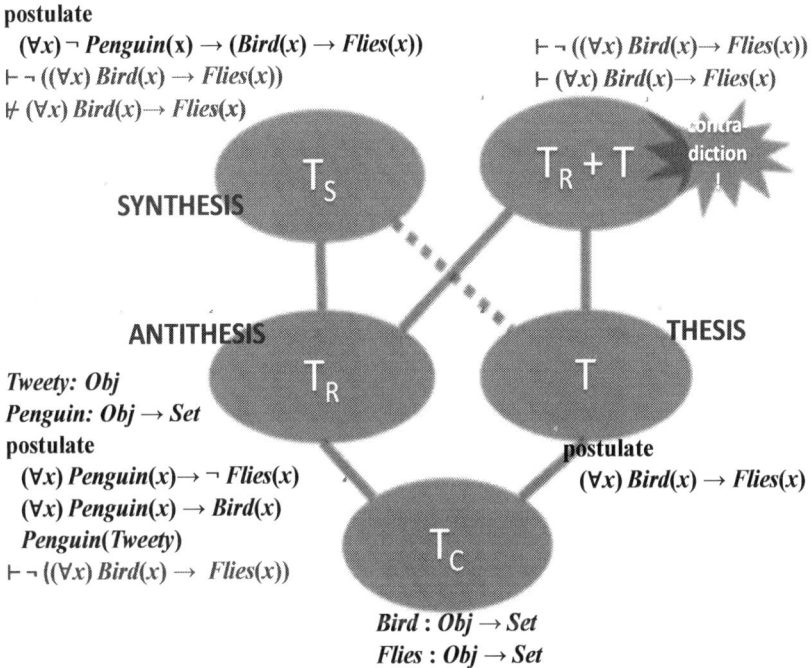

Fig. 2.Thesis, antithesis and synthesis

4.2 Rebuttal and change of theory

In our formulation, rebuttal to a thesis (T, A) proceeds as follows. The person who rebuts the claim A examines its proof in T and identifies its part that he does not agree. The part he agrees is the common ground theory T_C. We consider the case where A is already well-formed in T_C. The rebutter extends T_C to T_R and he proves $\neg A$ there. The thesis is rebutted in this sense. Note that the rebuttal is done in T_R, not in $T + T_R$ that is inconsistent.

The amendment is given by a synthesis (T_S, A'). The requirement that T_S extends T_R means that the rebuttal must be fully respected. The negation $\neg A$ should be provable in the amendment, in particular. The claim A of the thesis should not be provable in the amendment, but its content should be retained as much as possible. This corresponds to the requirement that $T_R \nvdash A$ but $T_S \vdash A'$.

Rebuttal is often regarded as an example of *non-monotonic reasoning* (McCarthy 1980) because the claim once proved becomes unprovable after adding the rebutter's counterexample to the original theory. Here is a presumption that a global theory is given, which is common to all arguments at each instant, and it can only grow as the vocabulary and axioms grow. Our formulation avoids the need for special non-monotonic logics by making explicit that different arguments are made in different theories. In particular, the rebutter need not argue in an extension of the 'current' theory, but can first remove the part that is responsible for the proof of the claim, namely $(T - T_C)$.

4.3 Arbitration

The conditions we put so far on the synthesis (T_S, A') do not capture our intention for it to be an arbitration between theory (T, A) and antithesis (T_R, T_C). Any theorem A' of any extension T_S of T_R counts as a synthesis, with no regard at all to A. We do not have an answer to the question 'Which theory should be considered to retain the content of the claim A as much as possible?', but we only note there are some subtleties here.

Consider the case where A is of the form $(\forall x)\, P[x]$ and a counterexample a with a proof of $\neg P[a]$ in T_R is given. It seems natural to restrict the range of x and consider A' of the form $(\forall x)\, D[x] \to P[x]$ for some choice of $D[x]$ with $T_R \not\vdash D[a]$. Then A' is consistent with $\neg P[a]$ and $(T_R + A', A')$ is a candidate synthesis. It also seems natural to require the choice of range restriction $D[x]$ to be as weak as possible, in order to retain the content of A as much as possible. However, this requirement determines $D[x]$ to be $P[x]$ and A' is $(\forall x)\, P[x] \to P[x]$, a purely logical tautology. Somehow, we manage to lose all the content of $(\forall x)\, P[x]$ in our attempt to retain it as much as possible.

This observation makes clear that identifying logically equivalent propositions as it does is far too coarse to discuss the 'contents' of a proposition in a theory. This is no surprise considering the difference between the statement of a deep mathematical theorem and the statement 'true'.

A well-known example of 'The penguin Tweety does not fly' written in Agda is given in Appendix C. There, $P[x]$ and $D[x]$ correspond to $Bird(x) \to Flies(x)$ and $\neg Penguin(x)$, respectively. This choice of $D[x]$ seems the only reasonable one for this example, but its justification is left for further study. One hint is the role $Penguin(\text{Tweety})$ plays in the proof of $\neg ((\forall x)\, Bird(x) \to Flies(x))$.

5 Conclusion

A framework for 'formal assurance cases' is proposed. The concept of a formal assurance case consisting of its theory part presenting a formal theory and its reasoning part presenting a formal proof in the theory is explained. Its concrete realisation in the Agda language is shown. The explicit theory part of a formal assurance case improves its assurance communication and together with its formality enables machine-checking and other machine processing.

The framework is also for accounting the evolving aspect of assurance cases in the interest of Open Systems Dependability. As one of the significant evolution processes, rebuttals to assurance cases and subsequent amendments are analysed within the framework.

Future work includes

- libraries for building up the theory parts of formal assurance cases such as basic ontologies and argumentation patterns
- more analysis on amendments to assurance cases to accommodate rebuttals but to reflect the original case's content 'as much as possible'
- study on evolution processes of assurance cases of the kind other than rebuttal to the conclusions, including attacks to inference rules and axioms and changes in environment and requirements.

Appendix A: The role of formal assurance cases in Open Systems Dependability

Modern systems tend to be huge and complex. They must exchange services with a wide variety of other interconnected systems. Those surrounding systems are managed according to their own principles and stakeholders, and their interfaces are subject to change for various reasons. The pervasive nature of the system means that it must serve a diverse set of stakeholders. Each has his/her own objective that changes from time to time and there may be no single authority responsible for the system. External conditions for the system, such as requirements and constraints, change frequently and unpredictably, and are hard to be grasped completely at any given time.

Similar uncertainty and incompleteness are also present within the system itself, i.e., about its functions, internal structure, and the boundary. Its subsystems are often managed by different parties and the integrators of the system may not have complete knowledge and control on them. Services and components may be dynamically added to or removed from the system during its operation by/for various stakeholders, making the system boundary ambiguous.

For these reasons, as well as the sheer complexity and scale of the system, it is very difficult for any stakeholder to specify, comprehend, or control the system and its management to any sufficient completeness and certainty. Unforeseen changes and unexpected failures of various degrees are a part of the system's nature. The use of the term open systems emphasises this aspect of modern systems.

To summarise, systems change and systems are vague. Not only the systems themselves but also their environment and requirements for them change all the time. The boundary of a system is vague; specifications are inherently incomplete; and different stakeholders have different presuppositions.

Open Systems Viewpoint is a viewpoint of systems that takes these problems into account, and dependability considered from this viewpoint is called *Open Systems Dependability*.

DEOS project identifies the requirements for Open Systems Dependability (Tokoro 2012). The requirements are divided into two parts: those for system life cycle processes and those for assurance cases of the system.

The set of requirements for the life cycle of a system consists of the following. The assurance case of the system plays an essential role in achievement of each requirement.

Consensus building to establish a consensus among stakeholders of the system as the basis of the system life cycle. The assurance case works as the communication tool and as the artefact that records the resulting consensus.

Accountability achievement to achieve confidence and trust in the system of interest and to share information about it among stakeholders and interconnected systems in the environment. The assurance case provides data necessary to account for decisions and actions taken. It also contains data for post failure investigation of the cause of failure.

Failure response to prepare for failures due to unexpected causes[2]. Usual risk treatment emphasises pre-failure actions such as risk prevention and mitigation, but post failure actions are required here. Nobody can identify all causes of failures, so there can be no complete prevention and mitigation. Response to failures depends on the situation; it should be agreed among stakeholders in advance. The assurance case describes the agreement.

Change accommodation to detect the change of requirements, environments and the system of interest itself, to reflect it and to take the action needed for continuing to provide the service required, thus continuing to keep the dependability of the system of interest. Therefore, the consensus is modified as a result of change accommodation, and the assurance case must be rewritten accordingly. The assurance case provides information on what needs be changed and how.

Assurance cases must be rigorous and unambiguous, so that no stakeholders misunderstand it. Rigor and unambiguity are requested to assurance cases independently of Open Systems Dependability, but they are more requested in this context, because much less implicit and tacit presumption exists there.

Formalisation is one of the effective means to make assurance case rigorous and unambiguous. This explains why the notion of formal assurance cases plays an essential role in Open Systems Dependability.

---

[2] To prepare for such failures are possible only through preparing what to do after such failure occurs; prevention and mitigation are not possible because the cause is not identified.

Appendix B: Example assurance case

```
module ExampleAssuranceCase where
open import Data.Sum
open import PoorMansControlledEnglish


----------------------------------------------------------------
-- Theory part
----------------------------------------------------------------
module Theory where
  postulate
    Probability-Type : Set
    impossible 1×10⁻³-per-year 1×10⁻⁶-per-year : Probability-Type
    _<_ : Probability-Type → Probability-Type → Set
  infix 1 _<_

  module C2-Control-System-Definition where
    postulate
      Control-System-Type : Set
      Control-System : Control-System-Type

  module C4-Hazards-identified-from-FHA where
    data Identified-Hazards : Set where
      H1 H2 H3 : Identified-Hazards
    postulate
      Probability-of-Hazard
        : Identified-Hazards → Probability-Type

  module C3-Tolerability-targets where
    open C4-Hazards-identified-from-FHA

    mitigation-target : Identified-Hazards → Probability-Type
    mitigation-target H1 = impossible
    mitigation-target H2 = 1×10⁻³-per-year
    mitigation-target H3 = 1×10⁻⁶-per-year

    Sufficiently-mitigated : Identified-Hazards → Set
    Sufficiently-mitigated h =
      Probability-of-Hazard h < mitigation-target of h

    postulate
      Eliminated : Identified-Hazards → Set

    argument-over-each-identified-hazard :
        H1 is Eliminated →
        H2 is Sufficiently-mitigated →
        H3 is Sufficiently-mitigated →
        ∀ h → h is Eliminated Or Sufficiently-mitigated
    argument-over-each-identified-hazard p1 p2 p3 H1 = inj₁ p1
    argument-over-each-identified-hazard p1 p2 p3 H2 = inj₂ p2
    argument-over-each-identified-hazard p1 p2 p3 H3 = inj₂ p3

  module C1-Operating-Role-and-Context where
    open C2-Control-System-Definition
    open C3-Tolerability-targets
```

```
open C4-Hazards-identified-from-FHA

postulate
  Software-has-been-developed-to-appropriate-SIL : Set

  Acceptably-safe-to-operate : Control-System-Type → Set

  argument-over-product-and-process-aspects :
    (∀ h → h is Eliminated Or Sufficiently-mitigated) →
    Software-has-been-developed-to-appropriate-SIL →
    Control-System is Acceptably-safe-to-operate
---------------------------------------------------------------
-- References to evidence
---------------------------------------------------------------
module Evidence where
  open Theory
  open C4-Hazards-identified-from-FHA
  open C3-Tolerability-targets

  postulate
    Formal-Verification    : H1 is Eliminated
    Fault-Tree-Analysis-2
      : Probability-of-Hazard H2 < 1×10⁻³-per-year
    Fault-Tree-Analysis-3
      : Probability-of-Hazard H3 < 1×10⁻⁶-per-year


---------------------------------------------------------------
-- Reasoning part
---------------------------------------------------------------
module Reasoning where
  open Theory
  open Evidence
  main =
    let open C1-Operating-Role-and-Context
        open C2-Control-System-Definition
    in
    Control-System is Acceptably-safe-to-operate
    by argument-over-product-and-process-aspects
      • (let open C3-Tolerability-targets
             open C4-Hazards-identified-from-FHA
         in
         (∀ h → h is Eliminated Or Sufficiently-mitigated)
         by argument-over-each-identified-hazard
           • (H1 is Eliminated
              by Formal-Verification)
           • (Probability-of-Hazard H2 < 1×10⁻³-per-year
              by Fault-Tree-Analysis-2)
           • (Probability-of-Hazard H3 < 1×10⁻⁶-per-year
              by Fault-Tree-Analysis-3))
      • (Software-has-been-developed-to-appropriate-SIL
         by ? )
```

Appendix C: Example of rebuttal written in Agda

```
module RebuttalExample where

open import Data.Bool
open import Data.Empty
open import Data.Nat
open import Data.Product
open import Data.Sum
open import Relation.Binary.PropositionalEquality
open import Relation.Nullary
open import Relation.Unary
open import PoorMansControlledEnglish

Contradiction = ⊥

module Initial-AC where
  module Theory where
    postulate
      Obj    : Set
      Bird   : Obj → Set
      Flies  : Obj → Set
      tweety : Obj
      tweety-is-a-bird : Bird tweety
      all-birds-fly    : ∀ {x} → Bird x → Flies x

  open Theory
  tweety-flies =
    Flies tweety
    by all-birds-fly
       • (Bird tweety
          by tweety-is-a-bird)

module Initial-AC-Decomposed where
  module Theory where
    module Common where
      postulate
        Obj    : Set
        Bird   : Obj → Set
        Flies  : Obj → Set
        tweety : Obj
        tweety-is-a-bird : Bird tweety
    module Objectionable where
      open Common
      postulate
        all-birds-fly : ∀ {x} → Bird x → Flies x

  open Theory.Common
  open Theory.Objectionable
  tweety-flies : Flies tweety
  tweety-flies = all-birds-fly tweety-is-a-bird
```

```
module Rebutting-Argument where
  module Theory where
    open Initial-AC-Decomposed.Theory.Common
    postulate
      Penguin              : Obj → Set
      a-penguin-is-a-bird  : ∀ {x} → Penguin x → Bird x
      a-penguin-does-not-fly : ∀ {x} → Penguin x → ¬ Flies x
      tweety-is-a-penguin  : Penguin tweety

  open Initial-AC-Decomposed.Theory.Common
  open Theory
  tweety-does-not-fly =
    ¬ Flies tweety
    by a-penguin-does-not-fly
       • (Penguin tweety by tweety-is-a-penguin)

module Contradiction where
  open Initial-AC-Decomposed.Theory.Common
  open Initial-AC-Decomposed.Theory.Objectionable
  open Rebutting-Argument.Theory
  open Initial-AC-Decomposed
  open Rebutting-Argument
  contradiction : Contradiction
  contradiction = tweety-does-not-fly tweety-flies

module Revised-AC where
  module Theory where
    open Initial-AC-Decomposed.Theory.Common
    open Rebutting-Argument.Theory
    postulate
      non-penguin-birds-fly
        : ∀ {x} → ¬ Penguin x → Bird x → Flies x

  open Initial-AC-Decomposed.Theory.Common
  open Rebutting-Argument.Theory
  open Theory
  -- WHAT? No synthesis here, just a concession.


module Undercutting-Argument where

  open Initial-AC-Decomposed.Theory.Common
  open Rebutting-Argument.Theory

  not-all-birds-fly =
    (¬ (∀ {x} → Bird x → Flies x))
    by λ (hypothesis : ∀ {x} → Bird x → Flies x) →
       Contradiction
       by a-penguin-does-not-fly
          • (tweety is Penguin by tweety-is-a-penguin)
          • (Flies tweety
```

```
                  by hypothesis
                    • (tweety is Bird
                       by a-penguin-is-a-bird
                         • (Penguin tweety by tweety-is-a-
penguin))))
```

Appendix D: Using a proof assistant to construct assurance cases[3]

D.1 Introduction

An assurance case is a documented body of *evidence* that provides a convincing and valid *argument* for specified *claims* that a system has critical properties for a given application in a given environment. Assurance cases are natural language documents, but it has been observed that their structure is analogous to that of formal proofs of a logical formula. Using this, but still keeping the flexibility of natural language description, we formulate our format D-Case for assurance cases in Agda, a programming and proof-description language based on constructive type theory. This approach can bring the following features into the assurance case development.

Correctness by construction. Agda provides a powerful dependent type system, so the interactive type checker of Agda system can perform static analysis of an assurance case, resulting in *correctness by construction*. The analysis includes fine dependency checking between parts of assurance cases.

Processing assurance cases. Agda's 'propositions as types, proofs as program' paradigm makes it possible to write programs that generate or analyse assurance cases with correctness guarantee.

Parameterised module. Agda's nested parameterised module works as the module system for assurance cases.

Natural notations. Mixfix operators with unicode character set can be defined for introducing easy-to-read notations.

The system D-Case/Agda (Takeyama 2011) implements this approach.

---

[3] The content of this Appendix was originally published as Fast Abstract (Takeyama et. al 2012) in Proceedings of DSN 2012 distributed as USB data. Reproduced with permission from OMNIPRESS.

D.2 D-Case in Agda

The concept of a D-Case (Tokoro 2012) extends that of an assurance case; it is not just a top-level control document for off-line assurance processes, but is on-line data from which a running system sources its failure response etc. as agreed by stakeholders. Here we concentrate on its notation, which is similar to GSN (Goal Structured Notation (Kelly and Weaver 2004, Origin Consulting Limited 2011)) and CAE (Claims, Arguments and Evidences (Bishop and Bloomfield 1998)). More formally, a D-Case description is a pair of a *formal theory* and a *proof tree* in it. The formal theory is defined in the logic of Agda with addition of postulated constants that represent atomic propositions, ad-hoc axioms and ad-hoc inference rules.

D.2.1 Abstract syntax

D-Case	::= Goal Argument
	| Context D-Case
Argument	::= Strategy { D-Case }
	| Evidence
	| Context Argument

We formulate proof trees in the Natural Deduction style. Introduction and discharge of assumptions are explained later.

- A goal statement of a D-Case is a proposition. A D-Case consists of either a goal statement (proposition) with an argument to substantiate it, or a context with another D-Case. The context introduces, defines, or explains the notions appearing in the D-Case.
- An argument is a proof tree without conclusion. An argument consists of either

  - several sub D-Cases combined by a strategy, which is a derived inference rule
  - a direct evidence of the goal statement, which is a postulated axiom rule
  - another argument in a specified context.

The graphical representation for the abstract syntax is shown in Figure D.1.

D.2.2 Concrete syntax in Agda

A D-Case (the proof part) is represented as an Agda term using the 'propositions as types, proofs as programs' correspondence. A piece of evidence is a piece of data. A goal is a data type. The type specifies what data counts as a verification that the goal is achieved, i.e., what data counts as evidence. A strategy is a function that constructs evidence of its goal from evidence of its sub goals.

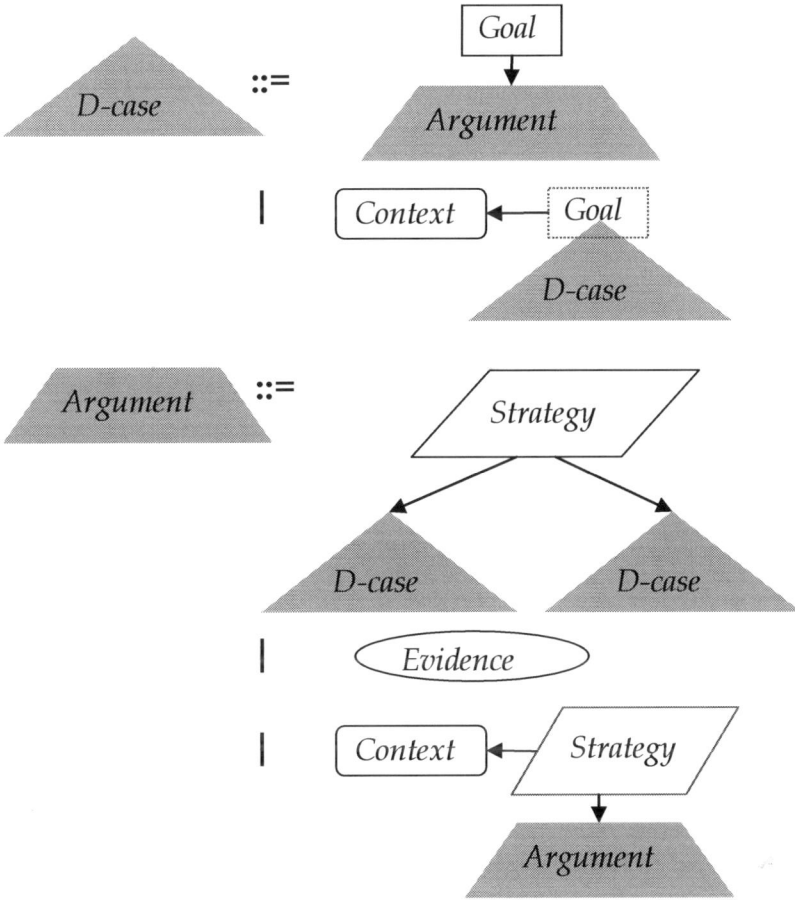

Fig. D.1. Graphical representation of abstract syntax

Although plain Agda suffices to express and check logical contents of assurance cases, a D-Case in Agda is written using specially defined Agda functions that form an embedded language. This provides D-Case writers with a presentation layer to express the structure of the D-Case explicitly, as distinct from lower-level or programmatic details of formalisation, and with natural language descriptions for its parts. D-Case/Agda system uses this explicit structure to translate between a D-Case in Agda and its graphical representation.

The syntax of D-Case in Agda is given by EBNF as follows; bold characters are literals, i.e., the above special functions, and *{}* is the EBNF notation for zero or more repetition.

$$
\begin{array}{lll}
\textit{D-Case} & ::= \textit{Goal} \ni \textit{Argument} \\
& \mid \quad \texttt{Context[}\; \textit{Context} \;/\; \textit{D-Case} \;] \\
& \mid \quad \textit{Argument} \\
\textit{Argument} & ::= \textit{Strategy} \{ \bullet \textit{D-Case} \} \\
& \mid \quad \textit{Evidence} \\
& \mid \quad \texttt{Context[}\; \textit{Context} \;/\; \text{Argument} \;] \\
& \mid \quad \forall \texttt{Intro}\{ \textit{Domain} \} \;\$\; \textit{Lambda-D-Case} \\
& \mid \quad \rightarrow\!\texttt{Intro}\{ \textit{FormalGoal} \} \;\$\; \textit{Lambda-D-Case} \\
\textit{Goal} & ::= \textit{FormalGoal} \\
& \mid \quad \langle\!\langle\, \textit{FormalGoal} \;/\; \textit{Description} \,\rangle\!\rangle \\
\textit{Strategy} & ::= \textit{FormalStrategy} \\
& \mid \quad \langle\, \textit{FormalStrategy} \;/\; \textit{Description} \,\rangle \\
\textit{Evidence} & ::= \textit{FormalEvidence} \\
& \mid \quad \langle\, \textit{FormalEvidence} \;/\; \textit{Description} \,\rangle
\end{array}
$$

FormalGoal   ::= *agda-term* (of type Set)
FormalStrategy   ::= *agda-term* (of the right function type)
FormalEvidence   ::= *agda-term* (of the right type)
Context   ::= *Description*
Description   ::= *agda-term* (of type String)
Lambda-D-Case   ::= **λ** agda-variable-identifier → *D-Case*
Domain   ::= *agda-term* (of type Set)

For type checking, the special functions are defined as follows.

- The value of $X \ni x$ is x, which must have type X.
- $x \bullet y$ is the function application; the function argument y must have the domain type of the function x.
- The value of $\texttt{Context[}\; x \;/\; y \;]$ is y.
- The values of $\langle\!\langle\, x \;/\; y \,\rangle\!\rangle$ and $\langle\, x \;/\; y \,\rangle$ are x.

Thus, to have a well typed D-Case term $G \ni t$ is to have a proof t of the goal proposition G. For translation to graphical representation, these are treated as primitive constants, so that any Agda program that computes to a D-Case term can be used as a representation.

While a Context is merely a string in this version, it can be more formally represented in Agda as local declarations in a `let`-expression.

For a goal 'for all x in domain D, $P(x)$', exhibiting a function that sends any object d in D to a *D-Case* with the goal $P(x)$ counts as a valid argument. When such a function is given as a λ-expression **λ** $x \rightarrow (P(x) \ni \textit{Argument})$, the Agda term $\forall \texttt{Intro}\{ D \} \;\$\; \boldsymbol{\lambda}\, x \rightarrow (P(x) \ni \textit{Argument})$ is an *Argument* for the goal $\forall(x : D) \rightarrow P(x)$. Its meaning is the same as the original λ-expression; $\forall \texttt{Intro}\{ D \}$ is the identity function on the function type. This should be seen as introducing a variable x for an assumed object in D to be used in the argument for $P(x)$.

The *Argument* →Intro{ G_1 } $ λ h → (G_2 ∋ *Argument*)) is similar, for the goal G_1 → G_2. The variable h is introduced for an assumed *Evidence* of G_1; the λ-expression maps it to a *D-Case* with the goal G_2 in which h can be used as an evidence for G_1.

Examples of D-Cases in Agda, some using the module mechanism of Agda, some using Agda programming for D-Case patterns and D-Case generations, etc., can be found in the distribution package of D-Case/Agda system (Takeyama 2011).

Appendix E: Terms for elements of an argument

	Statement to be asserted	Inference of a claim from subclaims	Information that directly supports a claim
CAE, ISO/IEC 15026-2	Claim	Argument	Evidence
GSN	Goal	Strategy	Solution
[Section 1- 4]	Claim	Strategy	Evidence
[Appendix D]	Goal	Strategy	Evidence
OMG SACM	Claim	AssertedInference	Evidence

Acknowledgments This work is supported by the project 'Study on User-Oriented Dependability' in the DEOS (Dependability Engineering for Open Systems) research area (programme) of JST CREST scheme, and the NII-AIST joint project 'Study on Evolution Process of Arguments.'

References

Agda Team (2012) Agda Wiki. http://wiki.portal.chalmers.se/agda/pmwiki.php. Accessed 5 October 2012

Basir et al (2009) Deriving Safety Cases from Machine-Generated Proofs. In Proceedings of Workshop on Proof-Carrying Code and Software Certification (PCC'09), http://eprints.soton.ac.uk/id/eprint/271267, Los Angeles, USA

Bishop P and Bloomfield R (1998) A Methodology for Safety Case Development. Industrial Perspectives of Safety-Critical Systems: Proceedings of the Sixth Safety-critical Systems Symposium. Birmingham

Hall JG, Mannering D and Rapanotti L (2007) Arguing safety with problem oriented software engineering. In the Proceedings of High Assurance Systems Engineering Symposium, 2007, HASE'07, 10th IEEE, 23–32

Kelly TP and Weaver RA (2004) The Goal Structuring Notation – A Safety Argument Notation, in Proceedings of the Dependable Systems and Networks 2004 Workshop on Assurance Cases

McCarthy J (1980) Circumscription – A Form of Non-Monotonic Reasoning, Artificial Intelligence, 13: 27–39

Origin Consulting Limited (2011) GSN Community Standard, Version 1

Toulmin SE (1958) The Uses of Argument, Cambridge University Press. Updated edition published in 2003 by the same publisher (ISBN 978-0-521-53483-3)

Takeyama M (2011) 'D-Case in Agda' Verification Tool (D-Case/Agda). http://wiki.portal.
    chalmers.se/agda/pmwiki.php?n=D-Case-Agda.D-Case-Agda. Accessed 9 October 2012
Takeyama M, Kido H, Kinoshita Y (2012) Using a proof assistant to construct assurance cases,
    Fast Abstract in Proceedings of Dependable Systems and Networks (DSN) 2012
Tokoro M (ed.) (2012) Open Systems Dependability – Dependability Engineering for Ever-
    Changing Systems, CRC Press (ISBN 978-1466577510)

A Formal, Systematic Approach to STPA using Event-B Refinement and Proof

John Colley and Michael Butler

Electronics and Computer Science, University of Southampton

Southampton, UK

Abstract System-Theoretic Process Analysis (STPA) from Leveson is a technique for hazard analysis developed to identify more thoroughly the causal factors in complex safety-critical systems, including software design errors. Event-B is a proof-based modelling language and method that enables the development of specifications using a formal notion of refinement. We propose an approach to hazard analysis where system requirements are captured as monitored, controlled, mode and commanded phenomena and STPA is applied to the controlled phenomena to identify systematically the safety constraints. These are then represented formally in an Event-B specification which is amenable to formal refinement and proof.

1 Introduction

System-Theoretic Process Analysis (STPA), described in (Leveson 2012), is a technique for hazard analysis developed to identify more thoroughly the causal factors in complex safety-critical systems, including software design errors. STPA has been applied to a wide range of safety critical applications (Leveson 2012). Event-B (Abrial 2010) is a proof-based modelling language and method that enables the development of specifications using a formal notion of refinement. The Rodin platform (Abrial et al. 2010) is the Eclipse-based IDE that provides automated support for Event-B modelling, refinement and mathematical proof. The Event-B method has also been used in the deployment of safety critical systems for automotive and railway applications.

We propose an approach to hazard analysis where system requirements are captured as *monitored*, *controlled*, *mode* and *commanded* phenomena and STPA is applied to the controlled phenomena to identify systematically the safety constraints. These are then represented formally in an Event-B specification, which is amenable to formal refinement and proof.

In Section 2 we provide an overview of Event-B with particular attention paid to formal Event-B refinement.

In Section 3 we show how our proposed approach to hazard analysis can be applied, using a domestic washing machine case study, to derive systematically the safety constraints expressed in *natural language*.

In Section 4 we illustrate how the natural language safety constraints can be represented formally in Event-B.

In Section 5 we present a summary of our approach and the direction of our future work.

2 Event-B

In Event-B, an abstract model comprises a *machine* that specifies the high-level behaviour and a *context*, made up of sets, constants and their properties, that represents the type environment for the high-level machine. The machine is represented as a set of *state variables*, v and a set of events, *guarded atomic actions*, which modify the state. If more than one action is enabled, then one is chosen non-deterministically for *execution*, an observable transition on the state variables which must preserve an *invariant* on the variables, $I(v)$.

A more concrete representation of the machine may then be created which refines the abstract machine, and the abstract context may be extended to support the types required by the refinement. *Gluing invariants* are used to verify that the concrete machine is a correct *refinement*: any behaviour of the concrete machine must satisfy the abstract behaviour. Gluing invariants give rise to proof obligations for pairs of abstract and corresponding concrete events. Events may also have parameters, which take, non-deterministically, the values that will make the guards in which they are referenced true.

Event-B refinement allows a model to be built gradually (Abrial and Hallerstede 2006), starting with an abstract model and then introducing successive, more concrete refinements. Adding variables achieves spatial extension and adding events temporal extension. Events in the abstract model may be refined by one or more events in the concrete model. These concrete events can modify the state of new variables introduced in the refinement, but must preserve the behaviour with regard to the variables declared in the abstract model. New events may also be introduced in the refinement. These events are not allowed to assign values to abstract variables, but can assign values to new variables introduced in the refinement.

3 The washing machine case study

We use this case study to explore a systematic method for identifying both functional and safety requirements. We start with an overview of the washing machine system.

3.1 System overview

We are concerned with developing a master controller, which, on receiving a set of user settings from the control panel, will control the water drum system and agitator motor to comply with those user settings.

3.2 Discovering the functional requirements

We investigate the functional requirements using a method that identifies the system phenomena and then structures the functional requirements according to these phenomena (Yeganefard and Butler 2012). The phenomena that we shall explore are the *monitored* phenomena, *commanded* phenomena, *controlled* phenomena and *mode* phenomena.

3.3 Monitored phenomena

First we examine the phenomena that will be monitored by the washing machine controller.

3.3.1 Drum water level

The controller will receive the current level from the water level sensor.

3.3.2 Drum water temperature

The controller will receive the current temperature from the water temperature sensor.

3.3.3 Door position

The controller will receive from the door sensor whether the door is closed or open.

3.3.4 Vibration level

The controller will receive from the vibration sensor the level of vibration.

3.4 The commanded phenomena

These are the phenomena that are driven by the user through the washing machine control panel.

3.4.1 Water level setting

The controller will receive the water level setting from the control panel. In this case two settings are possible: half load and full load.

3.4.2 Cycle setting

The controller will receive the cycle setting identifier from the control panel and decode the cycle setting. The cycle setting consists of

- the mode sequence, for example: idle, wash, rinse, spin, rinse, spin, idle
- the mode duration: how long each mode will run
- the spin speed.

3.4.3 Water temperature setting

The controller will receive the water temperature setting from the control panel: 30, 40 or 60 degrees Celsius.

3.4.4 Start signal

The controller will receive the start signal from the control panel.

3.5 The controlled phenomena

These are the phenomena that are driven by the master controller.

3.5.1 Door lock

- The controller will lock the door at the start of the cycle.
- The controller will unlock the door at the end of the cycle.
- The door will remain locked during the cycle.

3.5.2 Agitator motor

- The controller directs the speed and rotation direction of the agitator motor.
- The agitator motor will be stationary when the door is unlocked.

3.5.3 Water control valves

The controller activates and de-activates the hot and cold water valves to meet the water level and temperature requirements.

3.5.4 Water drain pump

The controller activates the water drain pump to meet the water level requirements.

3.5.5 Heater

The controller activates and de-activates the heater to meet the temperature requirements.

3.6 The mode phenomena

The controller modes are idle, washing, rinsing and spinning.

3.7 Discovering the safety requirements

The following two quotations from (Leveson 2012) encapsulate the approach to safety analysis, developed by Leveson, which we use in the case study.

> Any controller – human or automated – needs a model of the process being controlled to control it effectively.

> Accidents can occur when the controller's process model does not match the state of the system being controlled and the controller issues unsafe commands.

Simply trying to make components more reliable does not in itself make a system safer. Safety is enhanced when the controller(s) respond to component failures in a way which ensures that the resulting hazards are correctly and safely managed.

Consider a potential hazard arising from the heater sub-system of the washing machine. The water could overheat dangerously if the controller cannot monitor water temperature properly. If the temperature sensor is faulty, the controller could switch off the heater if the value read from sensor is out of operating range. If, however, the sensor reports a value within the operating range but the actual value is *out of operating range*, how can the controller respond to this hazard? Sensor redundancy, with the introduction of a voting system in the controller, can decrease the probability that the hazard will not be detected. An alternative approach, however, is for the controller to predict the rise in water temperature and compare it with the reported rise.

The controller needs independent verification of the sensed values to detect failure. This can be provided by values from a different sensor or the controller can generate predicted values in the absence of other sources of data.

3.8 System-Theoretic Process Analysis

Leveson proposes a rigorous approach, System-Theoretic Process Analysis (STPA), which consists of the following three steps.

1. Identify potentially hazardous control actions.
2. Derive the safety constraints.
3. Determine how unsafe control actions could occur.

STPA has been used by the US Missile Defense Agency to characterize the residual safety risk of the ballistic missile defense system (Perreira et al. 2006). A simulator of the interceptor flight computer is used to predict the expected behaviour and therefore to detect a failure in the system.

In our method, we perform a systematic analysis of the *controlled phenomena* identified in the requirements analysis: the door lock, the heater, the water drain pump, the water control valves and the agitator motor.

3.8.1 The door sub-system

Consider a model of the controlled door sub-system as shown in Figure 1.

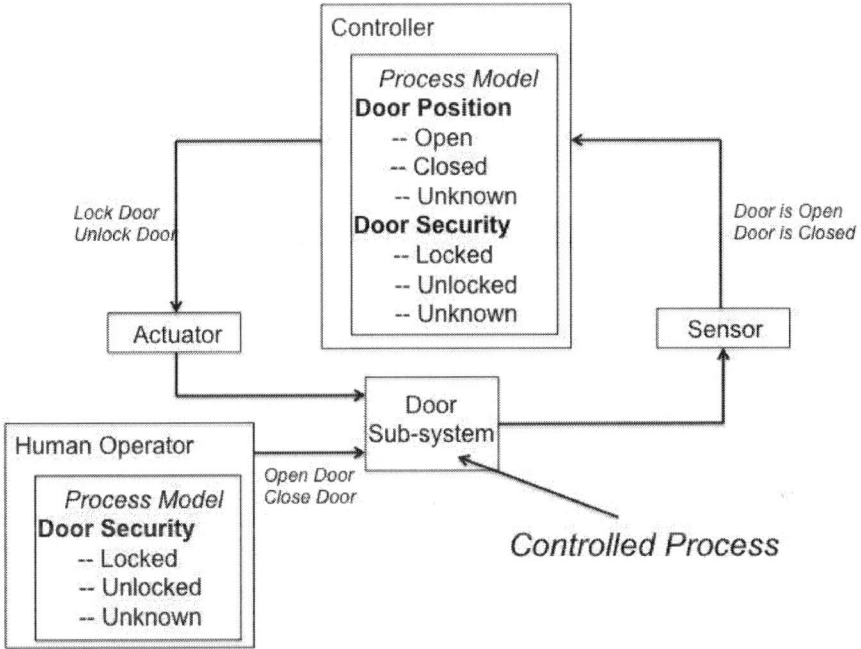

Fig.1. The controlled door sub-system

The main controller has a process model of the door sub-system. So also does the human operator. The operator can open or close the door directly. The controller uses an actuator to lock and unlock the door and a sensor to detect whether the door is open or closed.

Step 1: identifying potentially hazardous control actions

For each of the two controller actions, *Unlock Door* and *Lock Door*, we identify three potential causes of a hazard: *not providing* the action when it should, *providing* the action when it shouldn't and providing the action at the wrong time or in the wrong order. The results of the analysis are shown in Table 1.

   Failing to unlock the door is inconvenient but not hazardous. Unlocking the door when the drum is filled is hazardous because the operator will be able to open the door inadvertently and release potentially very hot water. Unlocking the door *before* the drum has been fully drained is also hazardous.

Table 1. Door hazards

Controller action	Not providing causes hazard	Providing causes hazard	Wrong timing or order causes hazard
Unlock Door	Not hazardous	Operator can open door with drum filled	Water not fully drained
Lock Door	Operator can open door with drum filled	Not hazardous	Water starts filling before lock

Failing to lock the door when the drum is filled is hazardous, but locking the door when the drum is empty is not. Locking the door *after* the drum has started filling is hazardous.

Step 2: deriving the safety constraints

Three safety constraints can be derived from Table 1.

1. The door must always be locked when there is water in the drum.
2. An *Unlock Door* command must never be issued until the water is fully drained.
3. A *Lock Door* command must be issued before starting to fill the drum.

The first is an *invariant* of the system. The second and third are *guards* that prevent an operation occurring in an unsafe way. These natural language invariants and guards can then be represented formally in an Event-B model, as we shall show in detail in Section 4.

Step 3: determining how unsafe control actions could occur

We now revisit the controlled door sub-system to determine systematically the potential causes of unsafe actions as shown in Figure 2.

The hazard is that the door is open when there is water in the drum. The potential causes of this hazard are then represented on the diagram. The controller or the operator can have an inadequate or incorrect process model of the door sub-system, the requirements may not be fully specified or implemented and the operator may not be properly trained. The actuators and sensors may fail. These potential causes of unsafe actions can be used to both improve the design and inform the test plan.

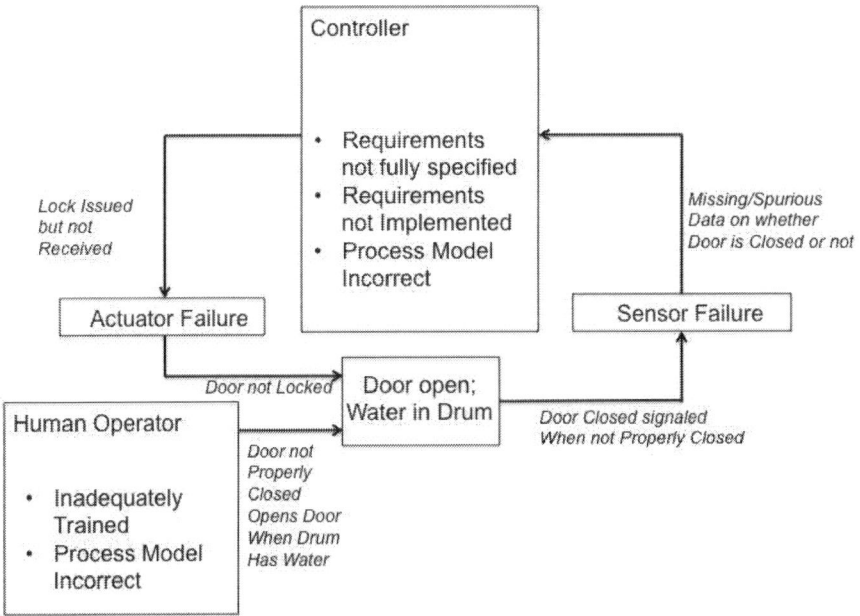

Fig.2. Potential causes of unsafe actions

4 Representing the safety constraints formally in Event-B

4.1 The Abstract Model: the Door Sub-system

To illustrate the method, we present first an abstract model of the washing machine door sub-system. We define an Event-B *context* as shown in Figure 3.

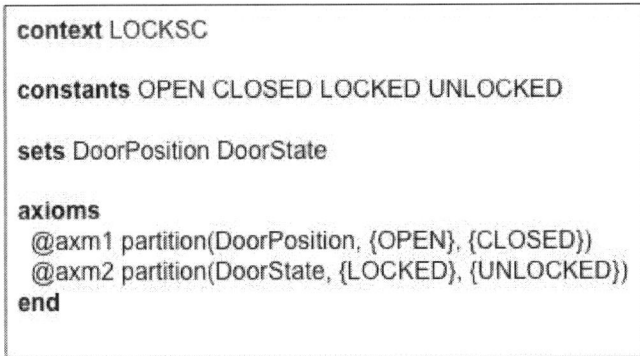

```
context LOCKSC

constants OPEN CLOSED LOCKED UNLOCKED

sets DoorPosition DoorState

axioms
    @axm1 partition(DoorPosition, {OPEN}, {CLOSED})
    @axm2 partition(DoorState, {LOCKED}, {UNLOCKED})
end
```

Fig.3. Door sub-system context

The *position* of the door can either be *OPEN* or *CLOSED* and the *state* of the door can either be *LOCKED* or *UNLOCKED*.

We then define an Event-B *machine*, which *sees* this context, as shown in Figures 4 and 5.

```
machine LOCKSM sees LOCKSC

variables dpos doorst

invariants
    @inv1 dpos ∈ DoorPosition
    @inv2 doorst ∈ DoorState
    @inv3 doorst = LOCKED ⇒ dpos = CLOSED

events
    event INITIALISATION
        then
            @act1 dpos ≔ OPEN
            @act2 doorst ≔ UNLOCKED
    end
```

Fig.4. Door sub-system machine initialisation

The variables *dpos* and *doorst* represent the door position, which is initialized to *OPEN*, and the door state, which is initialized to *LOCKED*. The *invariant @inv3* states that if the door is locked, then it must be closed.

The *events* of the machine are shown in Figure 5.

When the door is *open*, as indicated by the *guard @grd1* in the event *Close-Door*, then the door can be *closed*. The guards of event *OpenDoor* indicate that the door can only be opened if it is *closed* and *unlocked*. The event *LockDoor* is only enabled if the door is *closed* and *unlocked*. The event *UnlockDoor* unlocks the door if it is locked.

The proof obligations for the machine are generated and discharged automatically by the Rodin tool. In particular, we have proved that the invariant *@inv3* is preserved for all possible *interleavings* of the events.

4.2 The refined model: introducing the drum sub-system

In the formal refinement of the abstract model, we first introduce the *drum state* in the context shown in Figure 6, which *extends* the abstract context.

The drum is either *EMPTY*, *FILLING*, *FILLED* or *EMPTYING*. The *refined* machine *sees* the extended context, introduces the variable *drumst* to represent the state of the drum, refines the events of the abstract machine and introduces the events shown in Figure 7.

```
event CloseDoor
  where
    @grd1 dpos = OPEN
  then
    @act1 dpos := CLOSED
  end

event OpenDoor
  where
    @grd1 dpos = CLOSED
    @grd2 doorst = UNLOCKED
  then
    @act1 dpos := OPEN
  end

event LockDoor
  where
    @grd1 doorst = UNLOCKED
    @grd2 dpos = CLOSED
  then
    @act1 doorst := LOCKED
  end

event UnlockDoor
  where
    @grd1 doorst = LOCKED
  then
    @act1 doorst := UNLOCKED
  end
end
```

Fig.5. Door sub-system machine events

```
context LOCKSE1 extends LOCKSC

constants EMPTY FILLING FILLED EMPTYING

sets DrumState

axioms
  @axm1 partition(DrumState, {EMPTY}, {FILLING}, {FILLED}, {EMPTYING})
end
```

Fig.6. Extended context

```
event FillDrum
   where
      @grd1 doorst = LOCKED
      @grd2 drumst = EMPTY
   then
      @act1 drumst ≔ FILLING
   end

event Wash
   where
      @grd1 drumst = FILLING
   then
      @act1 drumst ≔ FILLED
   end

event EmptyDrum
   where
      @grd1 drumst = FILLED
   then
      @act1 drumst ≔ EMPTYING
   end

event Finish
   where
      @grd1 drumst = EMPTYING
   then
      @act1 drumst ≔ EMPTY
   end
```

Fig.7. New events in the refinement

The event *FillDrum* is only enabled if the door is *locked (@grd1)* and the drum is *empty (@grd2)*. The door can only be locked by the *LockDoor* event. These guards therefore fulfil the requirement of the safety constraint: '*A lock door command must be issued before starting to fill the drum*'.

To represent the safety constraint, '*The door must always be locked when there is water in the drum*', we introduce the invariant shown in Figure 8.

```
@inv2 drumst ≠ EMPTY ⇒ doorst = LOCKED
```

Fig.8. Safety constraint invariant

However, when we run the automatic prover, we find that this invariant cannot be proved for the *UnlockDoor* event. Inspecting the failing proof more closely, we see that the door can be unlocked while the drum is not *empty*. We must therefore *strengthen* the guards of the abstract event in this refinement by introducing the extra guard, *@grd2,* as shown in Figure 9.

This guard represents the safety constraint: '*An Unlock Door command must never be issued until the water is fully drained.*' When we re-run the prover, the invariant, *@inv2*, is now proved automatically. All three safety constraints derived during the safety analysis are now represented formally in the refined model.

1. The door must always be locked when there is water in the drum.
2. An *Unlock Door* command must never be issued until the water is fully drained.
3. A *Lock Door* command must be issued before starting to fill the drum.

```
event UnlockDoor refines UnlockDoor
  where
     @grd1 doorst = LOCKED
     @grd2 drumst = EMPTY
  then
     @act1 doorst := UNLOCKED
  end
```

Fig.9. Safety constraint guard

5 Summary and future work

We have presented an approach to hazard analysis where system requirements are captured as *monitored, controlled, mode* and *commanded* phenomena and STPA is applied to the controlled phenomena to identify systematically the safety constraints. These natural language constraints are then represented formally in an Event-B specification, which is amenable to formal refinement and proof. We have shown how the safety constraints are represented as either *invariants* or *guards* in the formal model. We build the model systematically using Event-B formal refinement. The Rodin environment automatically generates the required proof obligations, and the Rodin provers have been shown in this case study to discharge the proof obligations automatically. Where a proof obligation cannot be discharged, we have shown how the Rodin tool guides the user to improve the model.

We have illustrated our approach using the door lock phenomenon. Application of the method continues by analyzing and modelling in the same way the remaining *controlled phenomena*: the agitator motor, water control valves, water drain pump and water heater.

It is an important goal of our work to integrate Event-B based formal verification techniques into the overall system development flow. In particular, it is necessary to validate the specification against the original requirements. This cannot be achieved in an ad hoc manner. It is necessary to trace elements of the specification back to the requirements, and for this tool support is vital to ensure that there is a measurable way of ensuring that the requirements are covered by the specification. In future work, therefore, we shall integrate our approach with the requirements capture and tracing facility, ProR (Jastram 2010) that forms part of the Rodin platform. ProR provides a flexible and configurable environment to support requirements engineering, within which we will integrate requirements analysis and safety analysis within the Rodin toolset and workflow.

Acknowledgments   The research presented in this paper is funded by the FP7 ADVANCE (287563) project, Advanced Design and Verification Environment for Cyber-physical System Engineering, http://www.advance-ict.eu.

References

Abrial J-R (2010) Modeling in Event-B – System and Software Engineering. Cambridge University Press

Abrial J-R et al (2010) Rodin: an open toolset for modelling and reasoning in Event-B. STTT, 12(6):447–466

Abrial J-R, Hallerstede S (2006) Refinement, decomposition, and instantiation of discrete models: Application to Event-B. Fundamenta Informaticae, XXI

Jastram M (2010) ProR, an open source platform for requirements engineering based on RIF. SEISCONF

Leveson N (2012) Engineering a safer world: Systems thinking applied to safety. MIT Press (MA)

Perreira S et al (2006) A system-theoretic hazard analysis methodology for a non-advocate safety assessment of the ballistic missile defense system. Technical report, DTIC Document

Yeganefard S, Butler M (2012) Control systems: Phenomena and structuring functional requirement documents, 17th International Conference on Engineering of Complex Computer Systems (ICECCS)

Testing and Proving: Strange Bedfellows?

Robert Dewar

New York University and AdaCore

New York, USA

Abstract Traditionally, e.g. when using DO-178B, we have relied on structured and formalized testing to assure safety, but the limitations of testing are well known. On the other hand, it is not feasible to use proof techniques for an entire application. That's partly a limitation of our proving capabilities, but partly fundamental. For instance we can't easily prove that the specification itself is correct or that the hardware operates as expected. So we will always be stuck with some testing. This paper discusses how testing and proof are used in practice, and considers the issue of how to combine tests and proofs in a single application.

1 What does safety-critical mean?

We are gathered together at the Safety-critical Systems Symposium. So it seems reasonable to assume that we all know what safety-critical means. But do we in fact have a clear definition? We recently had an extensive discussion within AdaCore of exactly what qualifies as safety-critical, and we came to the conclusion that we didn't really know.

The classical definition is of course a system where a defect can cause loss of human life. But the trouble is the word 'cause' needs a lot of interpretation. Suppose we have a computer system that implements a 999 (911 in the USA) emergency call system. It fails and as a result an ambulance cannot be called and a patient dies. Is that a loss of human life caused by a software bug? Suppose a financial system fails and results in someone being unable to access their money, so they fail to make a payment and health insurance is terminated, and then they cannot afford life saving medication? Suppose during the harrowing (but non-fatal descent) of the infamous Malaysian Airlines plane caused by a software bug (Aviation-Safety 2005), someone had died of a heart attack brought on by the terror of the situation? It's easy to make a list like this that goes on forever, and find that we are surrounded by complex computer systems whose failure could indirectly cause a loss of life. Are these safety-critical systems?

Perhaps the answer is that if they do not directly cause the death, they don't qualify. But that doesn't really work either. If an avionics system fails, it may cause a plane crash. It is that crash that kills people, not the bug directly. If an air traffic control system fails and results in a midair collision, it is the collision that kills people, not the ATC bug directly.

Eventually we came to two conclusions. First that the term safety-critical is hard to define precisely, and trying to define exactly how direct the chain of causation has to be is not particularly useful. Second, and much more importantly, we are surrounded by complex computer systems that are critical and really must not fail or there can be very serious consequences. Whether these systems are technically safety-critical is not really terribly relevant. What is important is that we need to develop techniques which can be widely employed to ensure that these systems are reliable.

2 How are we doing? The age of the 'glitch'

Barely a week goes by that we do not read of some major disruption caused by a computer error which is almost always software related. It has become the style for companies and journalists alike to refer to these errors as glitches. Some examples:

- In a story on the terrible computer systems disruptions resulting from the United Airlines merger (Reuters 2012a), a consultant is quoted as saying, 'It doesn't look like it's a major meltdown; it looks like a glitch.'
- On 30 January 2012, JetBlue sent a message to all customers saying, 'We apologize. This morning we sent you the January TrueBlue statement, and it may have displayed the incorrect balance. This was a glitch in our email data, and we are working to fix it, after which time we will send you a new statement with the correct balance.'
- In the wake of the NatWest mess, we read (Metro, 2012) 'Millions of NatWest customers were left without access to their money yesterday because of a computer glitch.'
- Following the Penn State affair, we read (NY Times 2011), 'On Friday, the governor finally got the word. The grand jury indictment had been filed under seal, but because of a computer glitch it had mistakenly been made public.'

For dozens more examples, see the article by Jerome Taylor (Taylor 2012) in which he has collected a catalogue of 'glitches' causing major disruptions in financial markets, cloud computing, internet service, air travel, etc. And in every article, we see that ubiquitous word 'glitch'. One traditional definition of this word from www.thefreedictionary.com is, 'a minor malfunction, mishap, or technical problem'. Minor mishaps could happen to anyone, right? Well I am pretty sure that people desperate to get their money from NatWest did not consider the problem minor. The use of the word is a way of disclaiming responsibility. At least one online dictionary notices what is going on with this word: dictionary.

reference.com has a second meaning, 'Computers. any error, malfunction, or problem'. Note that the 'minor' has disappeared as a qualifier.

For some observers, such pervasive malfunctions are to be expected. I heard one law professor from Yale give a talk advocating a change in product liability standards for computer software on the grounds that it was obviously impossible to hold software to the same standards of reliability as other products. In the aftermath of the trading program 'glitch' that caused a company to lose half a billion dollars in 30 minutes (during which they were desperately trying to turn the program off), the idea of requiring testing was floated. An OpEd piece in the NY Times argued that it was absurd to require such programs to be tested in advance because the market was moving so rapidly.

Those of us sitting in this room know that this assessment is unreasonably pessimistic. By using appropriate techniques, we actually know how to make software pretty reliable – not perfect, but we actually do quite well. When it comes to avionics we have a standard in place: DO-178B (Wikipedia 2010). This standard is imperfect, but we have a pretty good record: there is, as far as I have been able to determine, no incident of a death on a commercial airline due to a software implementation bug. But in other fields we have not done so well. People have been killed by bugs in medical equipment (Rose 1994), and alarming bugs have appeared in automotive software. For example, in a recent news article (Reuters 2012b), we read, 'BMW said automatic transmissions may not remain in "park" position due to a software problem on cars equipped with keyless ignition and the Comfort Access option.' And further, 'BMW said it would begin notifying owners of the problem in November, but dealers will not be able to correct the software until March.' Pretty amazing – a serious safety problem, which won't be fixed for eight months! Interestingly these are both areas where regulation and certification standards are weak compared to avionics requirements.

3 Doing a better job on safety

Nearly every major software system has at least indirect safety concerns, so our conference here can be seen as having a wider scope than perhaps we imagined. So how can we do better and avoid the widespread 'glitches' that seem to plague so many large software systems? When it comes down to the details, we basically have two approaches for making our software more reliable and safer. We can test, or we can use formal techniques to prove that code is correct. Testing can be quite effective if it is done in a highly systematic manner as prescribed for example by DO-178B. But increasingly we look to formal methods and proof of correctness as another path to system safety. Most often, research tends to focus on one approach or the other. In this paper we will present the viewpoint that we must develop systems, tools and techniques that smoothly integrate the two approaches. We will first look at some general principles, then explore detailed technical issues that arise from mixing these approaches.

4 Testing vs proof

Neither testing nor proof can provide a 100% guarantee that our software is totally reliable. In the case of testing it is obvious that unless we can test every possible input (a rare situation), we can't be sure that testing will catch every case. For example, if you are testing a floating-point square root algorithm, it is quite possible to test every value for 32-bit floating-point, difficult but perhaps just conceivable to test every value for 64-bit floating-point, and out of the question to test every value for 128-bit floating-point. Typical real problems involve multiple inputs that cause a combinatorial explosion of possible test cases, rendering complete testing infeasible. It is certainly possible to make testing more reliable, e.g. by requiring complete coverage testing following MCDC principles as is required by DO-178B. But achieving 100% assurance is out of reach. Indeed even in the avionics field, we have avoided serious accidents due to software implementation bugs, but we have had some close calls.

A few decades ago, it became fashionable to assume that the right way to deal with this problem was to prove entire programs correct. But that is misleading for several reasons. First, it is an awfully tall order to prove a large program correct. By 'correct' we really mean showing that an implementation is equivalent to a detailed specification. But such specifications are themselves the source of bugs, and faithfully reproducing an error in specifications in the implementation is unhelpful. Furthermore, proof of correctness can still leave a system open to compromise from software tool errors (e.g. compilers generating wrong code), or hardware malfunctions. We will always have to rely on integration testing to catch errors in these categories, and no advances in proof technology can eliminate the need for such final integration testing.

5 What we can achieve with proof of correctness

What we can achieve is proofs that specific units meet their specifications. For instance that a sorting function really sorts its argument. That's potentially interesting, since we really can get to a point of being 100% sure that the algorithm is correct, something that is hard to achieve by testing. Of course we will need careful accurate specifications for these units. But if we can achieve such proofs, then that's potentially advantageous compared to unit testing.

Furthermore, there are important properties we can prove without even needing a specification for our program. For instance in C, arithmetic overflow is undefined, and C compilers take advantage of this, so that if you have an arithmetic overflow, the results may be unexpected. Similarly in C, it is undefined to reference an array out of bounds (the source of the infamous 'buffer overrun' errors that result in many security and safety issues in C programs). Every C function has an implicit requirement that the code is free of these two errors, and if we can prove that this requirement is met, we have achieved a big step in the direction of reliability without needing a formal specification of the program.

In practice, the C language is not very well suited to such proofs on a large scale, but there are other languages where this approach is more practical. For example, programs written in SPARK (Altran Praxis 2012) have very well defined semantics describing run-time errors (they are the errors that would cause exceptions in a full Ada program), and proving large programs free of such run-time errors is indeed practical (Amey and Chapman 2002).

6 The limits of partial correctness

Most often the practical level of proof of correctness extends to partial correctness. For example, a proof that if a function returns then it returns the right result (satisfies its postconditions). Now of course it is a good thing to be sure that it does not return with the wrong results, but not returning at all is a serious (and often hard to debug) problem. The extent to which a proof of partial correctness gives a warm feeling that the code is in fact correct depends on the situation.

A while ago, I attended a workshop on the SPARK language and methodology. One of the exercises was to write the body for the following function and write down the verification conditions (formulas whose validity ensures that a property from the program is respected):

```
function Sqrt (Arg : Positive) return Positive
   with Post => Sqrt'Result ** 2 <= Arg
       and then
       (Sqrt'Result + 1) ** 2 > Arg;
```

Doing this efficiently is just a little tricky, since you have to work out and write down correctly the appropriate Newton-Raphson iteration formula. Proving this formula correct does not seem easy. I misunderstood the assignment and thought that we had to not only write down the verification conditions but also prove them. I succeeded in doing this, and the instructor was impressed, but in fact I cheated. What I wrote was:

```
function Sqrt (Arg : Positive) return Positive is
   Result : Positive := Arg;
begin
   loop
      Result := {formula to improve the estimate}
      exit when Result ** 2 <= Arg and then (Result + 1)**2 > Arg;
   end loop;
   return Result;
end Sqrt;
```

OK, it's not really cheating, in the sense that this is a perfectly reasonable way to write the body of this function. But of course it is trivial to see that if the loop terminates, the post condition is met. Proving this body partially correct really gives very little insight into the correctness, let alone efficiency of the implementation. Indeed the 'proof' that this body is correct does not even need to look at the formula. Yet this is the crucial and only non-trivial element of this code.

How often does this kind of situation arise in practice? Hard to say. This particular example was not contrived but was taken from actual experience. Of course it is still of value to prove that the implementation is partially correct, but the above example is hardly one where we would feel comfortable in skipping unit testing. A slip-up in the formula might well mean that the function never works (terminates) for any possible input.

7 The limits of total correctness

It's certainly possible to prove total correctness for some functions. Let's keep going with the example in the previous section, and rewrite the body this way:

```
function Sqrt (Arg : Positive) return Positive is
  Result : Positive := 1;
begin
  loop
    exit when Result ** 2 <= Arg and then (Result + 1)**2 > Arg;
    Result := Result + 1;
    pragma Loop_Variant (Increases => Result);
  end loop;
  return Result;
end Sqrt;
```

Here the Loop_Variant pragma is an extension in the GNAT implementation of Ada specifically to aid in formulating total correctness proofs. It specifies that Result increases each time around the loop, which is trivial to prove true in this case. It's thus straightforward to prove that the function always returns, and returns the right result. An important part of this proof is that there is indeed a value that satisfies the postcondition. It is interesting to note that a requirement for proving freedom from run-time exceptions automatically requires this proof, since you have to demonstrate that the increment of Result cannot cause an arithmetic overflow.

Good, so this implementation is totally correct. But it's inefficient. How inefficient? A worst case input of Positive'Last on a typical machine with 32-bit integers requires about 46,000 iterations, which probably takes something like 310 microseconds on a fast modern machine (machines are fast these days), but might of course be slower on an embedded microprocessor. Nevertheless it's hard to guess if this is an efficiency problem in practice, so we might worry that proving eventual termination is not good enough.

Proving things about performance is tough, though there is certainly interesting work being done in this area. On the other hand, traditional unit testing is typically just about functionality, rather than performance. Indeed in some development regimes, unit testing is done on hardware that differs from the final target hardware. In such an environment, we leave performance worries for final integration testing, e.g. by measuring CPU usage for typical tests and convincing ourselves there is an adequate margin.

Perhaps some day, it will be routine to provide not only proofs of total correctness, but also proofs of adequate performance as measured against a specification that includes detailed timing requirements. But the fact that we can't easily do that today should not worry us too much. The primary interest here is in using proof to replace unit testing. In practice a proof of total correctness will be at least as good as, and often better than, comprehensive unit testing. Of course we have to be confident that the preconditions (things that must be true on entry to a subprogram), and postconditions (things that must be true on exit) are complete and properly specified, but if we don't know what inputs a function takes, and what results it computes, we can't test it properly in any case. The discipline of producing proper contracts for functions is equally helpful for testing and proof, and whatever we decide in terms of when to test and when to prove, it's a very valuable discipline to acquire, and languages (like Ada 2012, SPARK and Eiffel) that allow us to formalize contracts in the code are helpful.

8 Choosing between proof and testing?

For scientists, the answer to this question is easy. Do both when you can! The safer the better. However, this is not in general economically viable. Assuming a status quo of using a testing approach as in DO-178B, the issue is when we shall consider substituting proof for testing for a given unit in the program. There are four possible situations:

- cases where testing is practical, and proof is impractical
- cases where both are practical, but testing is cheaper
- cases where both are practical, but proof is cheaper
- cases where proof is preferable technically.

It's going to be a hard sell to use proofs when they are impractical, or more costly than testing. On the other hand if we can show that proof will be cheaper than testing and as reliable, then it's a simple choice to use a proof-based approach. Traditionally, management has worried that formal techniques are going to add unacceptably to the cost of certification. But the combination of ever improving formal techniques and fast machines is making proof-based approaches more practical.

One of the most interesting results from the Tokeneer project was the cost figures. Tokeneer is an NSA sponsored demonstration of a security-critical program where proof of correctness techniques were used to formally prove that security requirements were met (AdaCore 2008). The implementation was carried out in SPARK, and careful track was kept of the time required for implementation. The result was that the cost (measured in lines/day) was very reasonable, better than many conventional development projects.

So that's encouraging! Furthermore, that's not the whole story. That was the cost of initial development. If proof of correctness techniques can reduce the occurrence of serious bugs found late on – in the worst case after deployment – then the cost savings can increase. It is no surprise for example that Intel is very interested in formal methods. The infamous division bug in the Pentium (Edelman 1997) cost them a lot of money. If formal techniques could plausibly have prevented this bug, then they are definitely of interest.

So the third category above (cases where proof is cheaper) is a real focus for future work. This acts as an interesting viewpoint for future research. We are not seeking perfection, we are seeking approaches that are good enough (i.e. at least as good as current testing techniques) but cheaper. We are not always oriented this way in the academic community, but if we want our work to be used in the real world, then we always have to think in terms of costs.

9 Cases where proof is preferable technically

This is an interesting category to consider. Are there cases where testing falls short and proof techniques can do significantly better *in practice*? The emphasis is important here; it is easy to conjure up theoretical cases where testing will be inadequate, but do they occur often in practice? And can we show how it would be practical to use proof techniques in place of unit testing?

There certainly are such cases. I have encountered several examples in the course of my practical experience in building systems. Let's have a look at two particularly instructive examples.

I recently implemented an arbitrary precision package for the GNAT compiler (actually this was to implement the treatment of contracts as discussed later in this paper). As part of this, I implemented multiple precision division using Algorithm D from Knuth Volume 2 (Knuth 1975). I chose variable names exactly matching the Knuth description, and laid out data the same way. For instance here is an excerpt of code from that implementation:

```
-- D3 (continued). Now test if qhat >= b or v2*qhat > (rhat,uj+2):
-- if so, decrease qhat by 1, increase rhat by v1, and repeat this
-- test if rhat < b. [The test on v2 determines at at high speed
-- most of the cases in which the trial value qhat is one too
-- large, and eliminates all cases where qhat is two too large.]
```

```
while qhat >= b or else DD (v2) * qhat > LSD (rhat) & u (j + 2) loop
    qhat := qhat - 1;
    rhat := rhat + DD (v1);
    exit when rhat >= b;
end loop;
```

It's easy to see that the code exactly matches the Knuth algorithm. I had carefully read the code and convinced myself that it was a faithful translation, and reasonably extensive unit testing showed that the quotient and remainder were computed correctly. I did not feel the need for exhaustive testing since this is a well-known algorithm, widely implemented for many years.

It turns out that my faith was misplaced. A colleague who is particularly brilliant at reviewing code raised an issue of whether an expression elsewhere in the algorithm could overflow in some circumstances. Well I was unconvinced. How could there be an error in this algorithm from 1975 which had been used so widely? My colleague persisted and came up with a corner case test that failed. Furthermore he investigated and found that in 1995 (nearly twenty years later), this bug had been found and documented (Knuth errata 1995). Furthermore, this persistent colleague still wasn't happy with one detail of the fix. Sure enough there was another bug not corrected till 2005 (Knuth errata 2005).

Amazing! An algorithm that had been widely used for 30 years was plain wrong. During that time it had been extensively implemented in many different contexts, and widely tested in deployed systems. Usually that would be enough to generate sufficient confidence in an algorithm, but that confidence was misplaced in this case. Now we can't rely on amazing work by code review geniuses to find such errors. After all, many people had reviewed this algorithm. I myself recall teaching it in detail in an algorithms class in the mid 1970s. So let's ask ourselves if proof techniques would have helped here.

If you look at the original presentation by Knuth, he does prove some critical and important theorems about the algorithm. But he does not attempt to prove the whole algorithm, and the proofs he gives are not keyed to an actual implementation. So it is not surprising that they would miss something. It is of course easy to write the postcondition for this complex algorithm. It's just a division after all. So a proof of partial correctness would undoubtedly have run into the bug (and we would have failed to find a proof). Moreover, the problem was simply one of an intermediate calculation overflowing in a particular situation. So even if all we were doing was proving freedom from run-time errors, we would have found ourselves unable to prove that the expression in question was safe from overflow.

It sure looks like this is a case where relatively straightforward proof techniques could have found the error and avoided the embarrassment and possible disastrous consequences of a bug undetected for 30 years. Probably if my colleague had not been so sharp, I would have got away with this bug. But who knows? On my list of things to do is to actually attempt this proof in the future. If you want to regard this as a challenge to the reader, the relevant code can be found in the file s-bignum.adb in the GNAT sources (GNAT 2012).

10 Another example, where I didn't get away with it

Another example of a case where proof techniques would have definitely helped avoid an embarrassing bug occurred back in the 1970s when I was writing operating systems for Incoterm and Honeywell. In 1977 I wrote a complete operating system and real time executive called EXEC/15 for an 8088-based system marketed by Honeywell. Semaphores were the basic synchronization mechanism, and using the unusual call-on-condition instructions on this processor, I devised some very clever efficient techniques for semaphore P and V operations. They were something like (operating a bit from rusty memory here, no documentation survives):

```
INC     sem     # increase semaphore count (grab semaphore)
CNZ     semp    # call os routine if already grabbed (call on non-zero)
DEC     sem     # release semaphore count
CNZ     semv    # call os routine if someone waiting
```

The idea is to call the OS routines only if needed. The INC/DEC set condition codes atomically, and the call tests these codes atomically. Now the exact condition codes for the calls and the initial semaphore state are delicate here, and that's the point. It's very hard to spot race conditions for implementations like this. I had a friend working at Honeywell who was expert in race condition detection, and he was convinced the implementation was right and so was I. We did very extensive testing, but testing is a very unsatisfactory method of detecting race conditions, as every real time programmer writing concurrent code knows well.

I thought it would be a good idea to try to prove this implementation correct, but proving concurrent algorithms is also tricky, and I failed to find a proof. I blamed this on my lack of mathematical competence. And eventually we convinced ourselves the implementation was right, and tens of thousands of ROMS were burned embodying this implementation.

Well perhaps I should have had more confidence in my mathematical abilities. A year later, I was explaining the algorithm to a friend, and horrors! I saw a bug. A delicate race condition that no one had noticed before. No wonder I had not been able to prove the approach correct. The system had seemed to work perfectly in the field, but that's not surprising; race conditions can hide for a long time before surfacing in ugly circumstances.

I devised a simple fix, but this time I worked with Malcolm Harrison at the Courant Institute, and he was able to prove that the fixed implementation was indeed correct. This work is documented in a Courant Technical Report, but my attempts to dig this up have failed. Anyway, this time I was much more confident that I had got it right. The spectre of the expense of burning tens of thousands of new ROMS and distributing them raised itself. Luckily I was rescued, the application running above the executive turned out to have a serious unrelated bug that was causing real troubles, so the ROMS had to be reburned anyway, so I could just sneak in my change (which as far as we know had not caused any actual bugs in the field so far) without being responsible for the huge cost of ROM replacement.

But this was a valuable lesson. I should not have given up so easily in my attempt to find a proof of correctness of my algorithm. I was lucky that I was not solely responsible for a massively expensive retrofit operation, but I came uncomfortably close. Here for sure was a good example where proof of correctness would have been a far preferable approach to unit testing for this small piece of code. I am sure there are many other examples, but it is certainly instructive to take these two examples from real life experience with critical systems software development.

11 Combining testing and proof

It really seems pretty obvious that the way forward will involve a mixture of proof and testing techniques, so we need to consider the requirements for systems that will facilitate this combined approach.

First we need to recognize this dual approach in relevant safety standards. DO-178B read literally seems to require testing in all circumstances. Although there are cases in which use of proofs has been accepted as a substitute for coverage testing, this is not the most common interpretation of the standard. DO-178C makes important steps forward in this regard in that it is much more flexible in allowing the use of formal methods. Other safety standards need to evolve in the same direction.

Second we need tools and languages that will facilitate the combination of testing in an integrated manner. The Hi-Lite project (Open-DO 2012):

'targets ease of adoption through a loose integration of formal proofs with testing and static analysis, that allows combining techniques around a common expression of specifications. Its technical focus is on modularity, that allows a divide-and-conquer approach to large software systems, as well as an early adoption by all programmers in the software life cycle.'

12 The use of contracts

The notion of contracts as an element in programming languages is not a new one, having been extensively explored by Eiffel (Howard 1993). An important component is the notion of specifying preconditions and postconditions. If you write them comprehensively, then they act as a complete specification that determines the full requirements for a correct implementation of the subprogram.

Such a specification is essential if we are to attempt a proof of correctness. But it is also very useful as a documentation and testing aid if we are doing conventional testing. After all you can't very well write tests if you don't know the required inputs and the expected outputs. So here we have an ideal objective that will be useful for both proof and testing, and it is clear that the language we use as a vehicle for our hybrid approach should have both capabilities. Ada in its latest incarnation (Ada 2012) has added a complete notion of contracts. And indeed the Hi-Lite project uses Ada 2012 as the starting point for its design.

But, there is a significant problem. Contracts are used in quite different ways in the two contexts. If you are concentrating on the notion of execution and formulating run-time tests, then contracts are executable tests with normal language semantics. But if you are focusing on proof, then contracts (e.g. as they appear in the SPARK language) are mathematical statements to be proved. Consider the following example:

```
function Sproduct (X, Y, Z : Natural) return Natural
  with Pre => X**2 + Y**2 in Natural and Z**2 in Natural
    Post => Sproduct'Result = (X**2 * Y ** 2 / Z ** 2);
```

The difficulty here is that intermediate computations in the pre and post conditions may fail due to overflow. If we regard these as simply executable tests, we have to worry about this failure. But if we think of these as mathematical formulae, then we want to consider the values to be mathematical integers where operations cannot overflow, since the range is unbounded.

This is a potentially significant source of friction between the testing and proof worlds. Fortunately there is a good solution which has been implemented in the Hi-Lite context. The Ada language allows flexibility in the treatment of intermediate results. It is not required that overflow exceptions be raised. Instead you are allowed to have intermediate results out of range provided you get the right mathematical results in the end. What we have done for Hi-Lite is to implement an option to use multiple-precision arithmetic where necessary for intermediate computations. Using this option, the above contract works fine in both contexts. In the proof context, the expressions can be viewed as using mathematical integers, and at run-time in a testing context, multiple-precision arithmetic is used so that we cannot get overflow during the evaluation of the contract expressions.

13 Extended assertions

Ada includes the notion of an assertion:

```
pragma Assert (condition);
```

Like pre and post conditions, this can be viewed either as a mathematical assertion to be proved, or a run-time test that will test the given condition. As with pre and post conditions, we can specify the option to use multi-precision arithmetic, avoiding the possibility of overflow, and allowing the assertion expression to be treated mathematically.

In the context of Hi-Lite, it has proved useful to extend the notion of assertions, using the freedom granted by the Ada standard to add user-defined pragmas. The design of these pragmas is ongoing. The following is a snapshot showing the current design:

pragma Assert_And_Cut (condition);
pragma Assume (condition);
pragma Loop_Invariant (condition);

In terms of run-time semantics these are essentially identical to the normal Assert pragma, but in a proof context they are treated differently. Assert_And_Cut creates a cutpoint, which is essentially a summary of all the work done so far, so that the postconditions can be proved from the expression in this pragma along with the effects of all subsequent statements. Assume refers to an assumption that does not need to be proved. Either it is a result of external conditions, or perhaps it is a known theorem too difficult to prove in the context of a proof tool. Loop_Invariant is used within loops to express the familiar notion of a loop invariant (and optionally allows the use of the attribute Loop_Entry to refer to values of variables on entry to the loop).

Finally there is the Loop_Variant pragma, which as previously shown in the context of the integer square root example, aids proof of loop termination by specifying variables which must continually increase or decrease on each iteration of the loop. These additional assertion pragmas are easily implemented, and are helpful both for formal proof purposes and as formal documentation even if we are not attempting proof of correctness.

14 Intermixing testing and proofs

One problem with mixing tests and proofs is that testing does not provide a tight enough guarantee that we have a reasonable starting point for proving a subprogram called by code that has only been tested and not proved. Consider the following:

procedure Calc (X : Positive; Y : Wide_Wide_String) ...

where we intend to provide a proof of Calc, but all the calls of Calc will be from units that have only been tested and not proved. The Ada language allows invalid values to appear during the course of calculations. For example, in the above case, elements of Y may be outside the range of Wide_Wide_Character. That doesn't cause problems in terms of run-time semantics, since the Ada definition carefully constrains the effect of such invalid values. But it greatly complicates proofs. We really want to assume in a proof that all values are within their subtype range. If we were proving everything this assumption would be valid throughout and we would not have a problem.

But in this hybrid testing/proving environment we have a problem. In the Hi-Lite context, we solve that problem by providing an option to add an additional check that parameters are always valid, and in the case of composite values, that the elements are valid (i.e. within their declared range, and meeting any predicates declared for the subtype). This ensures that the proof does not start from wrong assumptions. These checks are run-time checks in the testing context. They add overhead, in some cases substantial, but like all run-time checks, if we can be sufficiently sure that the check never fails, it can be removed at runtime. Or alternatively, the check can be retained if the inefficiency is acceptable.

15 Tool integration

In typical previous systems, proof tools have been separated from the compiler technology used to actually execute the program. For instance a SPARK user uses the SPARK examiner and proof tools to do the development and formal proof of a program, using the correctness by construction approach, and then a quite separate compiler to actually compile the code once it has been proved. An important element of the Hi-Lite project is that we avoid this separation. A single tool operating in dual modes is used for compilation (needed of course when testing is required, or for final generation of the application) and proof (where it is connected to a back end that can carry out proofs). The importance and benefits of this tool integration are discussed extensively in (Dross et al. 2012).

References

Ada (2012) Ada 2012: the most advanced language for safe and secure software. http://www.adacore.com/adaanswers/about/ada-2012. Accessed 20 November 2012
AdaCore (2008) The Tokeneer project, a hands on look at an NSA funded, highly secure biometric control system. http://www.adacore.com/sparkpro/tokeneer. Accessed 20 November 2012
Altran Praxis (2012) SPARK technical references. http://www.altran-praxis.com/sparkTechnicalReferences.aspx. Accessed 20 November 2012
Amey P, Chapman R (2002) Industrial strength exception freedom. Proc ACM SigAda
Aviation-Safety (2005) Malaysian Airlines 'close call', August 2005. http://aviation-safety.net/database/record.php?id=20050801-1. Accessed 20 November 2012
Dross C, Kanig J, Shonberg E (2012) Hi-Lite: the convergence of compiler technology and program verification. High Integrity Language Technology, ACM SigAda International Conference Boston 2012
Edelman A (1997) The mathematics of the Pentium division bug. SIAM Rev 39(1):54-67. http://www-math.mit.edu/~edelman/homepage/papers/pentiumbug.ps. Accessed 20 November 2012
GNAT (2012) GNAT sources. http://libre.adacore.com/tools/gnat-gpl-edition/. Accessed 20 November 2012
Howard R (1993) The Eiffel programming language. http://www.drdobbs.com/tools/the-eiffel-programming-language/184409090. Accessed 20 November 2012
Knuth D (1975) The art of computer programming. Vol. 2, 2nd edition, section 4.3.2
Knuth errata (1995) Vol 2 errata. http://www-cs-faculty.stanford.edu/~uno/err2-2e.ps.gz. Accessed 20 November 2012

Knuth errata (2005) Vol 2 errata. http://www-cs-faculty.stanford.edu/~uno/all2-pre.ps.gz. Accessed 20 November 2012

Metro (2012) NatWest takes a bank holiday. Metro, London, Friday 22 June 2012

NY Times (2011) Abuse inquiry set tricky path for a governor. http://www.nytimes.com/2011/11/11/sports/ncaafootball/tom-corbett-pennsylvania-governor-couldnt-discuss-inquiry.html. Accessed 20 November 2012

Open-DO (2012) Project Hi-Lite. http://www.open-do.org/projects/hi-lite/. Accessed 20 November 2012

Reuters (2012a) New reservation system causes delays for United. http://www.nytimes.com/2012/03/05/business/united-airlines-reservation-system-causes-delays.html. Accessed 20 November 2012

Reuters (2012b) BMW to recall 7 Series for transmission flaw. http://news.yahoo.com/bmw-recall-7-series-transmission-flaw-143348883--sector.html. Accessed 20 November 2012

Rose BW (1994) Fatal dose: radiation deaths linked to AECL computer errors. Saturday Night. http://www.ccnr.org/fatal_dose.html. Accessed 20 November 2012

Taylor J (2012) The RBS and NatWest IT breakdown: life's a glitch (and then you cry). The Independent. http://www.independent.co.uk/life-style/gadgets-and-tech/features/the-rbs-and-natwest-it-breakdown-lifes-a-glitch-and-then-you-cry-7881221.html. Accessed 20 November 2012

Wikipedia (2010) DO-178B. http://en.wikipedia.org/wiki/DO-178B. Accessed 20 November 2012

Balancing Safety, Security and Functionality

Chris Hobbs and Akramul Azim

QNX Software Systems

Ottawa, Canada

Abstract Designing a system with safety requirements means balancing the system's safety, security and functionality (usefulness) requirements so that, while the system is adequately safe and secure, it is also useful. This paper draws on the authors' practical experience designing such systems to explore the relationships between these antagonistic requirements, and presents a simple example illustrating their implications for safe and useful system design.

1 Introduction

When designing a safe software-based application for an embedded device, the designer must balance the conflicting requirements of safety, security and usefulness, particularly in the context of the larger system within which the device will operate. These requirements are typically antagonistic, as illustrated by the classic example of emergency exit doors in a building: safety and usefulness demand that they be unlocked at all times, while security requires that they always be locked.

The need to balance these conflicting requirements raises a number of fundamental questions:

- Can the safety and usefulness estimates for the software system be accommodated in a single analysis, and thereby be handled by a single tool?
- Safety and usefulness are based on availability (does the system respond?) and reliability (does it respond correctly?). For both hardware and software these are concepts that can be treated statistically. Superficially, security appears to be different: security vulnerabilities arise from malicious actions. Can security be treated statistically, as are availability and safety?
- How can reduced safety be (responsibly) traded off against increased usefulness? In particular, how can the special failure modes of software (e.g., Heisenbugs) be used to make that tradeoff?

In this paper, Section 2 discusses the relationship between safety, usefulness and security and Section 3 expands this discussion to consider the impact that a device can have on its wider environment. Sections 4 to 6 use a simple example to illustrate how safety and usefulness can be traded off against one another.

2 Safety, security and usefulness

2.1 Usefulness

In this paper we use the term 'usefulness' primarily to avoid the ambiguous term 'available'. Consider a device that automatically stops a train before it passes its movement limit. If the device stops the train unnecessarily due to a fault, the device can still be, strictly, considered 'available' because it has actively kept the train safe. The unnecessarily stopped train is, however, not useful.

Table 1 lists the four states that are considered in this paper. Under some definitions of the term 'available', the device can be considered to be available in three of those four states. It is, however, performing a useful function in only one (operating, no dangerous condition).

Table 1. System states

	State	Device safe?	Device useful?	Stress on environment?
I	Operating, no dangerous condition	Yes	Yes	No
II	Safe state, no dangerous condition	Yes	No	Yes
III	Operating, dangerous condition	No	No	Yes
IV	Safe state, dangerous condition	Yes	No	Yes

2.2 Safety and usefulness

Designing a system that is safe is easy. Designing a system that is both safe and useful is more difficult. Designing a system that is useful and remains safe within its wider environment is even more difficult, and is a design consideration that is, unfortunately, often neglected.

The train that never moves, the traffic lights that are always red, the infusion device that never dispenses drugs are all safe, but they are useless.

When the train moves, the traffic lights turn green or the drug begins to flow, the system should handle all possible situations. However, in case conditions arise that the system is not able to handle, we define safe states for the system, and ensure that, to some level of probability, it moves into the appropriate safe state when it encounters such a condition. Reversion to the safe state is unusual and places stress on the higher level environment within which the (sub-)system operates. This stress must be considered in the higher-level design.

2.3 Security, safety and usefulness

System security affects both system usefulness and safety. A denial-of-service attack that is detected and contained might not be dangerous, but it could affect usefulness; an undetected spoofing of a GNSS signal could affect safety.

This problem is relatively new for embedded systems. In the past, these systems tended to be self-contained and physically isolated, thus implicitly protected from attack. This is no longer the case: railway braking systems, for example, communicate wirelessly with signalling equipment and receive GNSS signals; medical equipment uses Wi-Fi to communicate with databases; and operators use USB memory sticks to retrieve logging information, etc. All these interfaces to the outside world offer points through which the system can be attacked and compromised.

Observation 1. As Littlewood and Strigini (2004) point out, the uncertainty of safety, reliability and security is inherent: 'no system is completely secure, just as no system is completely safe, or completely reliable'.

While acknowledging that more research is needed, the authors of 'Disentangling the relations between safety and security' (Piètre-Cambacédès and Bouissou 2010) start to clarify the relationships between safety and security. Figure 1 is adapted from the SEMA classification provided in that reference. The primary difference between security and safety is whether the abnormal system behaviour is caused by deliberate and malicious action, or by accidental conditions. The system is subject to such conditions from its environment or from internal failures, and it increases the stresses on the larger system of which it is a part (Section 3).

Clearly, safety and security can be both antagonistic (e.g., physical redundancy might increase safety while also increasing the attack surface and thereby reducing security) and sympathetic (e.g., fine-grained logging can help anticipate both security and safety problems).

Some researchers argue that the tools commonly used to determine the anticipated level of safety (actually reliability and availability) of a system can also incorporate security information. For example, Johnson (2011) applies both semi-formal (the GSN) and formal methods (Boolean-Driven Markov Processes (BDMPs)) to evaluating the effect of security vulnerabilities in the GNSS system.

	Malicious	Accidental
Environment to System	Vulnerability exploitation	Unanticipated condition
System to Environment	Unnecessary move to safe state Necessary move to safe state Failure to move to safe state	
System to System	Unauthorised code on device	Internal bug

Security   Safety

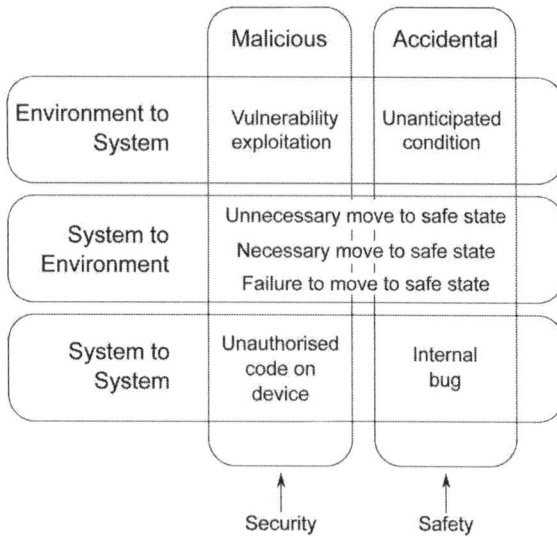

Fig. 1. Adapted SEMA classification

3 The wider environment

Several studies, including Thomas (2012), have pointed out that components, in particular embedded devices, may form part of 'accidental systems': systems brought together without full knowledge of the failure modes (or, in some cases, the existence) of all of the components.

Even if the system is not accidental, a component reverting to its safe state or, worse, suffering a dangerous failure, increases the burden on the wider system, which must now handle the situation: the 'system to environment' row in Figure 1. If a train suddenly stops (safe state) or passes its movement authority limit (dangerous failure), then the signalling system must have been designed to anticipate this danger and be able to respond correctly. If an infusion device stops supplying a drug (safe state) or starts providing the wrong dosage (dangerous failure) then the hospital must have manual procedures that can adequately handle this situation.

Observation 2. The term 'safe state' refers to a particular component, and a move by a component to its safe state normally makes the entire system of which it is a part less safe.

Experience 1. The designers of a device for performing medical procedures, Device T, recognised this problem of a system component moving to its safe state, and required that a trained human operator be present whenever T was operating – defining the acceptable larger environment. The human could have performed the work, but T was both faster and more accurate. If T moved to its safe state (stopped), the human would take over and complete the procedure. While this strategy addressed the possible failure of T, it introduced human factors related to the operator that increased the probability of the larger system (device and human operator) failing: loss of critical skills and boredom.

In effect, with T the problem has been transferred from the device to the higher level system. As Bainbridge (1983) notes:

> 'the automatic control system has been put in because it can do the job better than the operator, but yet the operator is being asked to monitor that it is working effectively ... if the decisions can be fully specified then a computer can make them more quickly, taking into account more dimensions and using more accurately specified criteria than a human operator can. There is therefore no way in which the human operator can check in real-time that the computer is following its rules correctly. One can therefore only expect the operator to monitor the computer's decisions at some meta-level ... The human monitor has been given an impossible task.'

4 Simple example

4.1 Description of the device

Consider a simple device consisting of a 'main process' that does something useful: perhaps it calculates whether a train's brakes should be applied, switches the colours of traffic lights, or dispenses a drug.

4.2 Safety requirement

This device is accompanied by a safety requirement; we will assume that the customer demands that the probability that a dangerous failure occurs per hour of operation be no greater than 10^{-7} (SIL3 in IEC 61508 terms).

Experience 2. As System U was about to be shipped, a programmer reading the code realised that, if the operator were to type a particular command with very regular and precisely-timed keystrokes, a safety check would be skipped, potentially exposing a service technician to a high voltage. To be a risk,

1. The dangerous condition would have to exist (unlikely).
2. The operator would have to type at precisely the correct rate (found in testing to be effectively impossible).
3. The service technician would have to access the circuit without manually checking for a high voltage (probable).

U was a low-volume, high-value product but, because no acceptable probability of dangerous failure had been agreed with the customer, shipment had to be stopped, and the development company had to absorb a substantial cost penalty while the software was changed.

In our example system, the main process is complex, so we aim to meet the safety requirement with implementation diversity by adding a 'safety function'. This safety function monitors the inputs, outputs and possibly internal states of the main system, and, using a much simpler algorithm, decides whether a dangerous situation has arisen (Figure 2).

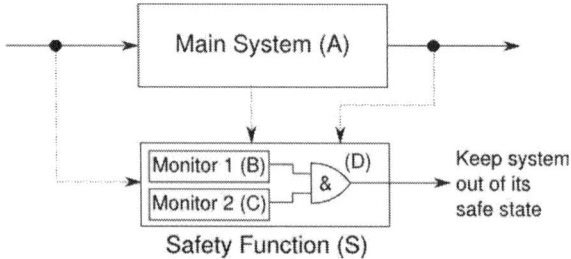

Fig. 2. A 1oo2 system

The AND gate in the safety function makes it appear at first glance to be a 2oo2 system: both monitors (B and C) must agree on a decision. However, like many software-based systems, these monitors decide whether the device should be held out of its safe state – the assumption being that, unless the software in both monitors agree that it should be allowed to run, the hardware will cause the device to revert to its safe state.

The safety function is, therefore, in the terminology of IEC 61508-6 really a 1oo2 system: any one monitor can cause the system to move to its safe state. An important implication of this distinction is that the safety function changes from being a low-demand sub-system to being a high-demand sub-system (every few milliseconds), or even a continuous sub-system.

Observation 3. Many low-demand hardware safety functions become high-demand or continuous systems when converted to software. Incidentally, this change reduces the probability of silent failure.

For the sake of discussion, we will assume that the probabilities of failure per hour and repair times are as given in Table 2. For simplicity, we (unrealistically) assume that all failures are immediately detected. These failure rates incorporate both 'accidental' (safety) and 'malicious' (security) failures (Figure 1).

Note that, for the components within the safety function, there are two failure modes:

1. to fail in such a way as to mimic the condition where a dangerous situation has been detected (i.e., fail safe)

2. to fail in such a way as to mimic the condition where a dangerous situation was not detected (i.e., fail unsafe).

With these two failure modes, there are a total of 54 (2 x 3 x 3 x 3) system states.

Table 2. Sample failure rates

Component failure	Failure rate (per hour)	Repair time (hours)	Repair rate (per hour)
A	10^{-4}	2	0.5
B or C move to 'fail safe'	5×10^{-5}	4	0.25
B or C move to 'fail unsafe'	5×10^{-5}	4	0.25
D move to 'fail safe'	500×10^{-9}	4	0.25
D move to 'fail unsafe'	500×10^{-9}	4	0.25

4.3 Usefulness requirement

One important value is missing from our description of the example device given in Section 4.2: for what percentage of the time does it have to do useful work? In our experience, omitting this requirement while including an upper bound on the probability of dangerous failure appears to be common. This omission means that the designer could produce a system that never released the brakes, that kept the traffic lights permanently red, or that never dispensed any drug, and still be able to defend the position that every requirement had been met.

When considering usefulness in a system design, it is important to take into account the failure rate of the main system, A (Figure 2), because it imposes an upper bound to the usefulness of the device. Anything we do by adding the safety function cannot improve that upper bound; it can only hinder it. Indeed, if the main system were 100% dependable, the safety function would *only* be a hindrance.

We will assume that the requirement for our example device states that meeting the system's safety requirement should not reduce the availability of the device by more than 5% from its failure rate given in the first line of Table 2.

Experience 3. System V controlled a major industrial process within a larger system. Its safety requirements were specified by international standards, but no requirements were given for its usefulness. The designers produced a design very similar to that shown in Figure 2, with disparate hardware and software in Monitors 1 and 2. Analysis of the design indicated that, had V been deployed as designed, the 'hair-trigger' safety function would have resulted in substantial outages (V remaining safe but adding stress to the larger system within which V operated).

4.4 Security requirement

If we assume that confidentiality is not a requirement for our example device (a hacker breaking into the system but doing no harm is acceptable), the security requirement becomes a combination of the safety and usefulness requirements: anticipated security breaches should compromise neither the safety requirement (Section 4.2) nor the usefulness requirement (Section 4.3). Thus, potential attacks must be included in the hazard and risk analysis. For the sake of this example, we assume that the resulting probabilities are incorporated into the numbers in Table 2.

5 System states

In a safety calculation there is normally only one state of interest: dangerous failure. This view is not adequate, however, when designing a device that must also be useful; Table 1 lists the four states that are then of interest.

Of these states, the most neglected in conventional analysis is possibly II: although there was actually no dangerous condition, the safety function thought that there was and has brought the device into its safe state unnecessarily, rendering the device useless and placing stress on the external environment. This state reflects the safety function adversely affecting the usefulness of the device due to a failure within the safety function itself.

Observation 4. Table 1 indicates that, of the four identified states, the device is actively dangerous in only one state, whereas it is useless and placing stress on its environment in three of them.

6 Design approaches for the example device

6.1 Tools

Designers need tools: mathematically-based, computer-assisted tools to help with the design process. 'Modeling safety and security interdependencies with BDMP' (Piètre-Cambacédès and Bouissou 2010) already mentioned contains a useful list of tools from the safety and security worlds that have been adapted for the other discipline (e.g., fault trees that have been used since the beginning of safety analysis have become threat or attack trees in the security world).

The designer, however, needs unified tools that will both incorporate safety and security threats and provide the probabilities associated with at least the four states listed in Table 1. Bouissou (2007), for instance, has proposed BDMPs as such a technique.

In order to make use of common tools it is, of course, necessary to accept that security threats can be considered statistically. For many years it was believed that software failure could not be handled statistically: it being thought that all software failures were systematic.

That argument has been long demolished, but it is still necessary to argue that security problems can be so considered (see Littlewood and Strigini 2004). The superficial difference between safety and security assessment, as identified by Littlewood and Strigini, is that for usefulness and safety one can imagine testing a large number of devices, measuring failure rates and building a statistical model: a frequentist approach. Security attacks, on the other hand (or at least the first exploitation of each vulnerability), are generally not reproducible and a frequentist interpretation cannot be used. However, from the point of view of the system owner, as illustrated in Experience 4 below, initial attacks appear as a stochastic process and, using a Bayesian (strength of belief) rather than frequentist view of probability, can be handled statistically.

Experience 4. System W was a large telecommunications system. One installation suffered repeated and highly embarrassing outages at random intervals. Many hypotheses as to why this one installation should be failing were tested (temperature fluctuations, EMI, etc.) but the random and infrequent nature of the failures made it difficult to find the cause. Eventually surveillance cameras were installed and it was found that a maintenance technician was deliberately bringing the system down so that he could be paid to fix it at overtime rates – a malicious rather than accidental failure. From the point of view of the telecommunications operator these were still stochastic failures, however.

If we accept that the availability, reliability and security of a software-based system can all be considered statistically, we can use enhancements of the well-known fault tree to derive all the necessary results. Although simple Boolean fault trees are not adequate, particularly when sequential operations, repair times and other duration-based tasks are taken into account, extensions such as dynamic fault trees, Bayesian networks and BDMPs can be used. These tools incorporate Markov models to allow inclusion of these types of duration- and sequence-based constructions into fault trees without a state explosion.

6.2 First design

A fault tree analysis of the example described in Section 4 indicates that the probability of being in each state is as given in the 'First design' column of Table 3. The only complexity associated with the fault tree is that, to obtain numbers for all four states, repair times as well as failure rates need to be taken into account. For example, the rate of entry to state IV is $\lambda_A(1 - (\lambda_D + \lambda_B\lambda_C)R_S)$ per time unit, where the λ_i are the failure rates of component i, and R_S is the repair time of the safety function. To handle this complexity, we can use either a BDMP or, in this case, more simply a fault 'tree' using the product $\lambda_i R_i$ rather than λ_i.

Table 3. State probabilities

State	Probability of state				Change
	First design		Second design		
I	0.999398		0.999798		+0.04%
II	402e-06	(3.5 hrs/yr)	2.04e-06	(1 min/yr)	-99%
III	0.408e-09		80e-09		+20%
IV	0.2e-3	(1.75 hrs/yr)	0.19992e-03	(1.75 hrs/yr)	-0.04%

The unrealistically high safety level (probability of dangerous failure $\approx 4 \times 10^{-10}/4 = 10^{-10}$)) indicates two things. Firstly we are close to the level described in the 1981 Fault Tree Handbook:

'When due consideration is not devoted to matters such as this, the naïve calculator will often produce such absurd numbers as 10^{-16} or.10^{-18}. The low numbers simply say that the system is not going to fail by the ways considered but instead is going to fail at a much higher probability in a way not considered.'

Secondly we have spare safety budget that can be used to balance the shortfall in usefulness.

Observation 5. It is sometimes difficult to reduce the safety of a device deliberately. However, we should remember that the initial design was arbitrary: we could have made it even safer by incorporating a 1oo3 safety function.

6.3 Second design

To improve the overall availability of our device, we can decide that the safety function should become a 2oo2 device: both Monitor 1 (B) and Monitor 2 (C) must agree before the device is allowed to revert to its safe state.

This design reflects the practical reality that, particularly if they are replicas, if the two monitors disagree, then the disagreement almost certainly indicates a problem with one of the monitors, not with the main system. If the two monitors are disparate (with different processors, different operating systems, different applications implementing different algorithms), then it could be argued that a disagreement is more likely to reflect a dangerous situation in the main system. This is by no means certain, however.

Experience 5. System V, described above, was implemented with disparate monitoring systems and analysis demonstrated that loss of synchronisation between them could cause momentary disagreement and consequently an unnecessary move to the safe state.

The 'Second design' column of Table 3 lists the new state probabilities. Note that the device still meets the requirements of SIL3 (probability of dangerous failure per hour $\approx 80.4 \times 10^{-9} \approx 0.2 \times 10^{-7}$), and that, significantly, the non-availability of the device has dropped from 5.3 hours/year to 1.77 hours/year. This number is close to the best that can be achieved: 1.75 hours/year, because of the underlying dependability of the main system. An important implication of this second design is that, although the device will be less dependable, it will still meet its SIL3 requirements, and it will place less stress on the system into which it is embedded.

In this simple example, we have achieved a better balance between safety and usefulness, and accommodated security by making use of its stochastic nature.

6.4 Alternative second design

As an alternative to making the safety function a 2oo2 subsystem, we can take into consideration the fact that software systems suffering from Heisenbugs may have a very short 'repair time', and that many systems can afford a potentially dangerous situation to persist for a short time without significantly affecting the risk of harm. This short time can be used to 'repair' a possibly errant piece of software. Often, in the case of a Heisenbug or soft memory error, simply repeating the same computation will lead to a different (and correct) answer, because the internal timing conditions are now different.

For example, a high-speed train travels about 100 metres per second: it could perhaps tolerate a 20 ms (2 metres) delay in applying the brakes, and this tolerance could allow the monitor to reboot and resynchronise. Similarly, a drug infusion device might have a flow rate of 100 ml/hr and for some drugs the system might be able to tolerate an additional second of drug flow, again giving time to restart the dissenting monitor.

Providing such a delay makes the gate (component D in Figure 2) more complex, which will adversely affect its failure rate. Analysis may find, however, that there is a net gain in overall usefulness and that, therefore, this design should be considered.

7 Summary

Today's system designer must balance an increasing number of constraints. We have discussed usefulness, safety and security, and noted that they can be antagonistic: improving one often means accepting a deterioration in another. There are, of course, many other constraints, for example, maintaining adequate system performance. As the number of such constraints increases, the designer needs both clear requirements and help in creating a balance between requirements.

Fortunately, the constraints we have discussed can all be mapped into probabilistic models, though in order to model the overall system, extensions are needed to our conventional fault tree tools; BDMPs and Bayesian networks are candidates for this.

We are continuing our exploration of these techniques and tools with industrial-scale systems.

References

Bainbridge L (1983) Ironies of automation. In: Automatica, 19(6):775–779

Bouissou M (2007) A generalization of dynamic fault trees through Boolean logic Driven Markov Processes (BDMP). In: Proceedings of ESREL 2007

Johnson C (2011) Using assurance cases and Boolean logic driven Markov processes to formalise cyber security concerns for safety-critical interaction with global navigation satellite systems. In: ECEASST, 45

Littlewood B, Strigini L (2004) Redundancy and diversity in security. In: ESORICS 2004, 9th European Symposium on Research in Computer Security, LNCS 3193. Springer

Piètre-Cambacédès L, Bouissou M (2010) Modeling safety and security interdependencies with BDMP (Boolean logic Driven Markov Processes). In: Proceeding of the 2010 IEEE International Conference on Systems, Man, and Cybernetics

Thomas M. (2012) Accidental systems, hidden assumptions and safety assurance. In: Dale C, Anderson T (eds) Achieving Systems Safety. Springer

Challenging the 'Safety Sausage Machine'

Paul Chinneck and Gavin Wilsher

Altran Praxis

Bath, UK

Abstract   As military systems become increasingly complex, so does the requirement to argue acceptable levels of safety. Many long-established design standards favour mitigating safety risk by design, and view mitigation by procedure of lesser value.

However, recent experience has shown that this 'design everything in' philosophy can remove flexibility – some military users regularly mitigate risk through a combination of procedure and design, and are generally happy to accept more risk to gain the flexibility that this brings.

A natural tension therefore exists between the 'classical' approach of designing in safety, and an alternative approach that adjusts the design/procedural split to gain operational flexibility.

1 Introduction

Altran-Praxis has extensive experience in providing safety engineering support to the unmanned aerial system (UAS) domain. The most high profile of the projects on which we have been actively engaged is the British Army's WATCHKEEPER programme. We have been involved in WATCHKEEPER for over 9 years and have developed an electronic safety case to support its initial release to service. This will be the first UAV of this weight class to be certified for use in UK airspace.

Two definitions at the outset – 'UAV' refers to the airborne vehicle (unmanned aerial *vehicle*), whilst 'UAS' refers to the wider system (unmanned aerial *system*), including all the associated ground equipment. UAS can include non-deployed equipment and/or services, such as training and support equipment. The terms are used in their proper context in this paper – UAV when only the air vehicle is in view, and UAS for the entire system.

In this paper, we have avoided using the term 'autonomous'. This word suggests the ability of the system to learn or think for itself, without external intervention, and indeed recent attempts to define this term use just that description. Many of the systems badged as 'autonomous' follow a defined route plan and react to system states or external influences using pre-programmed behaviour. The authors feel that a better term for this behaviour might be 'automatic'.

Due to the majority of the authors' work being with UAS that are automatic in their behaviour, the experience presented in this paper understandably focuses on those systems. However, the paper is designed not just to present some of the lessons learnt from current work, but to stimulate thinking about the wider challenges for UAS and perhaps the wider military equipment domain.

The structure of this paper is to firstly outline some of the uses and risks associated with UAS, then to secondly present and explore some examples that have been encountered whilst managing safety for these novel systems.

2 UAS risks and considerations

2.1 Humans in the loop

For automatic UAS, almost all of the human pilot involvement is to conduct the pre-flight activities; route planning and subsequent uploading to the vehicle (using ground-based systems). However, once airborne, the on-board control software effectively replaces the pilot, as no human intervention is required, even for internal system emergencies such as on-board failures.

Risk can generally be divided into two main areas – that caused by proximity of people to the UAS on the ground, and that caused by either overflying third parties or colliding with other air users. These two types of risk, whilst causing a similar severity of accident, are very different in the way they can be mitigated. Typically, the UAS proximity hazards are mitigated by procedure i.e. keeping people or other manoeuvring aircraft away from the UAV, whilst overflight hazards are dealt with more by design i.e. reducing the likelihood of failures and implementing safety features if they do arise.

2.2 Quick reactions

Currently, UAS are limited to operation in segregated airspace. Whilst some of this is perhaps due to a lack of confidence in their ability to always act as intended, a more concrete reason is the absence of a truly autonomous function (known as a pilot in manned aviation!) to sense impending collisions with other moving objects. Sense and avoid is seen as the 'silver bullet' to this issue, and various studies are underway to achieve a workable solution to this. Whilst not discussed in any depth in this paper, it is perhaps worth highlighting that sense and avoid is really just another reaction that the UAS must implement. It is however understandable why it attracts so much focus, as the extent of situations the UAS must deal with are almost endless.

Returning to the scope of this paper, 'failures' can include external influences, such as weather-induced stall, icing or birdstrike, or internal system failures, such as engine failure or datalink loss. The UAS must either be tolerant to these factors or allow for their occurrence in the declared level of safety it achieves. For instance, inability to withstand a birdstrike may be acceptable if the likelihood of one occurring makes the associated risk acceptably low.

Just as there are two main types of risk that the UAS poses (see earlier), the ways of dealing with risk from failures or external influences fall into two main groups. Risk can be mitigated by pre-defined flight rules, or by defining locations to which to land in the event of emergencies during flight. The latter are clearly important to pre-plan, as UAS that rely on datalink for completion of mission must be tolerant to loss of that datalink, which would make any subsequent request to change the UAV behaviour impossible.

Pre-defining flight rules to cope with failures brings a formidable challenge. As we have already seen, the manned pilot is a truly autonomous function, able to think for itself and make decisions based on continually changing information. Replicating this behaviour, not just in a small subset of states but for all foreseeable circumstances, is a challenging task.

2.3 The trade-off

Many factors must be considered when deciding a system's capability. Mission time, payload ability and performance are just a few, not to mention safety of course. Clearly the safety community would favour safety over everything else, but this may limit a user's capability to the point where use of the system is impracticable.

The fundamental issue that drives the standards to set the guidelines in the way they do is one of tolerability of risk. In a purely civilian environment, the societal view on the tolerability of risk is fairly fixed (in the west). Society tends not want to tolerate a higher level of risk (or even just a perceived higher level), particularly one over which it has no control, irrespective of the potential benefits to be gained. One only has to look at nuclear power generation to see the response to perceived increase in risk level.

And so comes the challenge. Is it helpful, or even necessary, to design absolutely everything into the system to try to make it require no human interaction during the mission? The early experience of the authors is that this is how many UAS used to be developed. However, one cannot completely divorce the safety of the system from the reason it exists, and for a military UAS, that reason is largely to capture intelligence in the form of pictures or video. It stands to reason then that removing the human completely when he or she is there anyway to perform their mission function is not logical.

Development standards, such as Def Stan 00-56 (MOD 2007), suggest that there is a clear order of preference in how to reduce risk. This order begins with eliminating the hazard (by design), moves down to reducing the risk by engineering mitigation (such as safety features or warning devices) and finishes with procedural mitigation (such as training or warning notices). But is this the right preference in every case? Let us explore:

2.4 A simple example

Consider the need for a UAV to perform an emergency landing at a pre-defined site. There are three broad ways the system could do this, as shown in Figure 1.

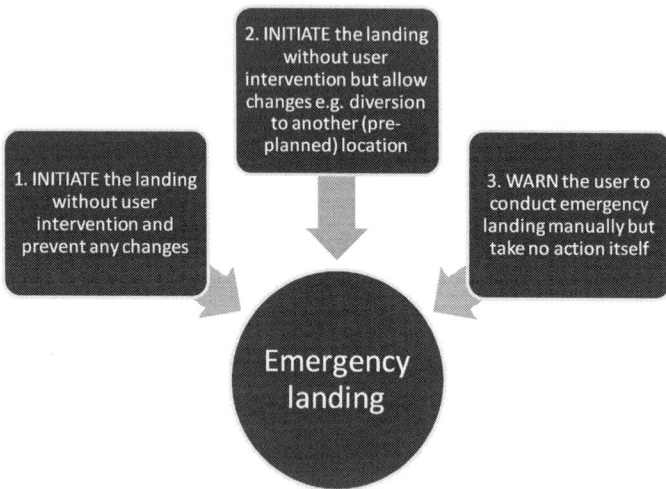

Fig. 1. Performing an emergency landing

Which of these is the 'right' answer? If we blindly follow the standards and 'design the hazard out' then we would select option 1, preventing human intervention from causing the UAV to impact the ground due to stress in what may be a high pressure situation. However, the real answer is probably that it depends – on factors such as weather, surrounding terrain, or confidence in the freedom of the landing site from third parties. From our experience, many users would totally discount the first option as too limiting, whilst any conscientious safety engineer would be horrified by the last one!

What may have made perfect sense to the designer in defining the UAV's behaviour may be different to the viewpoint of the operational commander in the heat of the mission. Weather conditions, other surrounding air traffic, the need to favour mission success over safety may all influence the judgement at the time.

So herein is the question this paper poses – is it right to remove decisions from the user in the interests of safety, because the standards demand it? Is it time to recognise that for UAS, this long-standing order of preference is being challenged and needs re-visiting? Typically, armed forces mitigate risk through a combination of procedure and design, and are generally happy to accept more risk to gain the flexibility that this brings. Automating everything and completely removing the human from the loop may solve one problem – but introduces others, not least reducing operational flexibility.

A natural tension therefore exists between the 'classical' design-in-safety approach (only relying on procedures where absolutely necessary), and an alternative approach that adjusts the split between designed-in safety and procedural safety (see Figure 2).

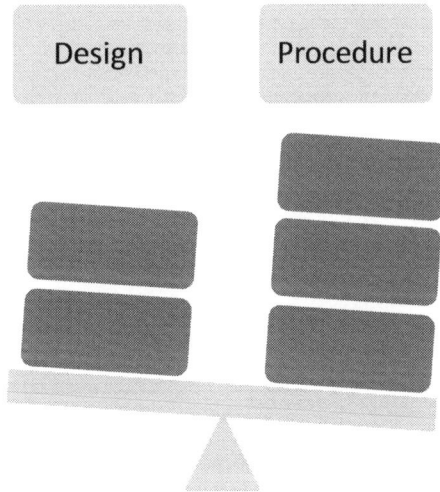

Fig. 2. The tension between design and procedure

The intent of highlighting this tension is to suggest potential answers to the question, and to raise the subject in the minds of the safety community with the hope of stimulating healthy debate. How it unfolds is largely up to the safety practitioners amongst us – those who face the challenge of applying standards in the real world every day.

2.5 Tolerability of risk

In a dynamic military environment, the concept of what is tolerable often changes according to the situation. So, taking the example posed previously, a UAS commander may be prepared to 'accept' the increased risk to life (and his asset) associated with leaving the failing UAS on station in order to benefit from the intelligence captured during the period before it fails. This is clearly at odds with the principle of designing the hazard out, which would divert the UAS to a designated landing site to reduce risk to life to a tolerable level (or at least one that was considered tolerable before the mission and before the UAS commander performed a dynamic cost benefit analysis and judged that the increased risk to life was now tolerable).

However, one could argue that this would be unacceptable for training purposes. One possible way of dealing with this is to introduce a 'training mode' into a UAS, which would prevent the user from making many of the above procedural trade-offs. Instead, potentially higher risk system behaviour could be prevented from being allowed to continue for the sake of mission success.

2.6 Making the designer's life easy

To the designer of a UAS, the military scenario above i.e. let the user decide what the UAS does in any given situation, simplifies the design process considerably. There is no longer a need to programme in a safe set of behaviours because the user will decide, on a case by case basis, what is tolerably safe.

Can this approach be acceptable? By not following the standards (which, it could be argued, define best practice) is the designer potentially negligent in some way? Is it acceptable to entrust the safety of life to a user who may be under such extreme pressure to deliver a capability that he may lose sight of the potential risks?

2.7 Making the user's life hard

In adopting the above approach and shifting a lot of the safety responsibility on to the user's shoulders, have we just made his job harder and therefore given him the opportunity to make mistakes that increase risk to life unnecessarily?

This approach not only relies on comprehensive training and well defined procedures and drills to manage the risks, it requires each user to remain current and always apply the training, procedures and drills. In practice, however good the user may be, people will make mistakes especially if they are under pressure.

3 So what?

So far, this paper has begun to challenge traditional safety engineering practice as applied to UAS operations and has posed many questions.

Let us now consider a number of practical, real-life examples. Firstly, let's go back to our original example with the three potential options for a failing UAS to take:

1. Initiate the landing without user intervention and prevent any changes e.g. diversion to a different location.
2. Initiate the landing without user intervention but allow changes to it e.g. change to a different (but still pre-planned) location.
3. Warn the user to land the UAV manually but take no action itself.

It would seem that a compromise may well provide the best balance between capability and inherent safety i.e. initiate the automatic landing without user intervention but allow any changes to it that the user may deem acceptable or appropriate.

The legal ramifications of this approach would also need consideration given that a user intervention to gain some benefit may result in loss of life.

A number of other examples are now discussed, based on actual experience learnt from many years of safety management of UAS. These examples cover both ground hazards and air hazards, as both aspects must be considered.

3.1 Propeller hazard

Propellers are frequently used on UAVs for propulsion. This clearly presents a considerable hazard to ground crews operating the UAV prior to its airborne deployment. We cannot practically engineer this hazard out (gas turbine engines are not practicable alternatives for smaller UAS, and in any case they present their own ground hazards) and so have to reduce the risk as far as is reasonably practicable using other engineering and human solutions. Engine start (and hence propeller rotation) is typically achieved through the use of a ground vehicle attached via cables. Once the engine is running, disconnecting these cables may take the user closer to the rotating propeller than feels comfortable. There are very good technical reasons for this layout of UAV, including a desire not to route high-voltage electrical cables close to (or through) the fuel tank (safety) and minimising the length of these heavy cables to increase flight endurance (capability).

The user is satisfied that this risk is tolerable because they follow strict procedures to manage the risk. But is following procedures a satisfactory approach in this case or would an engineered solution have been better? In safety terms alone (disregarding the technical reasons outlined above), good practice would most likely have placed the connector sockets further away from the propeller. If this was not practicable, other design mitigations could be envisaged e.g. cables that are designed to be released remotely, long reach release tools produced for this specific purpose, or introducing a cage around the propeller. Interestingly, conducting a formal cost benefit analysis indicated that further engineering effort was not necessary to reduce the risk to a level that would be deemed ALARP. However, the issue of what is deemed good practice still dominated, despite the absence of a financial reason to change the system. In this case, moving away from engineering solutions and towards human solutions may be viewed as a less satisfactory (not the lowest risk) solution, and may add support for following the traditional hierarchy more rigidly.

3.2 Runway incursion hazard

Operational UAS do not currently have a 'sense and avoid' capability when on the runway but tend to rely on an observer (along with local airfield procedures) to ensure people and assets are not at risk from the UAV during take-off (and landing). There is an inherent lag in this approach because the activities shown in Figure 3 are required.

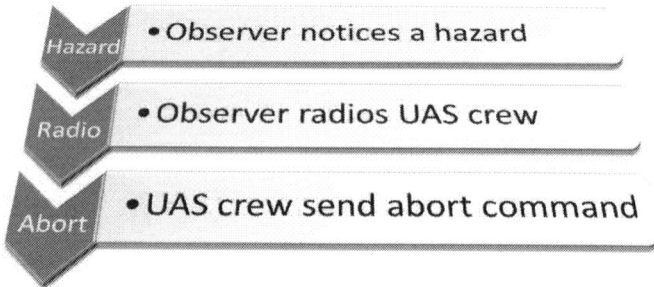

Fig. 3. The lag between hazard and abort

Of course, there is at least one other step required – that the UAV receives and responds to the abort command sent by the crew.

Some UAVs are fitted with cameras so that the 'pilot' may identify runway incursions himself but this is still not an engineering solution to hazard control and offers far from comprehensive visual coverage. Furthermore, many UAS are certified for use in zero visibility conditions. In these cases, the observer (and camera) is practically redundant and yet the UAV is still able to operate. Is this another case where not following the accepted hierarchy has become 'best practice' but in fact really should be replaced with an engineering solution?

3.3 To auto-land or not to auto-land (on loss of electrical power)?

In a similar way to our original example above, all aircraft failures could self-initiate an emergency landing. This would mean that no pilot intervention is required, even in emergencies.

Some emergencies are more critical than others. Engine failure is generally terminal, unless a re-start facility is provided, and loss of datalink (where the UAS implementation relies upon one) can also be irrecoverable. In these scenarios, no other action except landing would be the logical choice, and therefore the UAS automatically initiating landing is sensible.

However, take for example a loss of engine-sourced electrical power. Generally, UAS have a primary electrical power system (from an alternator), and a secondary (backup) system, usually a battery of some kind. The battery gives a finite amount of power in the event of the primary system failing. As system designers, we could enforce that the UAV land automatically on loss of primary electrical power, but this would mean that the remaining time on battery power (which may be significant) would be unavailable for mission use. Depending on the point at which primary electrical power is lost, this may be untenable for the mission commander, so in this case, the reliance on procedural mitigation would seem appropriate.

3.4 Airspace management

Current UAS operations are conducted only in segregated airspace. Control of this airspace is done almost exclusively by procedure, but a number of options are feasible for designing-in automatic management and reaction to airspace limits.

In some of the projects with which we have been involved, there were some discussions early in the lifecycle about two aspects of airspace, as shown in Figure 4.

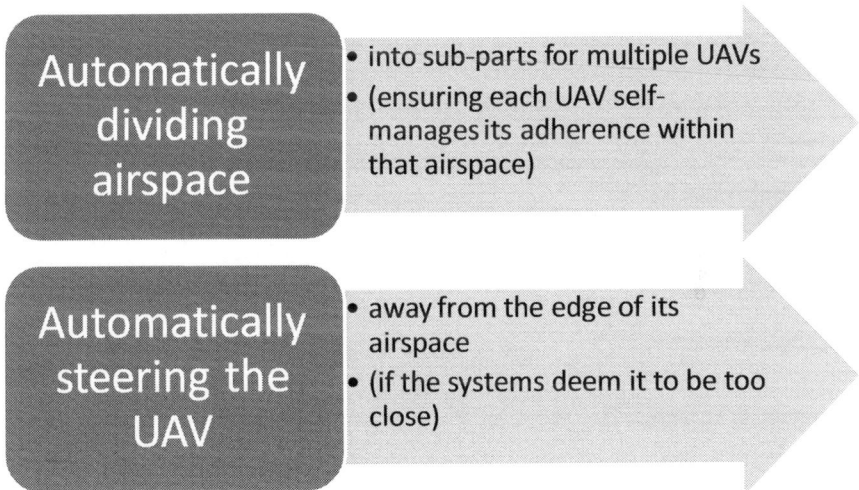

Automatically dividing airspace
- into sub-parts for multiple UAVs
- (ensuring each UAV self-manages its adherence within that airspace)

Automatically steering the UAV
- away from the edge of its airspace
- (if the systems deem it to be too close)

Fig. 4. Managing airspace automatically

Neither of these concepts was retained for very long, as it became increasingly clear (as extant UAS operations became more established) that the air traffic controllers were much better placed to manage the airspace than the UAS crews. Furthermore, for UAS that are subject to airspace limitations, the UAV should in theory never be too close to the edge of its airspace, if all the pre-flight checking and route management is working properly. If this has failed, to allow the UAV to be somewhere it shouldn't be, there seems to be little point in trying to use the same systems to enforce a 'steer-away' function, as that will be subject to the same failures that caused the UAV to stray in the first place.

3.5 Eyes in the sky

A very real situation for military UAS is what happens on the ground when an in-flight emergency occurs. If troops on the ground are already in contact with enemy forces, then the UAS failure may well deny them the eyes-on facility on which they were reliant. (Indeed, some military commanders are reluctant to send their forces out if the UAS is not available to give them coverage.) Losing the UAS information at such a critical point in the operation *will* almost certainly result in loss of life to those ground troops.

Users could avoid such an eventuality by insisting that the UAS remain on its mission until the last possible moment and accept the *potential* for loss of life it finally becomes unavailable. As with other combat systems, absence of the services provided by the UAS may itself cause loss of life – an issue rarely recognised by those not in direct contact with how modern military forces operate.

This kind of discussion may well strengthen the argument for challenging what would otherwise be classified as 'best practice'.

3.6 Bringing it all home

One final example. UAS operations are conducted more and more from busy shared airfields, despite our early experience indicating the opposite (sole-use remote strips) would be true. Many of the systems allow the operators to assign landing sites to use in the event of a malfunction, including the strip from which the UAS was launched. One can understand the logic here – landing a UAV at its 'home' strip is attractive, as it is then inside the fence, and much safer to the ground troops for its retrieval. However, it does bring risks – most notably that of landing a potentially damaged or malfunctioning UAV at a busy shared airfield, with the risks to other users that may pose. The UAV may not react as crews would expect; it may land short of the runway, or some other abnormal event that would conceivably pose extra risk to other users.

An idea that was suggested in one of the pieces of work with which we were involved was to warn the UAS crew that the nominated emergency landing site is their 'home' strip (and therefore potentially riskier than a remote location). This was eventually discounted, on the basis that the user would almost always try to land there if at all possible, and therefore would get too used to clearing an alert that reminded them about the risks it may pose. Negative training of this sort is something of which UAS users are very mindful, as it can lead to a mindset of 'just clearing the alert' without actually reading it.

3.7 What about ALARP?

With all these examples, the challenge exists, when not following the accepted 'best practice' approach to hazard control, of demonstrating that the resulting risks have been reduced to a level that is ALARP.

As system designers we need to be certain we have done all that we reasonably can to reduce risks. But how can we demonstrate ALARP if we have failed to follow the standard's basic requirements? The justification must be robust and defensible but justifying not following the standard can be very difficult. Some reviewers and regulators are more willing to accept this than others and ultimately, only a judge can decide whether everything that can be reasonably expected has been done (by then it is too late). Often, a cost benefit analysis can help with the justification but as we have alluded to previously in this paper, sometimes it may not help – especially if non-financial costs and benefits not related to reduction in risk to life are not considered.

It is of course true that ALARP for military operations may not impose the same level of risk mitigation as does peacetime or training use, even of the same system. This may not be as difficult a problem as might be perceived, if the suggestion from earlier in this paper is invoked i.e. a 'training mode' to prevent trade-offs being used to favour procedural mitigation over design. Over-use of procedure in a non-combat situation could well be questioned for correctness should an incident occur. This does of course bring challenges as to how to ensure realistic training, whilst protecting the users and third parties in more benign scenarios.

4 Conclusions

It was clear from the outset that we were never to resolve this issue with this paper (indeed that was never our intention). However, what we hope that the paper will achieve is some intelligent and constructive debate. What is evident is there cannot be a 'one size fits all' approach to risk reduction and management across all domains and technologies as appears to be mandated through the military (and other) safety standards.

The key to effectively reducing risk and balancing safety against the capability needs of the user would seem to be a flexible approach to the traditional 'best practice' hierarchy of hazard control i.e. reducing associated risks first through engineering solutions then using processes and procedures (the human element). How we document this flexible approach in a standard and provide guidance in its application is a challenge, but one that we believe can bring real benefit for both designer and user. This is true not just for UAS but for any modern system where the complex interaction of sub-systems, including humans, brings the need for re-assessing how we look at and deal with risk.

Acknowledgments   Grateful thanks are extended to Dave Hilton of Thales UK, for his permission to discuss some of our WATCHKEEPER experience in the public domain, and for the timely addition of a pertinent example for this paper!

Thanks also go to Stu Tushingham of Altran Praxis, for providing a comprehensive review of the content in this paper and adding some wider UAS experience.

References

Ministry of Defence (2007) Defence Standard 00-56 Issue 4 – Safety Management Requirements for Defence Systems

The Role of Human Factors in System Safety Analyses

Gabriele Schedl, Lukas Fritz

Frequentis AG

Vienna, Austria

Abstract A system is typically defined as a combination of people, procedures and equipment, but many safety analyses focus just on the equipment part. Even safety standards, e.g. IEC 61508, hardly cover human factors. One reason could be that most of the common safety tools can only be applied to hardware, some of them also to software, but they often neglect the human factors. Successful system safety cannot be addressed without this important contributor. The human factors engineering discipline needs to become an integrated part of system safety analyses. This paper will address some practical examples of the non-fulfilment of this requirement with the consequences and will also discuss some practical improvements of the current situation.

1 Introduction

Human factors as a domain is a multidisciplinary effort to compile, generate and apply knowledge about people at work. It focuses on optimizing the people element in a complex work system environment and further covers aspects of integrating people into systems which means getting the interfaces between humans and equipment right. Thereby also rules and procedures and the way people interact and communicate within their workplace teams are of interest. The aim is to improve safety and human performance within the whole lifecycle also taking into account managing of human errors, maintainability and subsequently also decommissioning of the system. The results of human factor assessment can then be applied to improve training, the design of the work environment and the respective system. As a consequence a thorough system safety assessment has to address the human element, considering how people may contribute to safety as well as risk (Eurocontrol 2007).

Workplaces in safety critical domains are often multi-component, multi-featured and integrated within a complex operational environment. To fully understand the human contribution to safety it is necessary to be aware of how human operational performance may be affected by the interrelation with the various components and features of the operational context as well as with other involved people. Within the ICAO Safety Management Manual (ICAO 2009) a conceptual tool, referred as the SHEL(L) model, for the visualization of these interactions and interfaces is introduced. Thereby the humans (liveware) at the front line of operations build the centre which has interfaces to the equipment, consisting of hardware and software, other persons in the workplace (liveware) and the operational environment.

Humans have a key role, as they are capable of recognizing operational events as possible threats and anticipate the associated risk as a basis for further decisions and actions. They are remarkably adaptable but are also subject to considerable variations in their performance. As humans are not standardized their capabilities to execute required tasks depends on their physical factors (e.g. strength, vision and hearing) as well as their psychological factors (e.g. experience, knowledge and adequacy of training). Day-to-day performance is further also affected by physiological reasons like illness or fatigue and additionally by their social environment (e.g. disputes with colleagues or family issues). These human frailties lead to unintended operational mistakes which pop up when least expected, not necessarily in demanding situations.

As modern systems, and especially safety critical systems, have the tendency to grow in their complexity, technology has to be introduced on a massive scale to fulfil all feature and service requirements. Therefore also the equipment-liveware interfaces become intricate and more difficult to assess entirely. The increasing risk that these interfaces are not properly considered during design may subsequently lead to a growing number of operational errors. A common strategy to prevent human induced operational errors is further automation of the systems. So humans remain in the function as supervisors and only take over in exceptional cases. This paradoxical effect, called irony of automation, means that in critical situations humans are performing tasks that had been intended to be fulfilled by machines in order to reduce the likelihood of human failures. The differentiation between human and technical failures is anyway very tricky, since all computers and systems have been designed by humans and therefore any failure at last can be attributed to human factors in the various stages of the entire system lifecycle or operational management (ICAO 2009, Badke-Schaub et al. 2008).

2 Coverage of human factors issues in safety standards

The implementation of a safety process according to a standard is both a moral responsibility and a business incentive for suppliers of safety critical systems as it is of utmost importance within a product liability case to show compliance to well accepted methods of hazard identification, risk management, safe product design and manufacturing.

2.1 Safety standards

2.1.1 IEC 61508

IEC 61508 (IEC 2010) is an international standard developed to facilitate the application of electrical/electronic/programmable electronic (E/E/PE) safety related systems so that functional safety can be achieved. It is designed to be generic (applicable to all kinds of industry) and is therefore also setting out the basic framework for sector specific standards. Whilst the scope of the standard covers all safety related systems based on E/E/PE technology, it focuses on complex systems which means computer based or programmable electronic systems where the exact behaviour under fault conditions cannot be completely determined. The standard aims to encompass all factors influencing the safety of the system and recognize the necessity of a full lifecycle approach that covers specification, design, installation, testing, commissioning, operation, maintenance and change management and decommissioning. Even though the emphasis of the technical content of the standard deals with claims and requirements considering hardware and software integrity, there are several references and requirements throughout the full safety lifecycle stages that take into account human factors (Brown 1999, Carey 2001).

A mentionable detail is that IEC 61508 explicitly notes:

> 'A person can form part of a safety-related system, for example, a person could receive information from a programmable electronic device and perform a safety action based on this information, or perform a safety action through a programmable electronic device, human factor requirements related to the design of E/E/PE safety-related systems are not considered in detail in this standard.'

In Part 1 (general requirements) for the hazard determination a requirement demands that all 'relevant' human factor issues shall be included and a reference to IEC 60300 (IEC 2001) is given for further guidance. A complete list of human factor requirements within part 1 over the whole safety lifecycle can be found in (Carey 2001) which assessed the first edition of IEC 61508 but can be directly applied also to the new second edition. Also in Part 2 (requirements for E/E/PE safety-related systems) in several requirements the impact of human factors is mentioned. The following example sums up the level of guidance provided:

> 'The design of the E/E/PE safety-related systems shall take into account human capabilities and limitations and be suitable for the actions assigned to operators and maintenance staff. Such design requirements shall follow good human-factor practice and shall accommodate the likely level of training or awareness of operators, for example in mass produced E/E/PE safety-related systems where the operator is a member of the public.'

Part 3 (software requirements) demands to take into account possible operator misuse for validation planning and gives the following basic advice regarding human factors for the human machine interfaces:

- An operator information system should use the pictorial layout and the terminology the operators are familiar with. It should be clear, understandable and free from unnecessary details and/or aspects.
- Information about the equipment under control (EUC) displayed to the operator should follow closely the physical arrangement of the EUC.
- If several display contents to the operator are feasible and/or if the possible operator actions allow interactions whose consequences cannot be seen at a glance, the information displayed should automatically contain at each state of a display or an action sequence, which state of the sequence is reached, which operations are feasible and which possible consequences can be chosen.

Part 5 (examples of methods for the determination of safety integrity levels) mentions to consider the impact of human factors for the calculation of the EUC risk.

If the E/E/PE system is basically acting as an autonomous protection system, the operator interface and performance can be treated as some kind of 'external part'; however in systems where people form part of the safety related system (e.g. air traffic control) the performance of the overall system has a high dependence on the quality of the user interface and in these cases the limited guidance and requirements regarding human factor issues given within IEC 61508 could be inadequate to provide the necessary level of assurance.

2.1.2 MIL-STD 882

Another important safety standard, especially within military industry, is MIL-STD 882 (Department of Defense 2012a), of which the latest issue E was published in May 2012. This standard uses the term human systems integration (HSI) for the integrated approach for analysis, design, assessment of requirements, concepts, and resources for system manpower, personnel, training, safety and occupational health, habitability, personnel survivability, and also human factors engineering. It includes several references to apply human factor engineering principles throughout the proposed safety process. Starting from requirements to include human factor aspects within the safety and hazard management plan, requirements for human factor integration can be found from the preliminary hazard analysis stage, subsystem hazard analysis (where it is stated that the human shall be considered as a 'component'), and system hazard analysis; further also in health hazard analysis, functional hazard analysis and system of system hazard analysis. However no guidance is given as to what is considered as acceptable or how these tasks have to be performed so it's left to the engineer's interpretation and judgment.

MIL-STD 1472G (Department of Defense 2012b), in its latest release, establishes general human engineering design criteria for military equipment and systems. The standard in detail defines acceptable conditions. However it is only referenced twice in the MIL-STD 882E and therefore is not fully integrated in its safety process.

2.1.3 DEF-STAN 00-56

Defence Standard 00-56 (Ministry of Defence 2007) is commonly used in the military industry in the UK. In Part 1 (requirements) human factor related issues are referenced as a possible mitigation for risk reduction and in the change management process in order to consider the impact of operator error. Part 2 (guidance) states on several instances (hazard identification, risk reduction and interface design) that human factors should receive appropriate consideration; regarding use of tools and techniques it always refers further to Defence Standard 00-25 (Ministry of Defence 2004). And it requires that safety requirements regarding the use of displays should specify the verification and validation of human actions.

A key issue that needs to be resolved is to what extent the criticality of the user can be determined by the criticality of the respective system and what measures have to be taken according to this safety integrity demand.

2.2 Assurance level allocation for human tasks

Eurocontrol has developed and established the Safety Assessment Methodology (SAM) (Eurocontrol 2006) in order to allow Air Traffic Management (ATM) service providers to show compliance towards European regulatory requirements. The SAM includes allocation of assurance levels for software (SWAL) and operational procedures (PAL). These assurance levels cover the whole lifecycle of the ATM system consisting of people, procedures and equipment from definition and design to operation and maintenance and are intended to provide a level of certainty that an acceptable level of safety can be achieved once the system is in operational service.

In (Mana et al. 2007) an extension to the current SAM has been proposed. Thereby a Human Assurance Level (HAL) has been introduced which should be applied to human tasks to help answer the following questions:

- What human factors need to be addressed on this project?
- What is the depth and scope of assurance required?
- What evidence is required to show that the human factors have been sufficiently addressed?

The allocation of the HAL follows the well known scheme of the other AL types. As illustrated in Figure 1 the probability P_h that the human failure generates a hazard has to be multiplied by P_e, the probability that the hazard generates the worst credible effect. The resulting probability has to be mapped in a qualitative set of levels to get an order of magnitude accuracy ranging from very possible to extremely unlikely.

Together with the classified severity, with 1 being a catastrophic outcome to 4 a minor effect, the required HAL can be taken from the matrix in Figure 2.

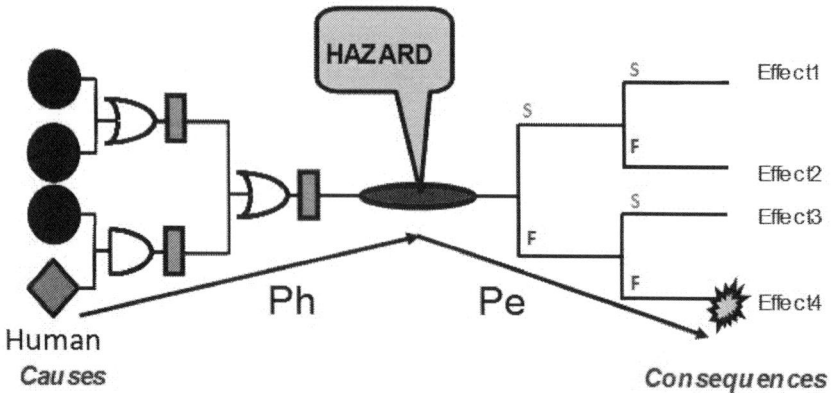

Fig. 1. Bow-tie model of AL allocation process

Probability Ph×Pe / Effect Severity	1	2	3	4
Very Possible	HAL1	HAL2	HAL3	HAL4
Possible	HAL2	HAL3	HAL3	HAL4
Very Unlikely	HAL3	HAL3	HAL4	HAL4
Extremely Unlikely	HAL4	HAL4	HAL4	HAL4

Fig. 2. AL allocation matrix

Additionally a set of objectives has been proposed for each AL for every phase of the lifecycle (definition, design, implementation, transfer into operation, and operation). As an example there are objectives for human reliability analysis, training, workplace ergonomics, monitoring and incident investigations. Even though the HAL framework has been restricted to be applied only to the ATM operations room staff (controller, supervisor and assistants) the AL allocation process could be integrated in almost any already existing safety process for human centric environments like control centres. It allows to consider the different criticality levels of human tasks and to apply the required effort to maintain safety in a systematic approach. If a HAL is further applied to a certain function/product the challenge for a supplier would then be to provide the evidence for execution of the required training as well as the fulfilment of human factor and human reliability requirements. It may also lead to development of supportive tools to manage briefing and shift handovers of a respective system. Even though the HAL framework was introduced in (Mana et al. 2007) and announced in the SAM newsletter, there has been no update of the SAM since 2006.

2.3 Human factor integration frameworks

As IEC 61508 does not cover human factor aspects in a sufficient manner an add-on framework has been funded and published by the Health and Safety Executive (Carey 2001). The proposed framework considers two main tasks, the incorporation of human tasks into the hazard and risk assessment process and it provides tables with human factor requirements for a given safety integrity level. The safety requirements process is refined by additionally allocating integrity requirements to human safety functions. This step is further subdivided into allocation of people and procedure requirements like demanded staff capabilities or training and user interface design requirements for the equipment. A mentionable topic considered within the framework is the analysis of various typical human-machine architectures. The focus and type of human factor issues that need to be handled vary distinctively between the discussed system classes. Further an exact mapping of the proposed process into the safety lifecycle and a description of the human factor activities is included.

In 2007 Eurocontrol released the updated version of their human factor case (Eurocontrol 2007). Its central objective is to provide a practical framework for project managers to address human factor issues throughout the entire project lifecycle. It is a structured approach to ensure that the design and implementation of new ATM systems can deliver performance improvements from a human perspective and also have a close look that safety is still kept at least at a comparable level. The proposed process consists of five stages:

- Fact Finding: recording of project information and identification of what will change and who will be affected
- Issues Analysis: identification and prioritisation of project specific HF issues by a group workshop and/or expert interviews
- Action Plan: description of actions and mitigation strategies
- Action Implementation: implementation of the planned tasks and provision of a human factors case report
- Human Factors Case Review: independent review of the case and suggestion of recommendation.

The guidance material provides additional information about how each stage can be implemented. To be most cost effective the case should be initiated at the earliest possible phase. Further it is explicitly noted that the case is not the human factor element of a safety case. It however can be used to inform a safety case by identifying and addressing safety relevant issues.

Based on the Eurocontrol case and Defence Standard 00-25 the human capability domain of the UK Ministry of Defence published its slightly expanded human factor integration case concept (Bruseberg 2008). It provides detailed explanation and examples for specifying, tracking and documentation of human factors integration requirements.

3 Applicability of standard safety methods

A typical safety process relies on methods like Fault Tree Analysis (FTA), Failure Mode and Effects Analysis (FMEA) or Functional Failure Analysis (FFA) to identify safety critical issues that may cause a hazard. Later on in the project lifecycle with the aid of these techniques it is possible to quantify the hazard probability of a respective design which further allows proper risk management. These techniques initially have been designed to identify and address equipment based problems. As a system consists of people, procedures, equipment and the interrelation between them, a focus just on the technical part will not suffice to assure that a system is acceptably safe. A human error hazard analysis with the aim to identify critical system demands regarding compatibility with human capabilities has to consider the people factor within its operational environment in the assessment. This is also of importance in order to recognise system areas with increased vulnerability to human errors. Initial information for these techniques can be taken from field experience, reviews and publically accessible incident and accident databases.

Further the well-known FTA could be extended by including human actions that could cause a system failure. Thereby fault trees can help to identify situations where the system is most vulnerable to human errors. Taking into account the complexity of the operational environment during normal and also contingency operation it is however difficult to assign a single reasonable figure for the human reliability. Human reliability assessments (HRA) aim to predict human errors and quantify their likelihood of occurrence based on actual performance studies or simulations. In literature lots of methods are presented, for example THERP (Swain and Guttman 1983), SPAR (Gertman et al. 2005) or CREAM (Hollnagel 1998), that render possible to model the human error probability. These results can be additionally refined using performance shaping factors like fitness for duty. However, as for every modelling approach, verifications have to be done via real-time simulations or operation in shadow mode to show that the applied model is a sufficient predictor of the respective operational reality. A sound human analysis however not only focuses on human errors but also considers potential positive contributions of humans to reduce risk or abilities to improve performance.

As complementary approach to the FTA, a top-down method, the Human Factors Process Failure Mode and Effects Analysis (HPFMEA) is considered in (Hobbs et al. 2008). That bottom-up technique identifies how operators interact with their interfaces, what errors are possible and what are the resulting consequences. The principles of both methods are identical for the equipment as well as for the human analysis and therefore even for projects without a dedicated human factor engineer an educated and trained safety engineer should be capable of performing them and thereby enriching the information about the potential safety risk of a system.

Another important technique for identification of human induced hazards is the Human-HAZOP. The methodology is similar to HAZOP studies for process and equipment analyses, except that instead of system functions operator or maintenance tasks are investigated and the causes of failures are credible human errors or incapability.

4 Human factor aspects in project lifecycle

Due to challenging time schedules and limited budgets it is a common pattern in projects to ask for human factors expertise once the system design is already finalized in order to solve problems resulting from not sufficiently considering humans and their interaction with the equipment in the design phase. This inadequate human factors integration costs not only in terms of safety and mission success, but also increases the overall complexity of the system, which increases the time needed to perform tasks, complicates training, maintenance which decreases the system capabilities and further also reduces competitiveness in the market. As illustrated in Figure 3 it is most cost effective to invest in human factors right from the beginning of the project in a proactive manner. In this initial lifecycle phase it is much cheaper to change the system design than only to react to emerging issues.

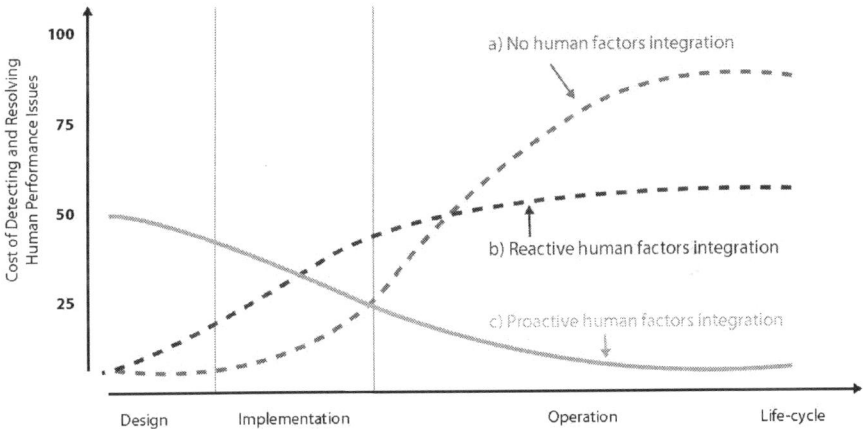

Fig. 3. Cost scenarios of three human factor implementation strategies, from (Eurocontrol 2010)

Investment into human factor integration will therefore help to reduce costs for the design and manufacturing industry as well as for the organisations using these systems operationally. Good usability leads to an increased rate of acceptance within the staff that have to operate the new system. Reduced resistance to change will ease the transition phase into operation and limit the amount of required training. Several frameworks have been proposed in literature implementing the human factor process within a developing process of safety critical systems.

5 Exemplary practical issues

In an organisation providing control centre services the human factor aspects are usually important and considered in implementation of procedures and in ergonomics of operator positions. However, sometimes a gap at the interface between the acquirer (the service provider organization) and our role as an equipment supplier can be experienced.

In tenders safety related human factor requirements hardly ever exist. Furthermore acquirer-supplier human factor/usability workshops quite often focus only on ergonomic issues, colour scheme and button arrangements to recreate the formerly known patterns. The safety department is hardly ever involved or safety a topic at all in these sessions.

Therefore system safety regarding human factor issues is mostly only considered during the internal product development process but not during the specific project implementation. An output of the internal product development safety process is also a set of safety recommendations from the supplier to the customer. These recommendations cover safety related issues identified during supplier safety assessment and certainly cannot be mitigated by the supplier but by the operating organisation.

Examples are a recommended cyclic check of some equipment parts, the demand to continuously monitor the system or that always a spare operator position should be available. The recommendations should become safety requirements on the acquirer side. In a desirable case there should also be a feedback loop that the implementation has happened.

Practical experience also showed that a system that has been regarded safe from a supplier point of view may not be safe in the environment the acquirer uses the equipment. An example is the installation of redundant equipment parts where a survey exhibited that the cable connection done by the system acquirer prevented a hot swappable replacement, so both equipment parts had to be disconnected and therefore redundancy is lost.

6 Practical improvements

Frequentis is active in different technology sectors (e.g. voice and data communication, electronic flight strips, control centre tools) and also in various business domains like air traffic management, public transport, public safety and maritime. Even though criticality and safety awareness is quite different in all these areas, a joint approach of human factor and safety department has been established to extend the already existing 'lessons learned' driven safety database with human factor based requirements. Reported human factor issues and practical experience within projects and products form the basis of this new requirement set.

The internal development process demands to take over all applicable safety requirements into the specification of the respective product or project right from the start, which is done under auspices of the safety engineer in charge. This development process step is applicable to all business areas and domains regardless of their criticality classification and should give assurance that problems experienced in the past should not recur in new products. This set of requirements is then tagged in the specification requirement database as safety related. The added benefit of this partnership for those concerned with human factors is that safety requirements are mandatory. This is a change from the usual situation of human factors during design phase, where achieving human factors integration is sometimes a process of negotiation between design and human factor issues. These requirements cover aspects of user interface displays like freeze recognition, prevention of the obstruction of safety relevant data, and range and sanity checks of user input. Further they also deal with alarm issues like minimum time until indication, required alarm modalities and many other aspects.

For an equipment supplier with limited knowledge of the exact operational environment and procedures, especially in the defence sector, it is commonly only possible to provide an equipment safety case. Nevertheless human factors have been considered in several spots of the argumentation structure, from hazard identification, supported by human factor experts, to the implementation in design and testing of the resulting safety requirements. Also the feedback loop regarding usability and customer acceptance is considered. Further people related aspects like demanding capabilities and respective evidence for the people who are involved in the development and assurance chain of the system under investigation are taken into account. A generic top level argument structure of a GSN based equipment safety case can be seen in Figure 4.

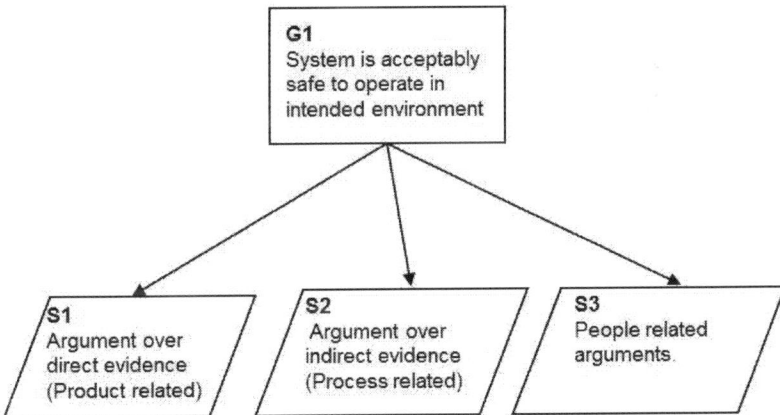

Fig. 4. High level structure of a safety case in GSN notation

7 Discussion

In companies there are usually dedicated departments for human factors engineering and system safety which have almost no connections. Would it be meaningful to implement trans-divisional training or certification to strengthen the integrative approach? This attempt may also foster the relation between the different departments and ease teamwork, and opens possibilities for role allocation as employees can be used more versatilely.

The SHEL(L) model clearly depicts the various interfaces within an operational organisation but there is also another aspect which deserves attention, the interaction between supplier and acquirer organisations. Additionally a typical safety critical system is built by many supplier companies, each delivering some parts/functionalities of the respective system which altogether have to be integrated. How could this interplay be covered from a human factors point of view?

8 Conclusion

The coverage of human factor aspects within commonly used safety standards is limited. In order to improve this situation several frameworks that integrate the human factors within the project lifecycle have been proposed in literature. However there seem to be no closed feedback loop, as even newer versions of the safety standards do not show an improved consideration of human factor issues.

From a supplier point of view the dissemination of operationally safety related human factor aspects from the acquirer organisation often does not happen and therefore only the equipment-operator interface can be considered during the development process, which may result in the negligence of safety related environmental and operational aspects.

References

Badke-Schaub P et al (2008) Human factors – psychologie sicheren handelns in risikobranchen, Springer Medizin Verlag
Brown SJ (1999) Human factors and safety integrity – IEC 61508, Int Conf on Human Interfaces in Control Rooms, Cockpits and Command Centres
Bruseberg A (2008) The HFI case concept: guidance on specifying, tracking and documenting human factors integration requirements, acceptance criteria and evidence
Carey M (2001) Proposed framework for addressing human Factors in IEC 61508, Contract Research Report for HSE
Department of Defense (2012a) MIL-STD-882E, System safety
Department of Defense (2012b) MIL-STD-1472G, Human engineering
Eurocontrol (2006) Safety assessment methodology, v2.1
Eurocontrol (2007) The human factors case: guidance for human factors integration
Eurocontrol (2010) Human performance in air traffic management safety – a white paper
Gertman D et al (2005) The SPAR-H human reliability analysis method NUREG/CR-6883

Hollnagel E (1998) Cognitive reliability and error analysis method – CREAM, Oxford Elsevier Science

Hobbs A et al (2008) Three principles of human-system integration. In Proc of 8th Australian Aviation Symposium

ICAO (2009) Safety management manual – Doc 9859 – 2nd edition

IEC (2001) IEC 60300, Dependability management – 1st edition

IEC (2010) IEC 61508, Functional safety of electrical/electronic/programmable electronic safety related systems – 2nd edition

Mana P et al (2007) Assurance levels for ATM elements: human (HAL), operational procedure (PAL), software (SWAL). In IEEE Inst of Eng and Tech Int Conf 2007

Ministry of Defence (2004) Defence Standard 00-25 Human factors for designers of systems

Ministry of Defence (2007) Defence Standard 00-56 Safety management requirements for defence systems – 4th edition

Swain AD and Guttman HE (1983). Handbook of human reliability analysis with emphasis on nuclear power plant applications NUREG/CR-1278

AUTHOR INDEX

16594512R00177

Made in the USA
Charleston, SC
30 December 2012